ATTACK ON TITAN

6

HAJIME ISAYAMA

"Attack on Titan" Character Introductions

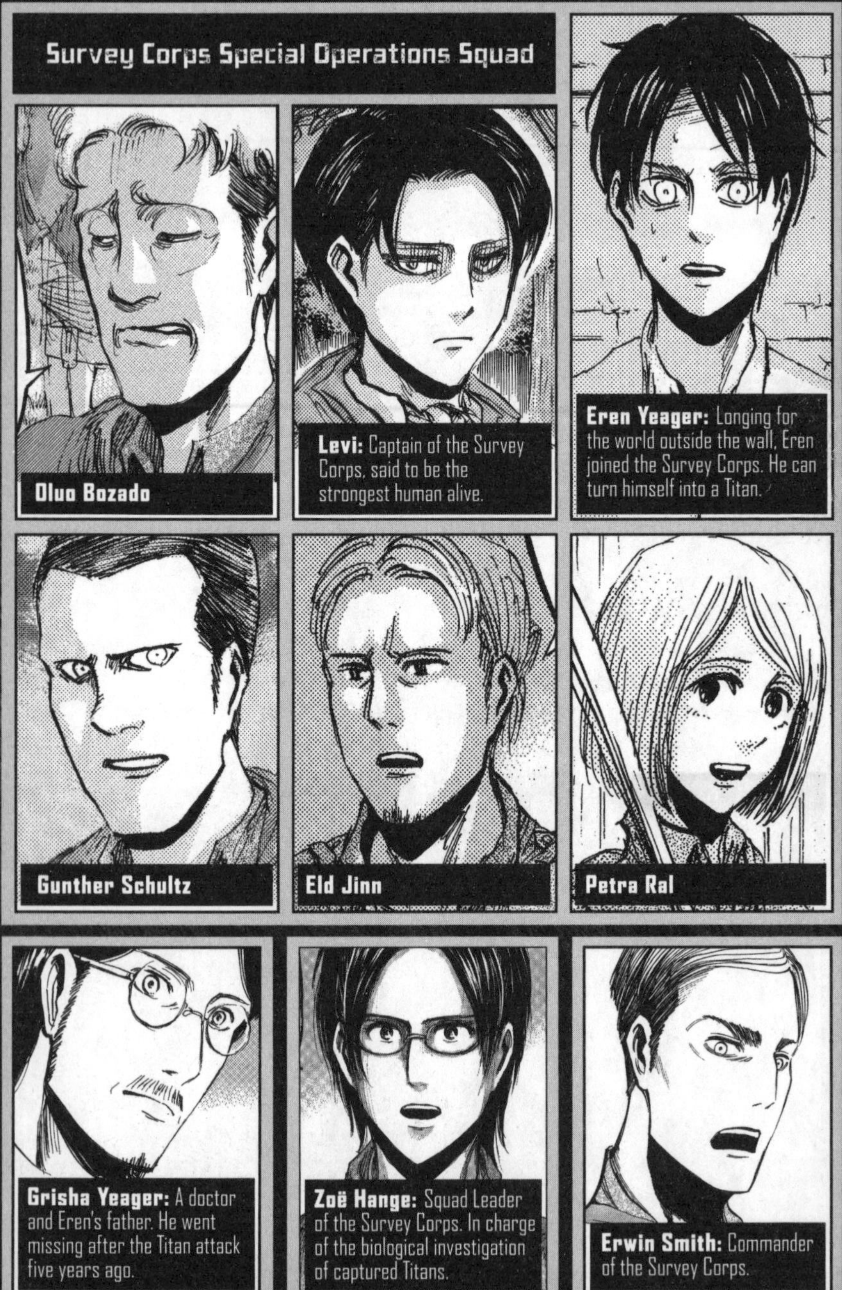
Survey Corps Special Operations Squad
Oluo Bozado
Levi: Captain of the Survey Corps, said to be the strongest human alive.
Eren Yeager: Longing for the world outside the wall, Eren joined the Survey Corps. He can turn himself into a Titan.
Gunther Schultz
Eld Jinn
Petra Ral
Grisha Yeager: A doctor and Eren's father. He went missing after the Titan attack five years ago.
Zoë Hange: Squad Leader of the Survey Corps. In charge of the biological investigation of captured Titans.
Erwin Smith: Commander of the Survey Corps.

104th Corps

Armin Arlert:
Eren and Mikasa's childhood friend. Though Armin isn't athletic in the least, he is an excellent thinker and can produce unique ideas. A member of the Survey Corps.

Mikasa Ackerman:
Mikasa graduated at the top of her training corps. Her parents were murdered before her eyes when she was a child. After that, she was raised alongside Eren, whom she tenaciously tries to protect.

Connie Springer: Effective at vertical maneuvering, but is slow on the uptake, so his comprehension of tactics is less than stellar. A member of the Survey Corps.

Jean Kirstein: Superior at vertical maneuvering. Jean is honest to a fault, which often puts him at odds with other people. A member of the Survey Corps.

Bertolt Hoover: Has a high degree of skill in everything he's been taught, but is indecisive and lacks initiative. A member of the Survey Corps.

Reiner Braun: Graduated second in his training corps. Reiner is as strong as an ox and has the will to match. His comrades have a great deal of trust in him. A member of the Survey Corps.

Marco Bott: Yearned to join the Military Police Brigade so he could serve the king. Marco died during the Titan mop-up operation.

Annie Leonhart: Annie's small stature belies her great skill in the art of hand-to-hand combat. She's a realist through and through, and tends to be a loner. A member of the Military Police Brigade.

Krista Lenz: Extremely short, with a friendly, warm-hearted personality. A member of the Survey Corps.

Sasha Blouse: Sasha is very agile and has remarkable instincts. Owing to her unconventionality, she isn't suited for organized activity. A member of the Survey Corps.

ATTACK on TITAN

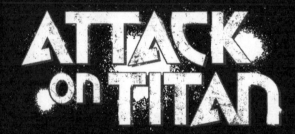

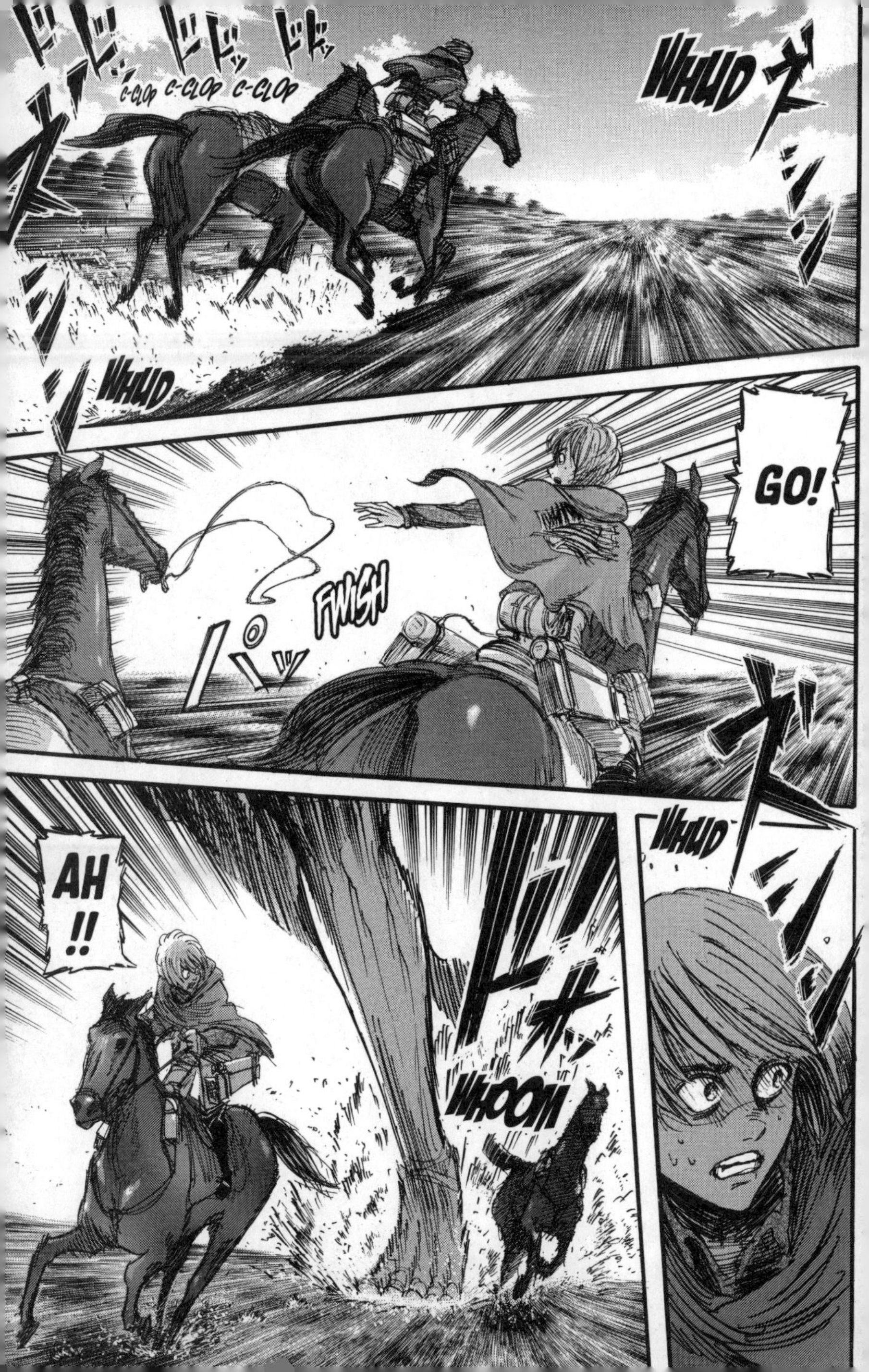
WHUD
C-CLOP C-CLOP C-CLOP
WHUD
GO!
FWISH
WHUD
AH!!
WHOOM

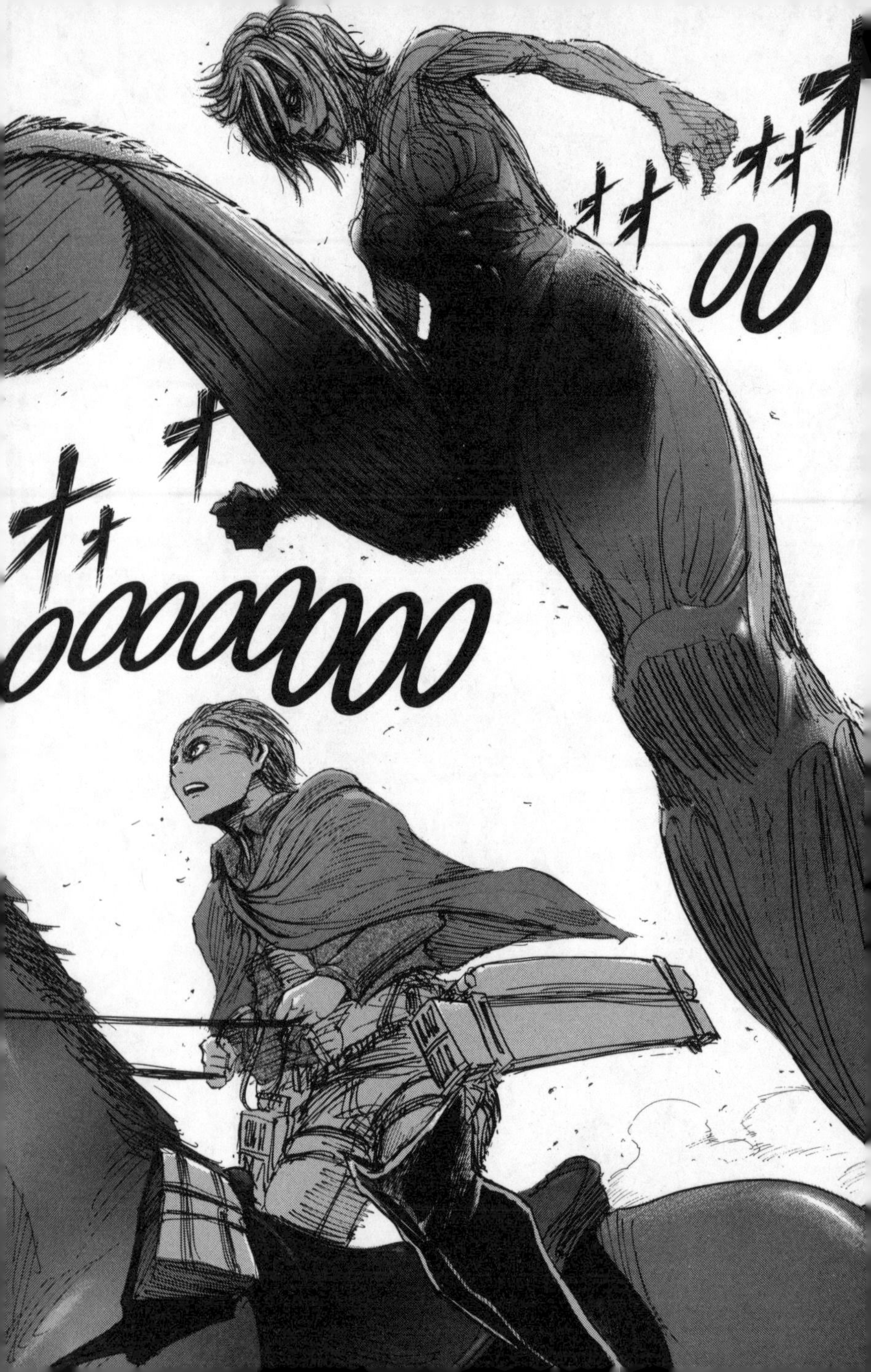
オオオオオ
OO
オオオ
OOOOOOO

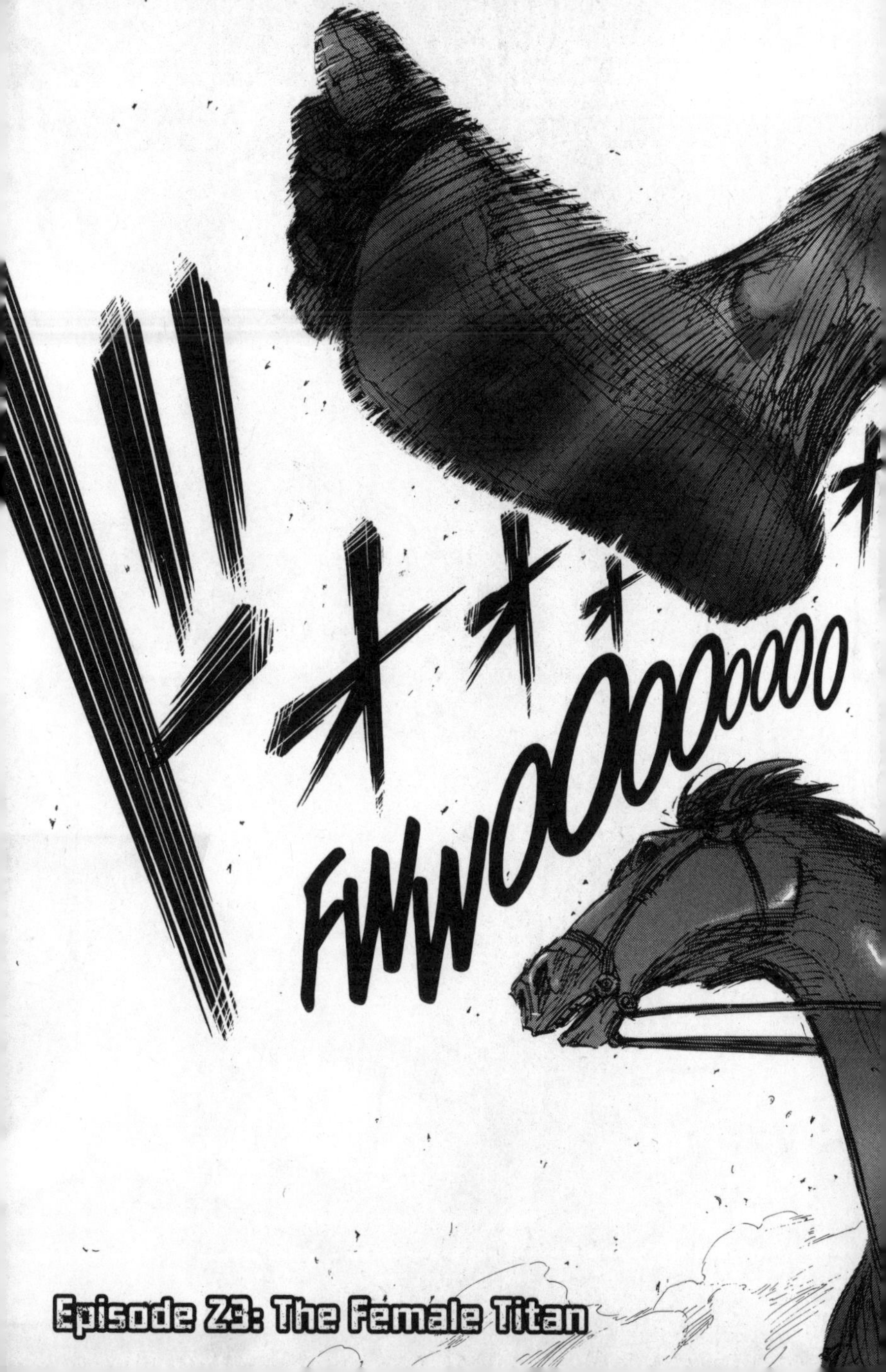
ドオオォォ
FWWOOOOOOOO

Episode 23: The Female Titan

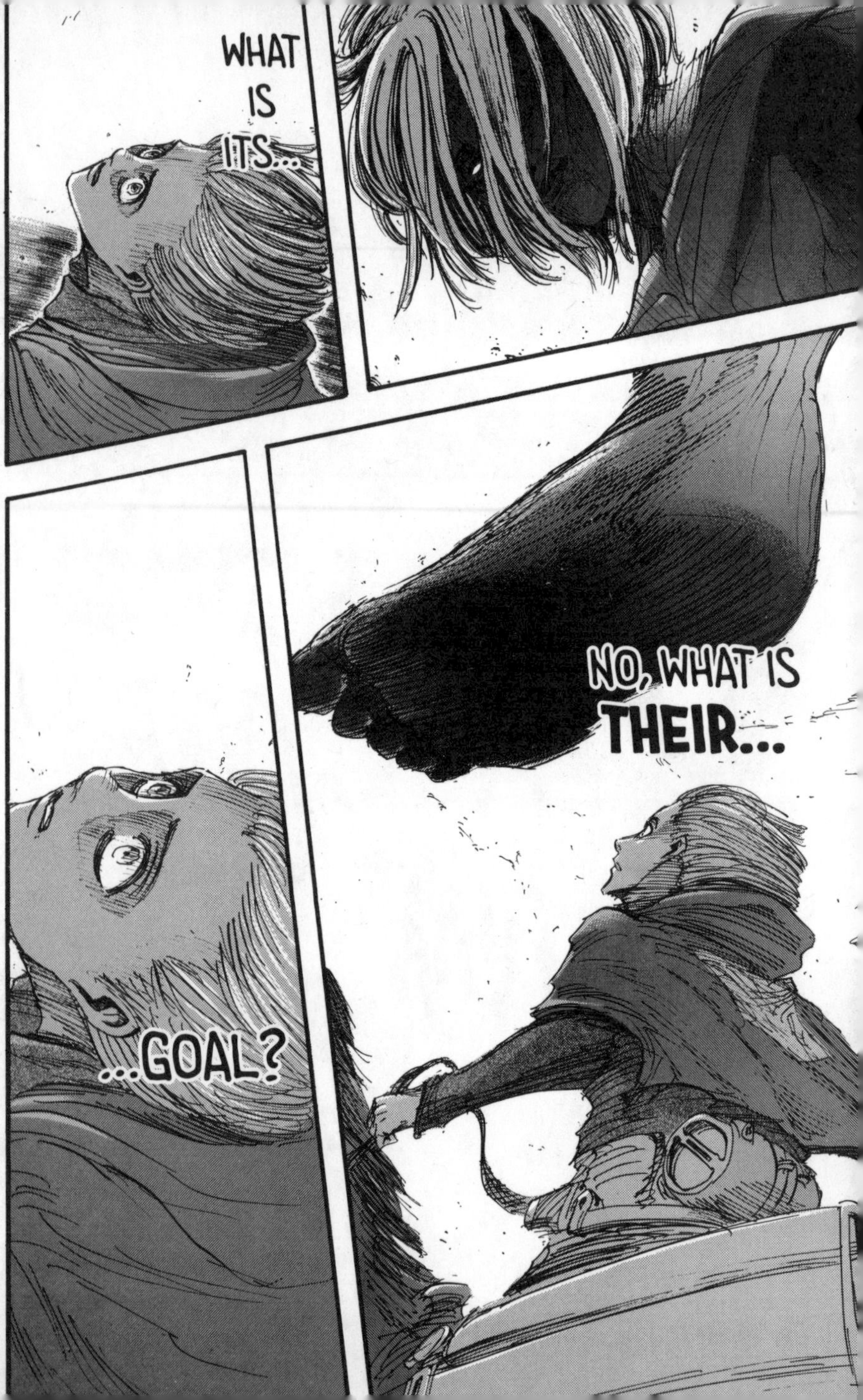
WHAT IS ITS...
NO, WHAT IS THEIR...
...GOAL?

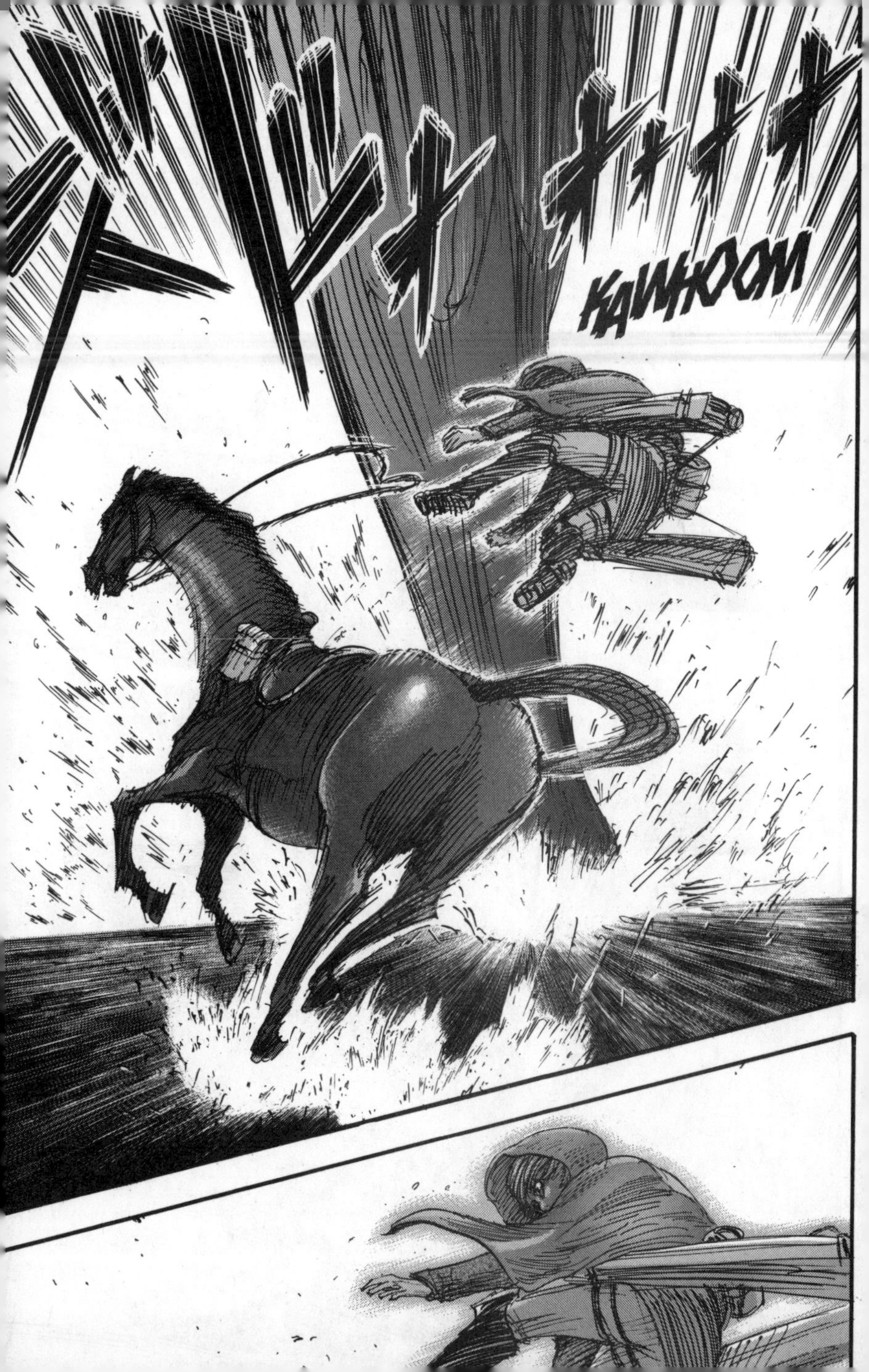
KAWHOOM

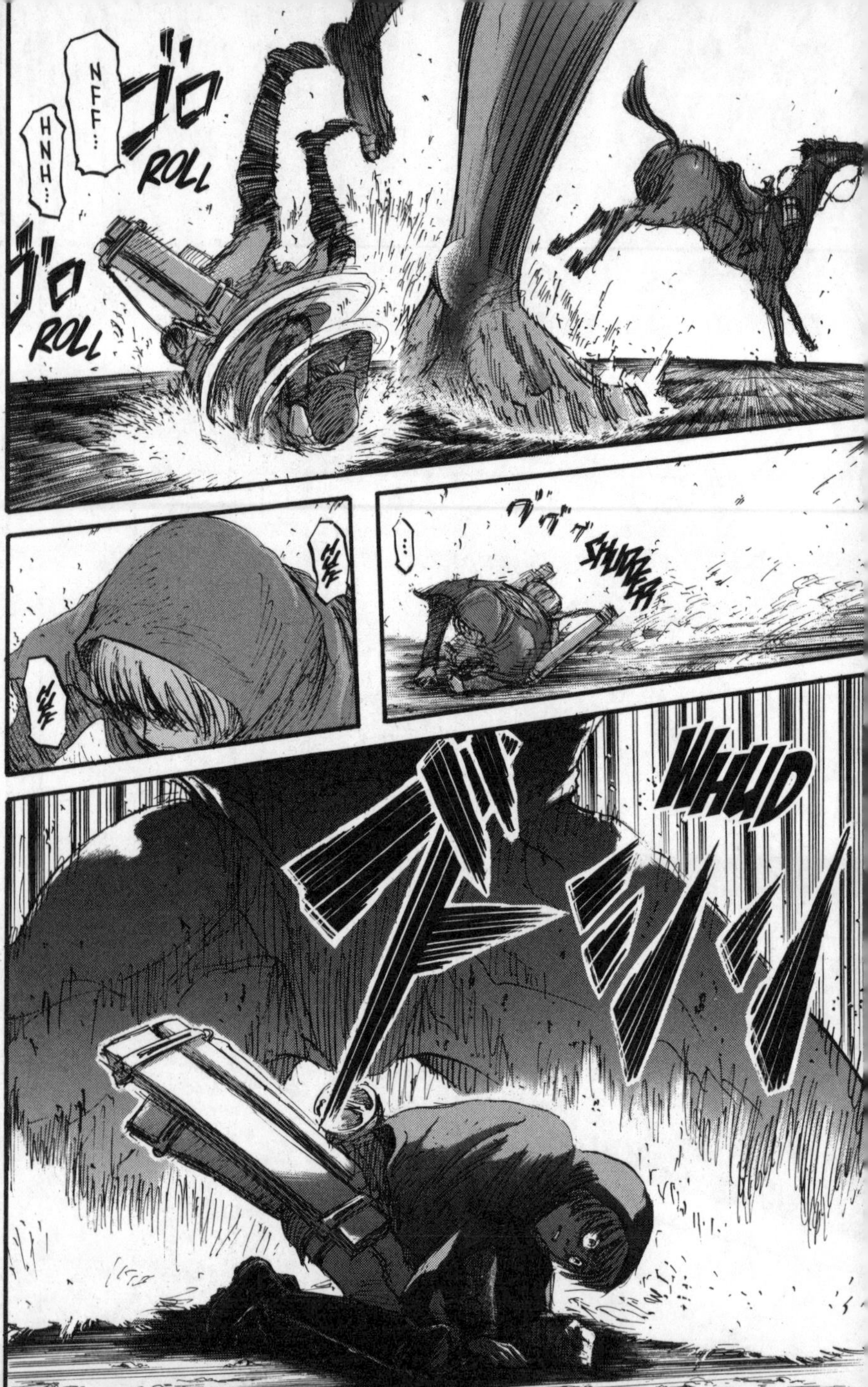
NFF...
HNH...
ゴロ
ROLL
ゴロ
ROLL
...
ズシン
WHUD

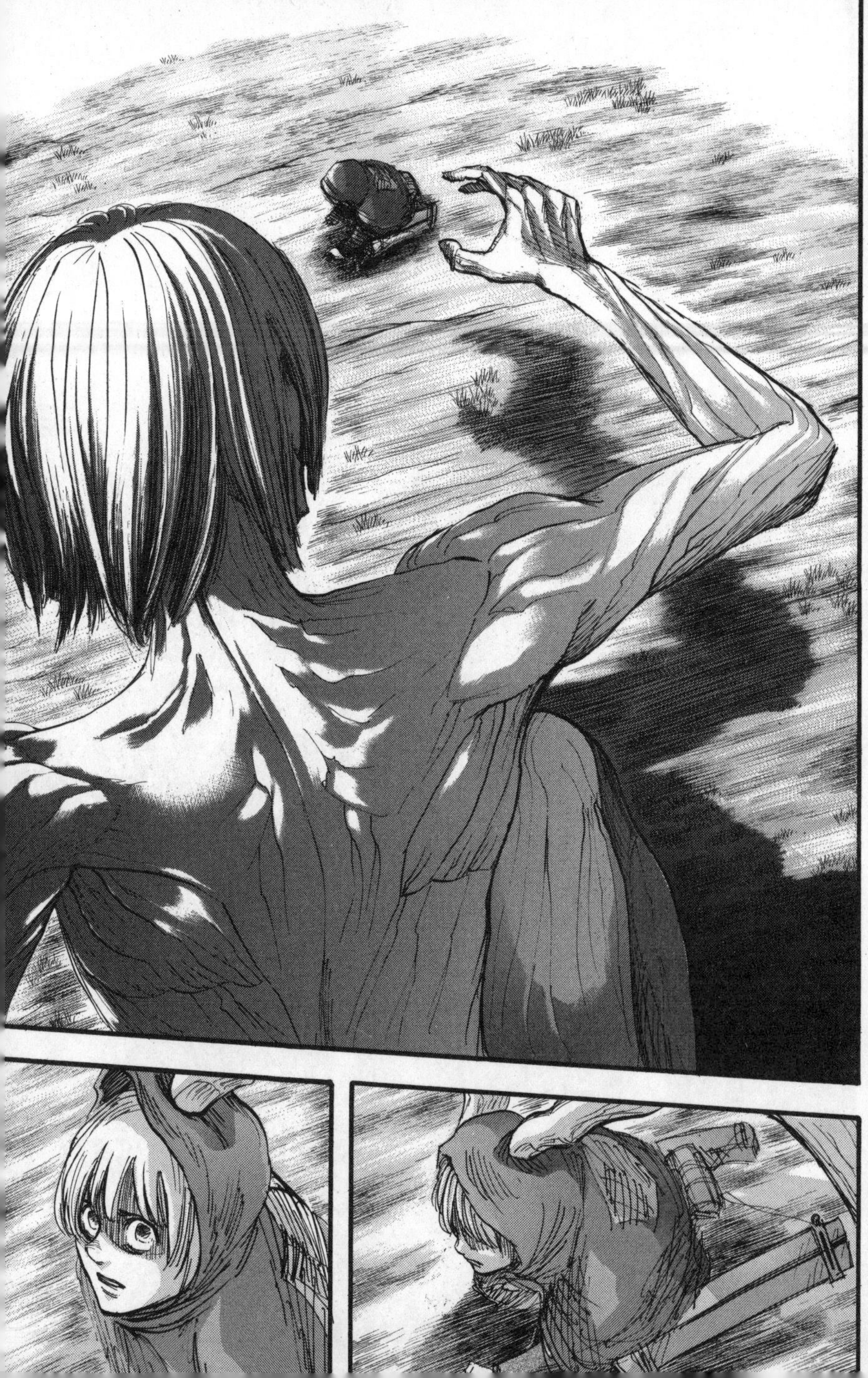

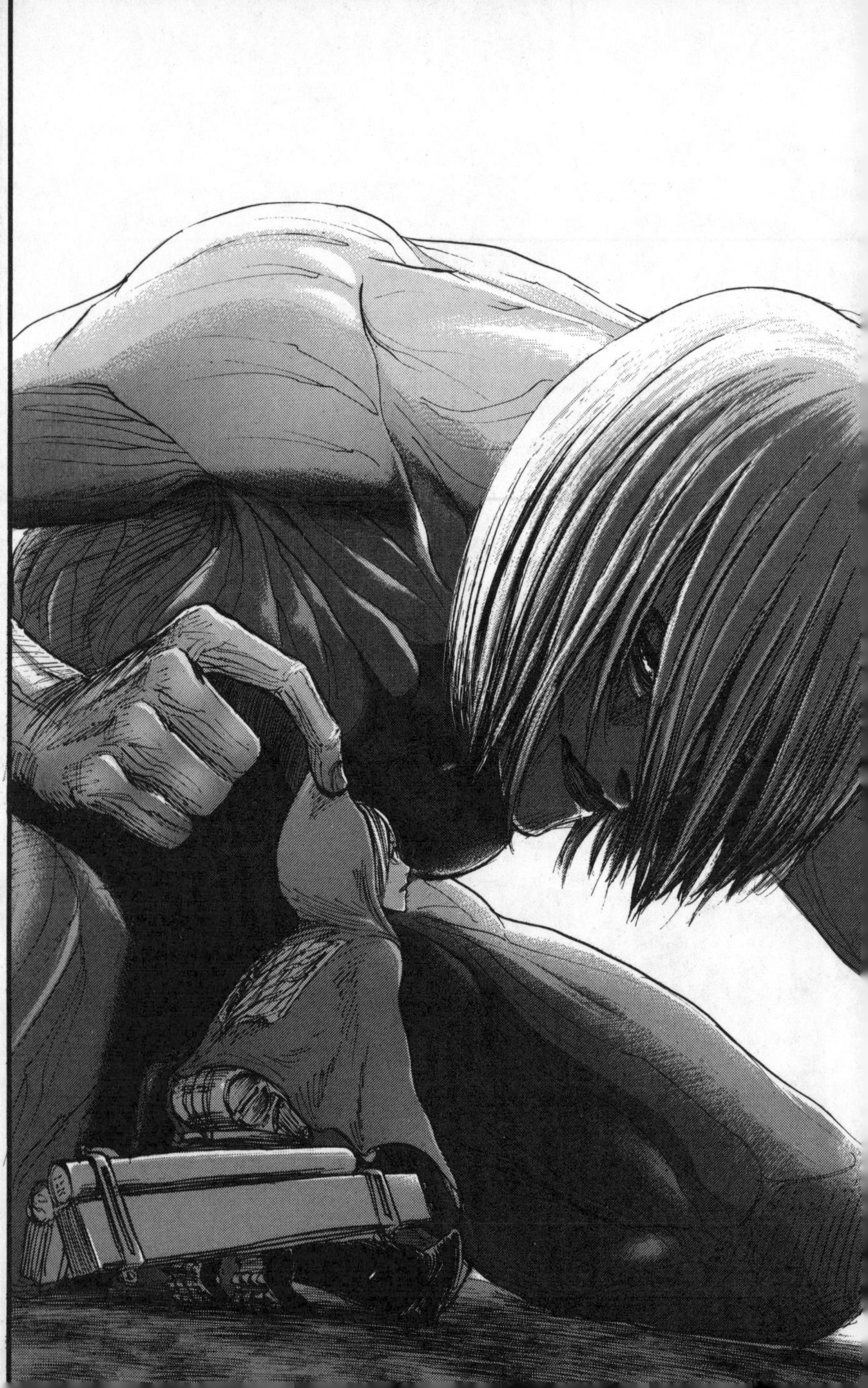

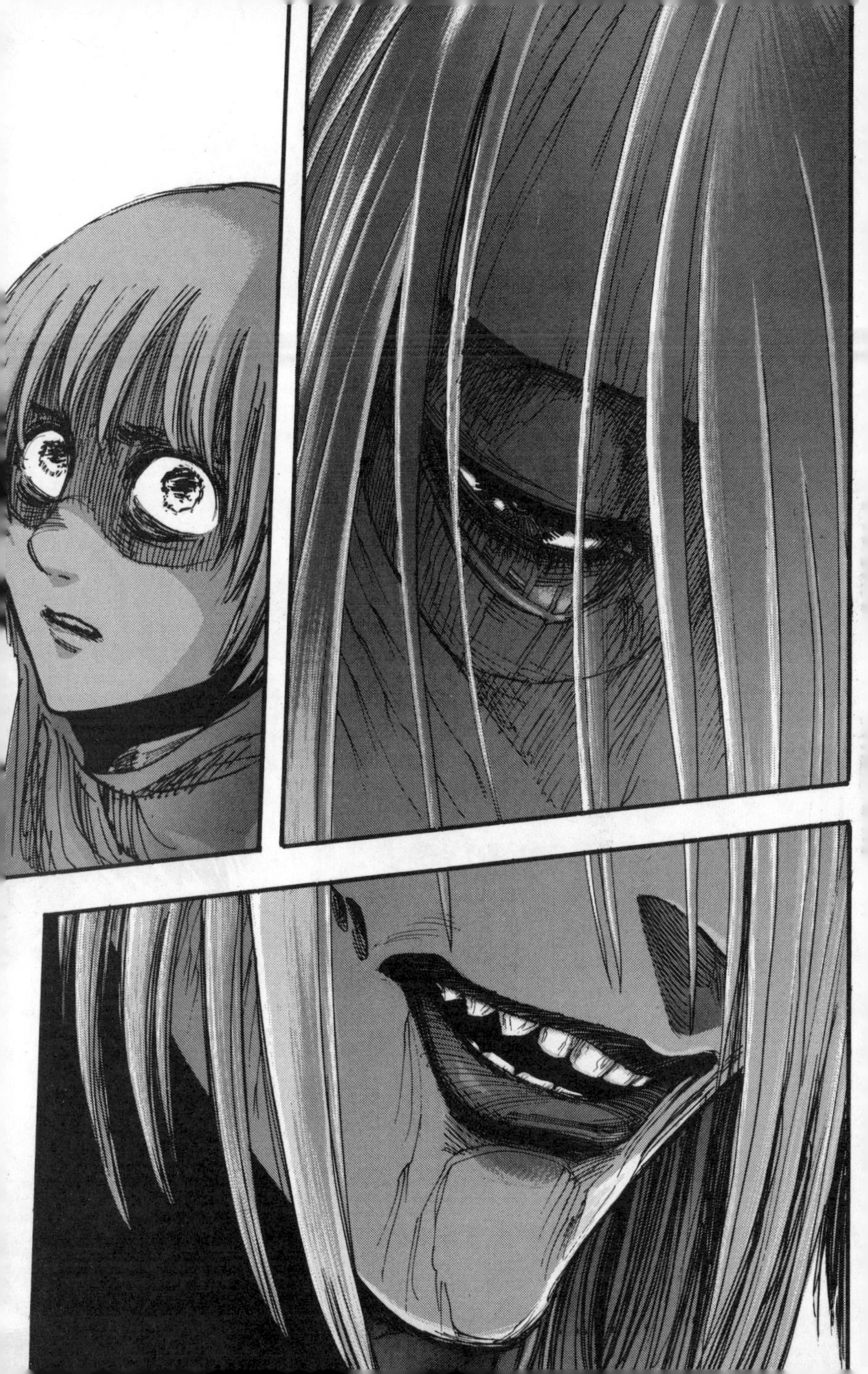

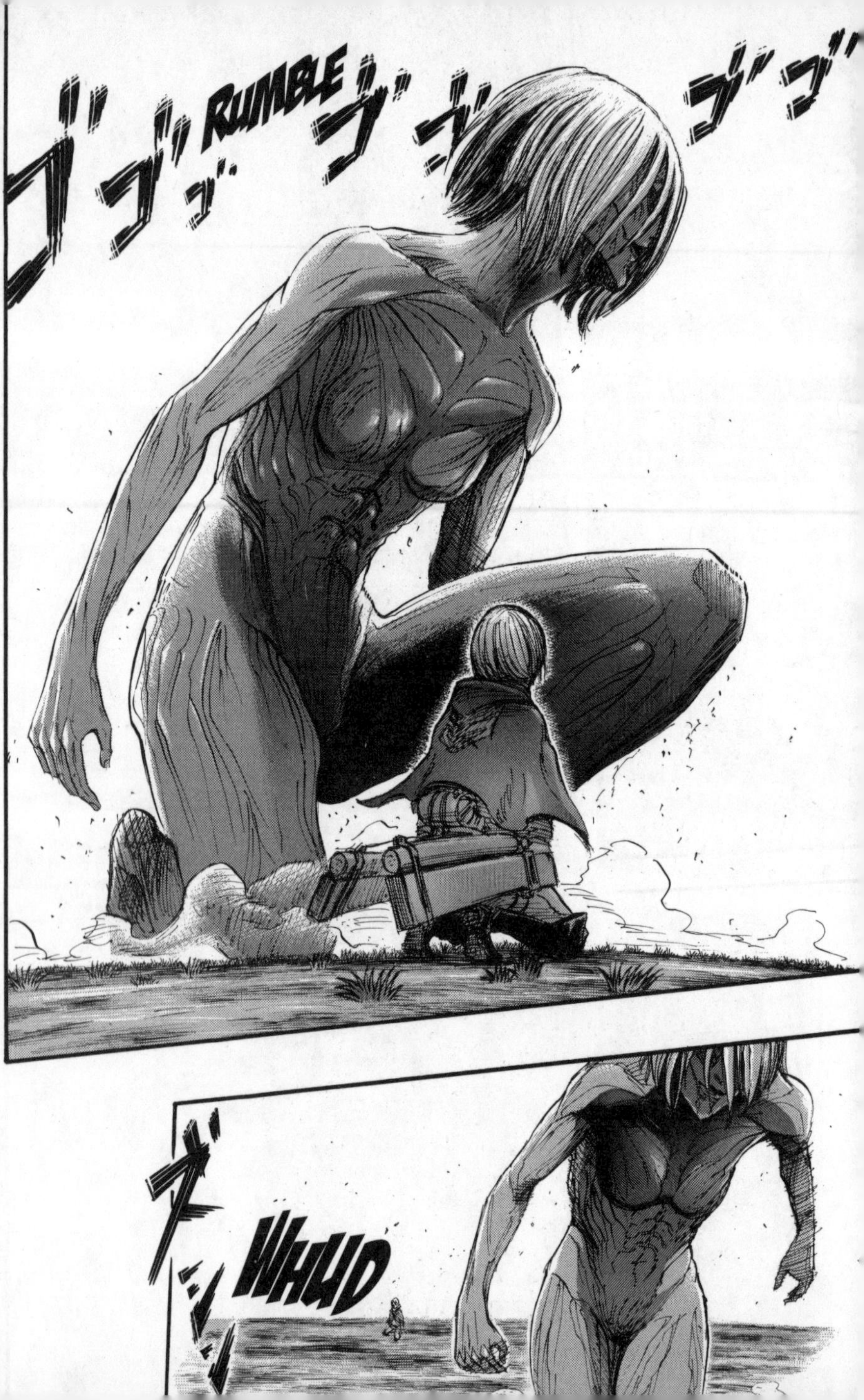
ゴゴゴゴゴゴ
RUMBLE
ズン
WHUD

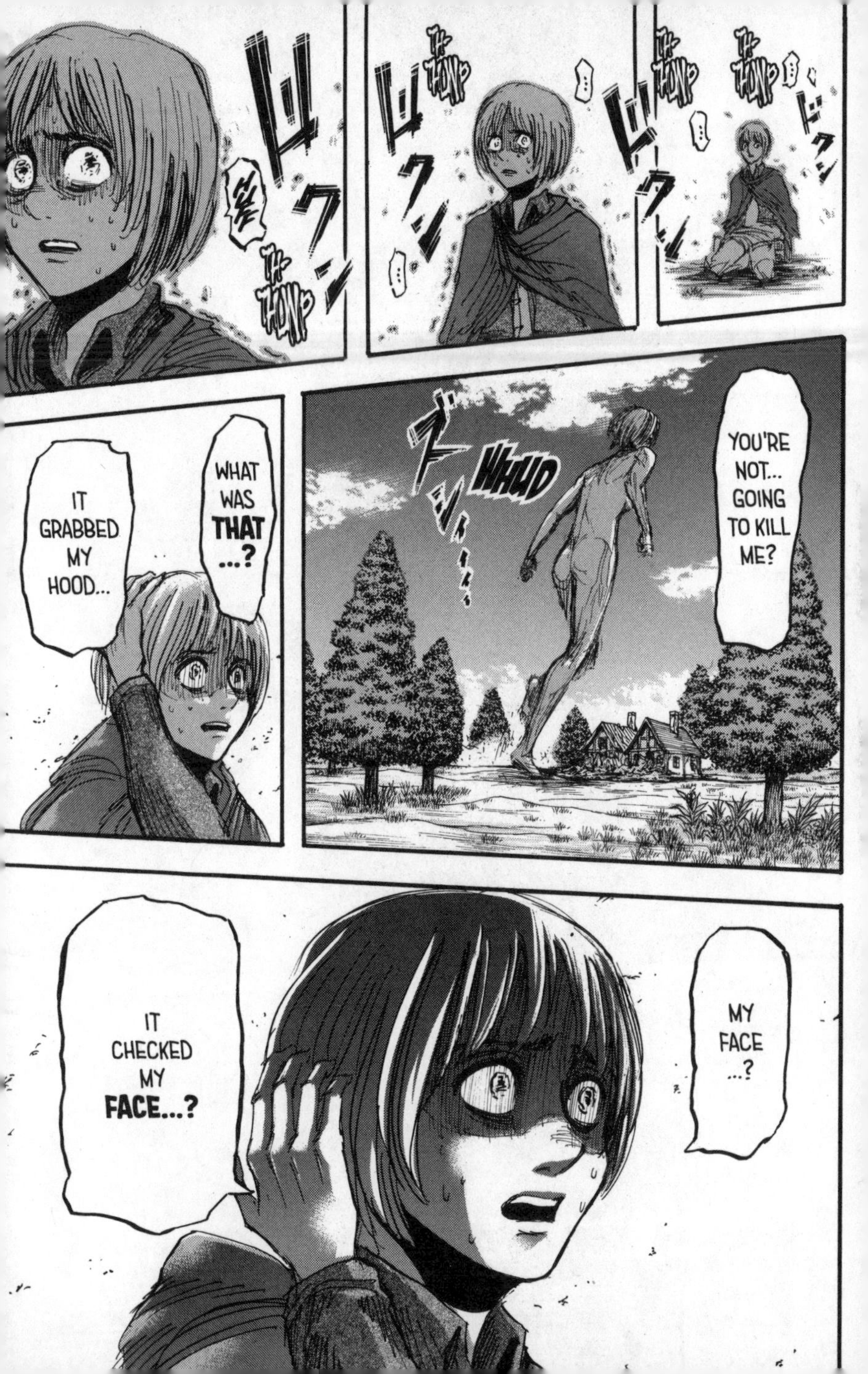

...
THA THOMP
THA THOMP
ドクン
...
...
ドクン
THA THOMP
...
ドクン
THA THOMP
YOU'RE NOT... GOING TO KILL ME?
WHUD
WHAT WAS **THAT** ...?
IT GRABBED MY HOOD...
MY FACE ...?
IT CHECKED MY **FACE...?**

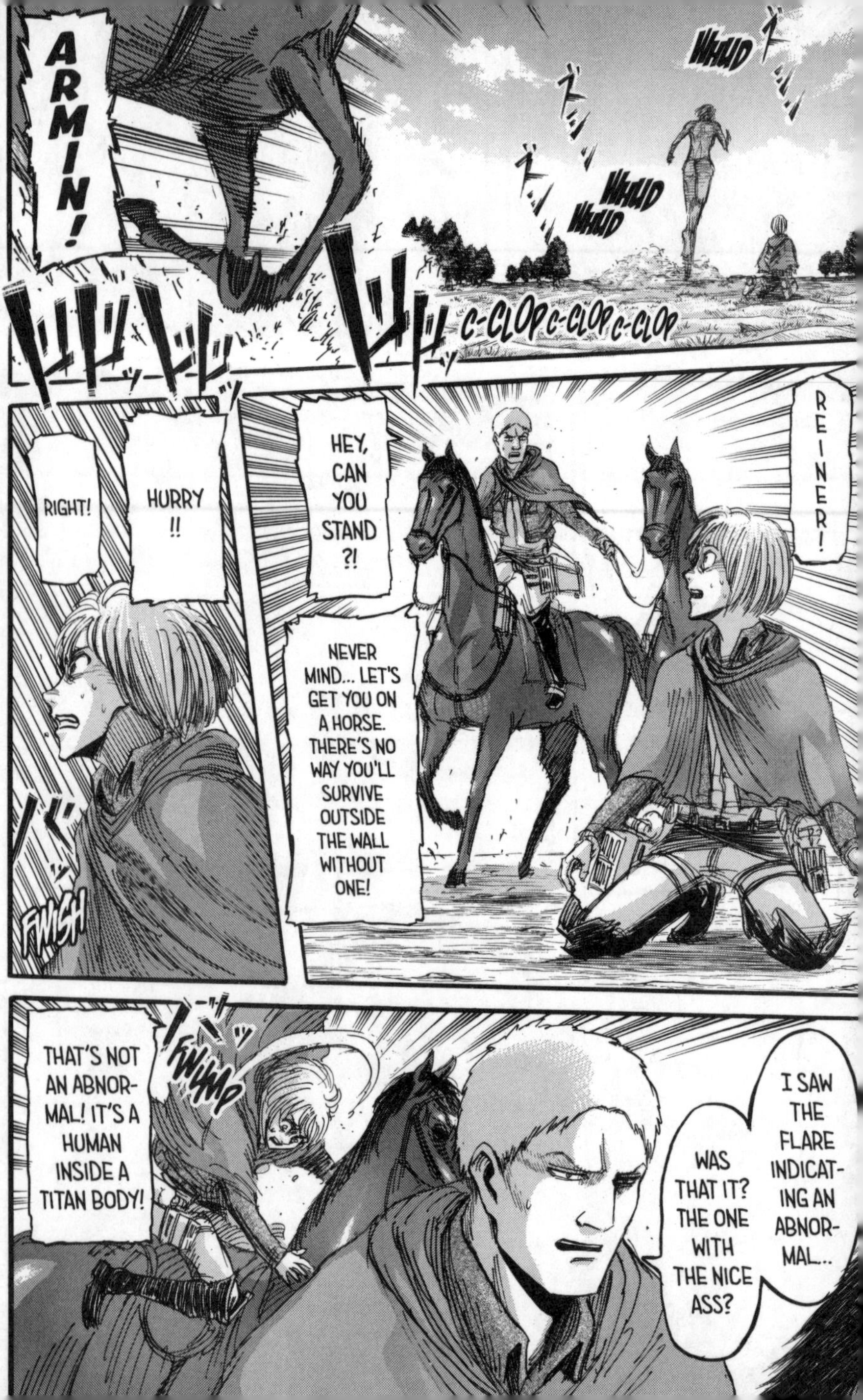
WHUD
WHUD
WHUD
ARMIN!
C-CLOP C-CLOP C-CLOP
REINER!
HEY, CAN YOU STAND?!
NEVER MIND... LET'S GET YOU ON A HORSE. THERE'S NO WAY YOU'LL SURVIVE OUTSIDE THE WALL WITHOUT ONE!
HURRY!!
RIGHT!
FWISH
I SAW THE FLARE INDICATING AN ABNORMAL...
WAS THAT IT? THE ONE WITH THE NICE ASS?
THAT'S NOT AN ABNORMAL! IT'S A HUMAN INSIDE A TITAN BODY!

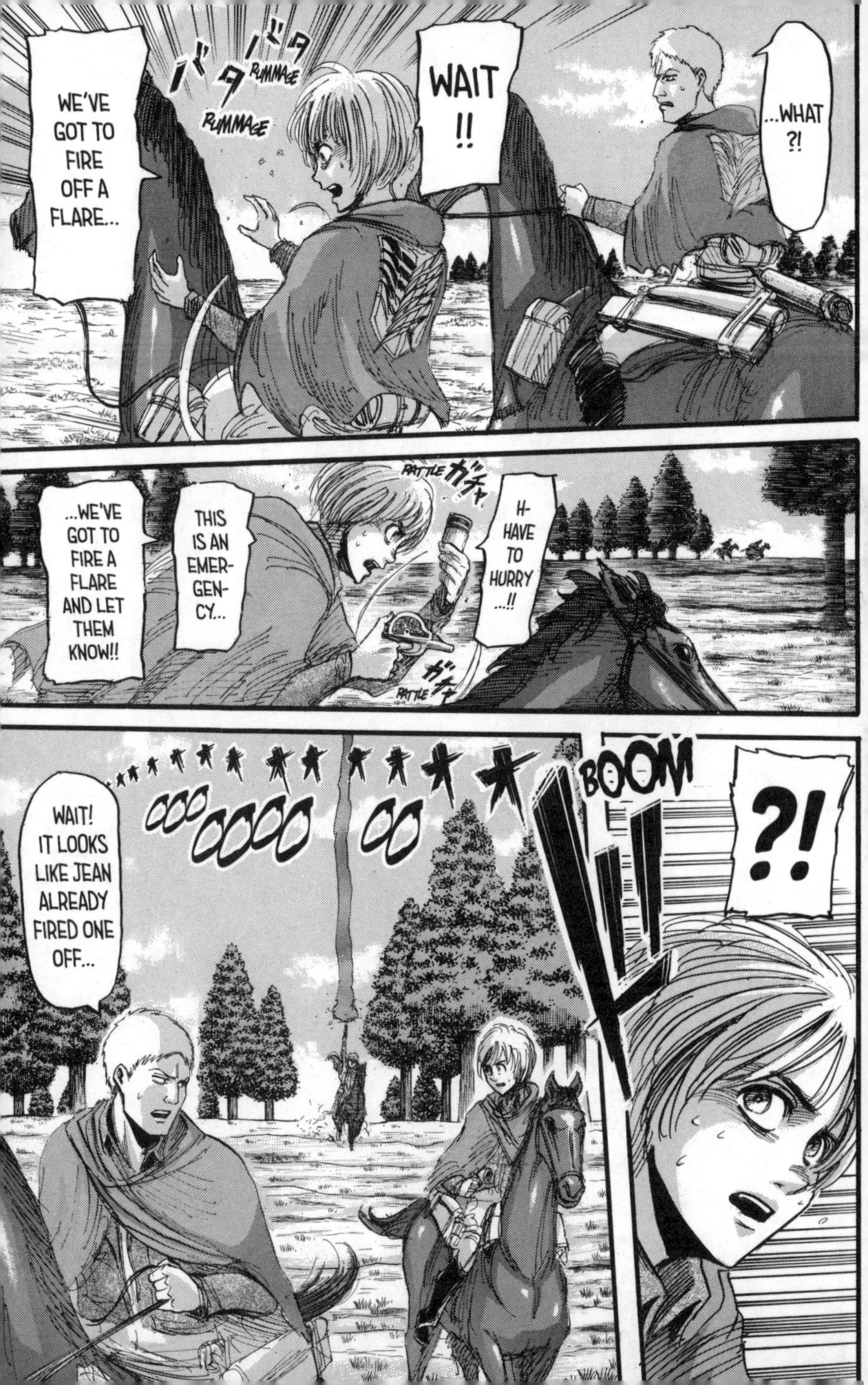
...WHAT ?!
WAIT !!
バタバタ
RUMMAGE
RUMMAGE
WE'VE GOT TO FIRE OFF A FLARE...
H-HAVE TO HURRY ...!!
RATTLE ガチャ
THIS IS AN EMER-GEN-CY...
...WE'VE GOT TO FIRE A FLARE AND LET THEM KNOW!!
ガチャ RATTLE
?!
BOOM
OOOOOOO OO
WAIT! IT LOOKS LIKE JEAN ALREADY FIRED ONE OFF...

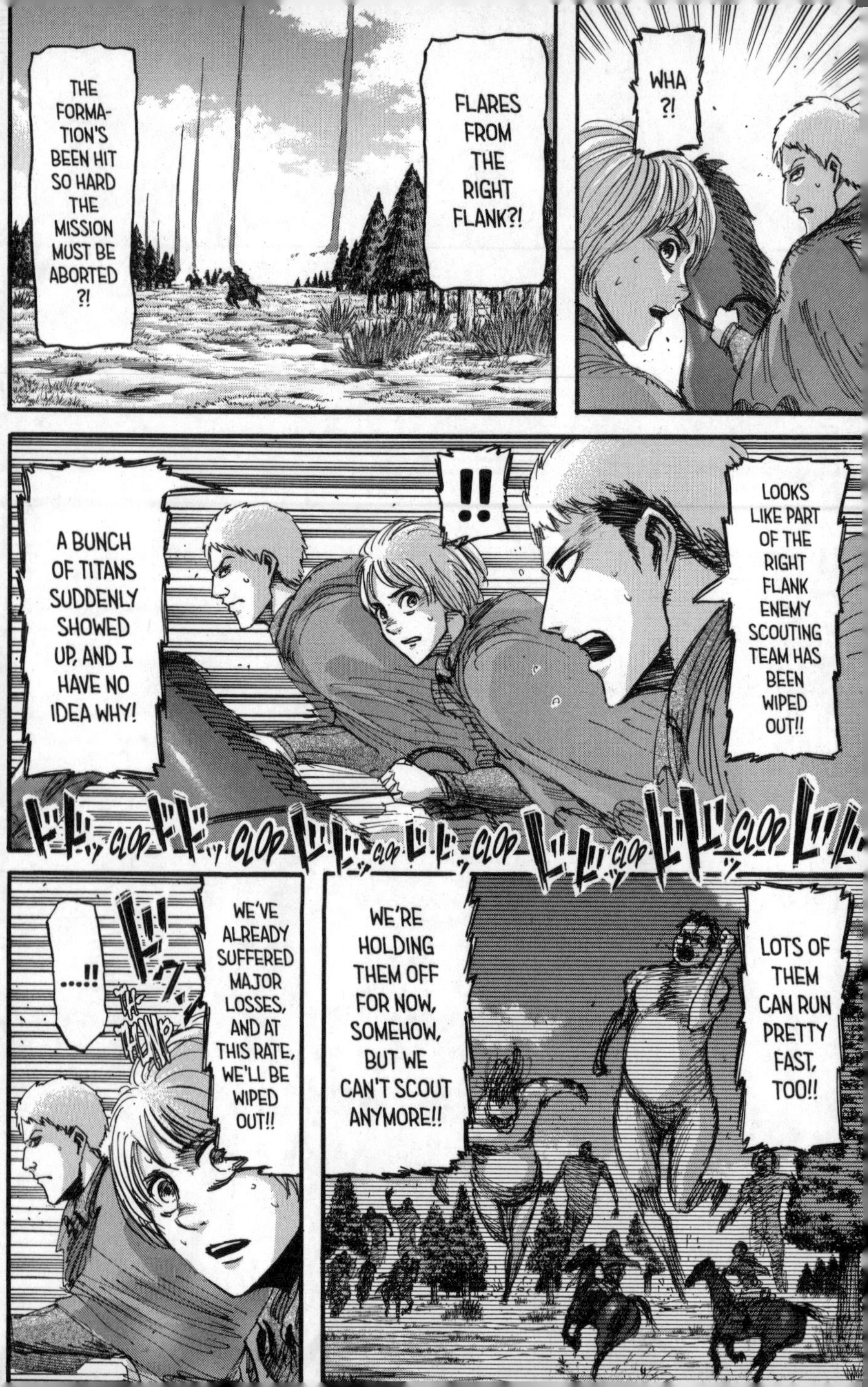
WHA ?!
FLARES FROM THE RIGHT FLANK?!
THE FORMATION'S BEEN HIT SO HARD THE MISSION MUST BE ABORTED ?!
LOOKS LIKE PART OF THE RIGHT FLANK ENEMY SCOUTING TEAM HAS BEEN WIPED OUT!!
!!
A BUNCH OF TITANS SUDDENLY SHOWED UP, AND I HAVE NO IDEA WHY!
CLOP
CLOP
CLOP
CLOP
CLOP
CLOP
LOTS OF THEM CAN RUN PRETTY FAST, TOO!!
WE'RE HOLDING THEM OFF FOR NOW, SOMEHOW, BUT WE CAN'T SCOUT ANYMORE!!
WE'VE ALREADY SUFFERED MAJOR LOSSES, AND AT THIS RATE, WE'LL BE WIPED OUT!!
...!!

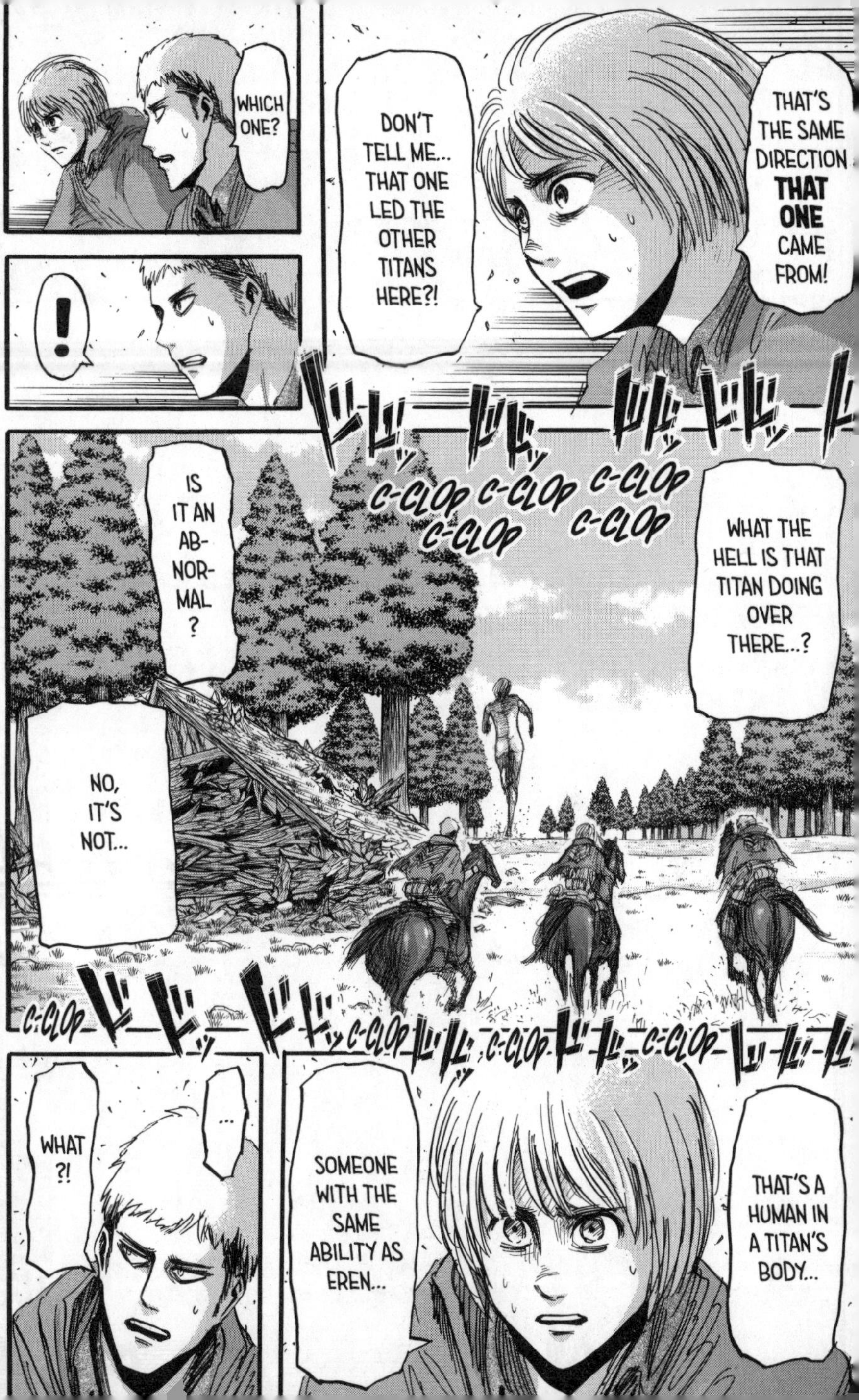
THAT'S THE SAME DIRECTION **THAT ONE** CAME FROM!
DON'T TELL ME... THAT ONE LED THE OTHER TITANS HERE?!
WHICH ONE?
!
C-CLOP C-CLOP C-CLOP C-CLOP C-CLOP
WHAT THE HELL IS THAT TITAN DOING OVER THERE...?
IS IT AN AB-NOR-MAL?
NO, IT'S NOT...
C-CLOP C-CLOP C-CLOP C-CLOP
THAT'S A HUMAN IN A TITAN'S BODY...
SOMEONE WITH THE SAME ABILITY AS EREN...
...
WHAT?!

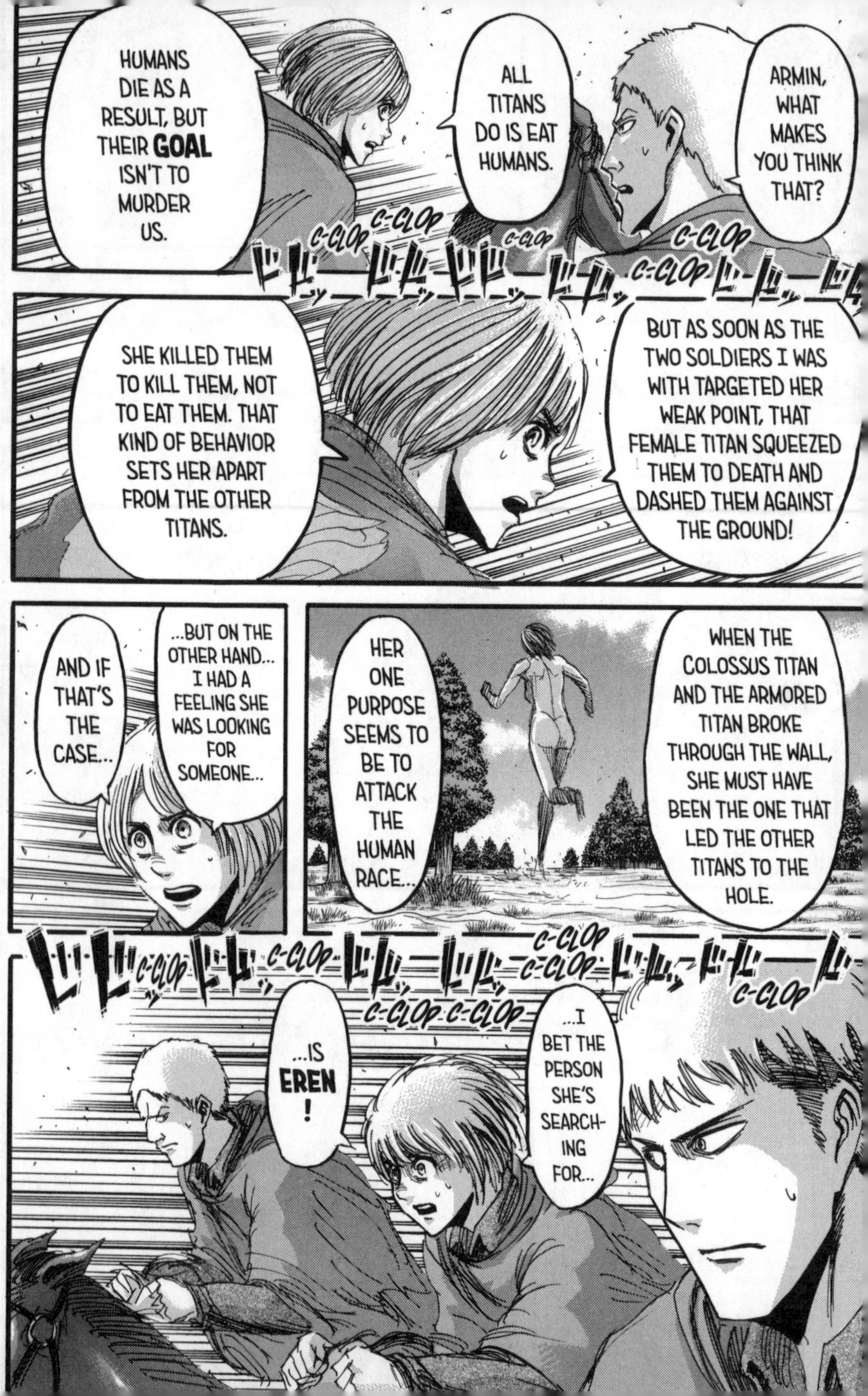
ARMIN, WHAT MAKES YOU THINK THAT?
ALL TITANS DO IS EAT HUMANS.
HUMANS DIE AS A RESULT, BUT THEIR **GOAL** ISN'T TO MURDER US.
C-CLOP C-CLOP
C-CLOP
C-CLOP C-CLOP
C-CLOP
BUT AS SOON AS THE TWO SOLDIERS I WAS WITH TARGETED HER WEAK POINT, THAT FEMALE TITAN SQUEEZED THEM TO DEATH AND DASHED THEM AGAINST THE GROUND!
SHE KILLED THEM TO KILL THEM, NOT TO EAT THEM. THAT KIND OF BEHAVIOR SETS HER APART FROM THE OTHER TITANS.
WHEN THE COLOSSUS TITAN AND THE ARMORED TITAN BROKE THROUGH THE WALL, SHE MUST HAVE BEEN THE ONE THAT LED THE OTHER TITANS TO THE HOLE.
HER ONE PURPOSE SEEMS TO BE TO ATTACK THE HUMAN RACE...
...BUT ON THE OTHER HAND... I HAD A FEELING SHE WAS LOOKING FOR SOMEONE...
AND IF THAT'S THE CASE...
C-CLOP C-CLOP C-CLOP C-CLOP
C-CLOP C-CLOP C-CLOP
...I BET THE PERSON SHE'S SEARCHING FOR...
...IS **EREN**!

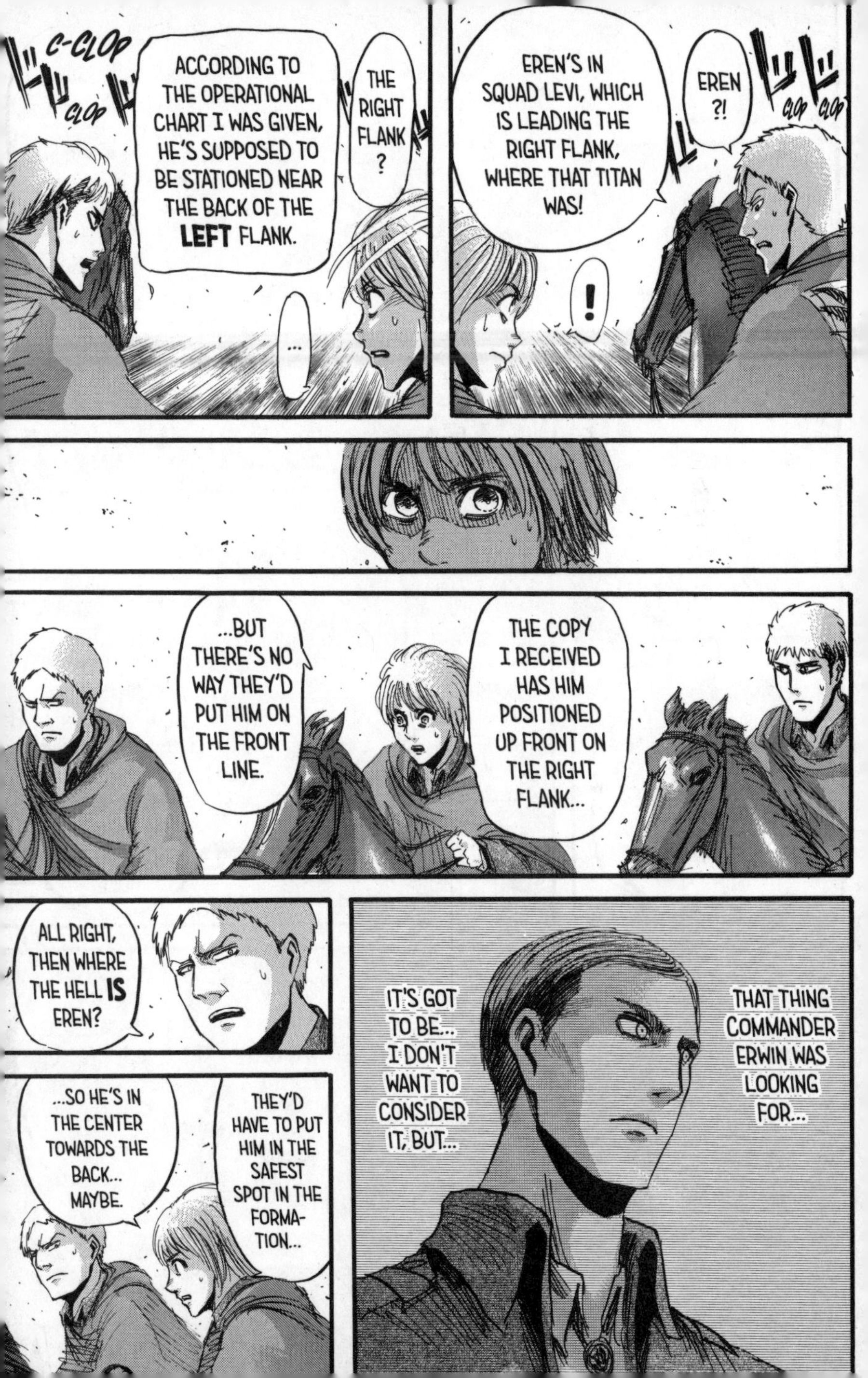
CLOP CLOP
EREN ?!
EREN'S IN SQUAD LEVI, WHICH IS LEADING THE RIGHT FLANK, WHERE THAT TITAN WAS!
!
THE RIGHT FLANK ?
C-CLOP CLOP
ACCORDING TO THE OPERATIONAL CHART I WAS GIVEN, HE'S SUPPOSED TO BE STATIONED NEAR THE BACK OF THE **LEFT** FLANK.
...
THE COPY I RECEIVED HAS HIM POSITIONED UP FRONT ON THE RIGHT FLANK...
...BUT THERE'S NO WAY THEY'D PUT HIM ON THE FRONT LINE.
THAT THING COMMANDER ERWIN WAS LOOKING FOR...
IT'S GOT TO BE... I DON'T WANT TO CONSIDER IT, BUT...
ALL RIGHT, THEN WHERE THE HELL **IS** EREN?
THEY'D HAVE TO PUT HIM IN THE SAFEST SPOT IN THE FORMATION...
...SO HE'S IN THE CENTER TOWARDS THE BACK... MAYBE.

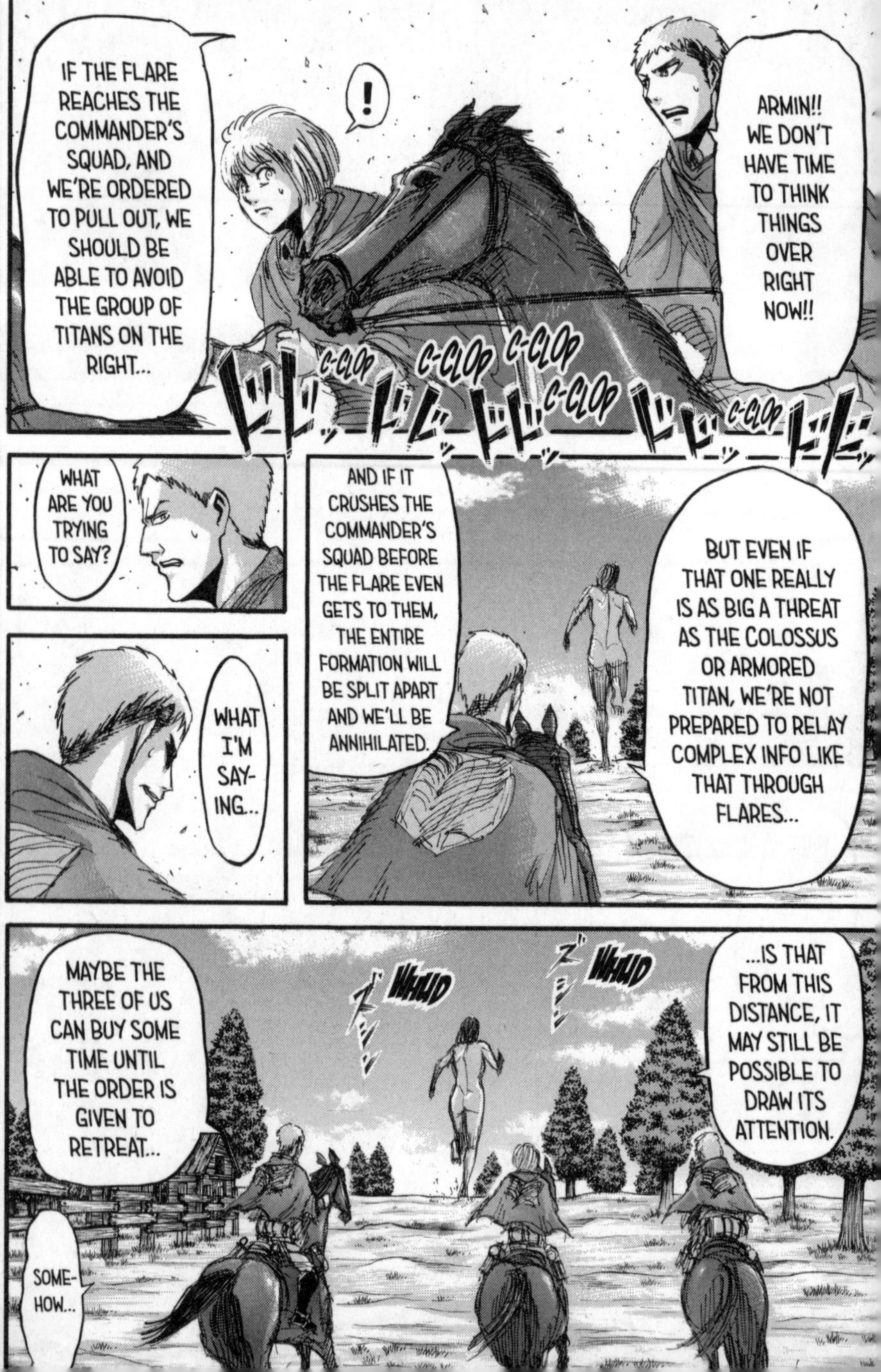
ARMIN!! WE DON'T HAVE TIME TO THINK THINGS OVER RIGHT NOW!!
!
IF THE FLARE REACHES THE COMMANDER'S SQUAD, AND WE'RE ORDERED TO PULL OUT, WE SHOULD BE ABLE TO AVOID THE GROUP OF TITANS ON THE RIGHT...
C-CLOP
C-CLOP
C-CLOP
C-CLOP
C-CLOP
BUT EVEN IF THAT ONE REALLY IS AS BIG A THREAT AS THE COLOSSUS OR ARMORED TITAN, WE'RE NOT PREPARED TO RELAY COMPLEX INFO LIKE THAT THROUGH FLARES...
AND IF IT CRUSHES THE COMMANDER'S SQUAD BEFORE THE FLARE EVEN GETS TO THEM, THE ENTIRE FORMATION WILL BE SPLIT APART AND WE'LL BE ANNIHILATED.
WHAT ARE YOU TRYING TO SAY?
WHAT I'M SAY-ING...
...IS THAT FROM THIS DISTANCE, IT MAY STILL BE POSSIBLE TO DRAW ITS ATTENTION.
WHUD
WHUD
MAYBE THE THREE OF US CAN BUY SOME TIME UNTIL THE ORDER IS GIVEN TO RETREAT...
SOME-HOW...

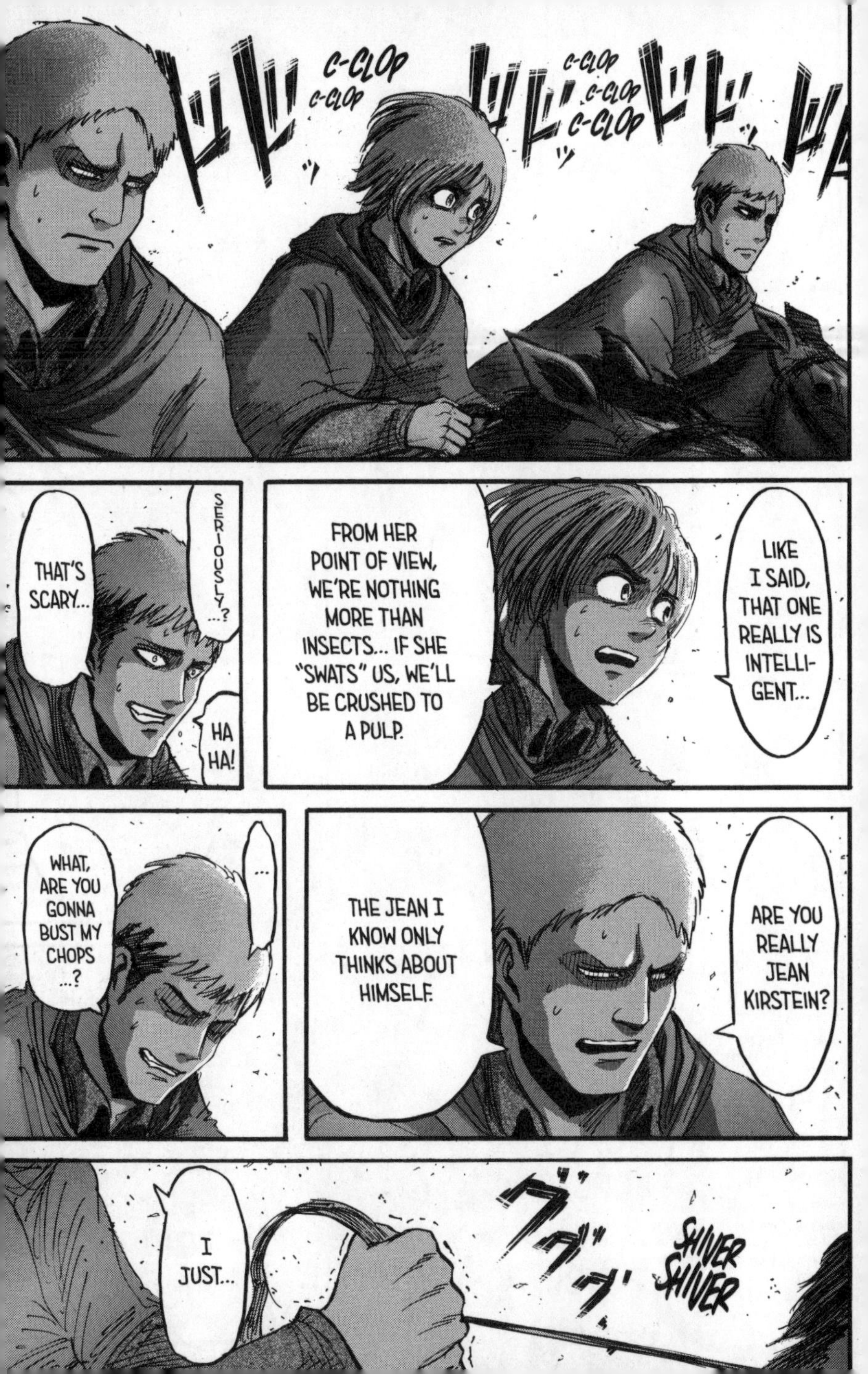
C-CLOP
C-CLOP
C-CLOP
C-CLOP
C-CLOP
LIKE I SAID, THAT ONE REALLY IS INTELLI-GENT...
FROM HER POINT OF VIEW, WE'RE NOTHING MORE THAN INSECTS... IF SHE "SWATS" US, WE'LL BE CRUSHED TO A PULP.
SERIOUSLY...?
HA HA!
THAT'S SCARY...
ARE YOU REALLY JEAN KIRSTEIN?
THE JEAN I KNOW ONLY THINKS ABOUT HIMSELF.
...
WHAT, ARE YOU GONNA BUST MY CHOPS ...?
SHIVER SHIVER
I JUST...

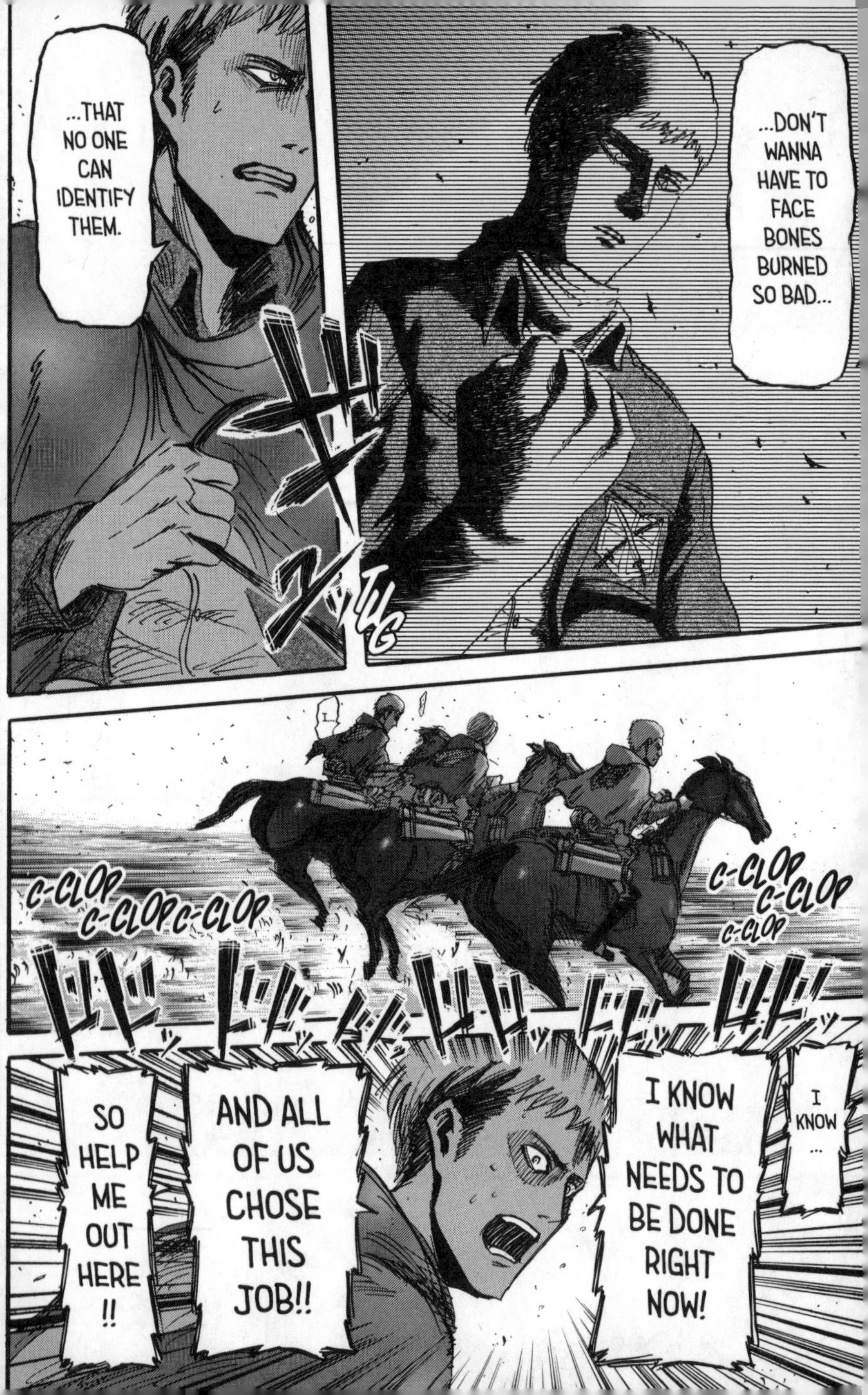
...DON'T WANNA HAVE TO FACE BONES BURNED SO BAD...
...THAT NO ONE CAN IDENTIFY THEM.
TUG
I...
!
C-CLOP C-CLOP C-CLOP
C-CLOP C-CLOP C-CLOP
I KNOW ...
I KNOW WHAT NEEDS TO BE DONE RIGHT NOW!
AND ALL OF US CHOSE THIS JOB!!
SO HELP ME OUT HERE !!

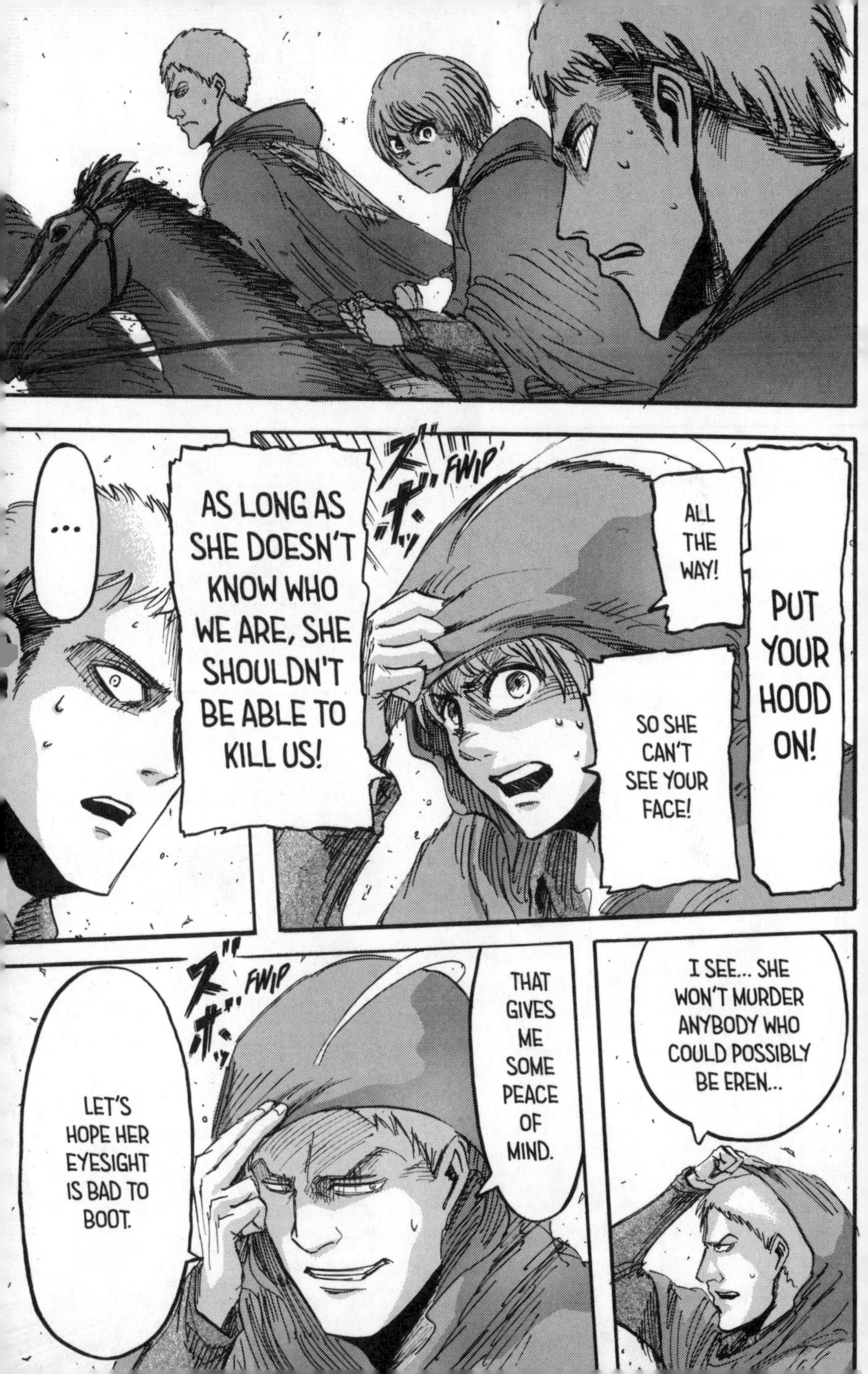
PUT YOUR HOOD ON!
ALL THE WAY!
SO SHE CAN'T SEE YOUR FACE!
FWIP
AS LONG AS SHE DOESN'T KNOW WHO WE ARE, SHE SHOULDN'T BE ABLE TO KILL US!
...
I SEE... SHE WON'T MURDER ANYBODY WHO COULD POSSIBLY BE EREN...
THAT GIVES ME SOME PEACE OF MIND.
FWIP
LET'S HOPE HER EYESIGHT IS BAD TO BOOT.

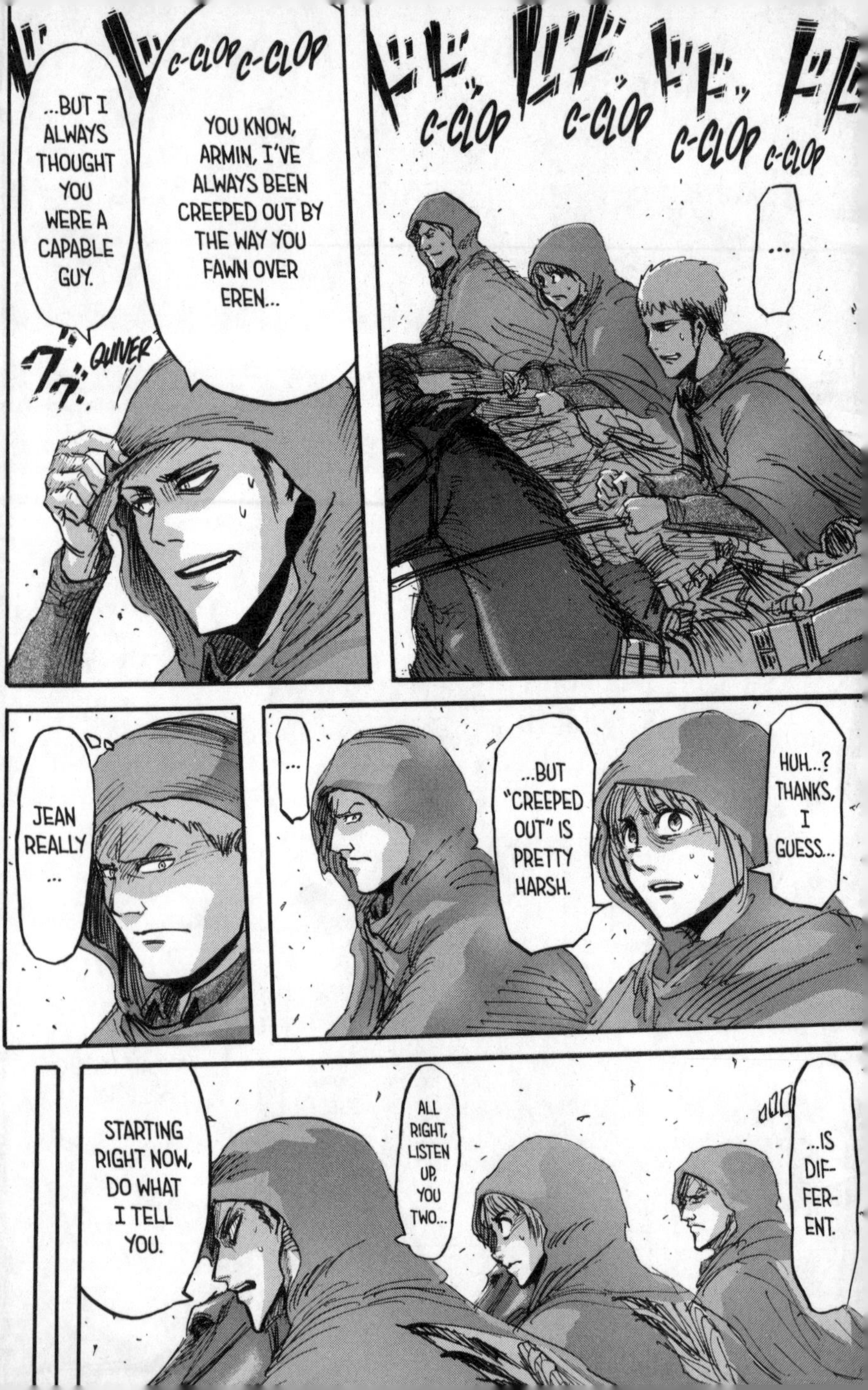
C-CLOP C-CLOP C-CLOP C-CLOP
...
C-CLOP C-CLOP
YOU KNOW, ARMIN, I'VE ALWAYS BEEN CREEPED OUT BY THE WAY YOU FAWN OVER EREN...
...BUT I ALWAYS THOUGHT YOU WERE A CAPABLE GUY.
QUIVER
HUH...? THANKS, I GUESS...
...BUT "CREEPED OUT" IS PRETTY HARSH.
...
JEAN REALLY ...
...IS DIF-FER-ENT.
ALL RIGHT, LISTEN UP, YOU TWO...
STARTING RIGHT NOW, DO WHAT I TELL YOU.

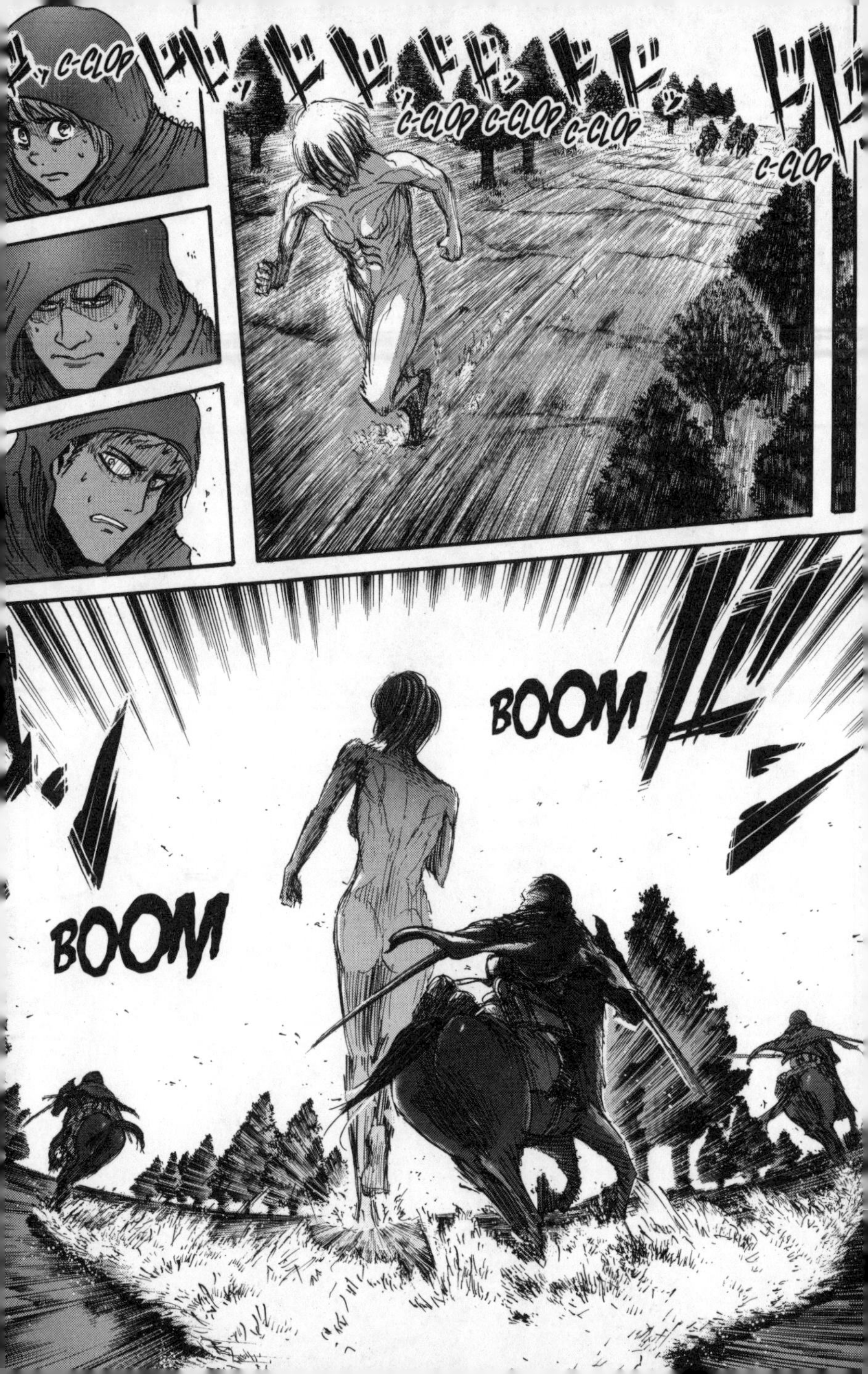
C-CLOP C-CLOP C-CLOP
C-CLOP
C-CLOP
BOOM
BOOM

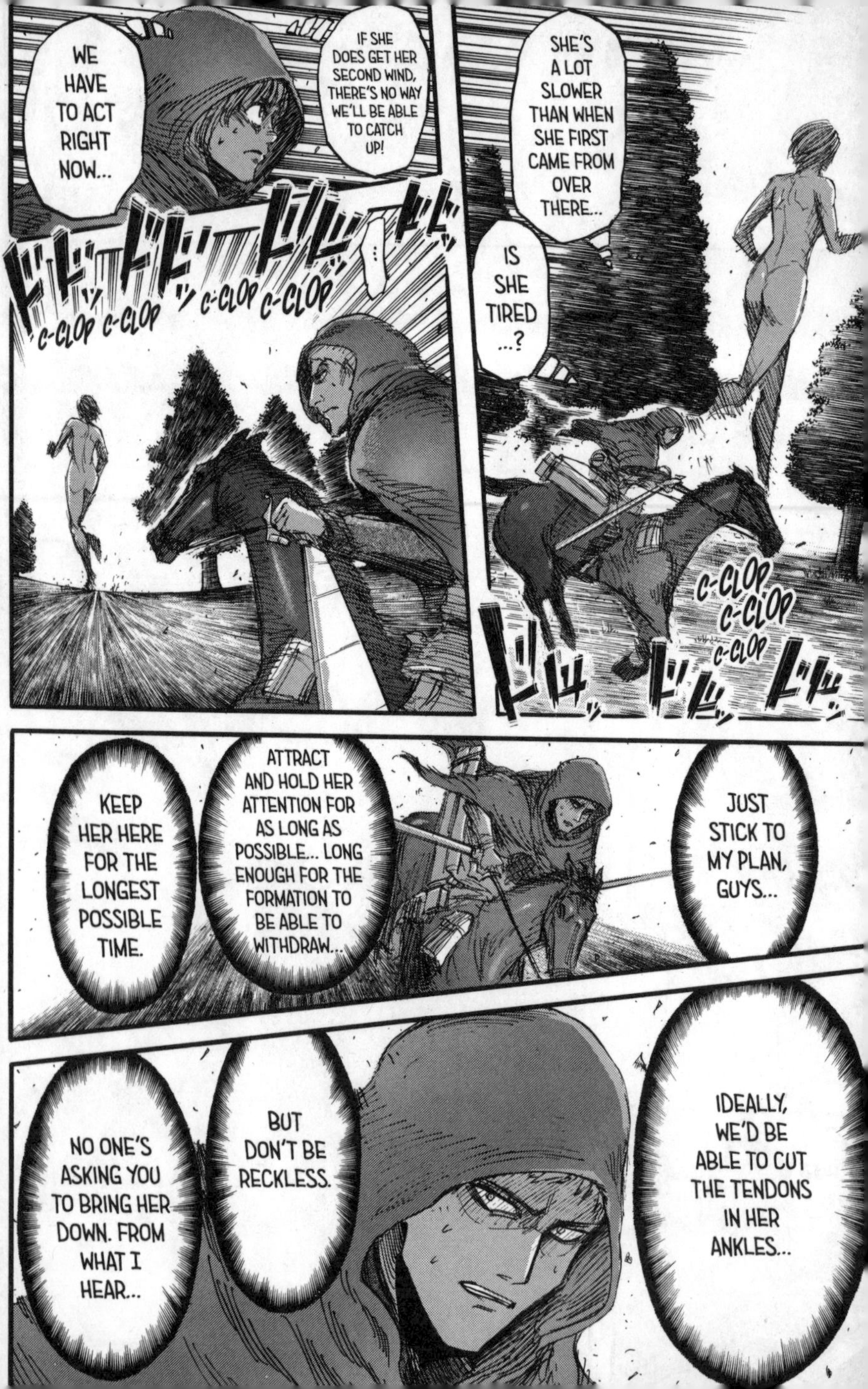
SHE'S A LOT SLOWER THAN WHEN SHE FIRST CAME FROM OVER THERE...
IS SHE TIRED ...?
C-CLOP C-CLOP C-CLOP
IF SHE DOES GET HER SECOND WIND, THERE'S NO WAY WE'LL BE ABLE TO CATCH UP!
WE HAVE TO ACT RIGHT NOW...
...
C-CLOP C-CLOP C-CLOP C-CLOP
JUST STICK TO MY PLAN, GUYS...
ATTRACT AND HOLD HER ATTENTION FOR AS LONG AS POSSIBLE... LONG ENOUGH FOR THE FORMATION TO BE ABLE TO WITHDRAW...
KEEP HER HERE FOR THE LONGEST POSSIBLE TIME.
IDEALLY, WE'D BE ABLE TO CUT THE TENDONS IN HER ANKLES...
BUT DON'T BE RECKLESS.
NO ONE'S ASKING YOU TO BRING HER DOWN. FROM WHAT I HEAR...

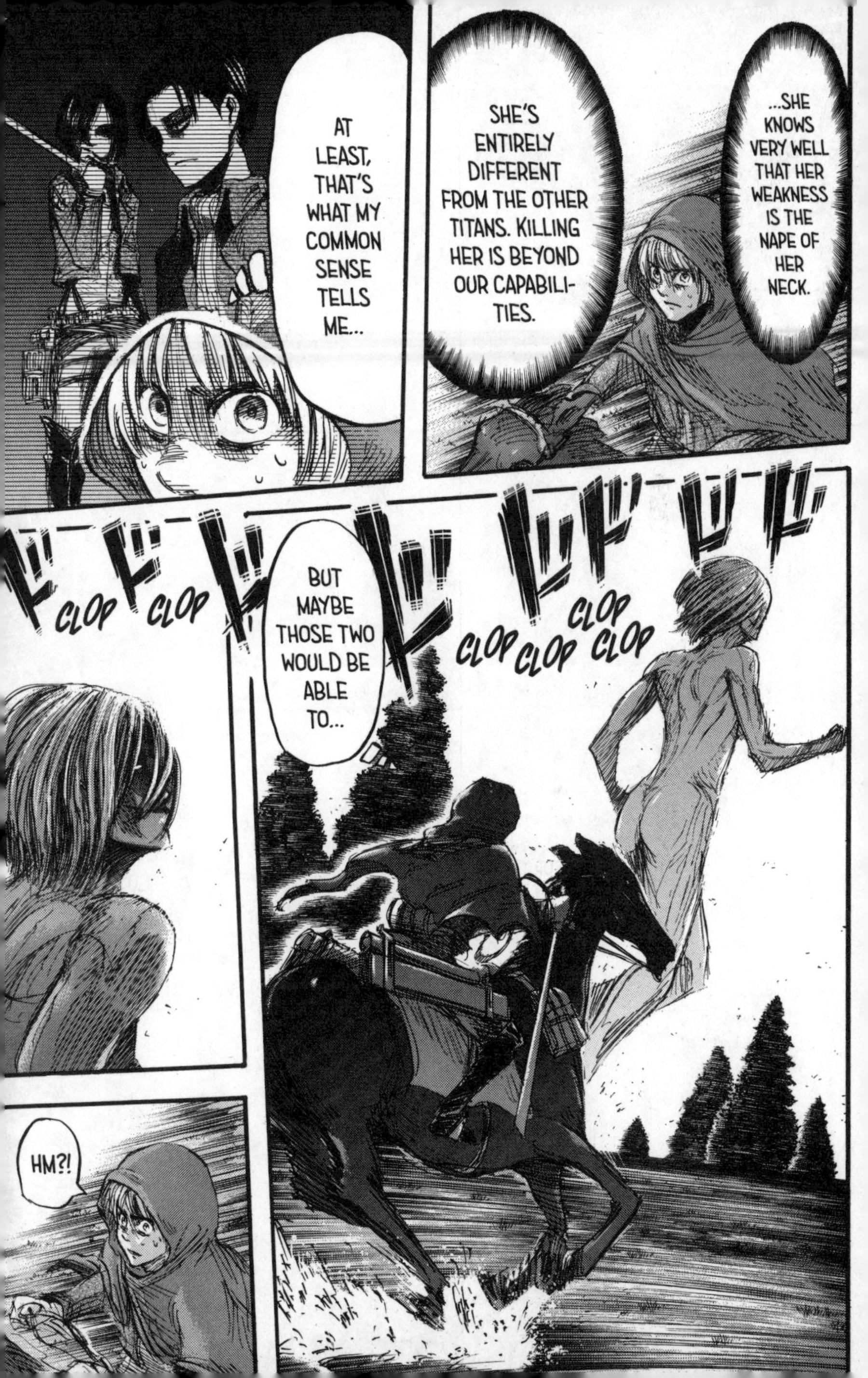
...SHE KNOWS VERY WELL THAT HER WEAKNESS IS THE NAPE OF HER NECK.
SHE'S ENTIRELY DIFFERENT FROM THE OTHER TITANS. KILLING HER IS BEYOND OUR CAPABILI-TIES.
AT LEAST, THAT'S WHAT MY COMMON SENSE TELLS ME...
CLOP CLOP CLOP CLOP
BUT MAYBE THOSE TWO WOULD BE ABLE TO...
CLOP CLOP CLOP
HM?!

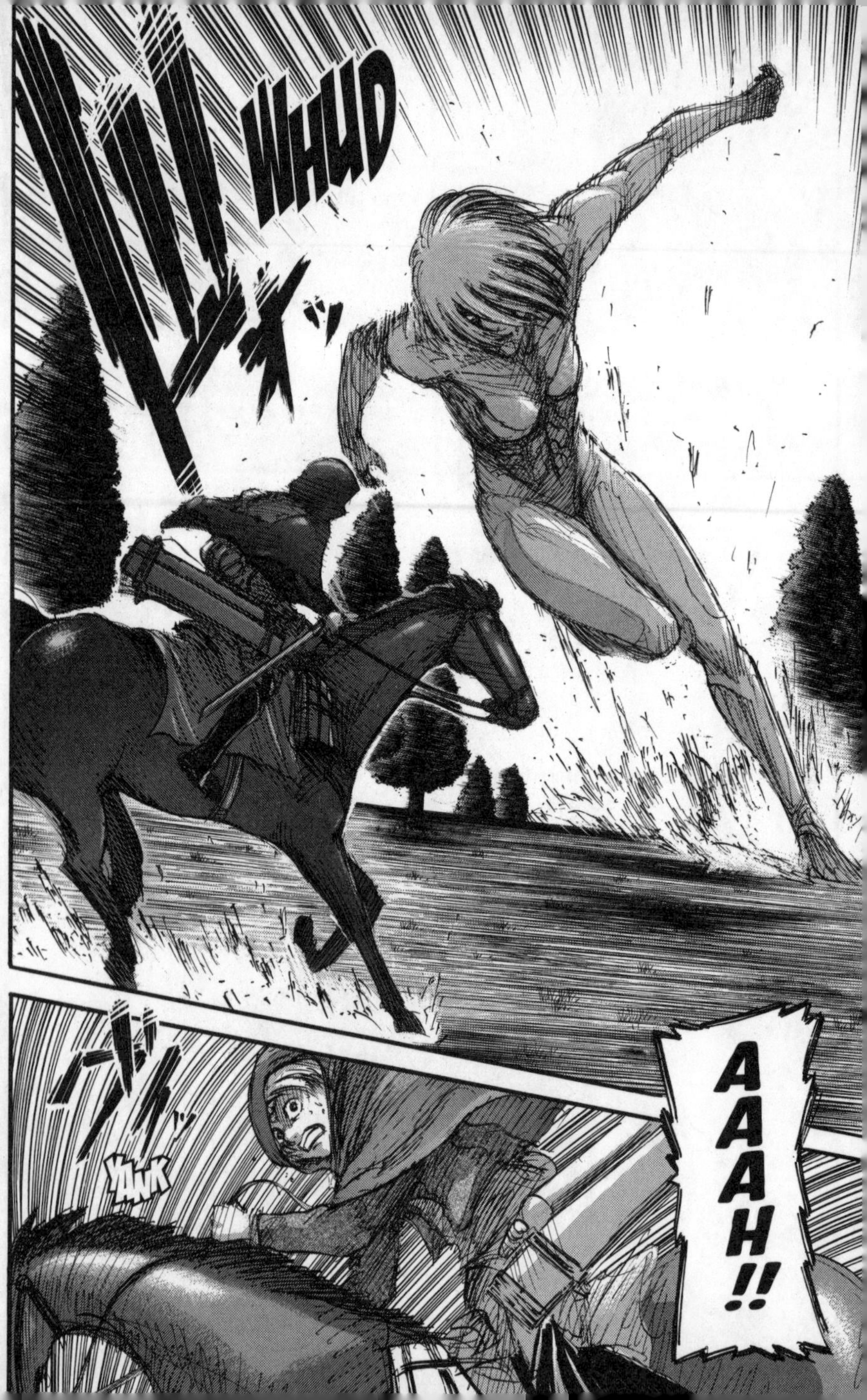
WHUD
AAAH!!
YANK

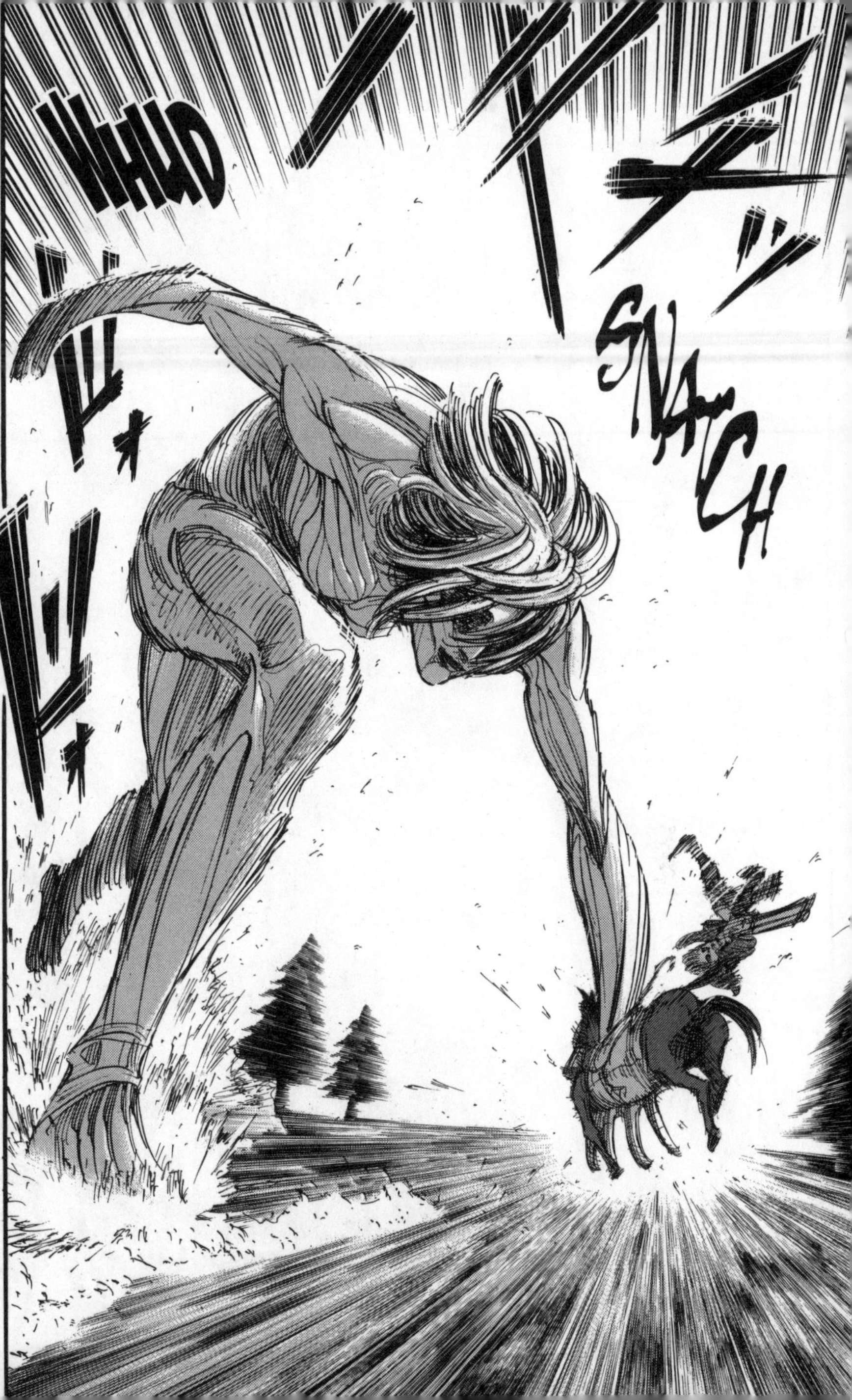
THUD
SNATCH

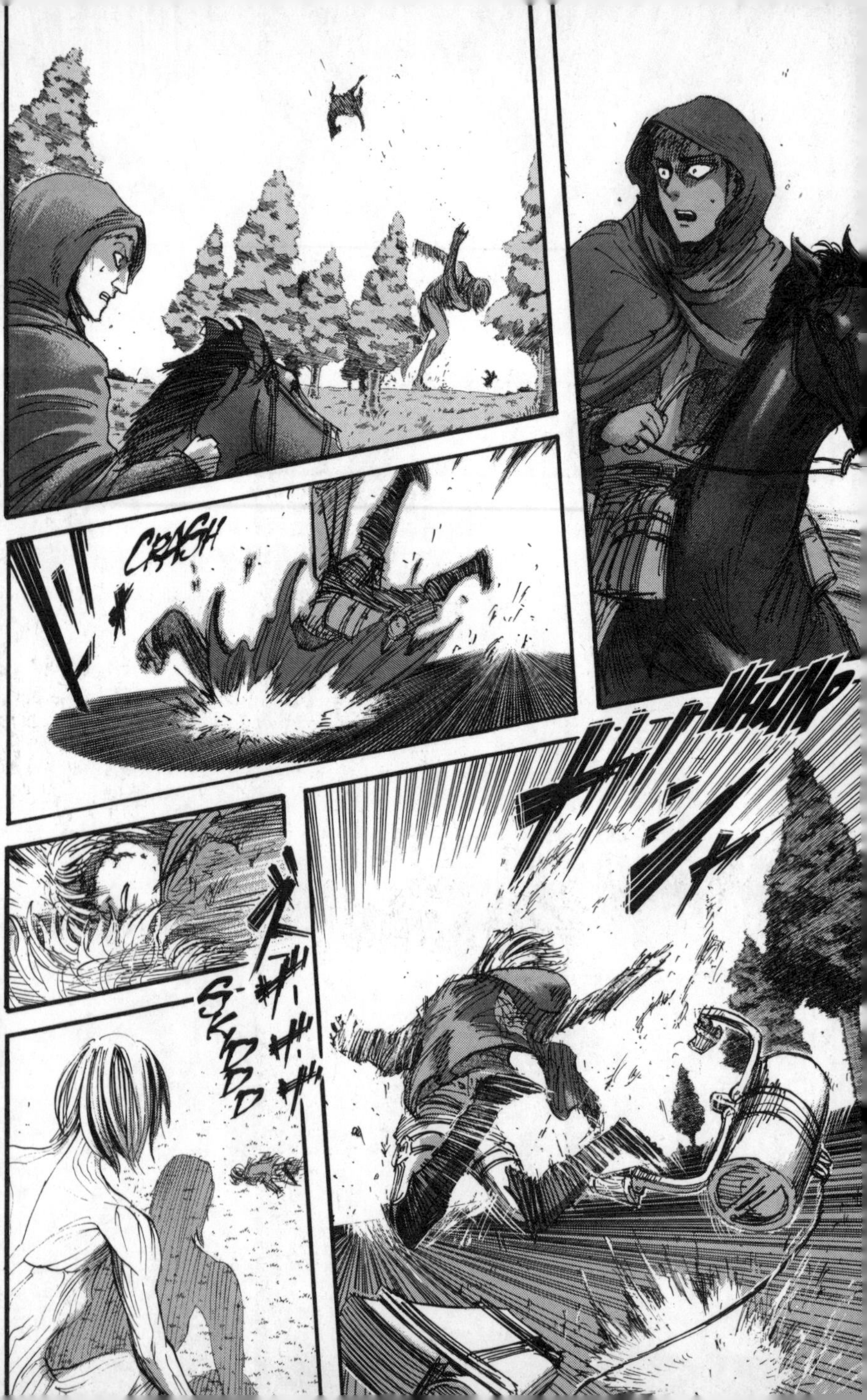
CRASH
WHUMP
SKIDDD

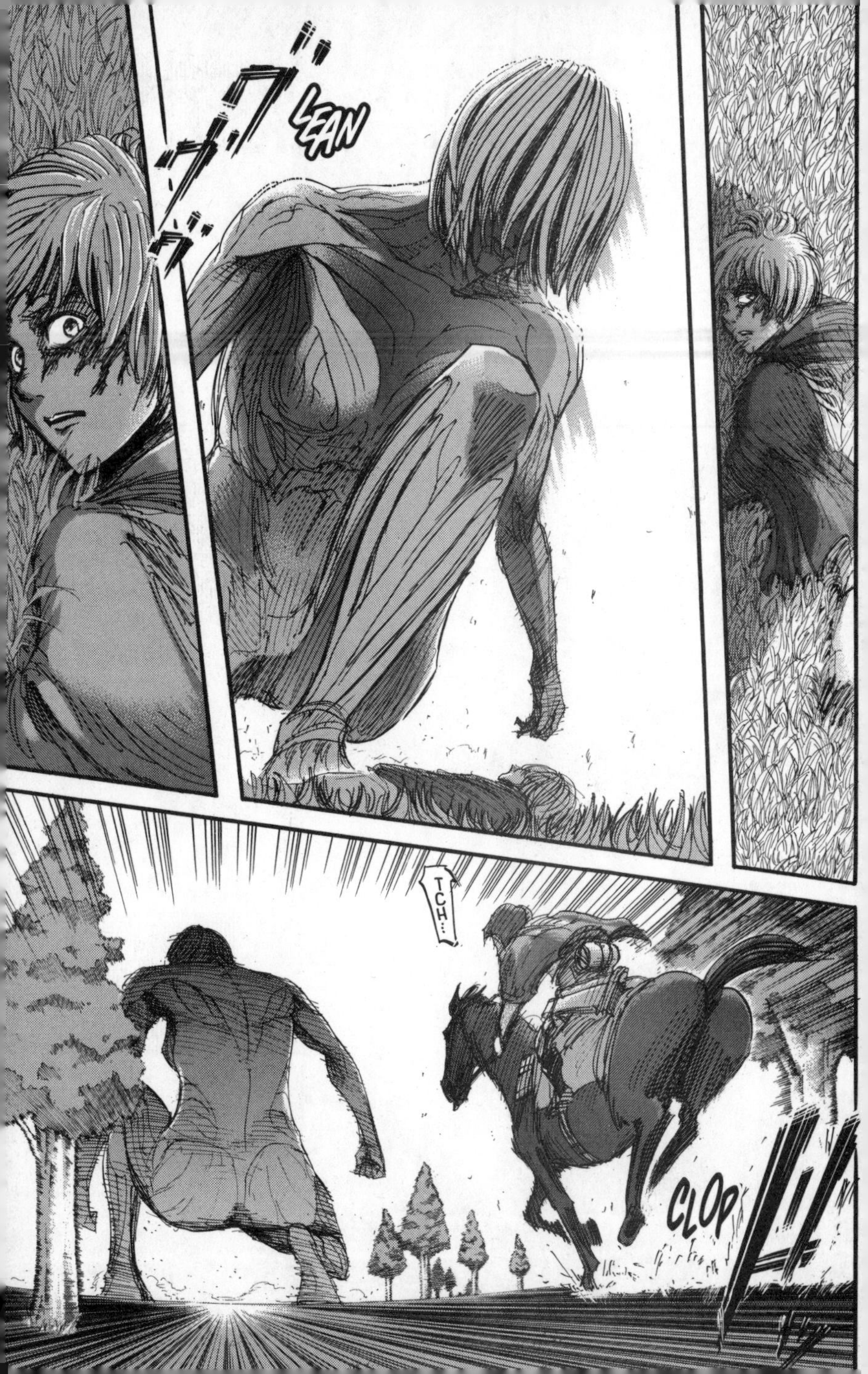
LEAN
TCH...
CLOP

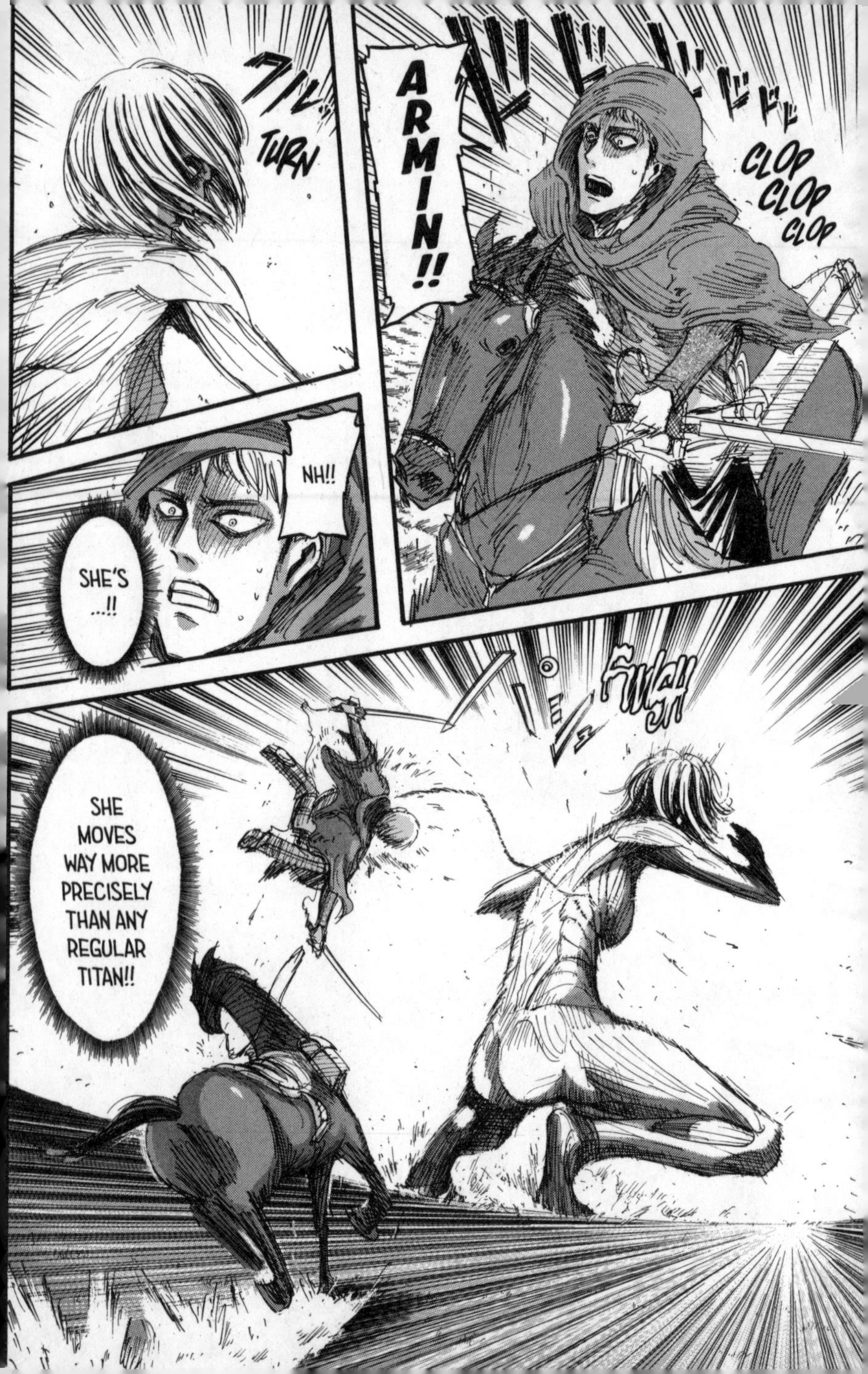
ARMIN!!
CLOP CLOP CLOP
TURN
NH!!
SHE'S ...!!
FWISH
SHE MOVES WAY MORE PRECISELY THAN ANY REGULAR TITAN!!

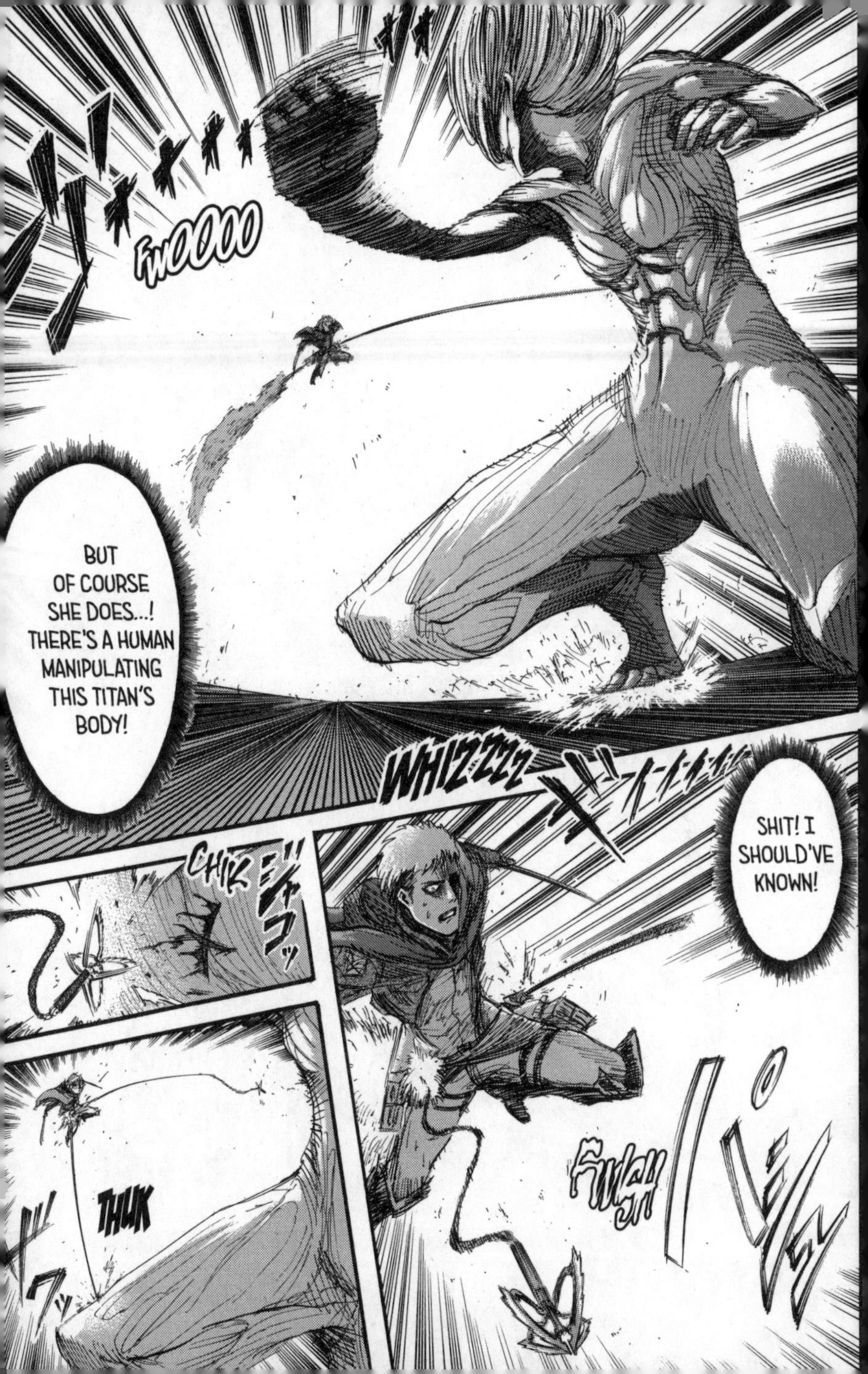
FWOOOO
BUT OF COURSE SHE DOES...! THERE'S A HUMAN MANIPULATING THIS TITAN'S BODY!
WHIZZZZ
SHIT! I SHOULD'VE KNOWN!
FWIGH
CHIK
THUK

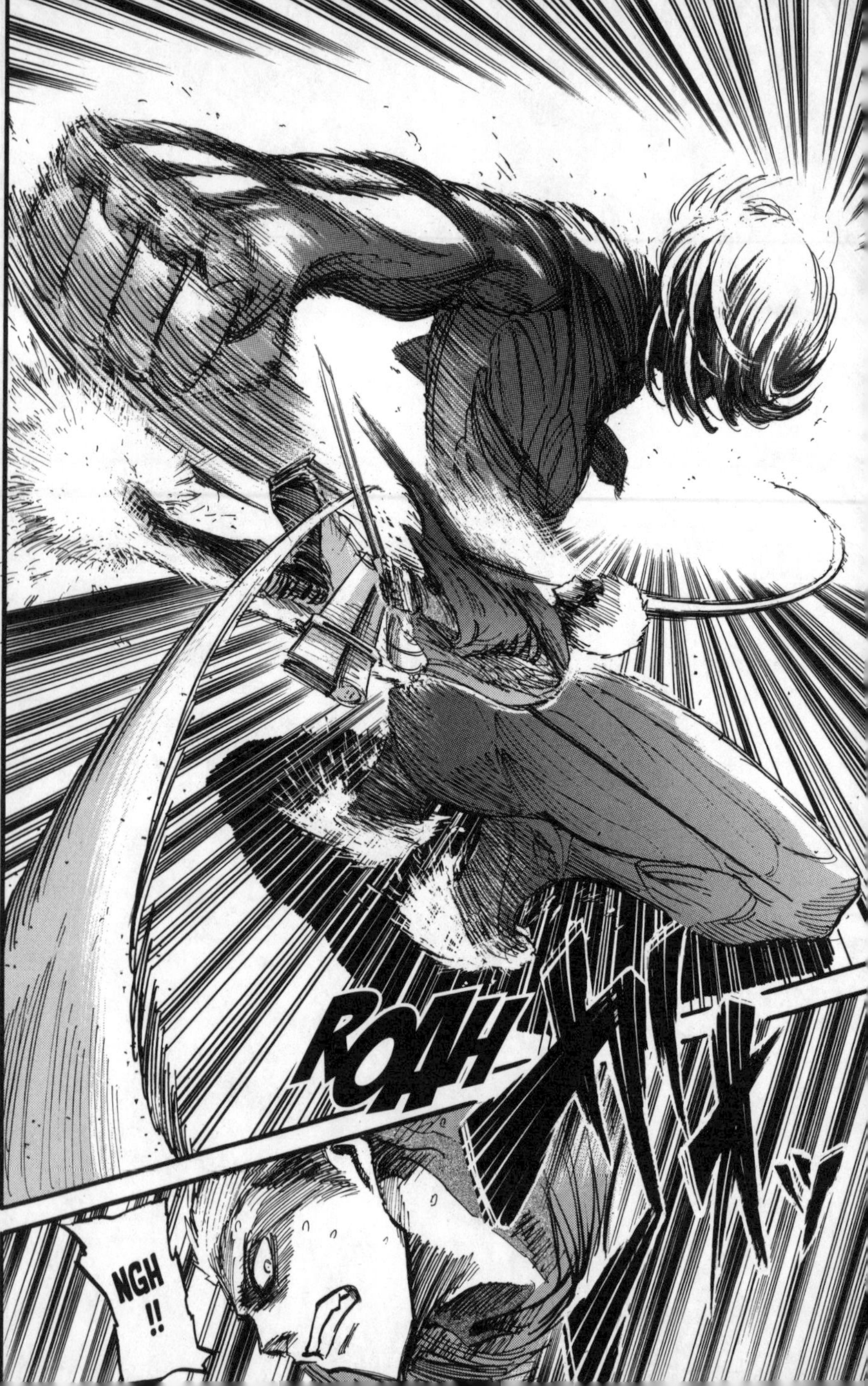
ROAH
NGH !!

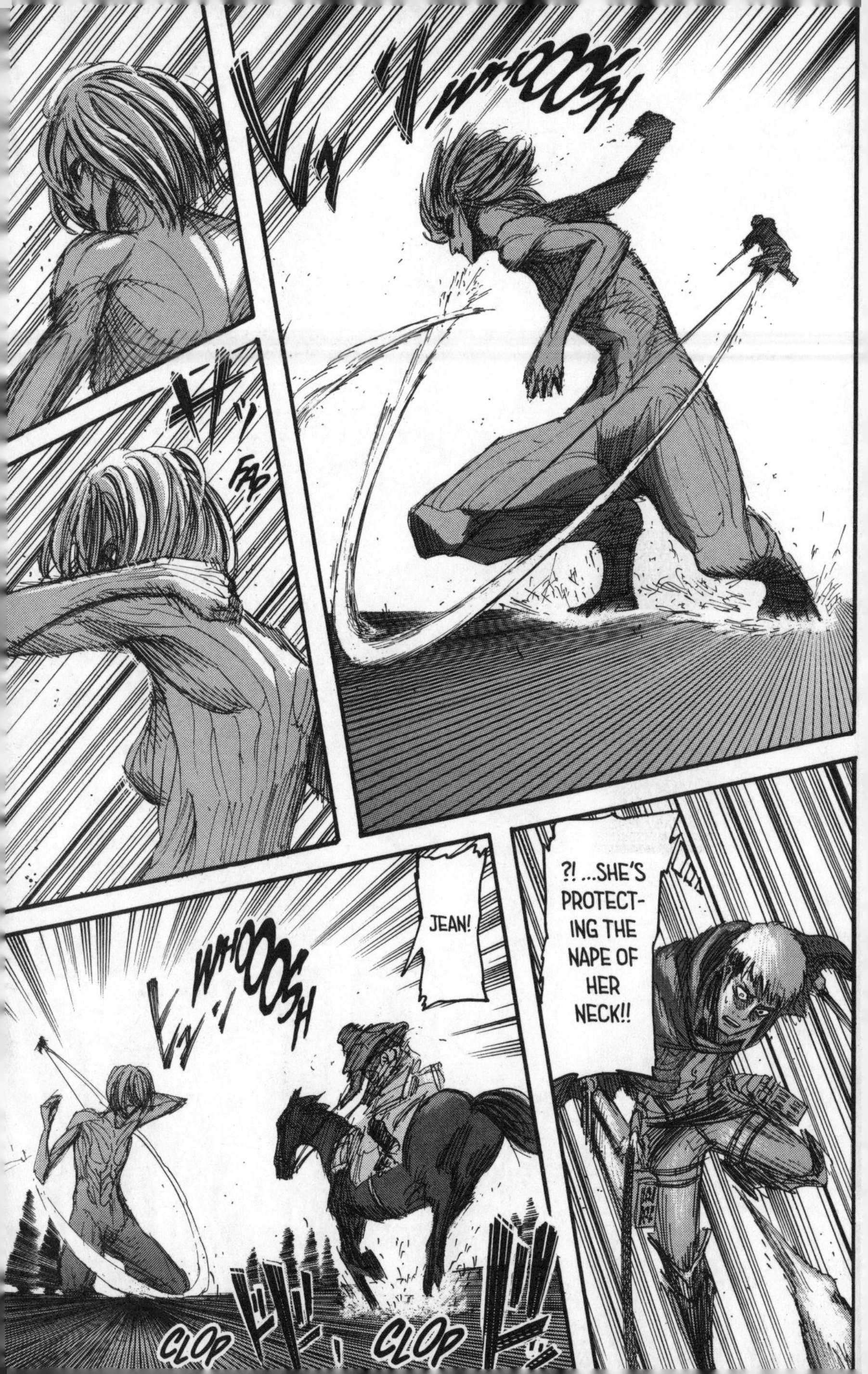
WHOOOSH
?! ...SHE'S PROTECTING THE NAPE OF HER NECK!!
JEAN!
WHOOOSH
CLOP
CLOP

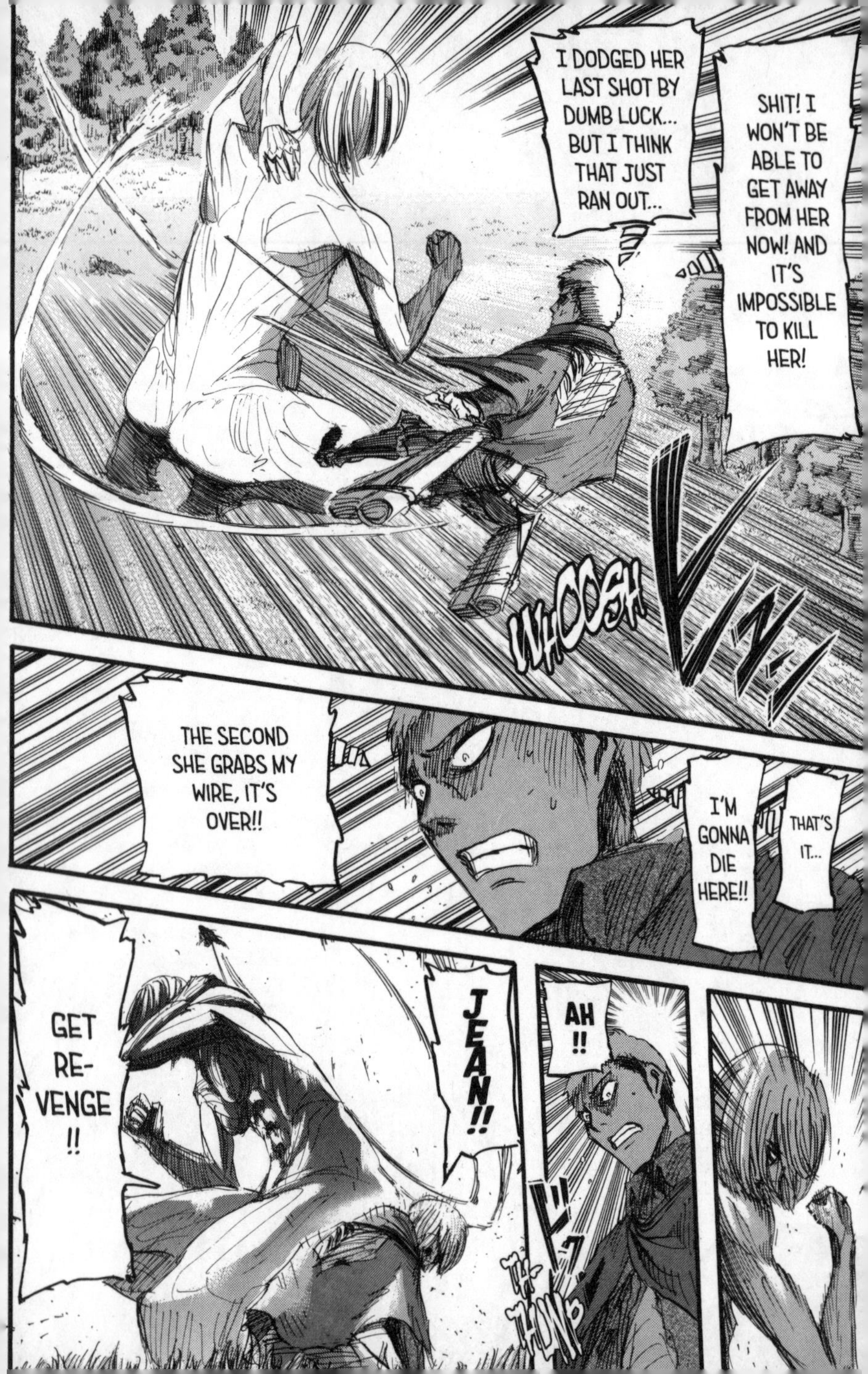
I DODGED HER LAST SHOT BY DUMB LUCK... BUT I THINK THAT JUST RAN OUT...
SHIT! I WON'T BE ABLE TO GET AWAY FROM HER NOW! AND IT'S IMPOSSIBLE TO KILL HER!
WHOOSH
THAT'S IT...
I'M GONNA DIE HERE!!
THE SECOND SHE GRABS MY WIRE, IT'S OVER!!
AH!!
JEAN!!
GET RE-VENGE!!

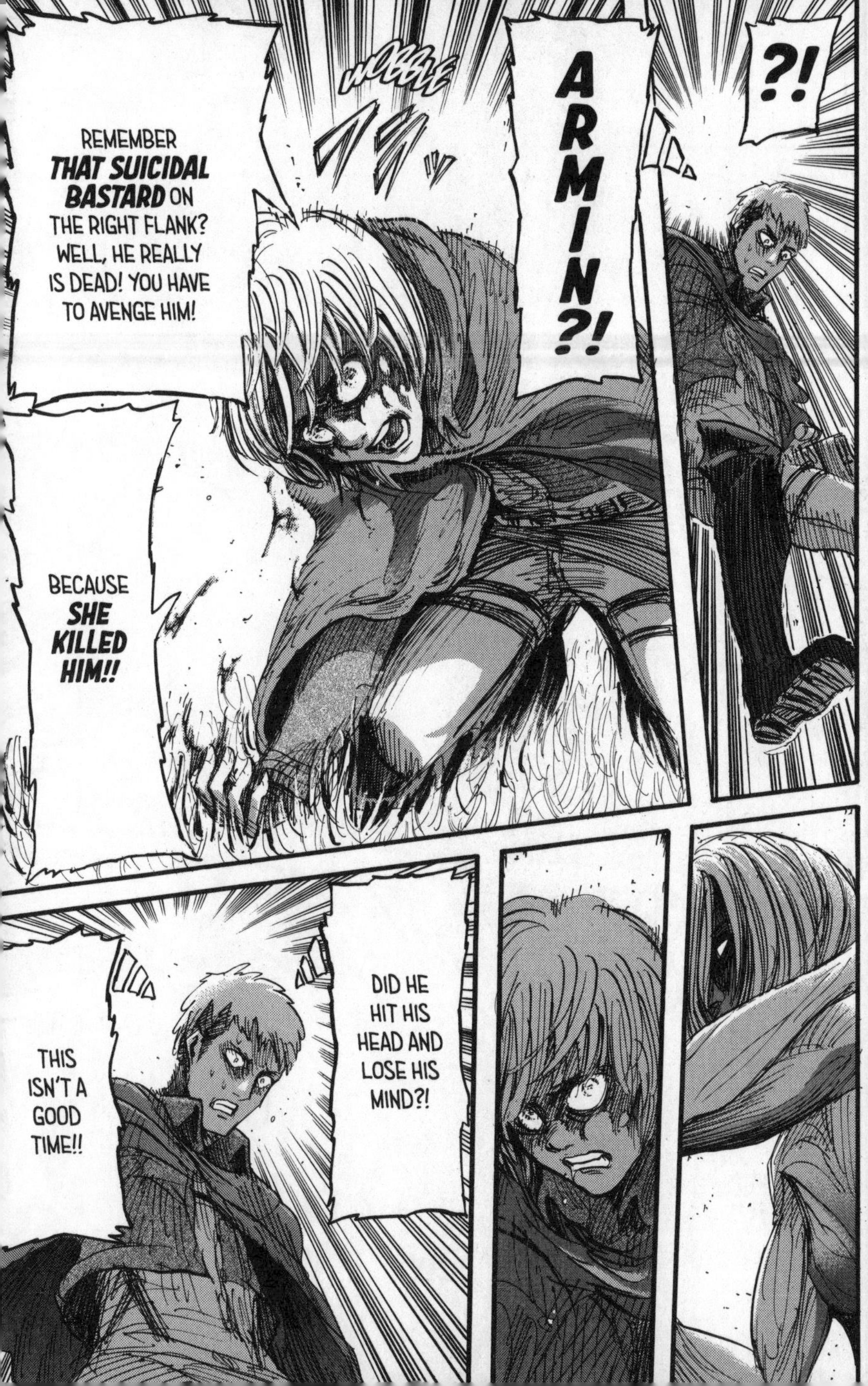
?!
ARMIN?!
WOBBLE
REMEMBER THAT SUICIDAL BASTARD ON THE RIGHT FLANK? WELL, HE REALLY IS DEAD! YOU HAVE TO AVENGE HIM!
BECAUSE SHE KILLED HIM!!
DID HE HIT HIS HEAD AND LOSE HIS MIND?!
THIS ISN'T A GOOD TIME!!

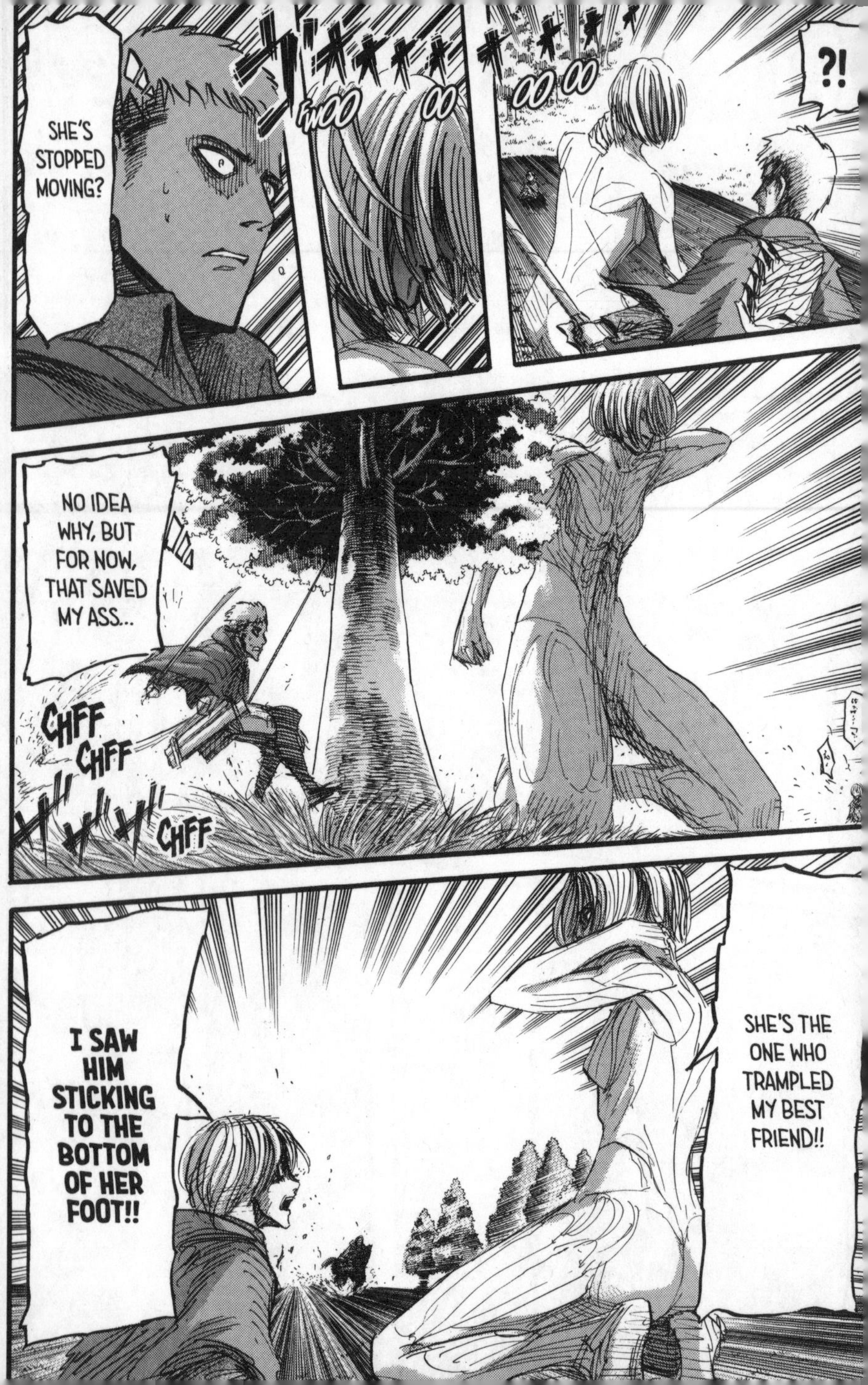
?!
FWOO
OO
OO OO
SHE'S STOPPED MOVING?
NO IDEA WHY, BUT FOR NOW, THAT SAVED MY ASS...
CHFF
CHFF
CHFF
SHE'S THE ONE WHO TRAMPLED MY BEST FRIEND!!
I SAW HIM STICKING TO THE BOTTOM OF HER FOOT!!

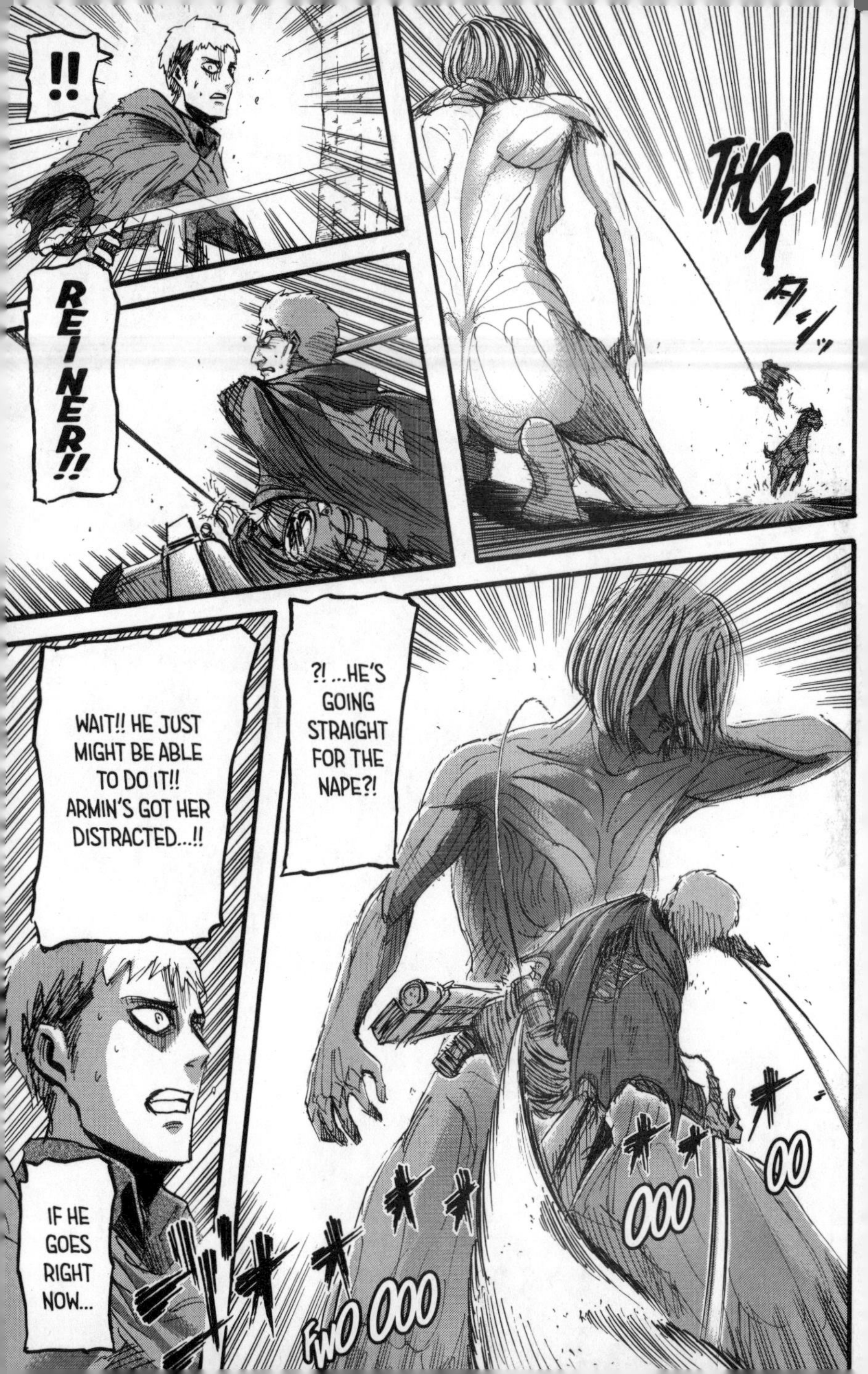
THOK
タッ
!!
REINER!!
?! ...HE'S GOING STRAIGHT FOR THE NAPE?!
OO
OOO
FWO OOO
WAIT!! HE JUST MIGHT BE ABLE TO DO IT!! ARMIN'S GOT HER DISTRACTED...!!
IF HE GOES RIGHT NOW...

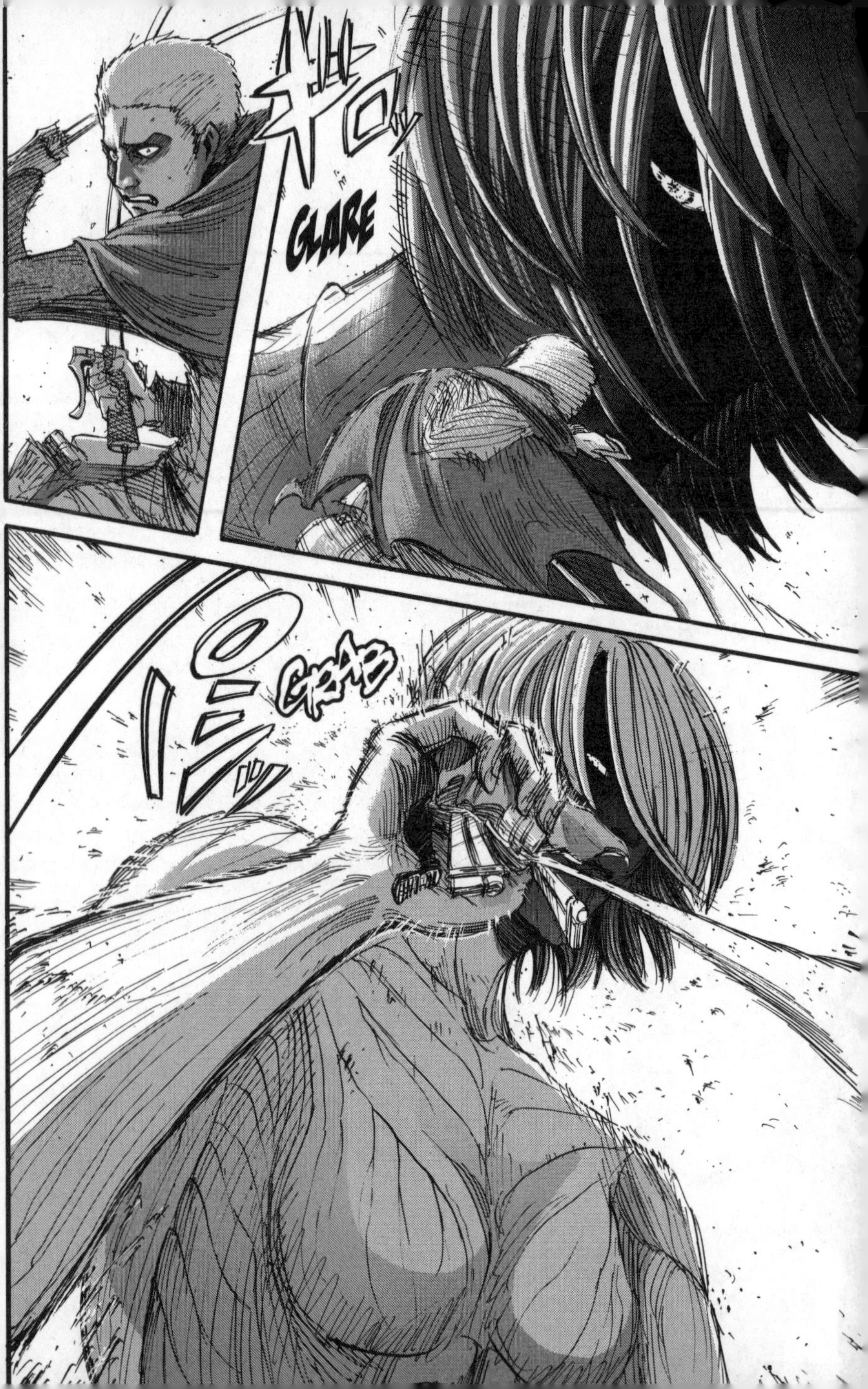
GLARE
GRAB

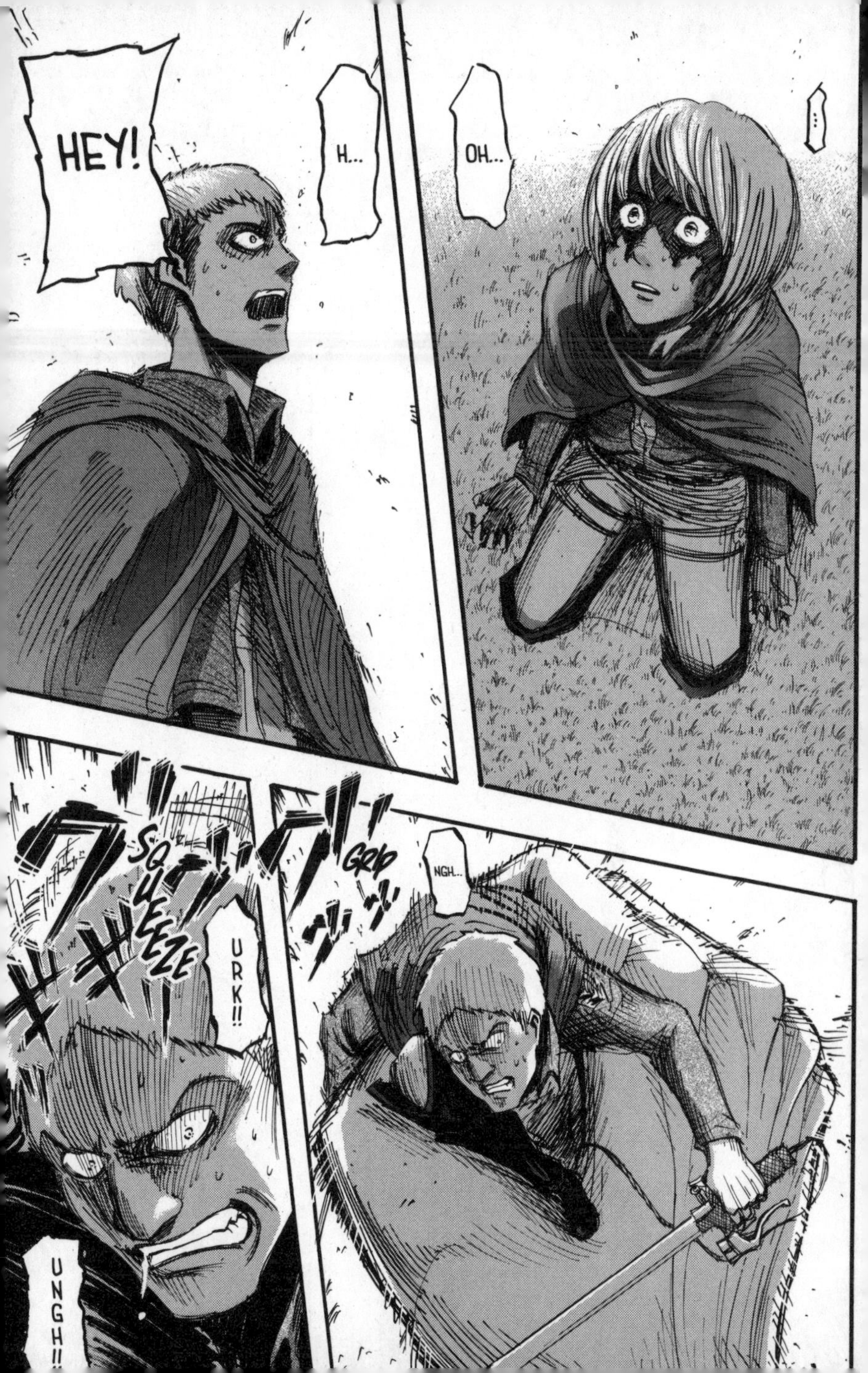
...
OH...
H...
HEY!
NGH...
GRIP
SQUEEZE
URK!!
UNGH!!

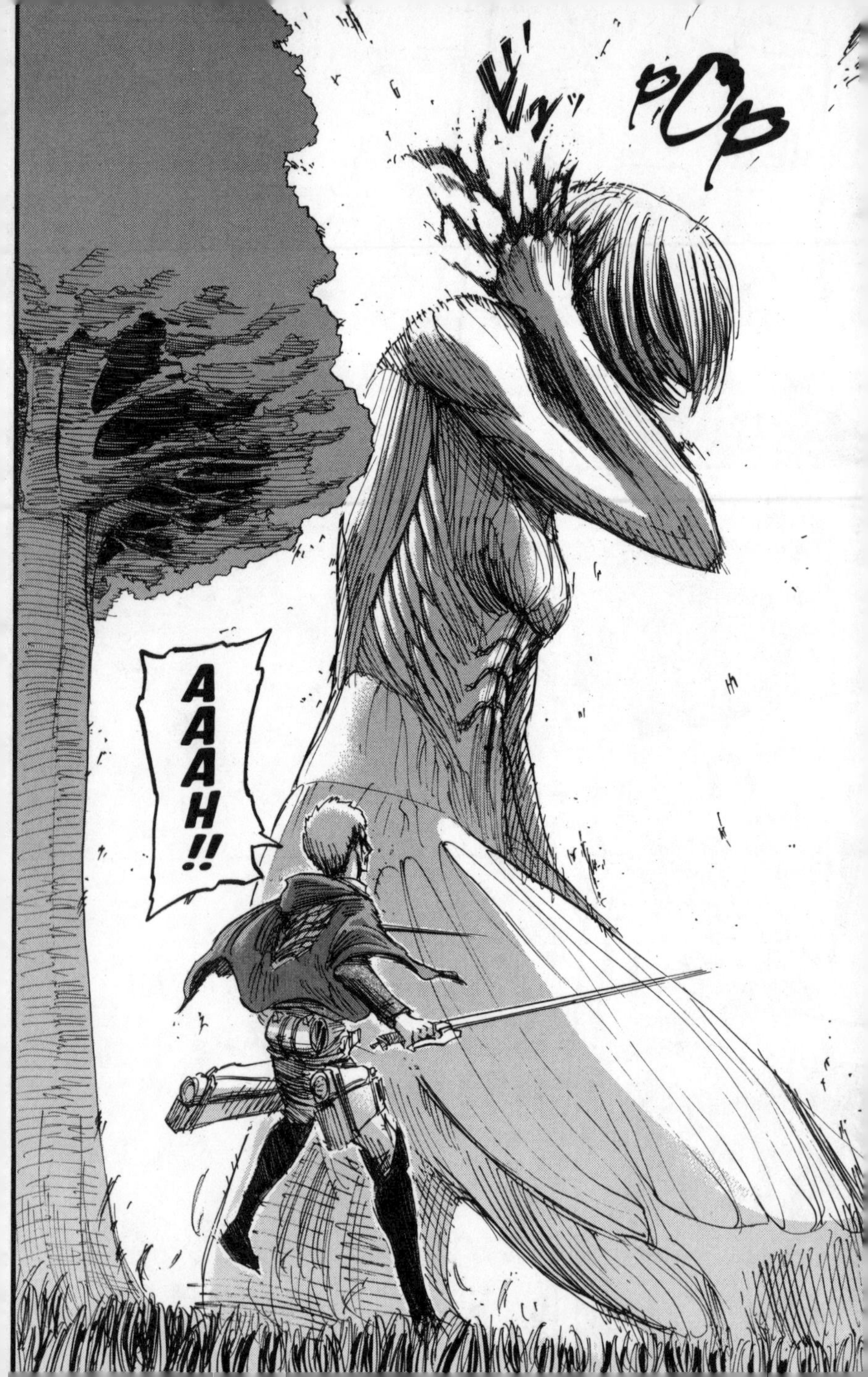
POP
AAAAH!!

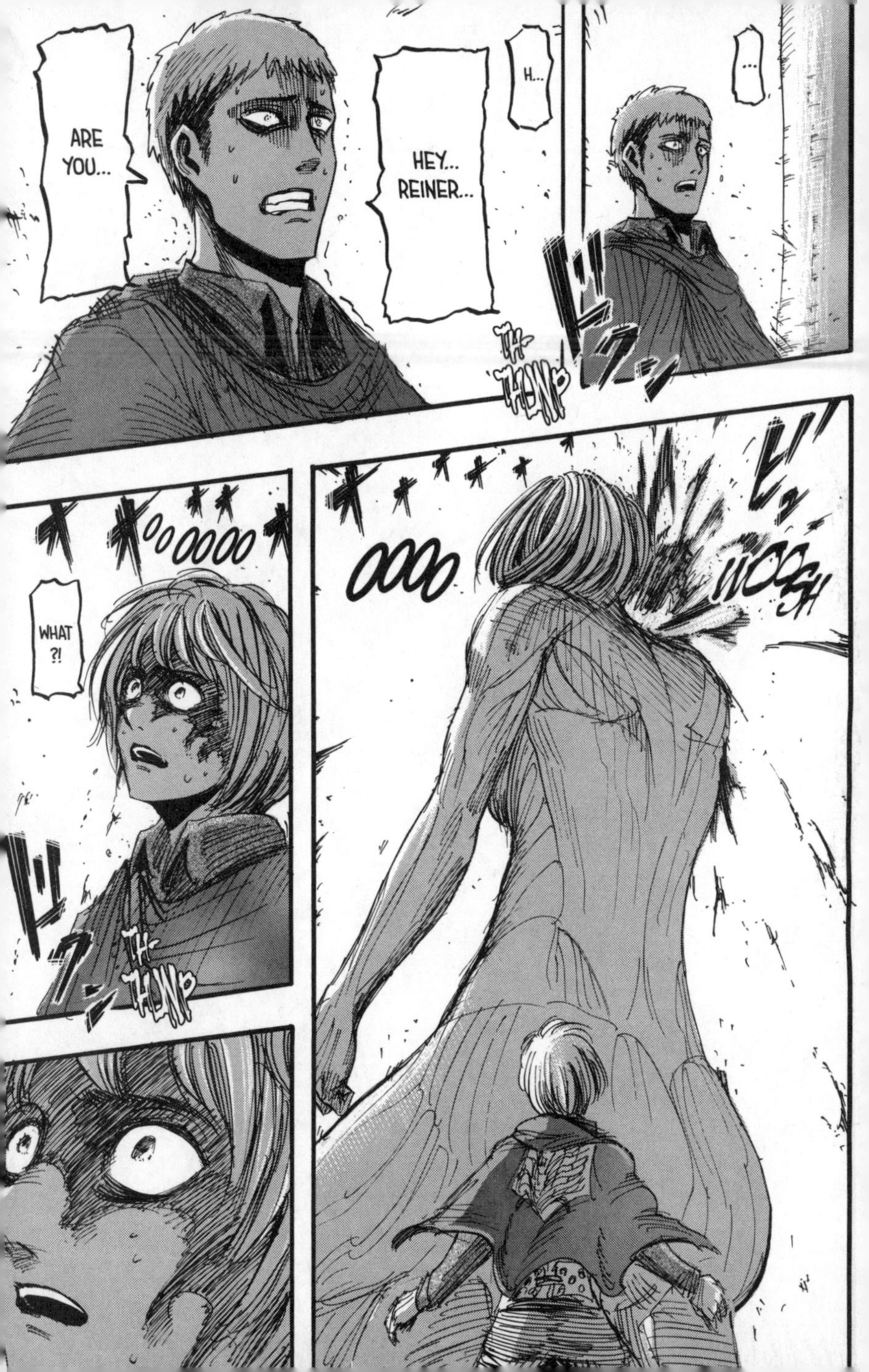
...
TH-THUMP
H...
HEY... REINER...
ARE YOU...
WOOSH
OOOO
OOOOOO
WHAT ?!
TH-THUMP

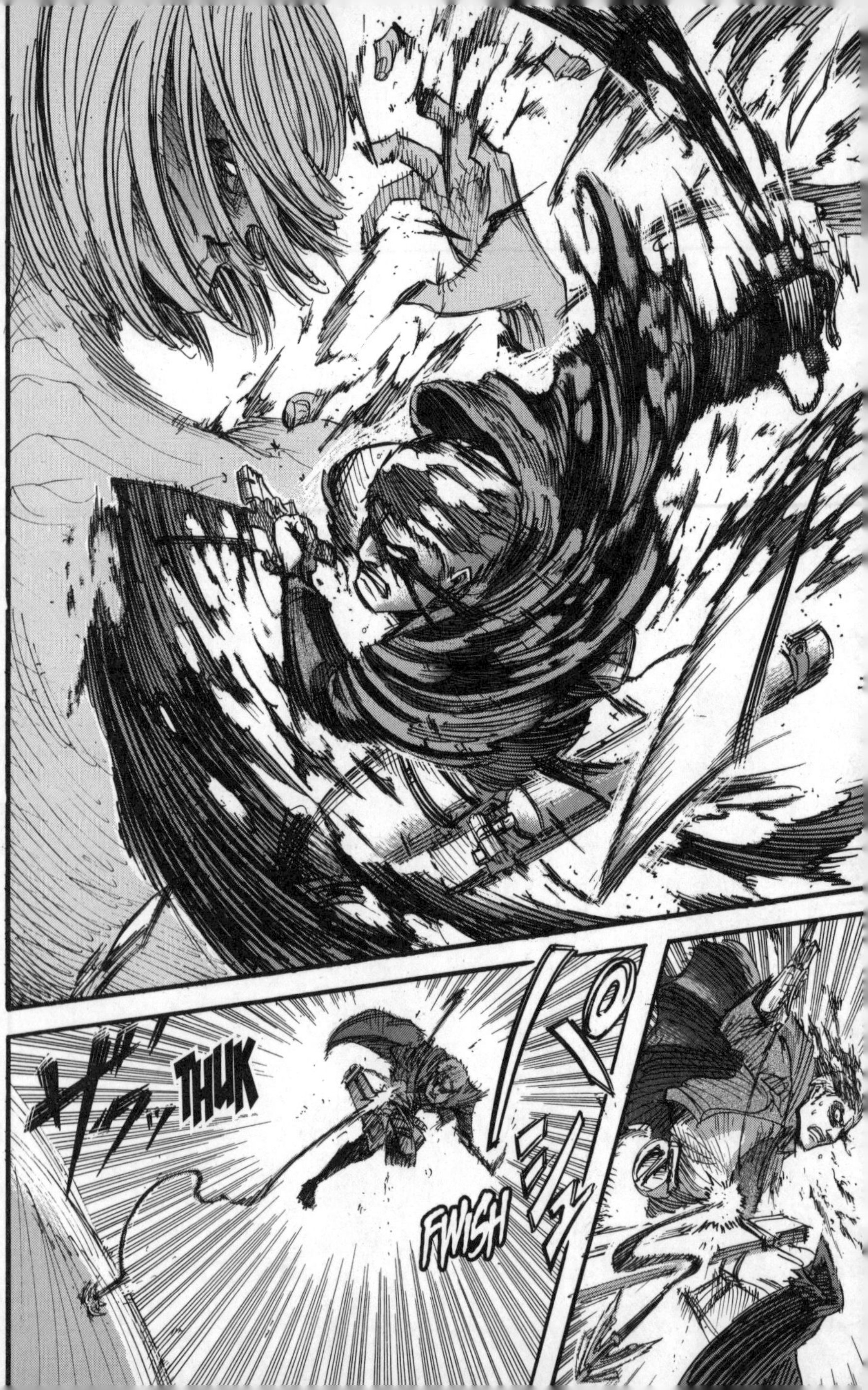
THUK
FWISH

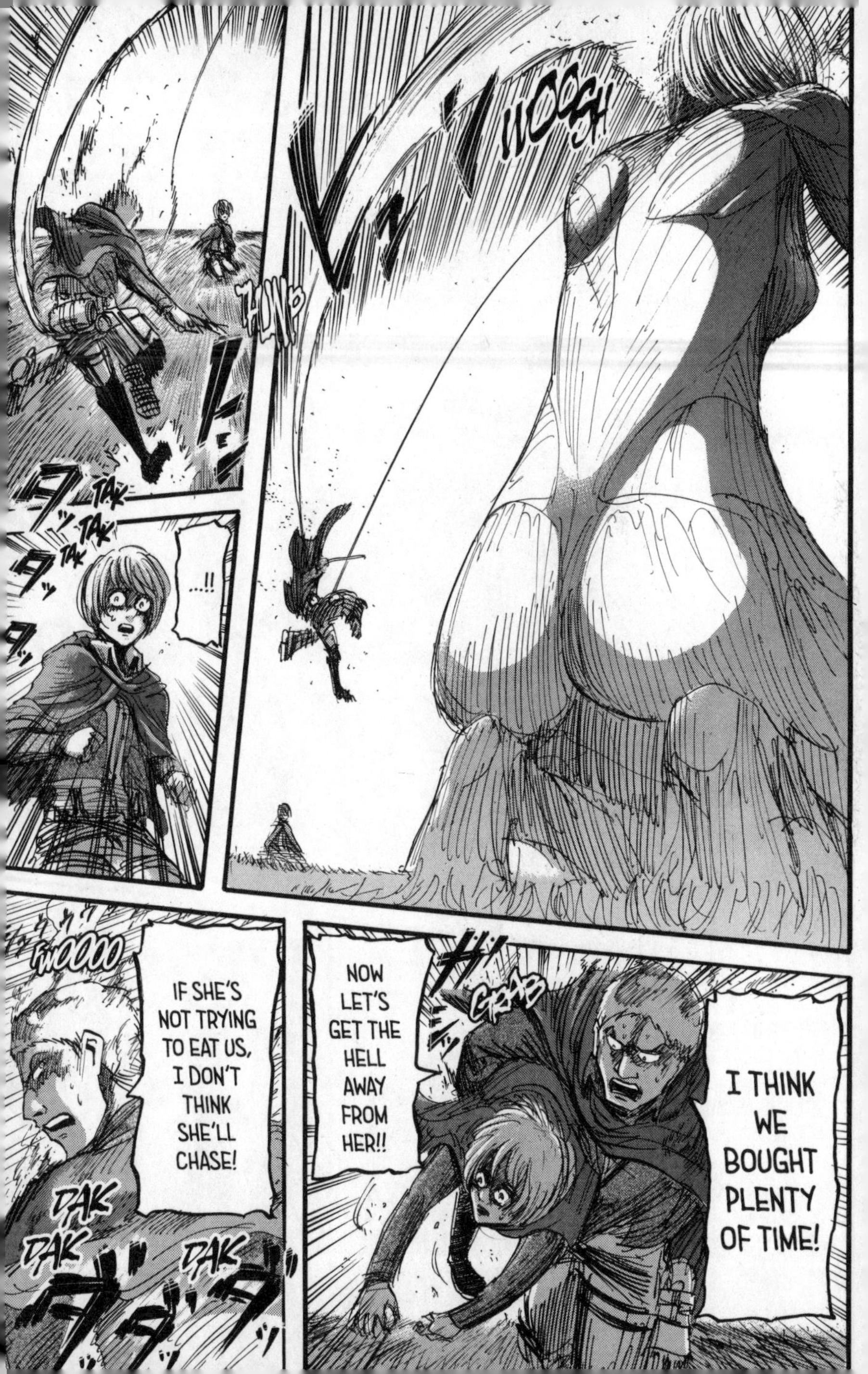

WOOSH
THUMP
TAK
TAK
TAK
...!!
GRAB
I THINK WE BOUGHT PLENTY OF TIME!
NOW LET'S GET THE HELL AWAY FROM HER!!
FWOOOO
IF SHE'S NOT TRYING TO EAT US, I DON'T THINK SHE'LL CHASE!
DAK
DAK
DAK

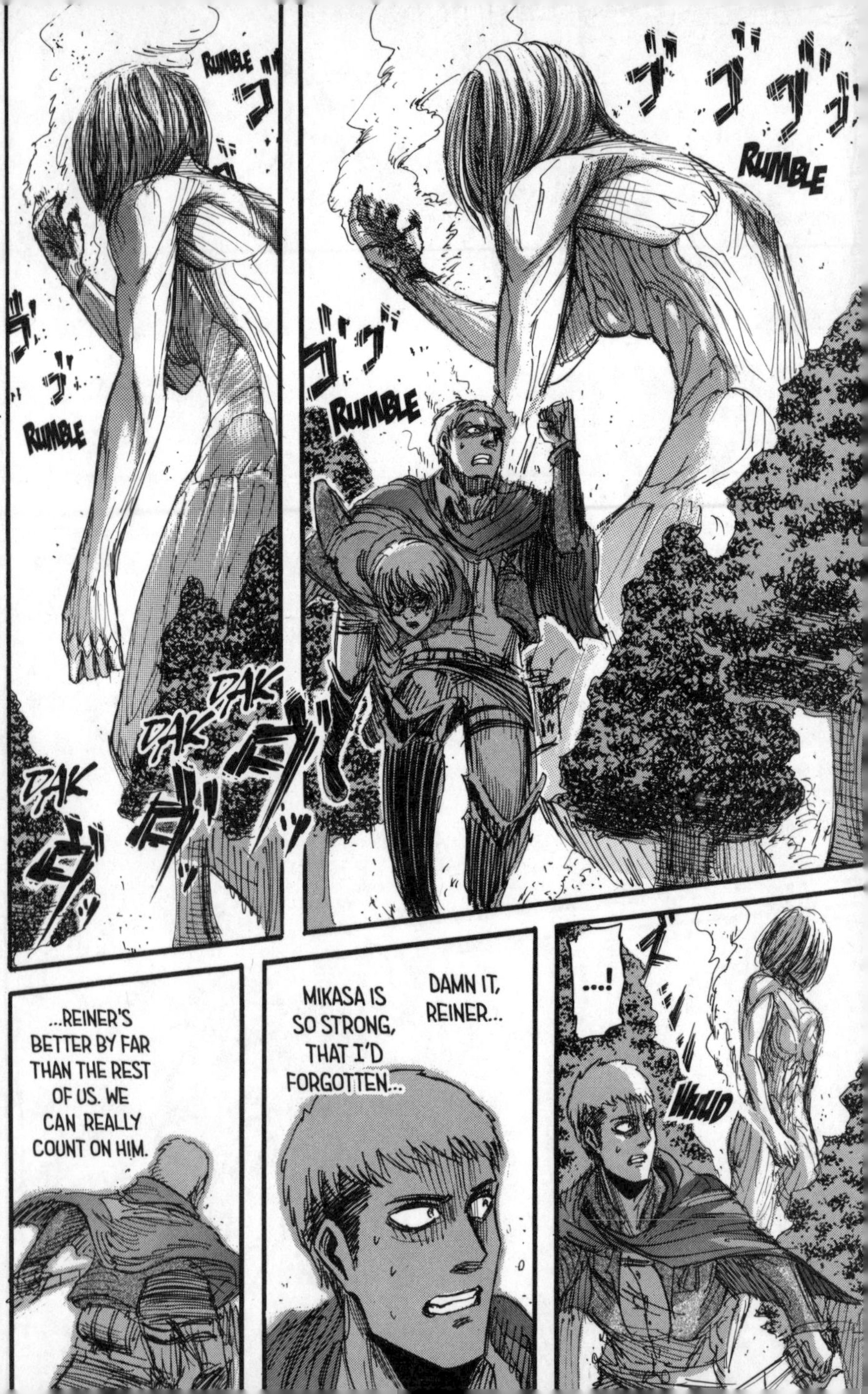
RUMBLE
RUMBLE
RUMBLE
RUMBLE
DAK
DAK
DAK
...!
WHUD
DAMN IT, REINER...
MIKASA IS SO STRONG, THAT I'D FORGOTTEN...
...REINER'S BETTER BY FAR THAN THE REST OF US. WE CAN REALLY COUNT ON HIM.

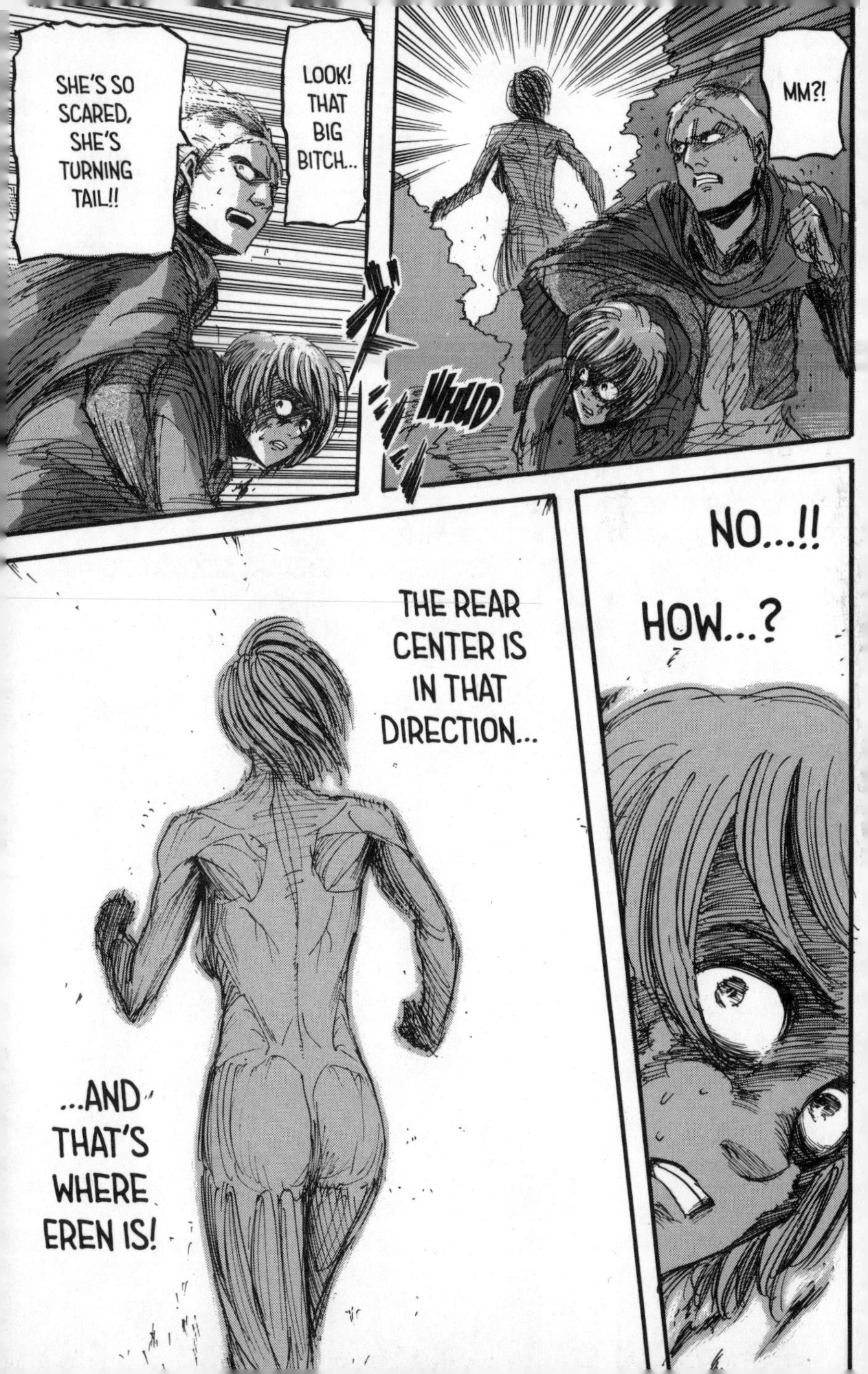
MM?!
WHUD
LOOK! THAT BIG BITCH...
SHE'S SO SCARED, SHE'S TURNING TAIL!!
NO...!!
HOW...?
THE REAR CENTER IS IN THAT DIRECTION...
...AND THAT'S WHERE EREN IS!

Current Publicly Available Information

11. Yeast

A UNIQUE TYPE OF YEAST IS PRODUCED BEHIND WALL SHEENA. AT A GLANCE, IT LOOKS LIKE A LUMP OF FERMENTED SOYBEANS THE SIZE OF A HUMAN HEAD. IT'S A WELL-KNOWN FACT THAT STORING THE YEAST IN SHEDS OR TENTS THAT ALSO CONTAIN FODDER, WHEAT, SOYBEANS, OR DRY-CURED MEAT SLOWS DOWN THE DECOMPOSITION PROCESS IMMENSELY. IT'S A GIVEN THAT THIS YEAST PRESERVES FOOD BY TRANSFORMING IT, ALTHOUGH THERE IS AS YET NO SCIENTIFIC THEORY TO EXPLAIN IT. THE PLACEMENT OF YEAST STORAGE PLANTS IN EVERY AREA SO THAT SUPPLIES CAN BE STOCKPILED IS PART OF THE HUMAN RACE'S STRATEGY TO TAKE BACK WALL MARIA.
(WITH THANKS TO UKYŌ KODACHI AND KIYOMUNE MIWA)

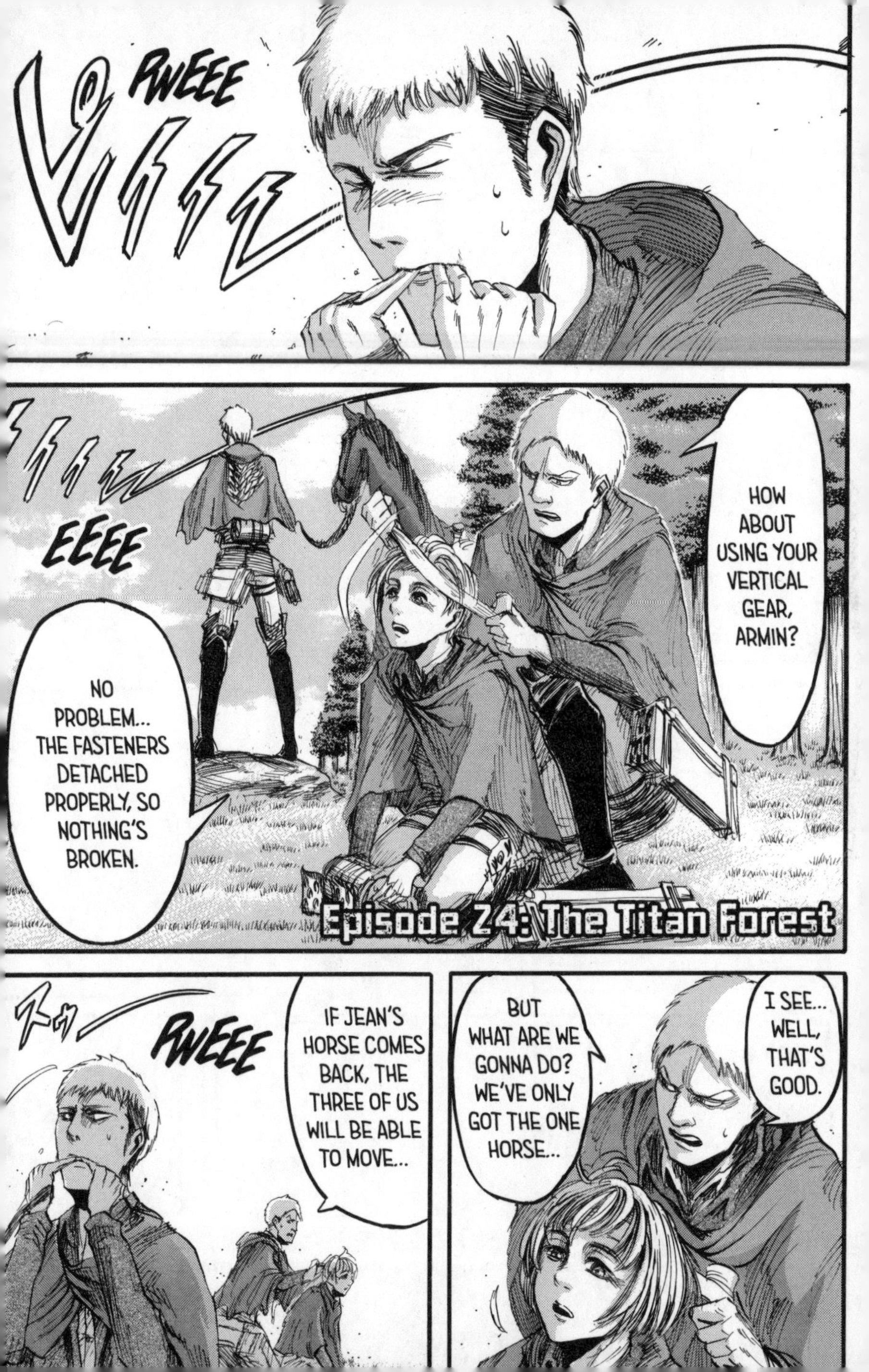
PWEEE
HOW ABOUT USING YOUR VERTICAL GEAR, ARMIN?
EEEE
NO PROBLEM... THE FASTENERS DETACHED PROPERLY, SO NOTHING'S BROKEN.
Episode 24: The Titan Forest
I SEE... WELL, THAT'S GOOD.
BUT WHAT ARE WE GONNA DO? WE'VE ONLY GOT THE ONE HORSE...
IF JEAN'S HORSE COMES BACK, THE THREE OF US WILL BE ABLE TO MOVE...
PWEEE

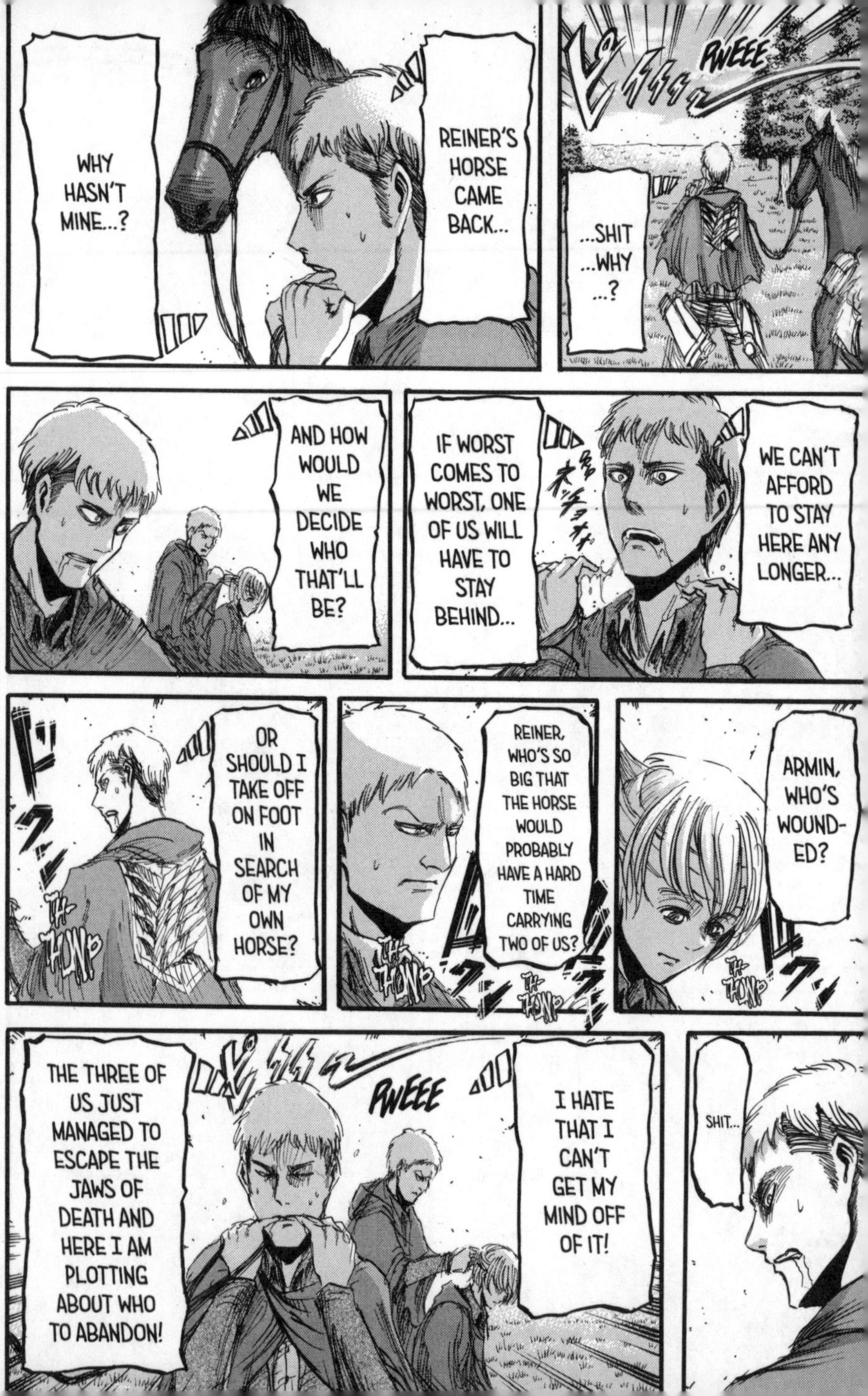
PWEEE
...SHIT ...WHY ...?
REINER'S HORSE CAME BACK...
WHY HASN'T MINE...?
WE CAN'T AFFORD TO STAY HERE ANY LONGER...
IF WORST COMES TO WORST, ONE OF US WILL HAVE TO STAY BEHIND...
AND HOW WOULD WE DECIDE WHO THAT'LL BE?
ARMIN, WHO'S WOUND-ED?
THA-THOMP
REINER, WHO'S SO BIG THAT THE HORSE WOULD PROBABLY HAVE A HARD TIME CARRYING TWO OF US?
THA-THOMP
THA-THOMP
OR SHOULD I TAKE OFF ON FOOT IN SEARCH OF MY OWN HORSE?
THA-THOMP
SHIT...
I HATE THAT I CAN'T GET MY MIND OFF OF IT!
PWEEE
THE THREE OF US JUST MANAGED TO ESCAPE THE JAWS OF DEATH AND HERE I AM PLOTTING ABOUT WHO TO ABANDON!

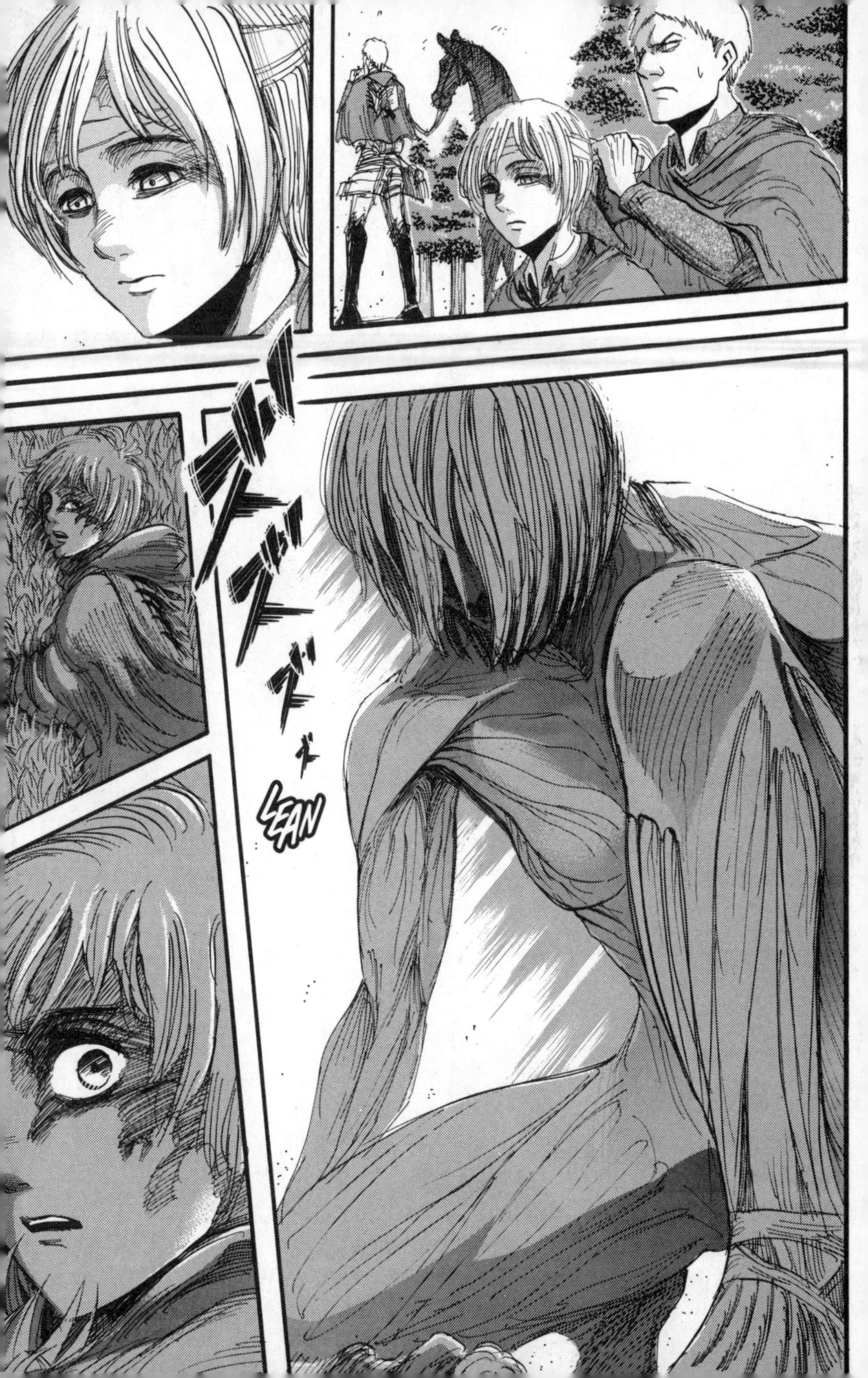
LEAN

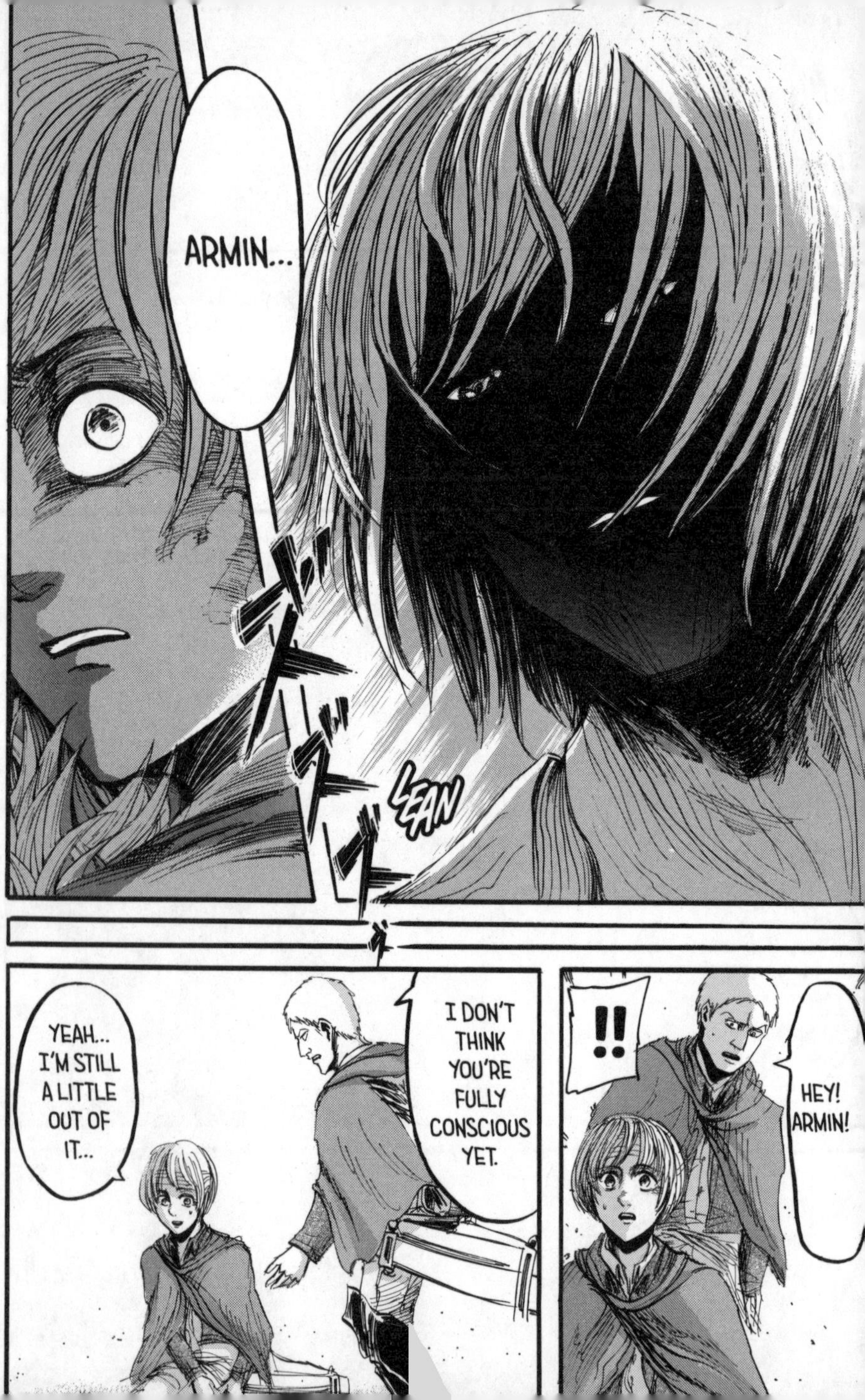
ARMIN...
LEAN
!!
HEY! ARMIN!
I DON'T THINK YOU'RE FULLY CONSCIOUS YET.
YEAH... I'M STILL A LITTLE OUT OF IT...

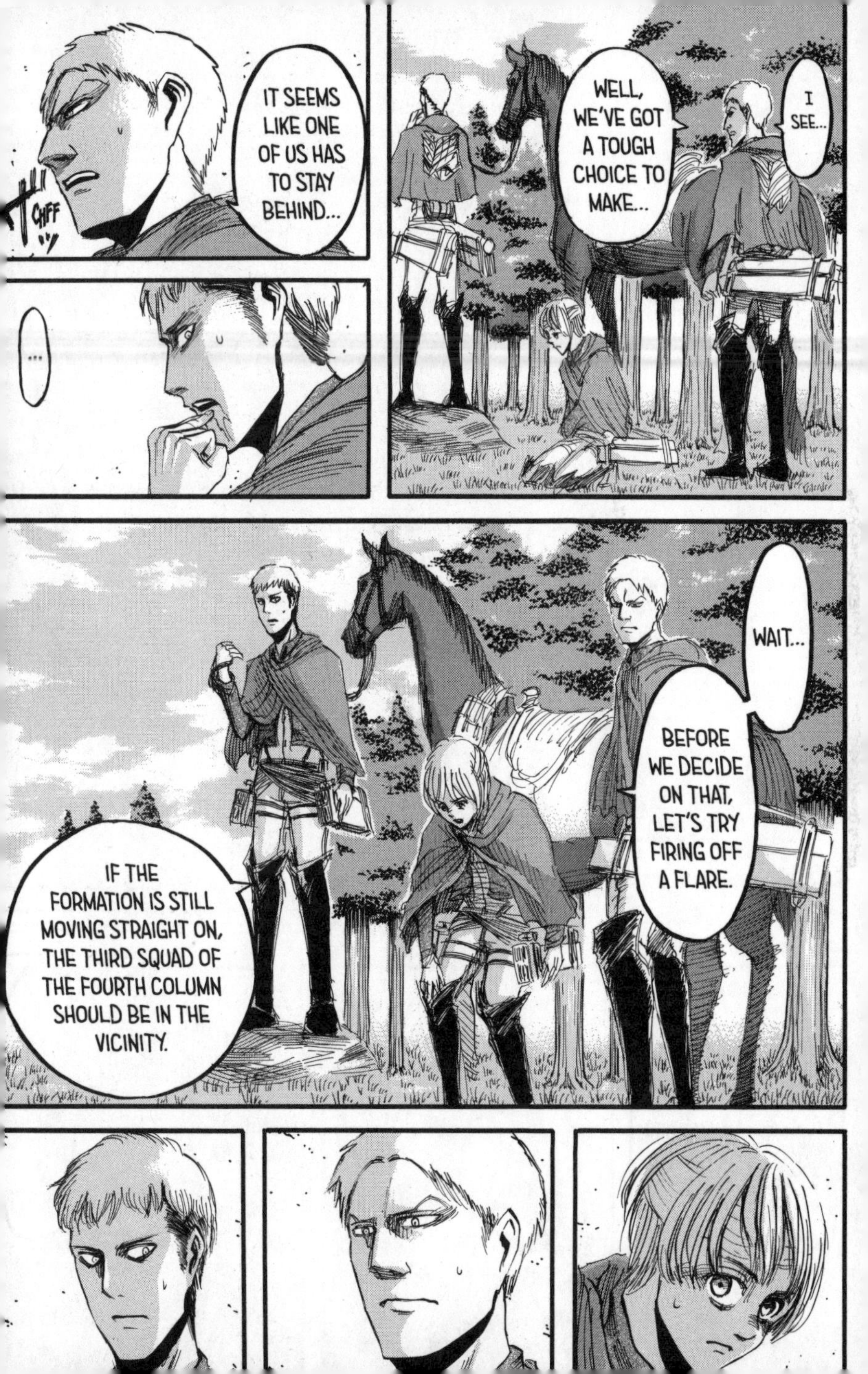
I SEE...
WELL, WE'VE GOT A TOUGH CHOICE TO MAKE...
IT SEEMS LIKE ONE OF US HAS TO STAY BEHIND...
CHFF
...
WAIT...
BEFORE WE DECIDE ON THAT, LET'S TRY FIRING OFF A FLARE.
IF THE FORMATION IS STILL MOVING STRAIGHT ON, THE THIRD SQUAD OF THE FOURTH COLUMN SHOULD BE IN THE VICINITY.

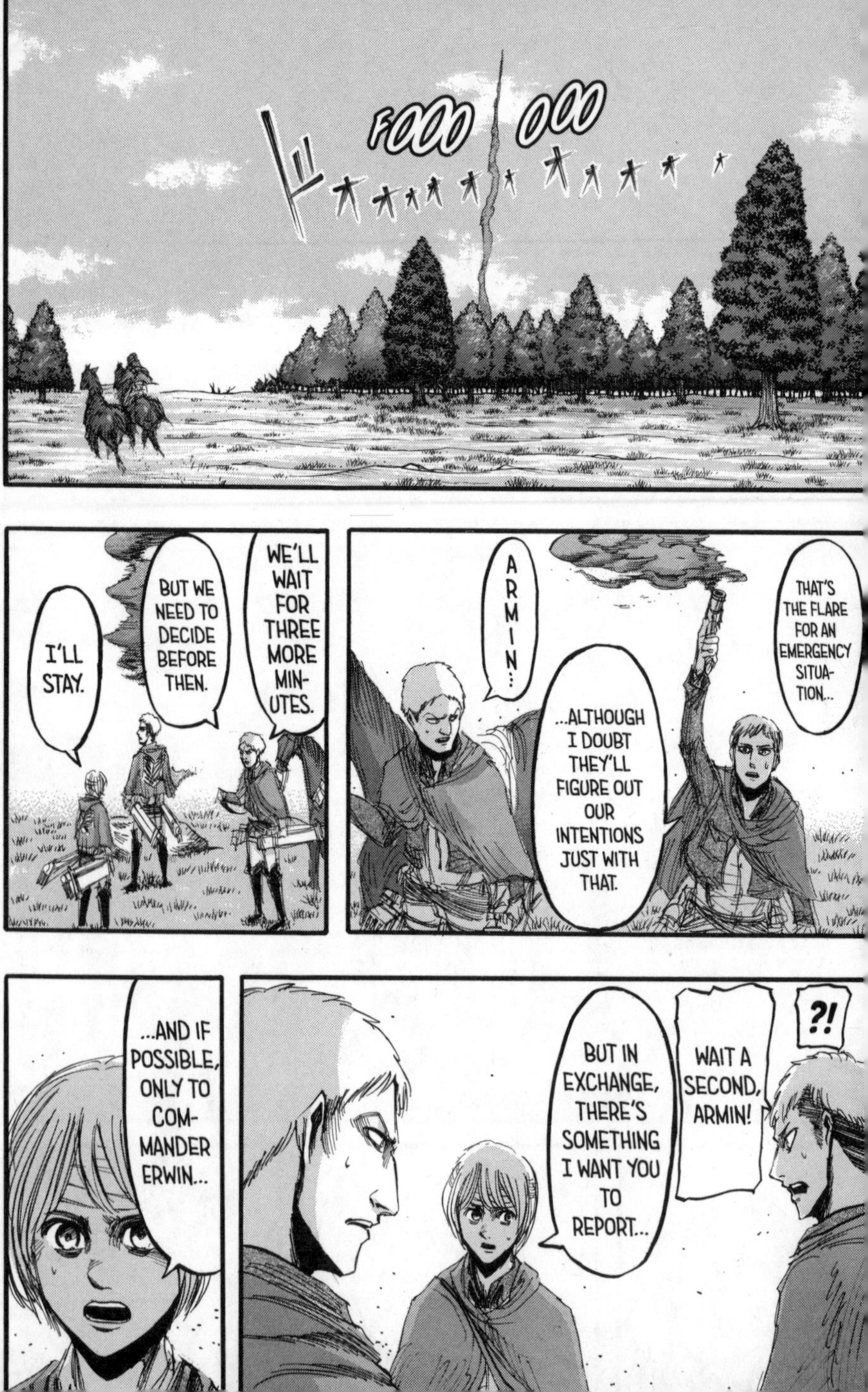

FOOOOOO
THAT'S THE FLARE FOR AN EMERGENCY SITUATION...
ARMIN...
...ALTHOUGH I DOUBT THEY'LL FIGURE OUT OUR INTENTIONS JUST WITH THAT.
WE'LL WAIT FOR THREE MORE MINUTES.
BUT WE NEED TO DECIDE BEFORE THEN.
I'LL STAY.
?!
WAIT A SECOND, ARMIN!
BUT IN EXCHANGE, THERE'S SOMETHING I WANT YOU TO REPORT...
...AND IF POSSIBLE, ONLY TO COMMANDER ERWIN...

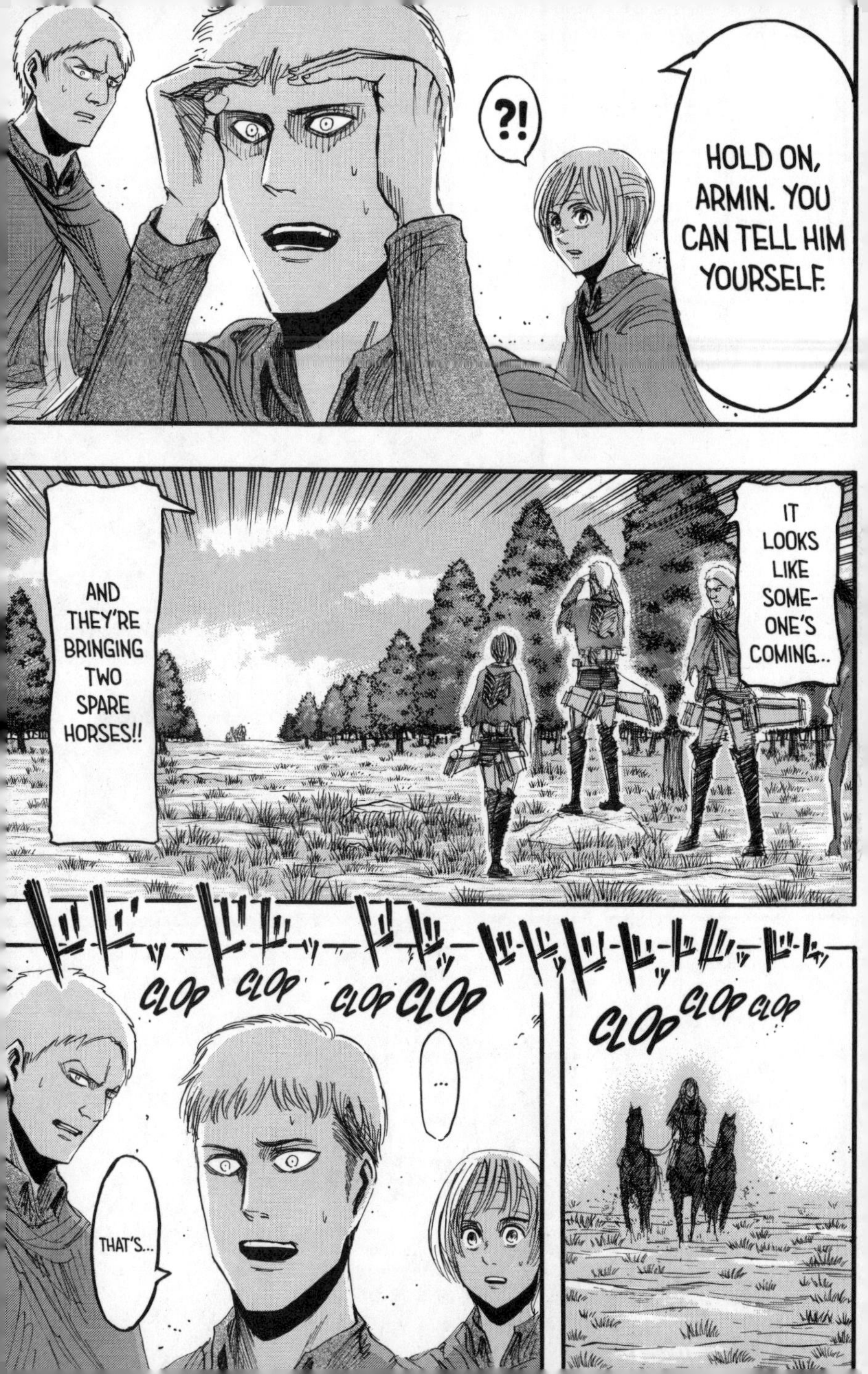
HOLD ON, ARMIN. YOU CAN TELL HIM YOURSELF.
?!
IT LOOKS LIKE SOME-ONE'S COMING...
AND THEY'RE BRINGING TWO SPARE HORSES!!
CLOP CLOP CLOP
CLOP CLOP CLOP CLOP
...
THAT'S...

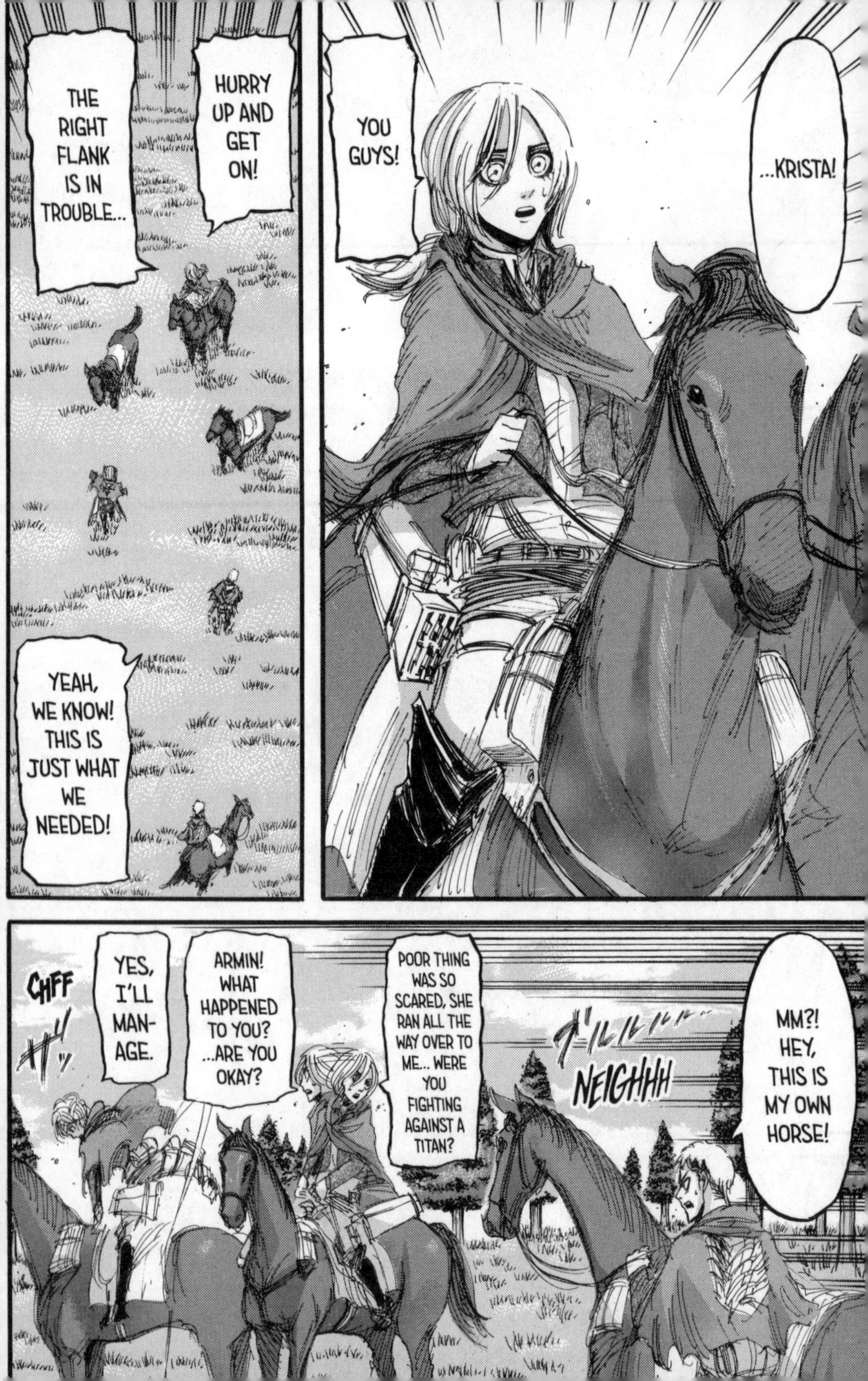
...KRISTA!
YOU GUYS!
HURRY UP AND GET ON!
THE RIGHT FLANK IS IN TROUBLE...
YEAH, WE KNOW! THIS IS JUST WHAT WE NEEDED!
MM?! HEY, THIS IS MY OWN HORSE!
NEIGHHH
POOR THING WAS SO SCARED, SHE RAN ALL THE WAY OVER TO ME... WERE YOU FIGHTING AGAINST A TITAN?
ARMIN! WHAT HAPPENED TO YOU? ...ARE YOU OKAY?
YES, I'LL MAN-AGE.
CHFF

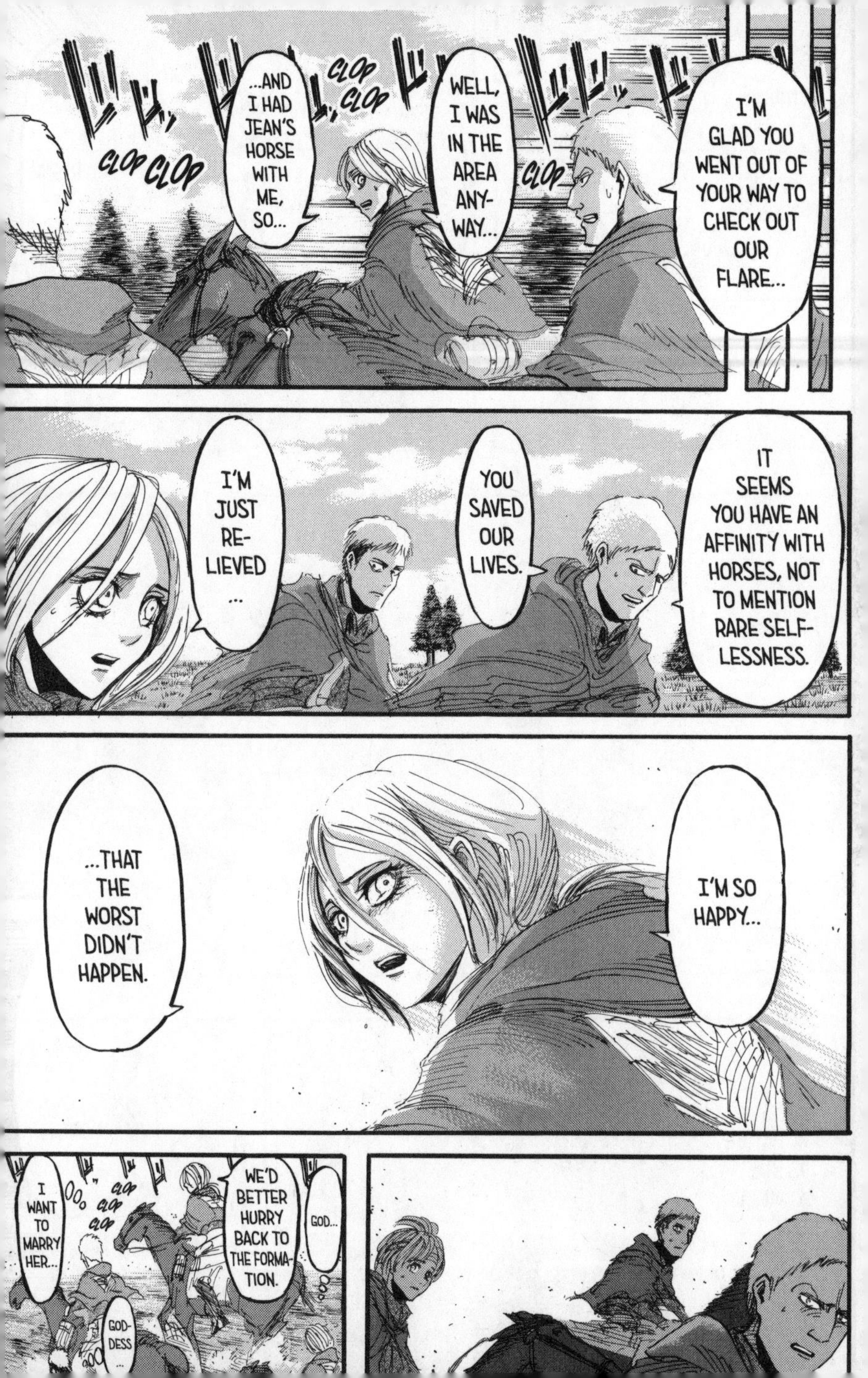
I'M GLAD YOU WENT OUT OF YOUR WAY TO CHECK OUT OUR FLARE...
CLOP
WELL, I WAS IN THE AREA ANYWAY...
CLOP CLOP
...AND I HAD JEAN'S HORSE WITH ME, SO...
CLOP CLOP
IT SEEMS YOU HAVE AN AFFINITY WITH HORSES, NOT TO MENTION RARE SELF-LESSNESS.
YOU SAVED OUR LIVES.
I'M JUST RE-LIEVED...
I'M SO HAPPY...
...THAT THE WORST DIDN'T HAPPEN.
GOD...
WE'D BETTER HURRY BACK TO THE FORMA-TION.
CLOP CLOP CLOP
I WANT TO MARRY HER...
GOD-DESS...

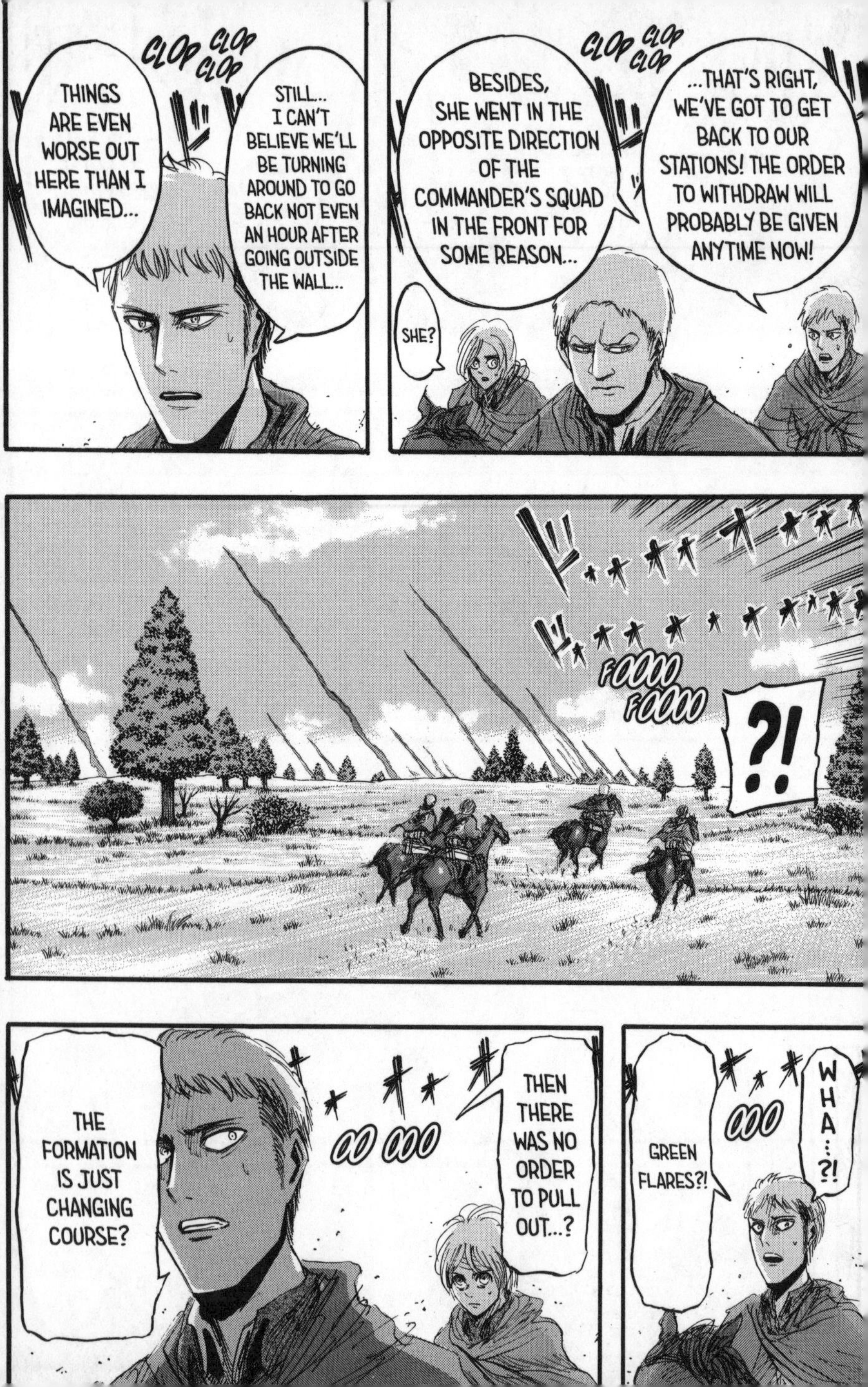
CLOP CLOP CLOP
...THAT'S RIGHT, WE'VE GOT TO GET BACK TO OUR STATIONS! THE ORDER TO WITHDRAW WILL PROBABLY BE GIVEN ANYTIME NOW!
BESIDES, SHE WENT IN THE OPPOSITE DIRECTION OF THE COMMANDER'S SQUAD IN THE FRONT FOR SOME REASON...
SHE?
CLOP CLOP CLOP
STILL... I CAN'T BELIEVE WE'LL BE TURNING AROUND TO GO BACK NOT EVEN AN HOUR AFTER GOING OUTSIDE THE WALL...
THINGS ARE EVEN WORSE OUT HERE THAN I IMAGINED...
FOOOO FOOOO
?!
WHA...?!
OOO
GREEN FLARES?!
THEN THERE WAS NO ORDER TO PULL OUT...?
OO OOO
THE FORMATION IS JUST CHANGING COURSE?

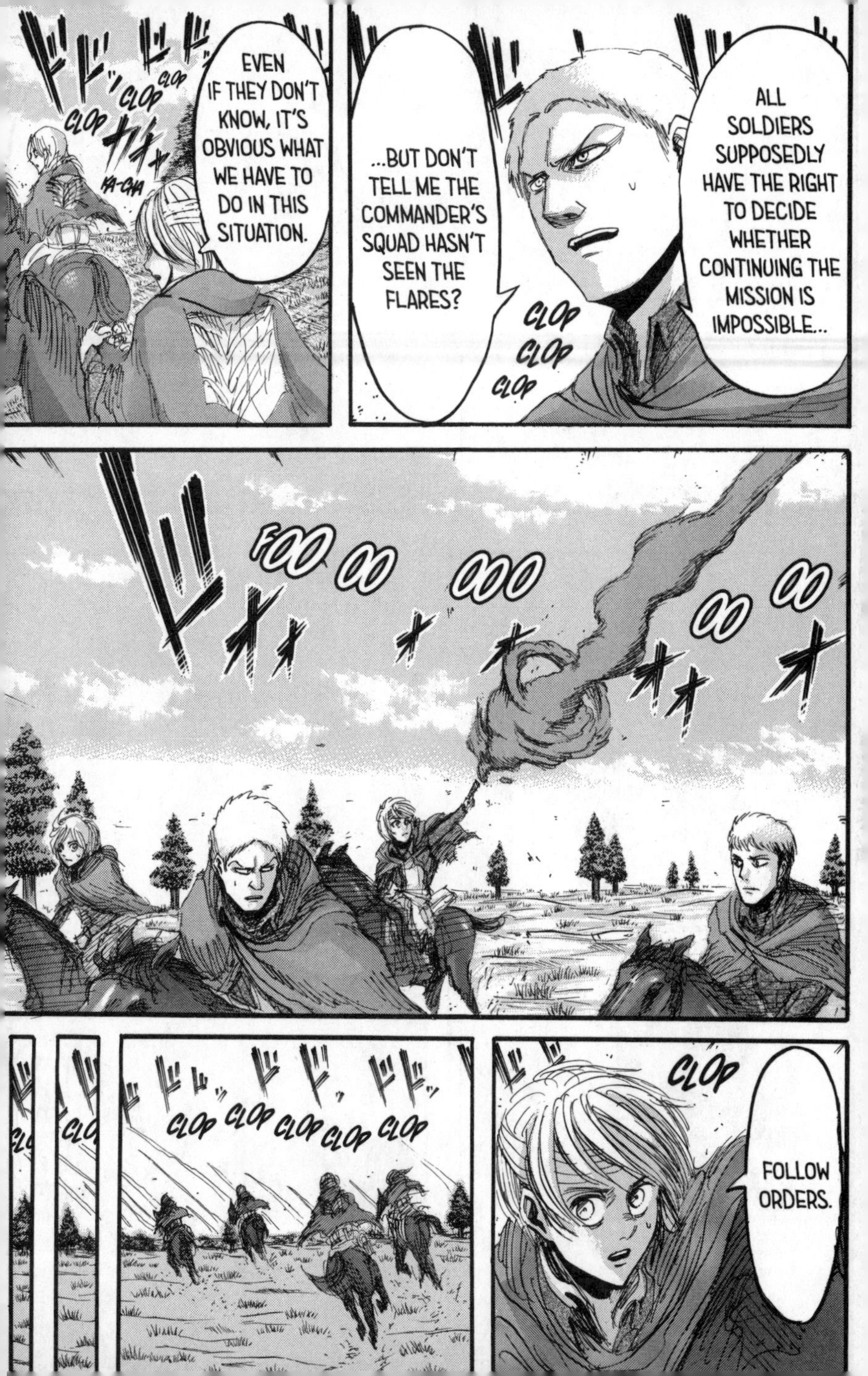
ALL SOLDIERS SUPPOSEDLY HAVE THE RIGHT TO DECIDE WHETHER CONTINUING THE MISSION IS IMPOSSIBLE...
...BUT DON'T TELL ME THE COMMANDER'S SQUAD HASN'T SEEN THE FLARES?
CLOP
CLOP
CLOP
EVEN IF THEY DON'T KNOW, IT'S OBVIOUS WHAT WE HAVE TO DO IN THIS SITUATION.
CLOP
CLOP
CLOP
KA-CHA
FOO OO OOO OO OO
CLOP
FOLLOW ORDERS.
CLOP CLOP CLOP CLOP CLOP

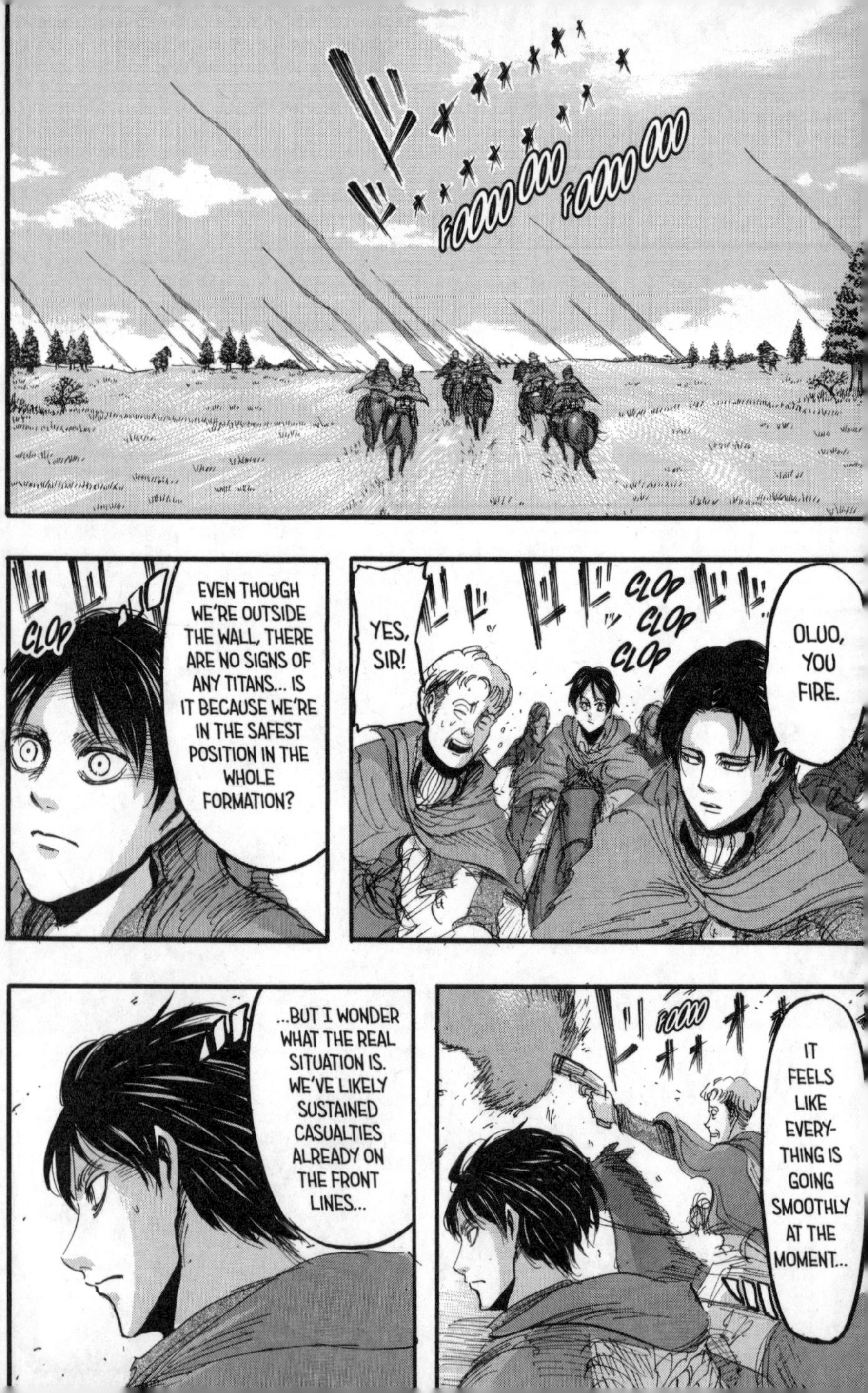
FOOOO OOO
FOOOO OOO
OLUO, YOU FIRE.
CLOP CLOP CLOP
YES, SIR!
CLOP
EVEN THOUGH WE'RE OUTSIDE THE WALL, THERE ARE NO SIGNS OF ANY TITANS... IS IT BECAUSE WE'RE IN THE SAFEST POSITION IN THE WHOLE FORMATION?
FOOOO
IT FEELS LIKE EVERY-THING IS GOING SMOOTHLY AT THE MOMENT...
...BUT I WONDER WHAT THE REAL SITUATION IS. WE'VE LIKELY SUSTAINED CASUALTIES ALREADY ON THE FRONT LINES...

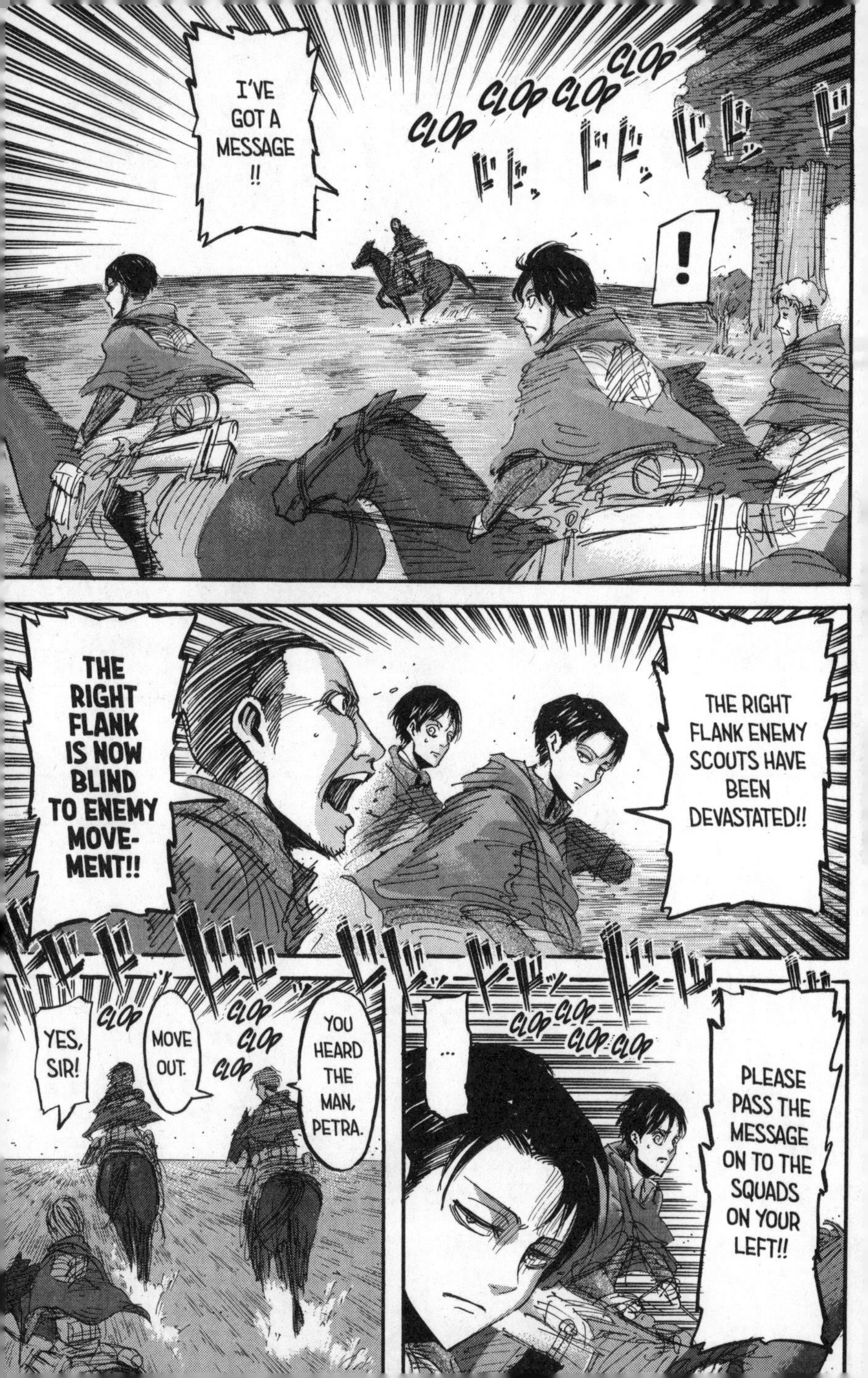
CLOP
CLOP CLOP
CLOP
CLOP
I'VE GOT A MESSAGE !!
!
THE RIGHT FLANK ENEMY SCOUTS HAVE BEEN DEVASTATED!!
THE RIGHT FLANK IS NOW BLIND TO ENEMY MOVEMENT!!
PLEASE PASS THE MESSAGE ON TO THE SQUADS ON YOUR LEFT!!
CLOP CLOP
CLOP CLOP
...
YOU HEARD THE MAN, PETRA.
CLOP CLOP CLOP
MOVE OUT.
CLOP
YES, SIR!

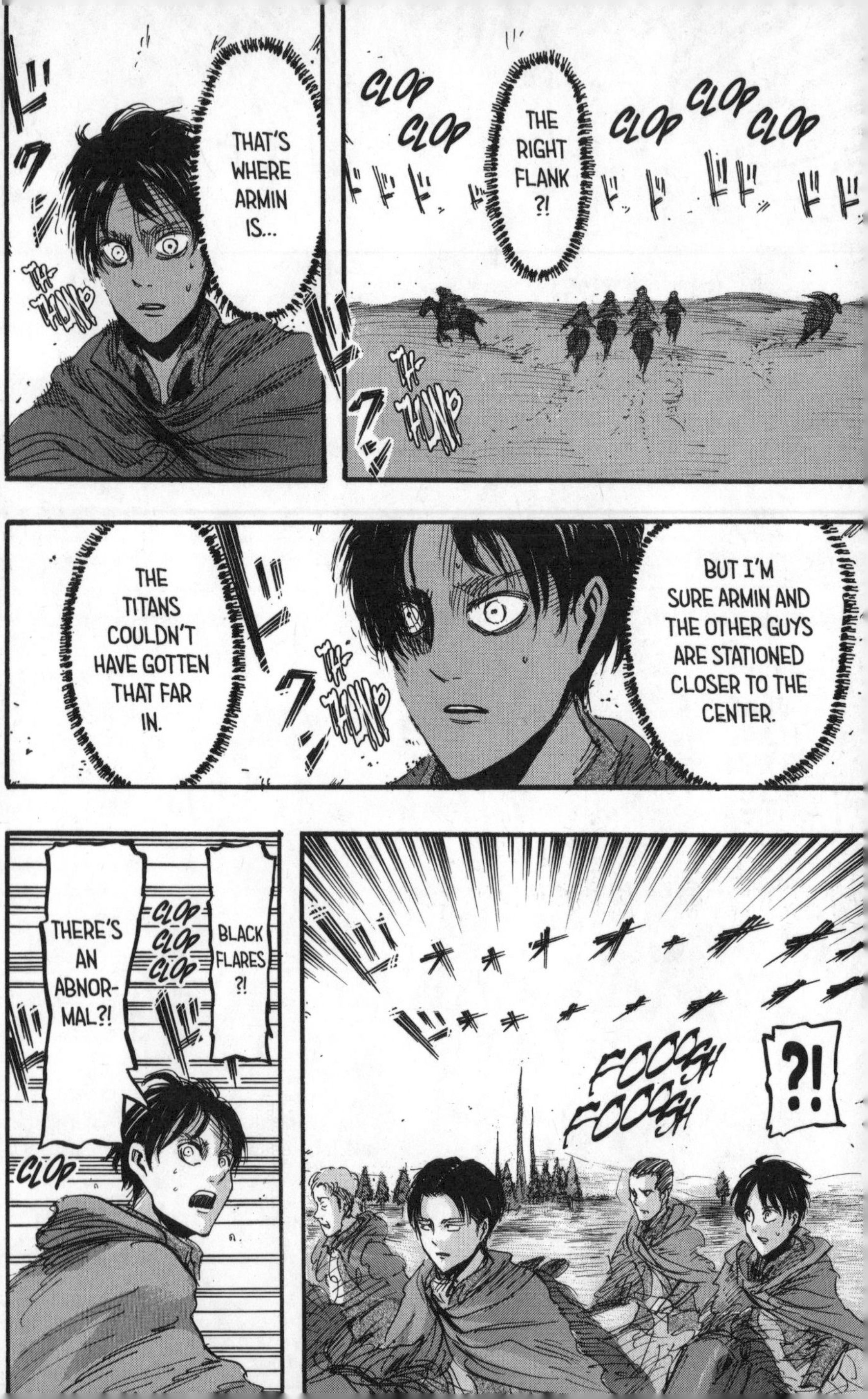
CLOP
CLOP
THE RIGHT FLANK ?!
CLOP CLOP CLOP CLOP
THA THUMP
THAT'S WHERE ARMIN IS...
THA THUMP
BUT I'M SURE ARMIN AND THE OTHER GUYS ARE STATIONED CLOSER TO THE CENTER.
THA THUMP
THE TITANS COULDN'T HAVE GOTTEN THAT FAR IN.
?!
FOOOSH FOOOSH
BLACK FLARES ?!
CLOP CLOP CLOP
THERE'S AN ABNOR-MAL?!
CLOP

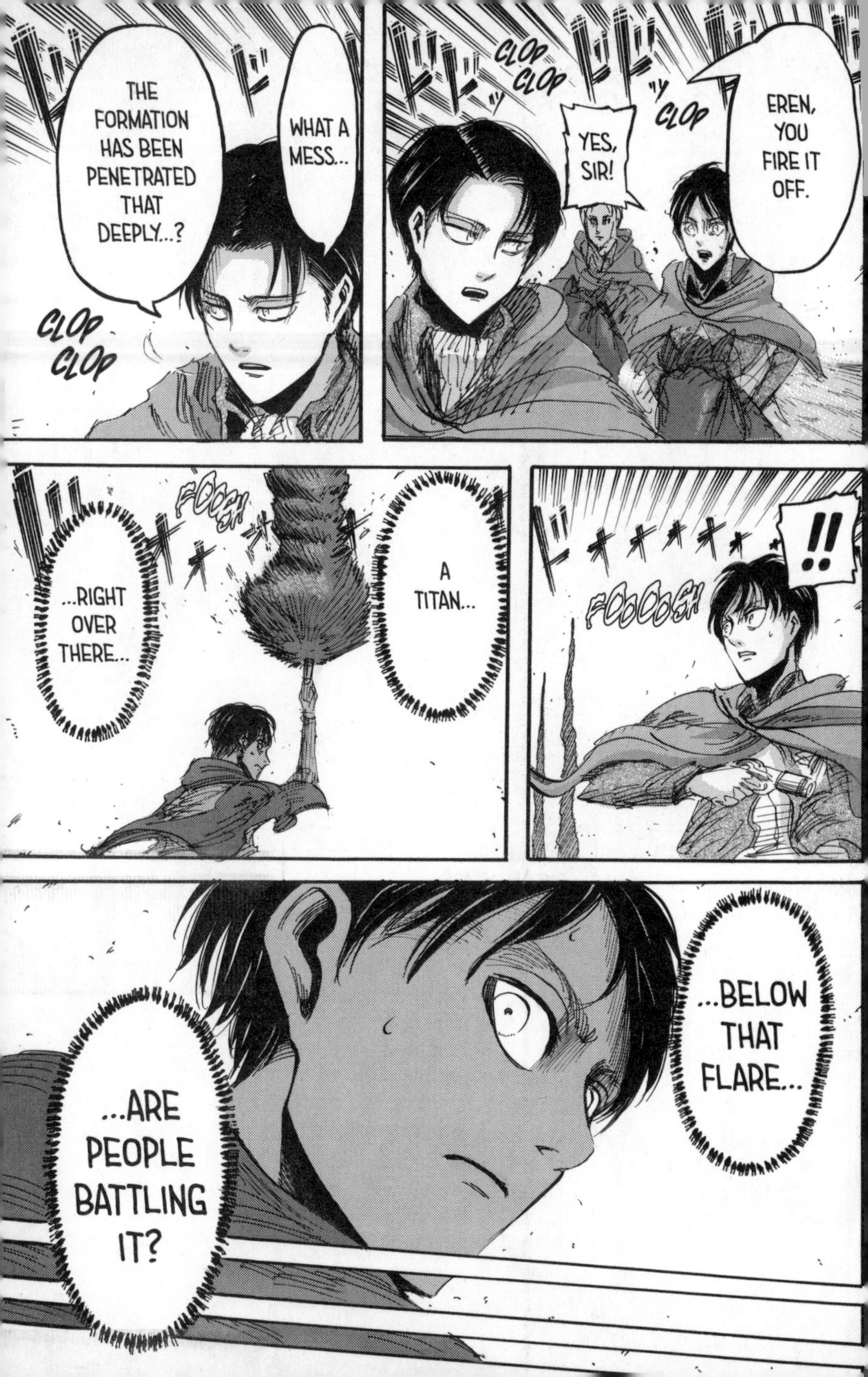
EREN, YOU FIRE IT OFF.
CLOP
YES, SIR!
CLOP CLOP
WHAT A MESS...
THE FORMATION HAS BEEN PENETRATED THAT DEEPLY...?
CLOP CLOP
!!
FOOOOSH
A TITAN...
FOOSH
...RIGHT OVER THERE...
...BELOW THAT FLARE...
...ARE PEOPLE BATTLING IT?

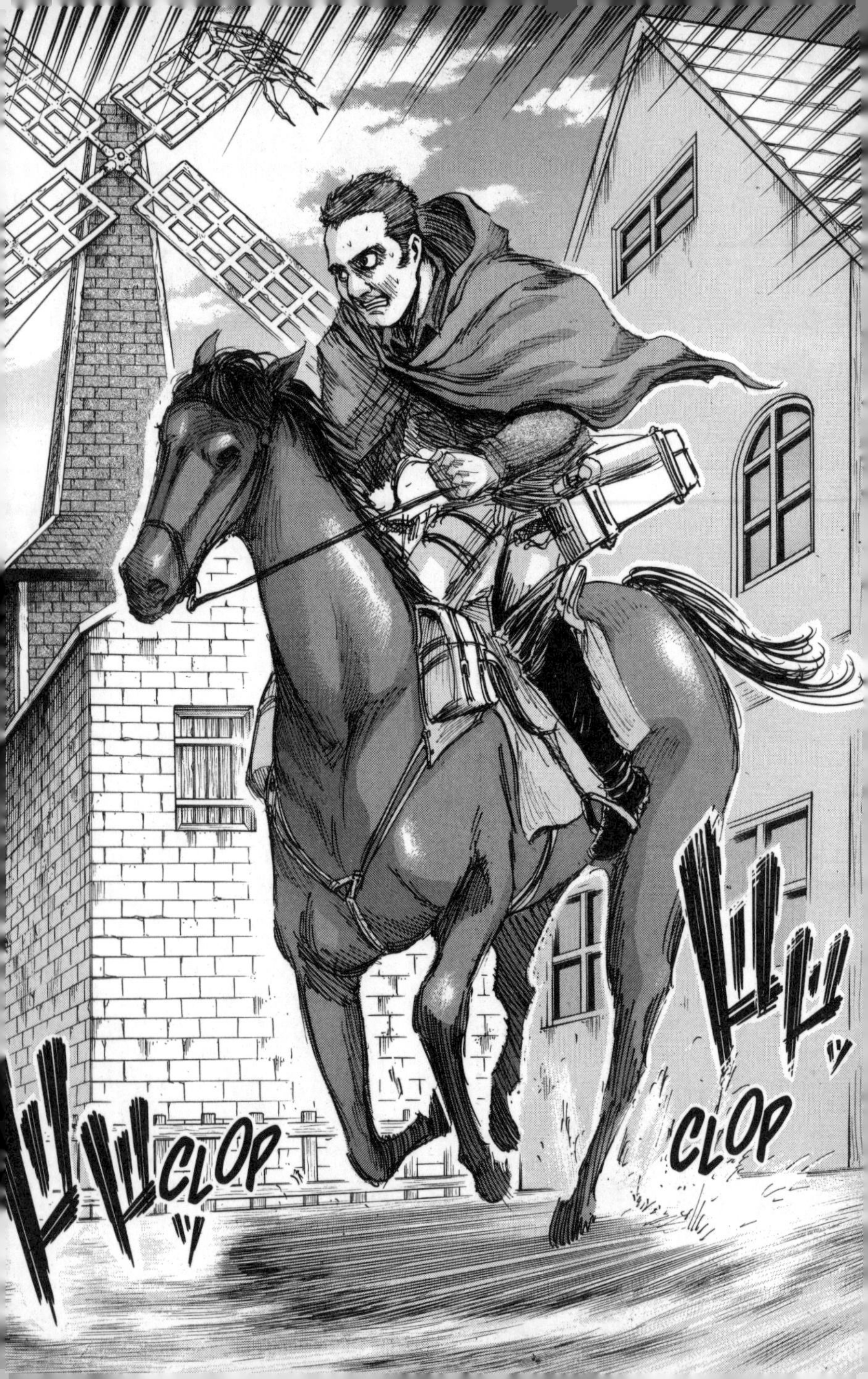
ドドッ
CLOP
ドドドッ
CLOP

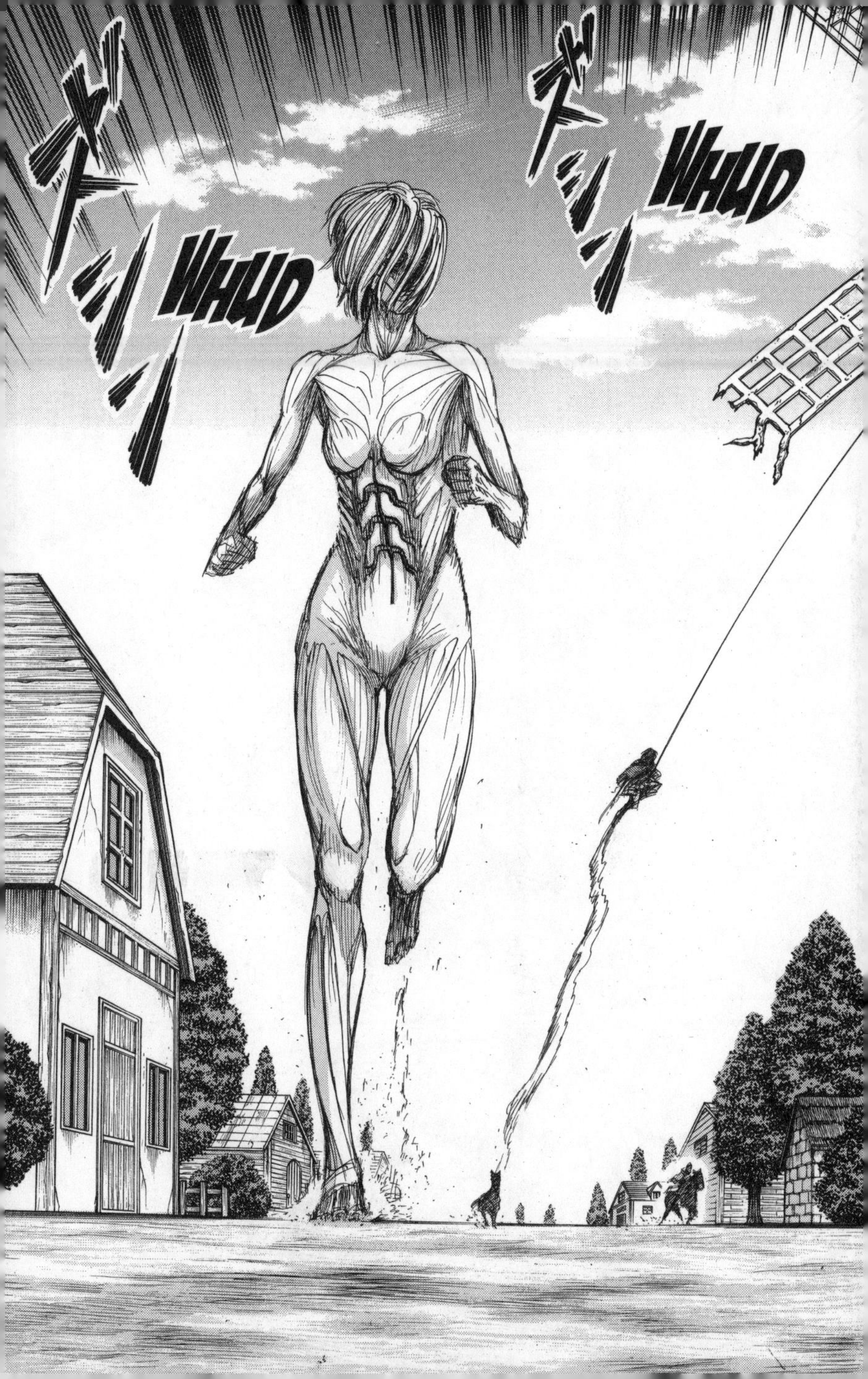
ズシン
WHUD
ズシン
WHUD

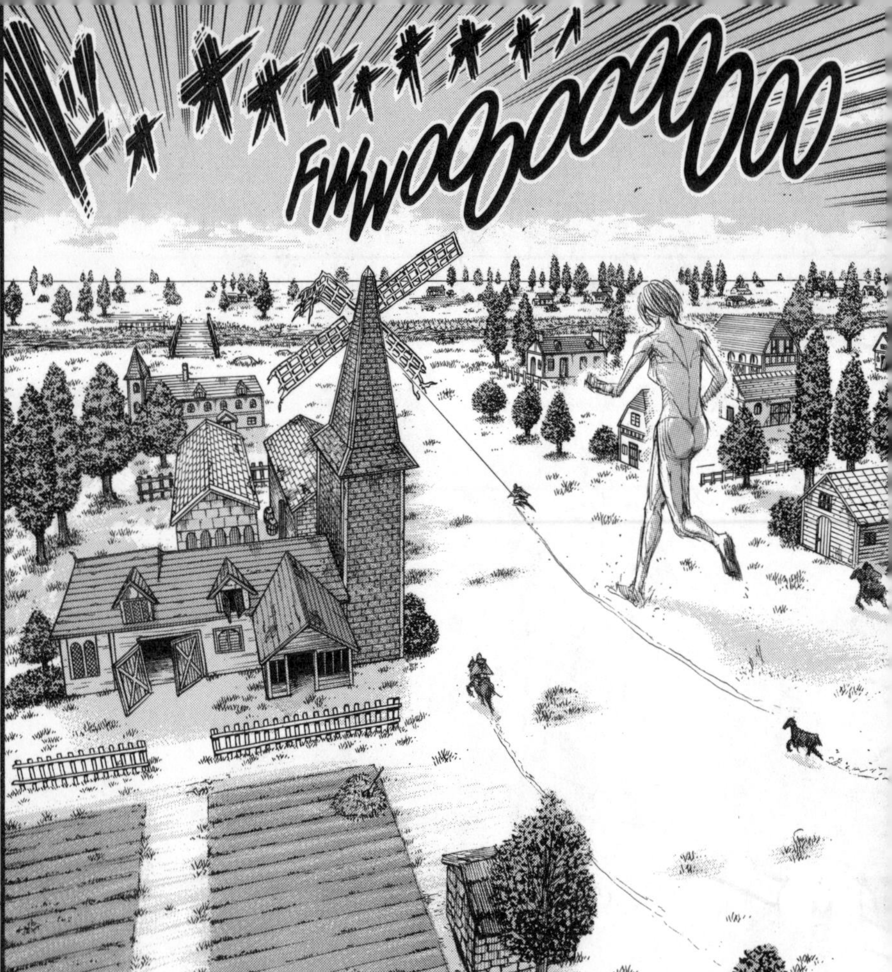
ドォォォォォォォォォ
FWOOOOOOOOOO
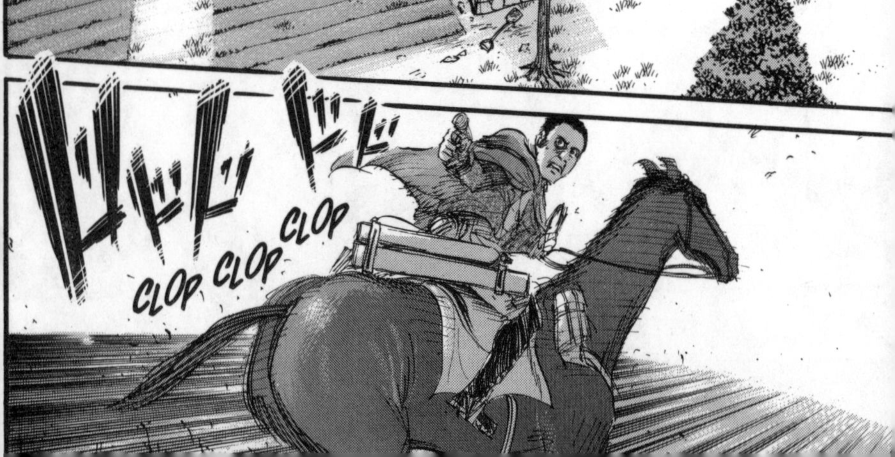
ドッドッ ドド
CLOP CLOP CLOP

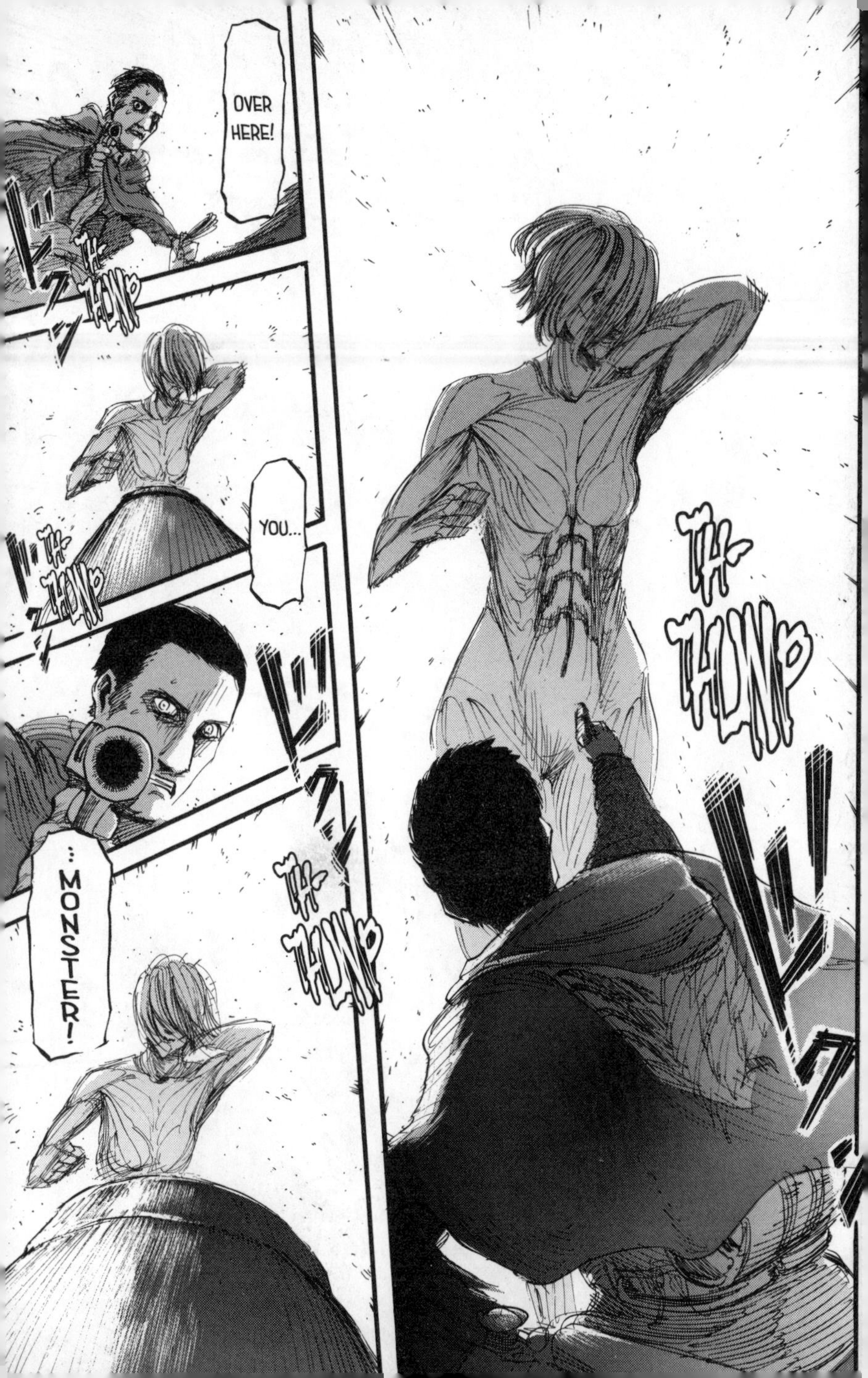
TH-THUMP
OVER HERE!
TH-THUMP
YOU...
TH-THUMP
TH-THUMP
...MONSTER!

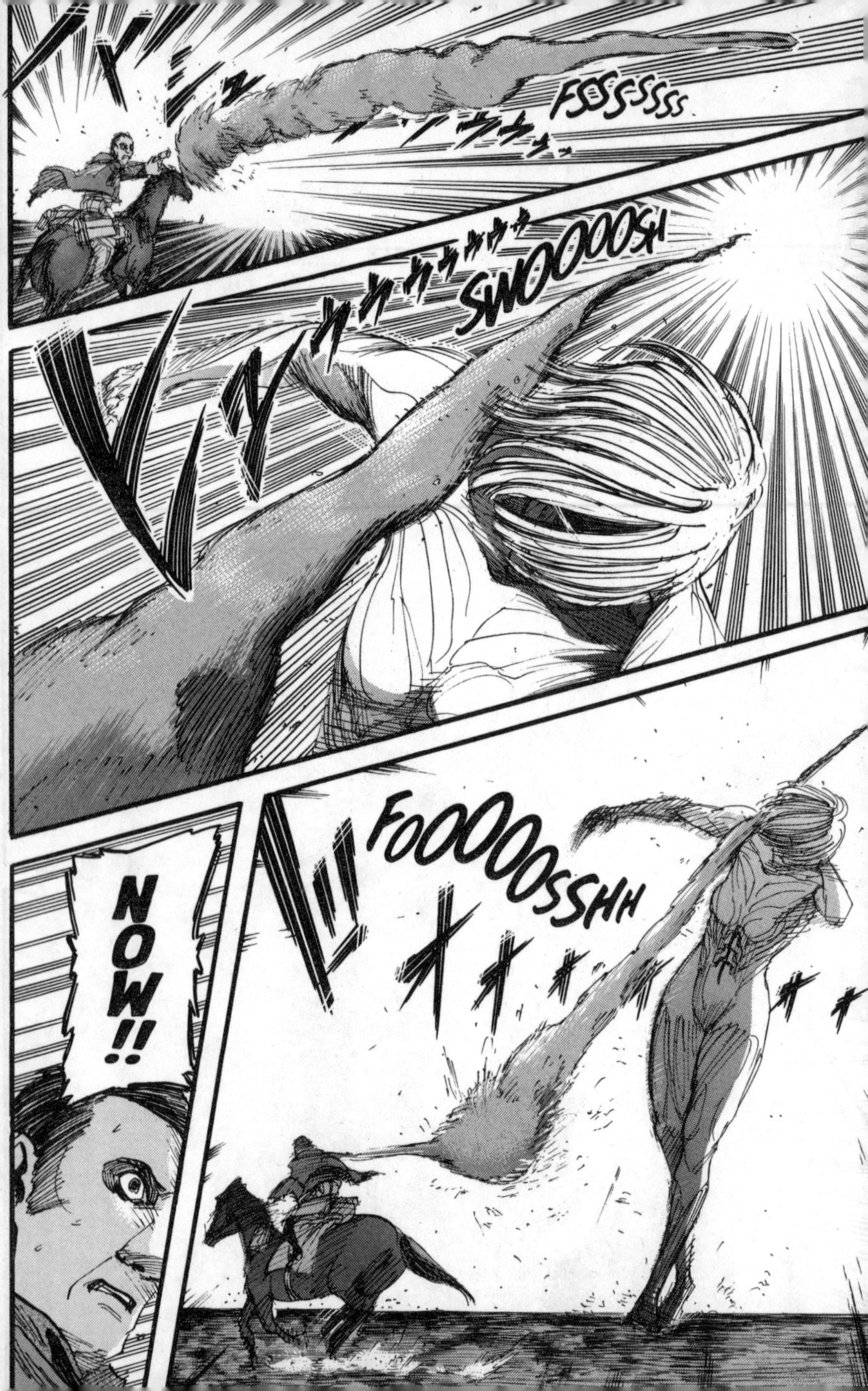

FSSS-SSSS
SWOOOOOSH
FOOOOOSSHH
NOW!!

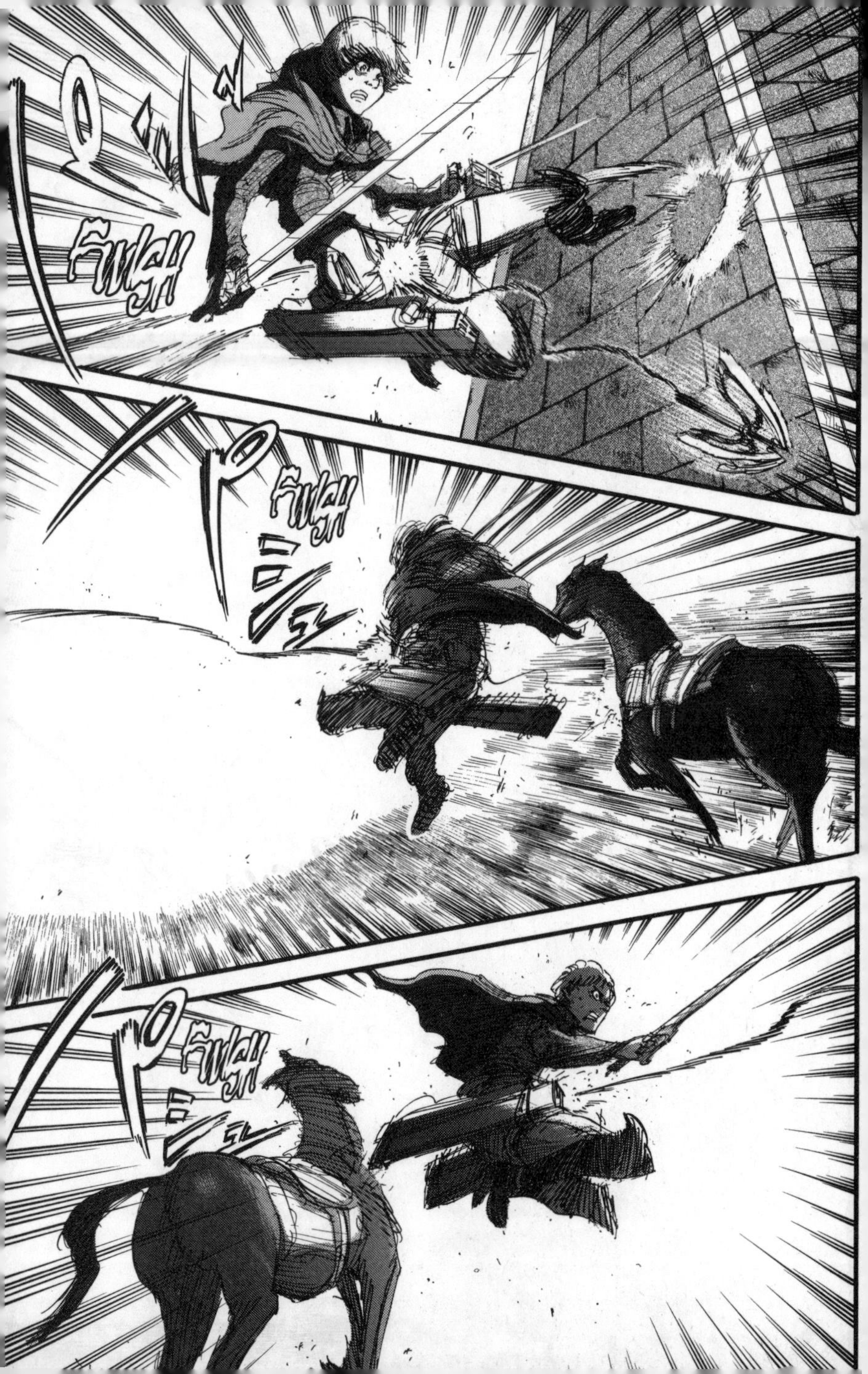
Fwigh
Fwigh
Fwigh

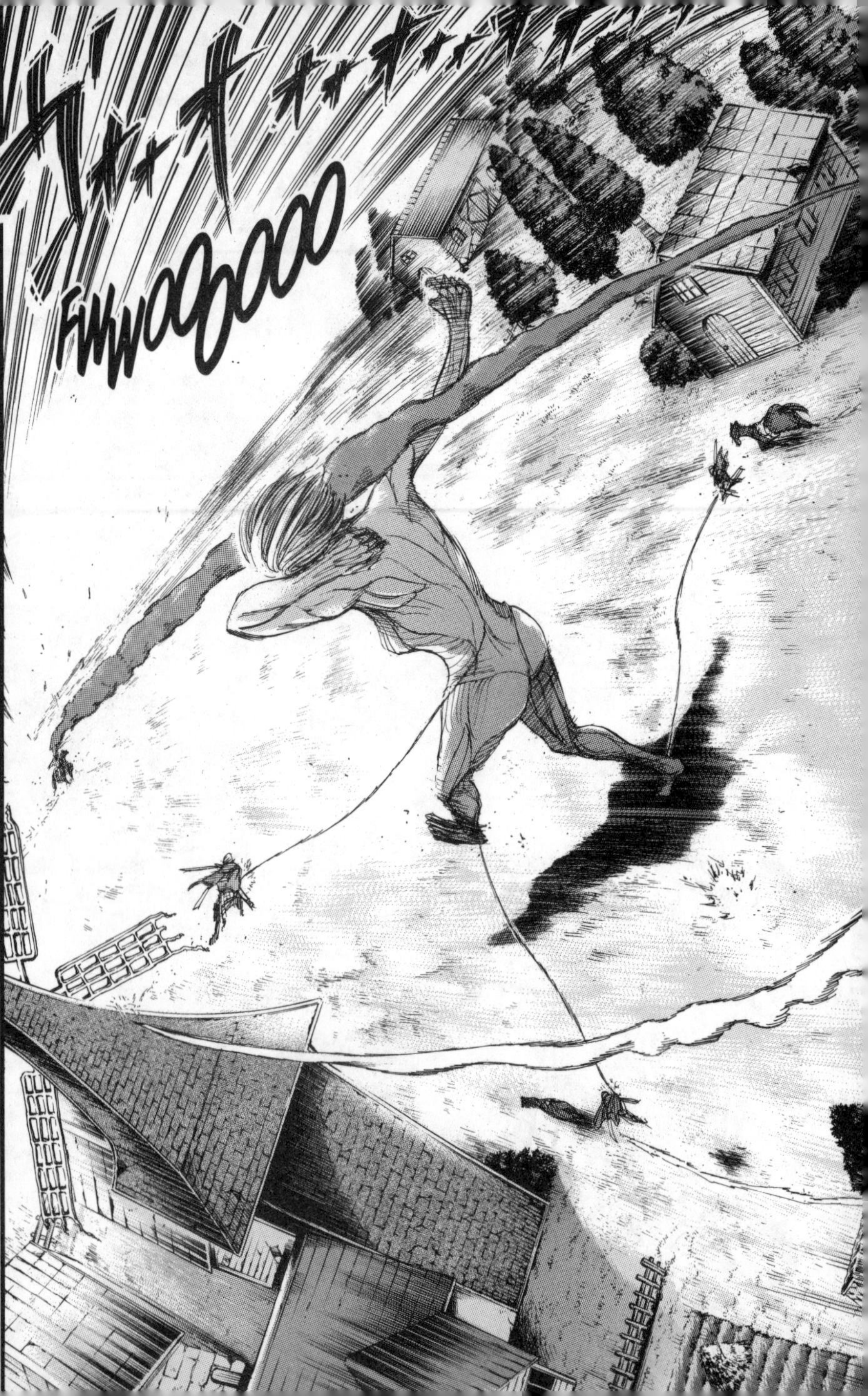
FWWOOOOO

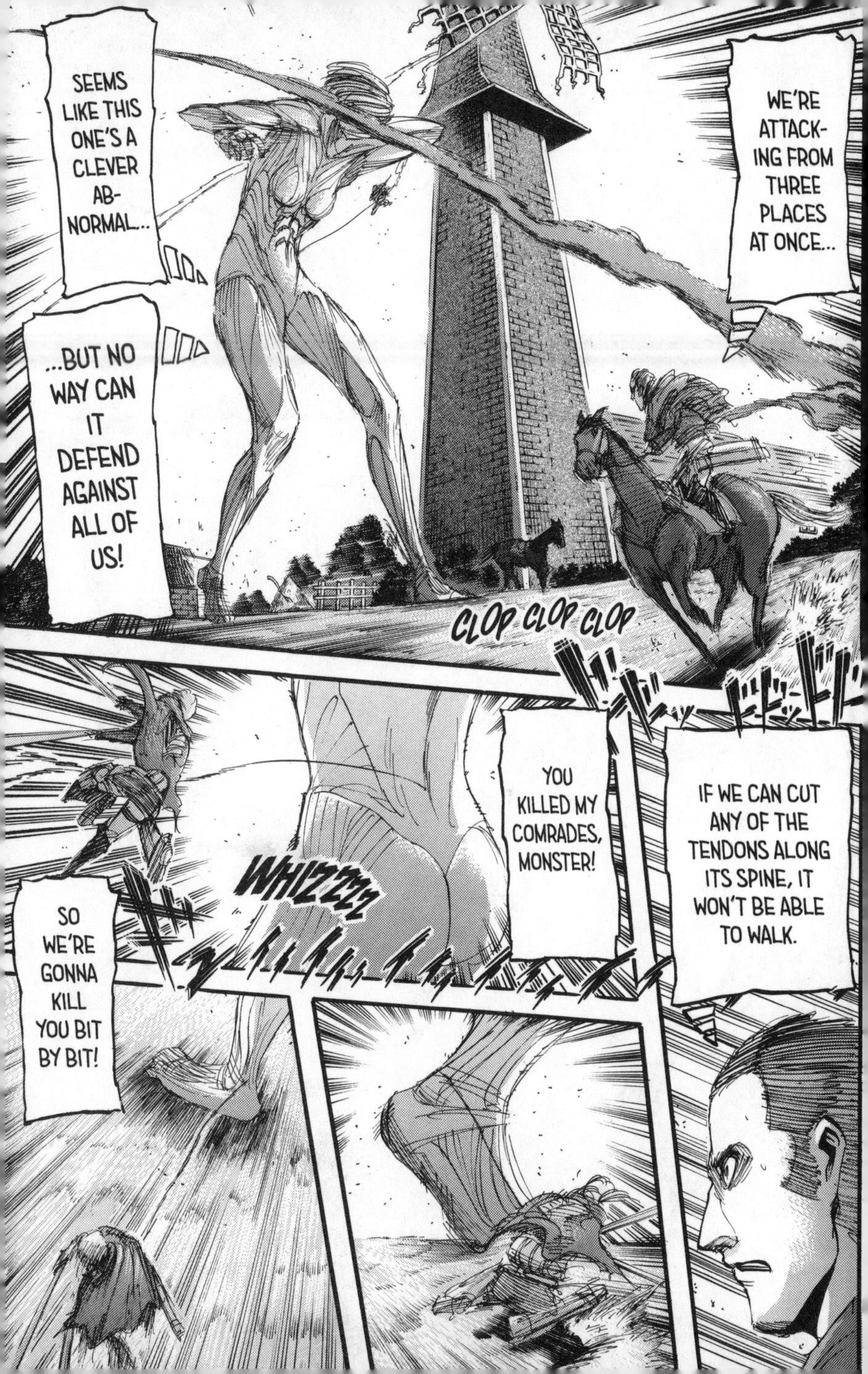
WE'RE ATTACKING FROM THREE PLACES AT ONCE...
SEEMS LIKE THIS ONE'S A CLEVER ABNORMAL...
...BUT NO WAY CAN IT DEFEND AGAINST ALL OF US!
CLOP CLOP CLOP
IF WE CAN CUT ANY OF THE TENDONS ALONG ITS SPINE, IT WON'T BE ABLE TO WALK.
YOU KILLED MY COMRADES, MONSTER!
WHIZZZZ
SO WE'RE GONNA KILL YOU BIT BY BIT!

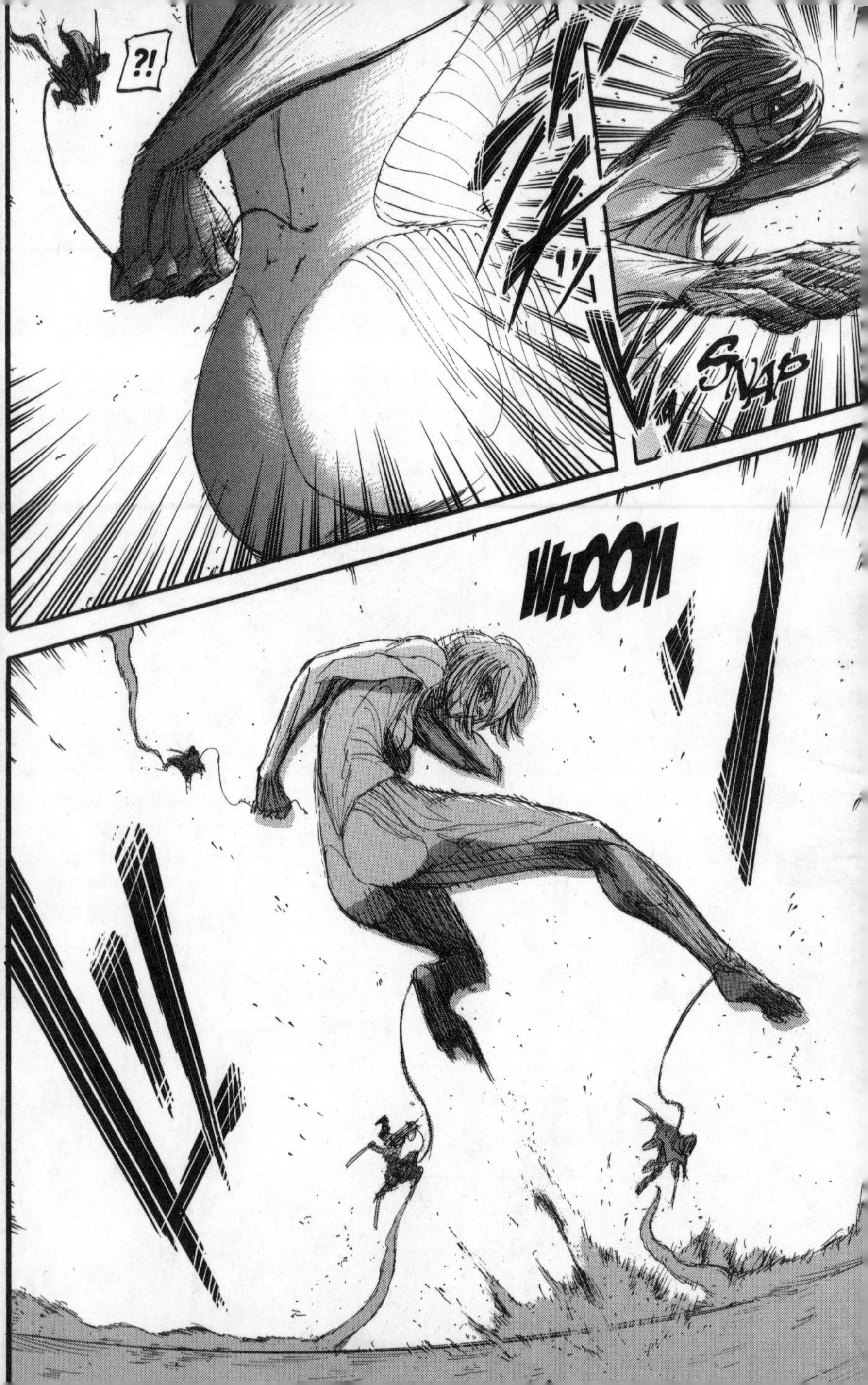
SNAP
?!
WHOOM

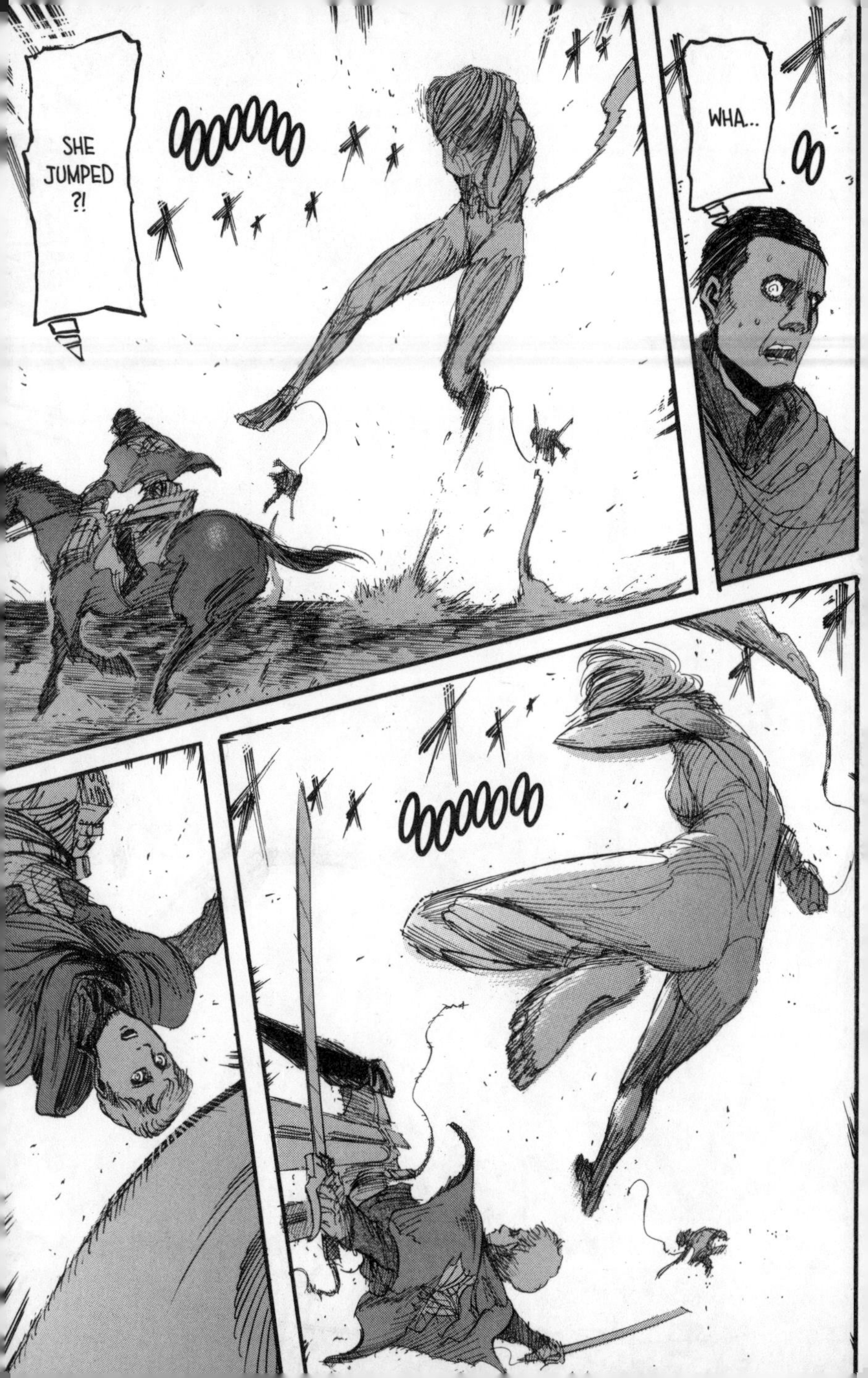
WHA..
oo
SHE JUMPED ?!
oooooooo
ooooooo

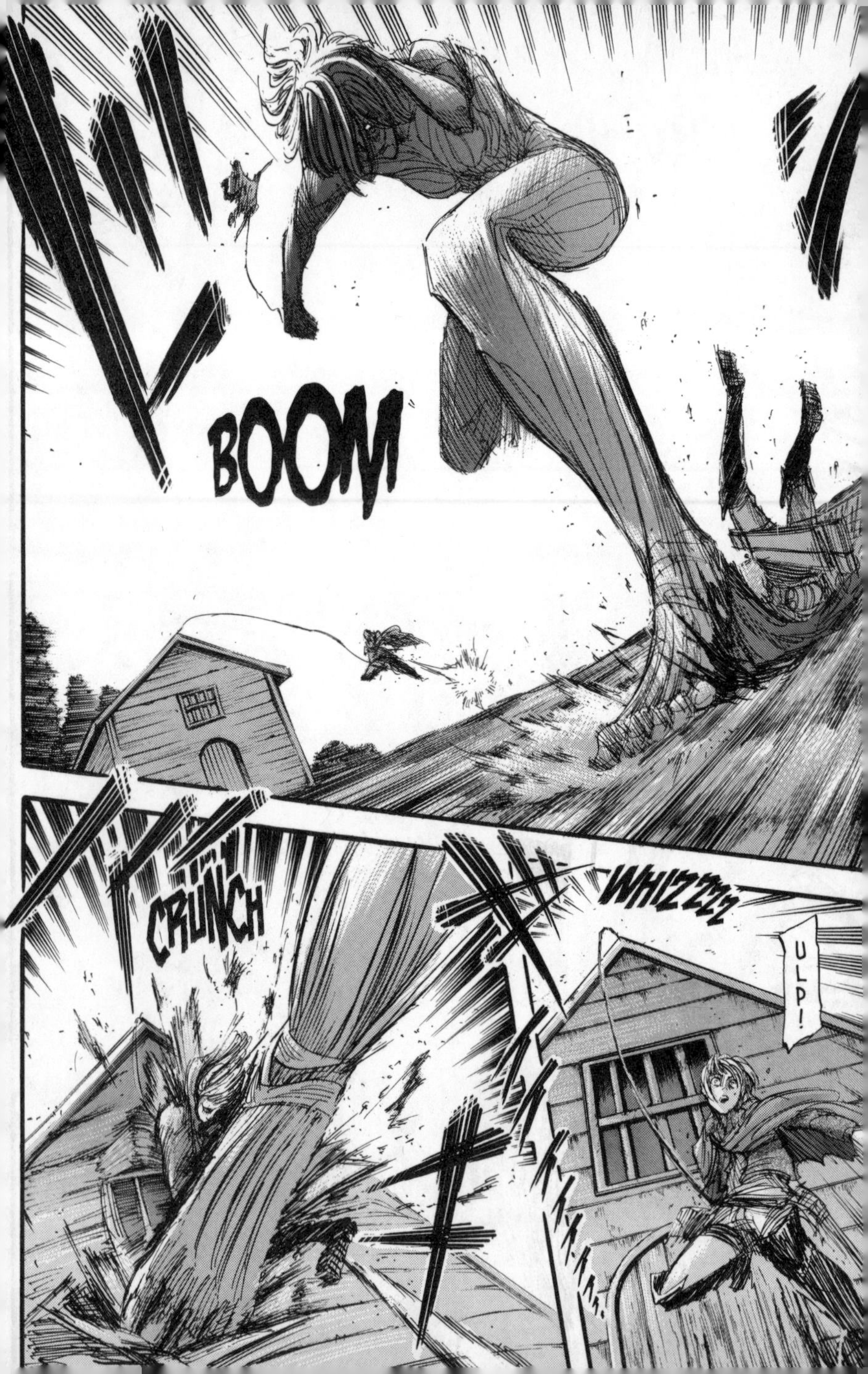
BOOM
WHIZZZZ
ULP!
CRUNCH

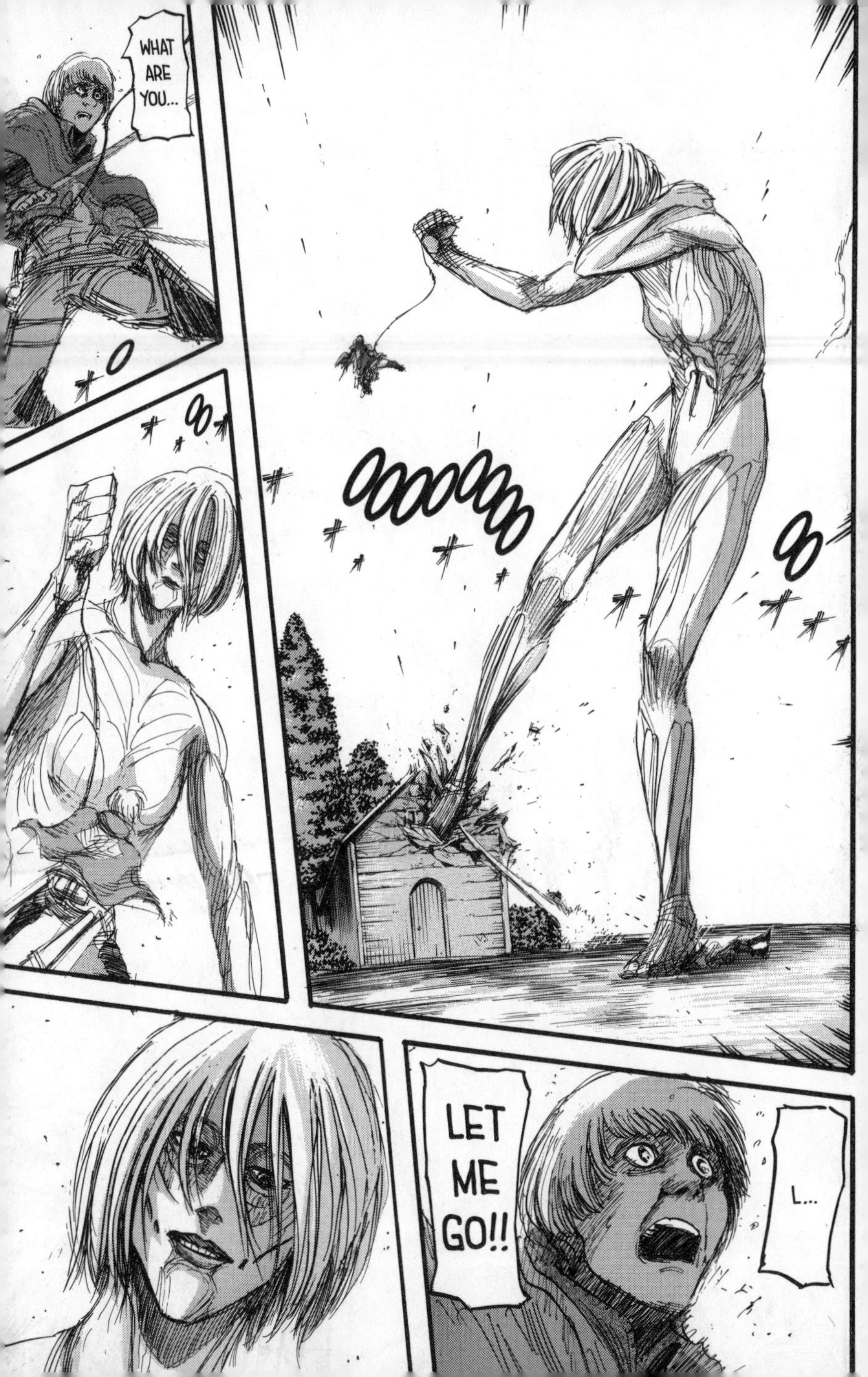
WHAT ARE YOU...
I...
LET ME GO!!

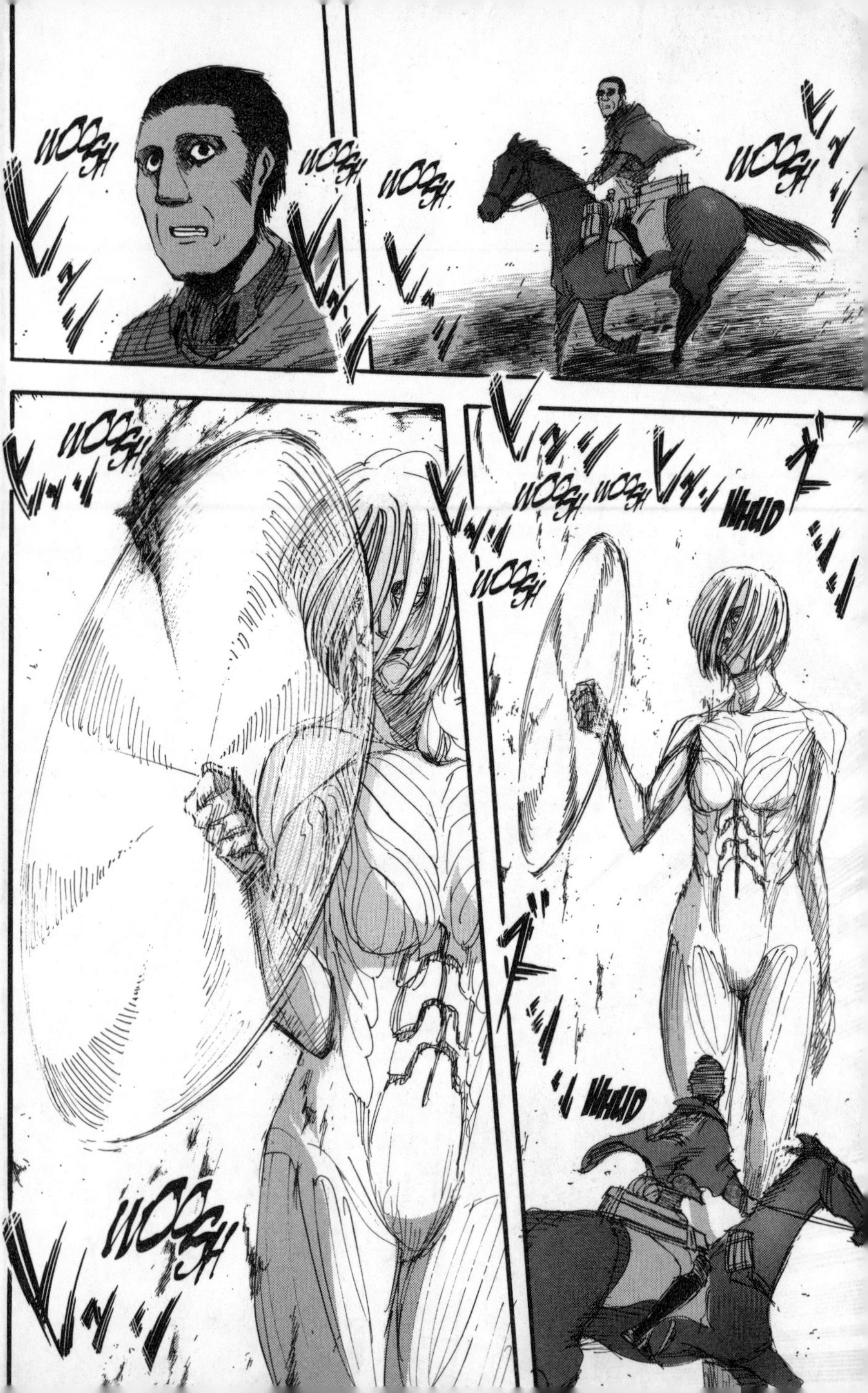
WOOSH
WOOSH
WOOSH
WOOSH
WHUD
WOOSH
WOOSH
WOOSH
WHUD
WOOSH
WOOSH

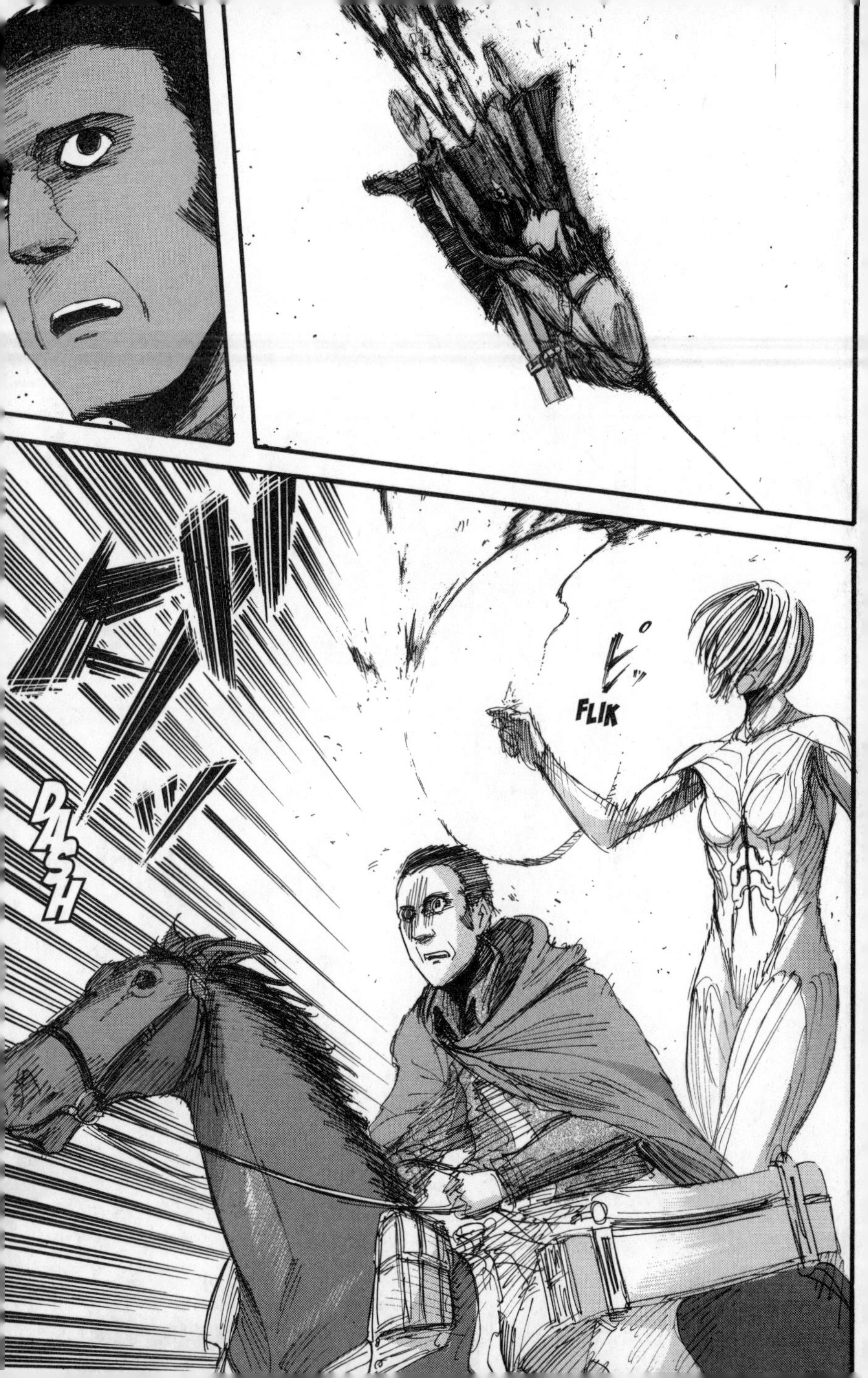

FLIK
DASH

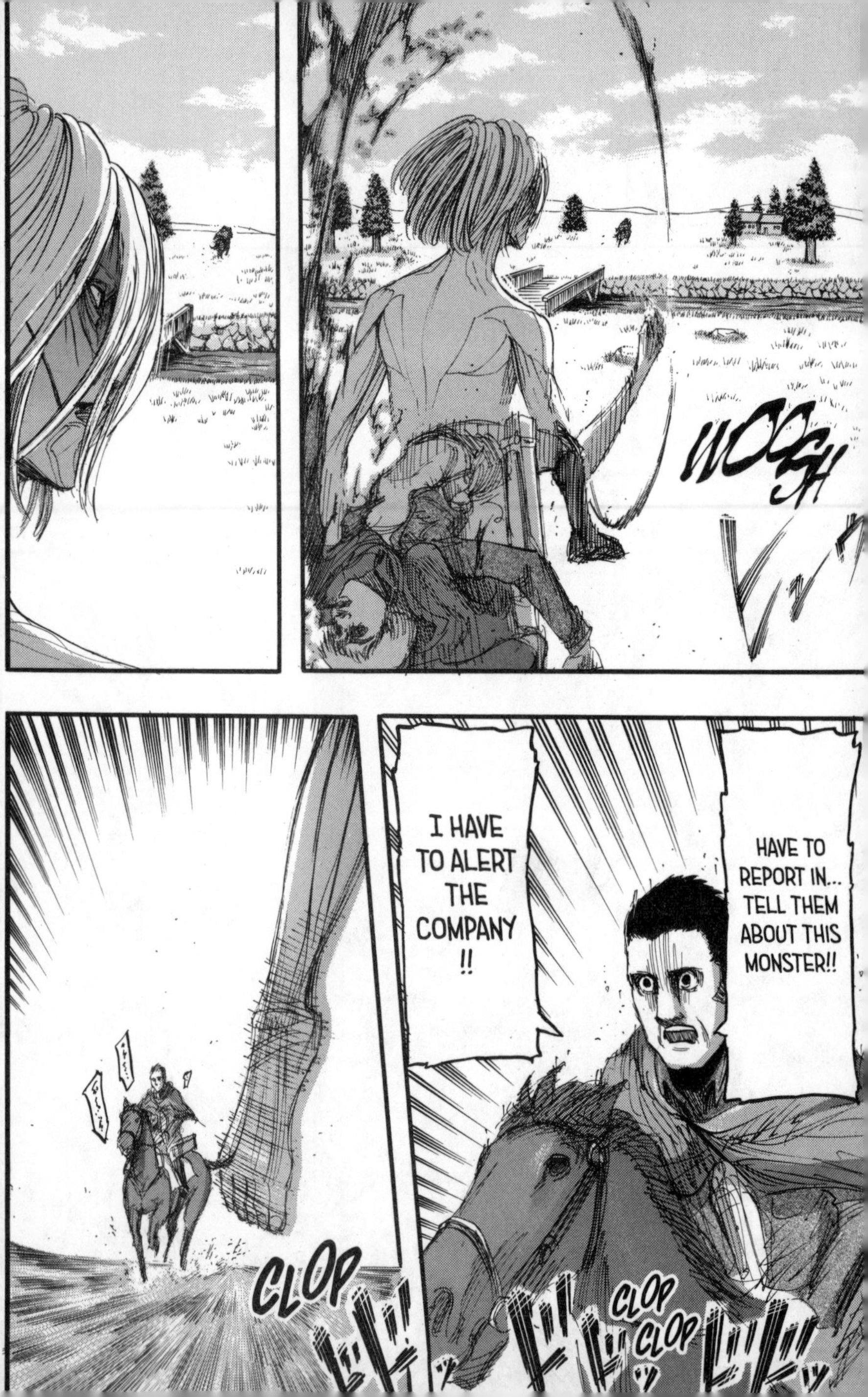
WOOSH
HAVE TO REPORT IN... TELL THEM ABOUT THIS MONSTER!!
I HAVE TO ALERT THE COMPANY !!
CLOP
CLOP
CLOP

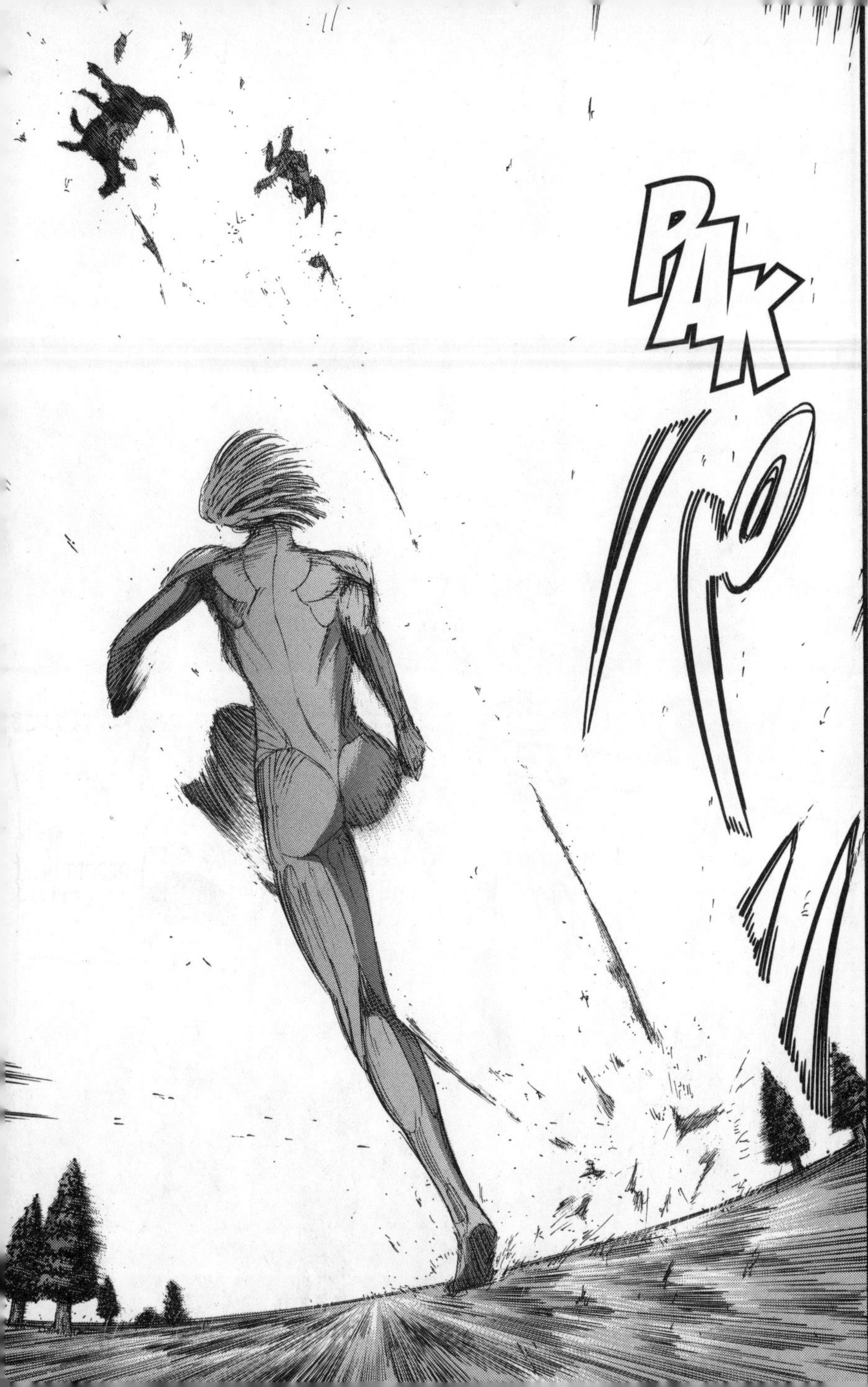
PAK

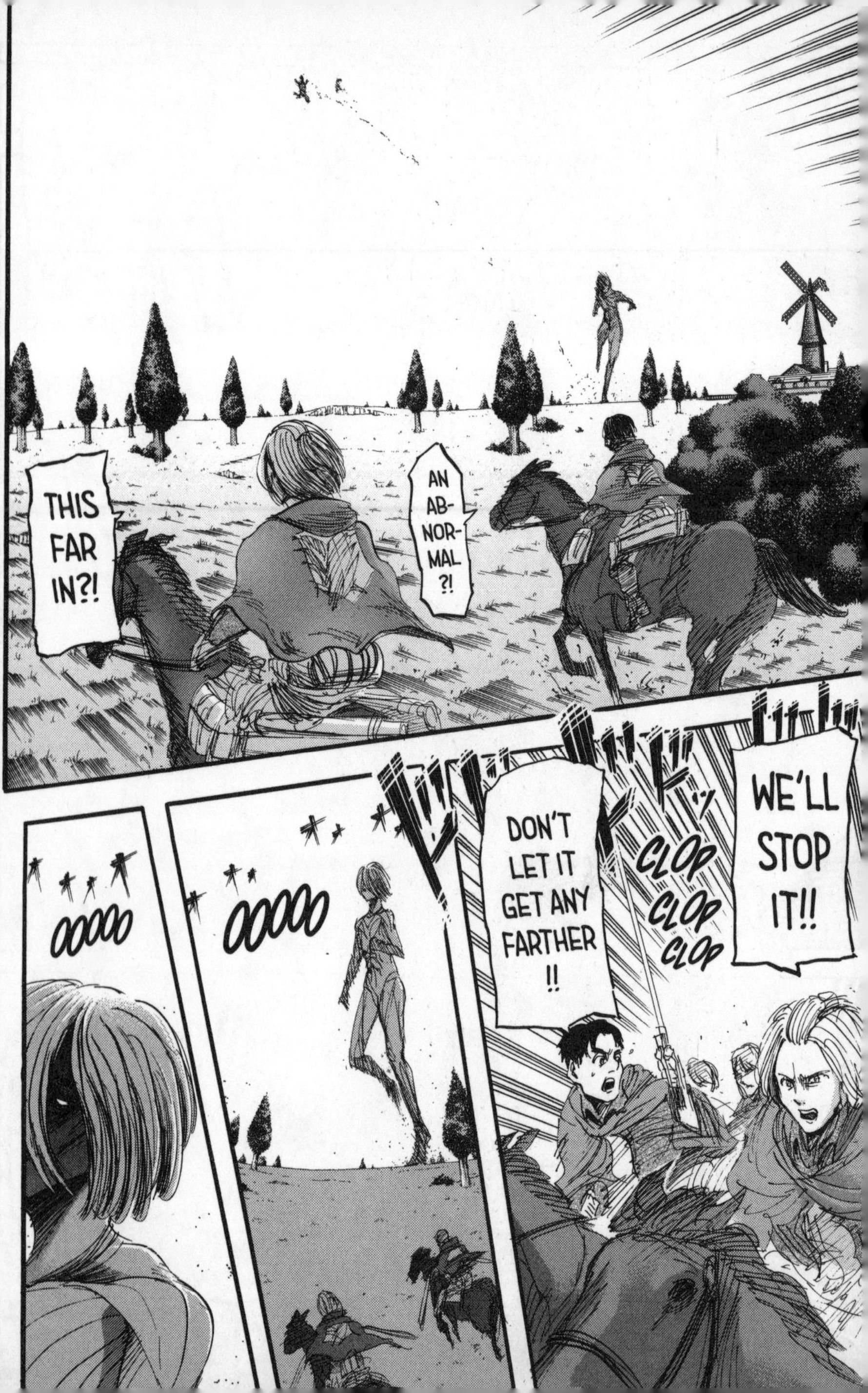
AN ABNORMAL?!
THIS FAR IN?!
WE'LL STOP IT!!
CLOP CLOP CLOP
DON'T LET IT GET ANY FARTHER!!
OOOOO
OOOOO

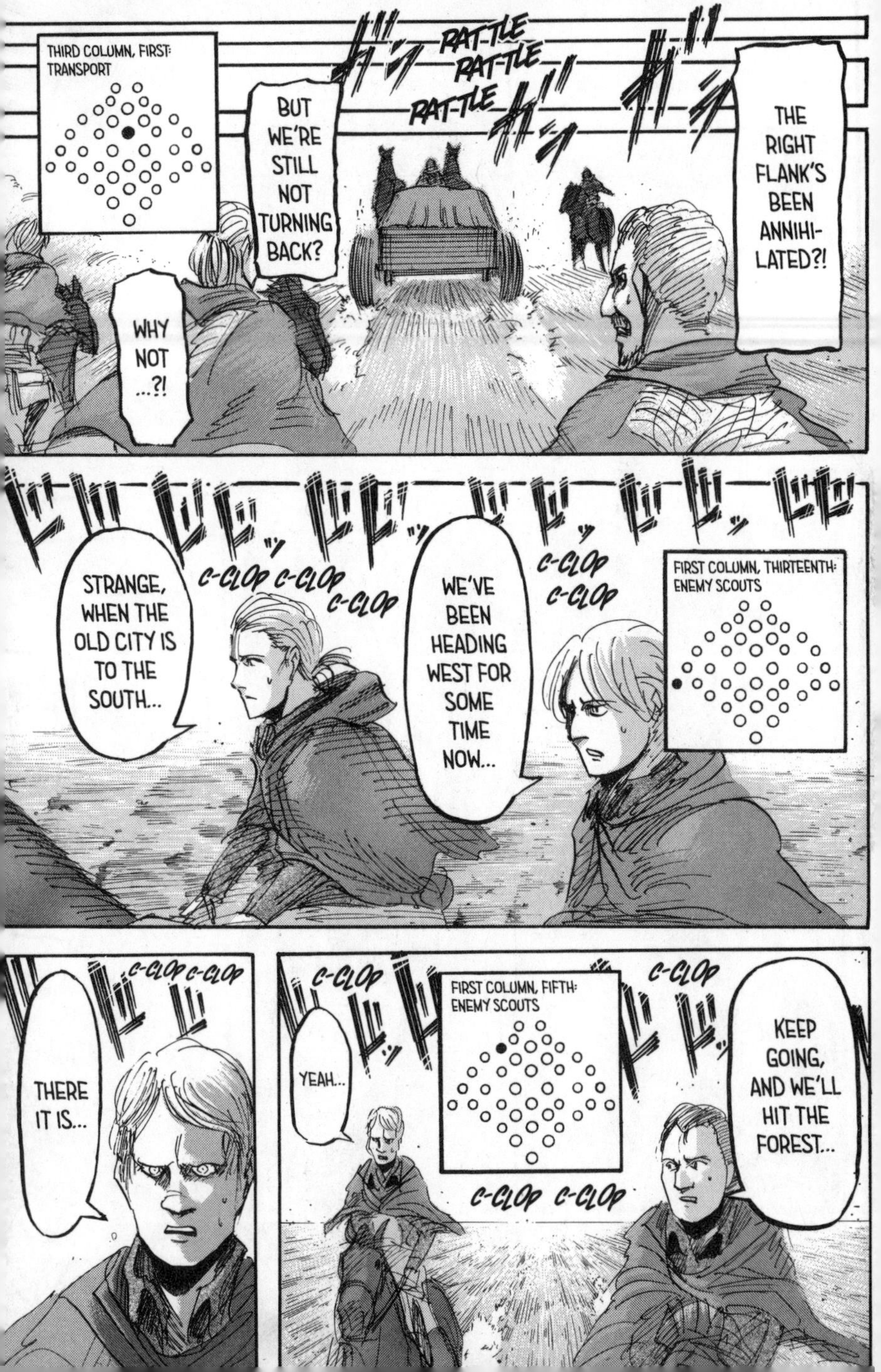

RATTLE RATTLE RATTLE
THE RIGHT FLANK'S BEEN ANNIHILATED?!
BUT WE'RE STILL NOT TURNING BACK?
THIRD COLUMN, FIRST: TRANSPORT
WHY NOT ...?!
FIRST COLUMN, THIRTEENTH: ENEMY SCOUTS
C-CLOP C-CLOP
WE'VE BEEN HEADING WEST FOR SOME TIME NOW...
C-CLOP C-CLOP C-CLOP
STRANGE, WHEN THE OLD CITY IS TO THE SOUTH...
C-CLOP
KEEP GOING, AND WE'LL HIT THE FOREST...
FIRST COLUMN, FIFTH: ENEMY SCOUTS
C-CLOP
YEAH...
C-CLOP C-CLOP
C-CLOP C-CLOP
THERE IT IS...

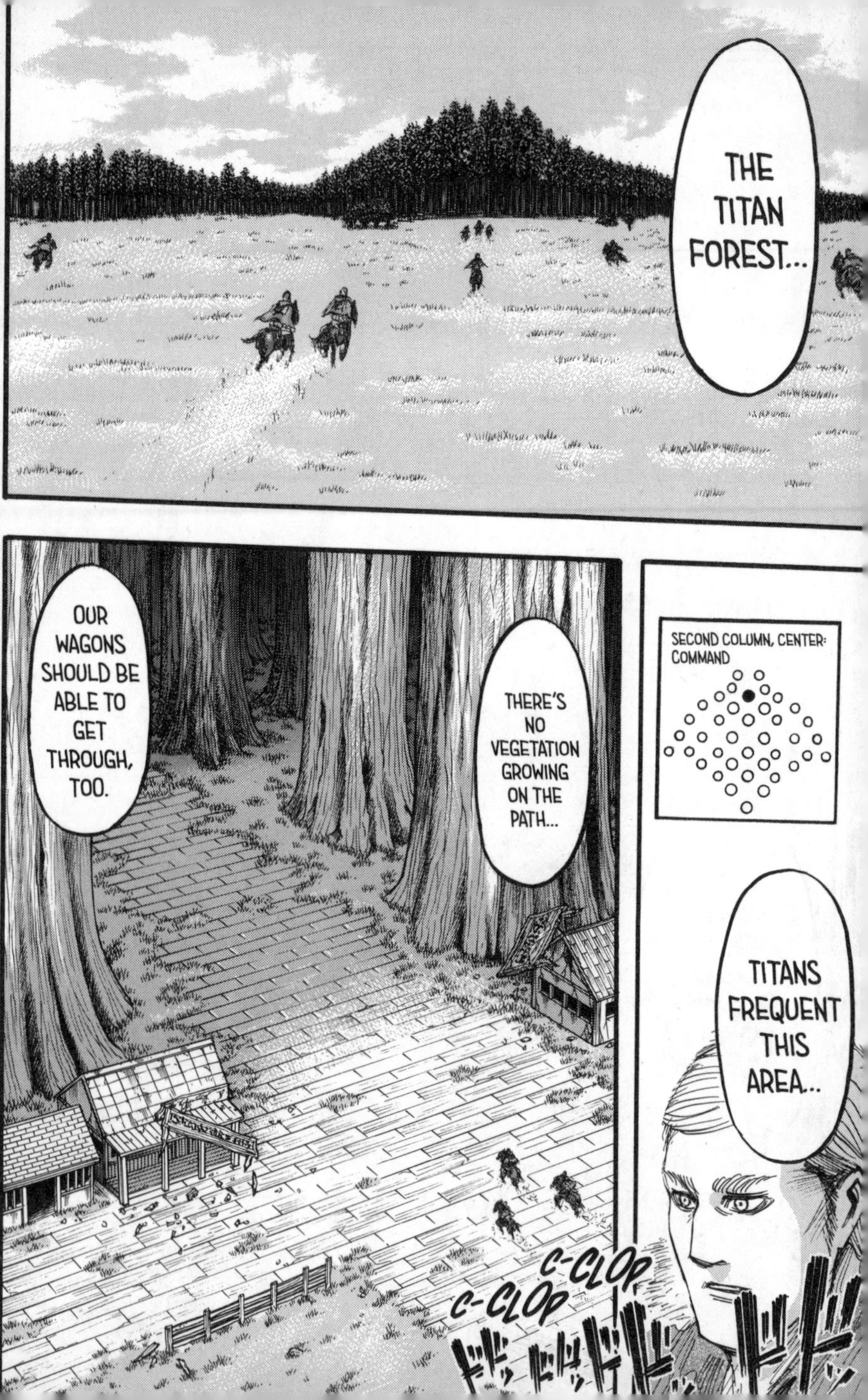
THE TITAN FOREST...
SECOND COLUMN, CENTER: COMMAND
TITANS FREQUENT THIS AREA...
C-CLOP
C-CLOP
THERE'S NO VEGETATION GROWING ON THE PATH...
OUR WAGONS SHOULD BE ABLE TO GET THROUGH, TOO.

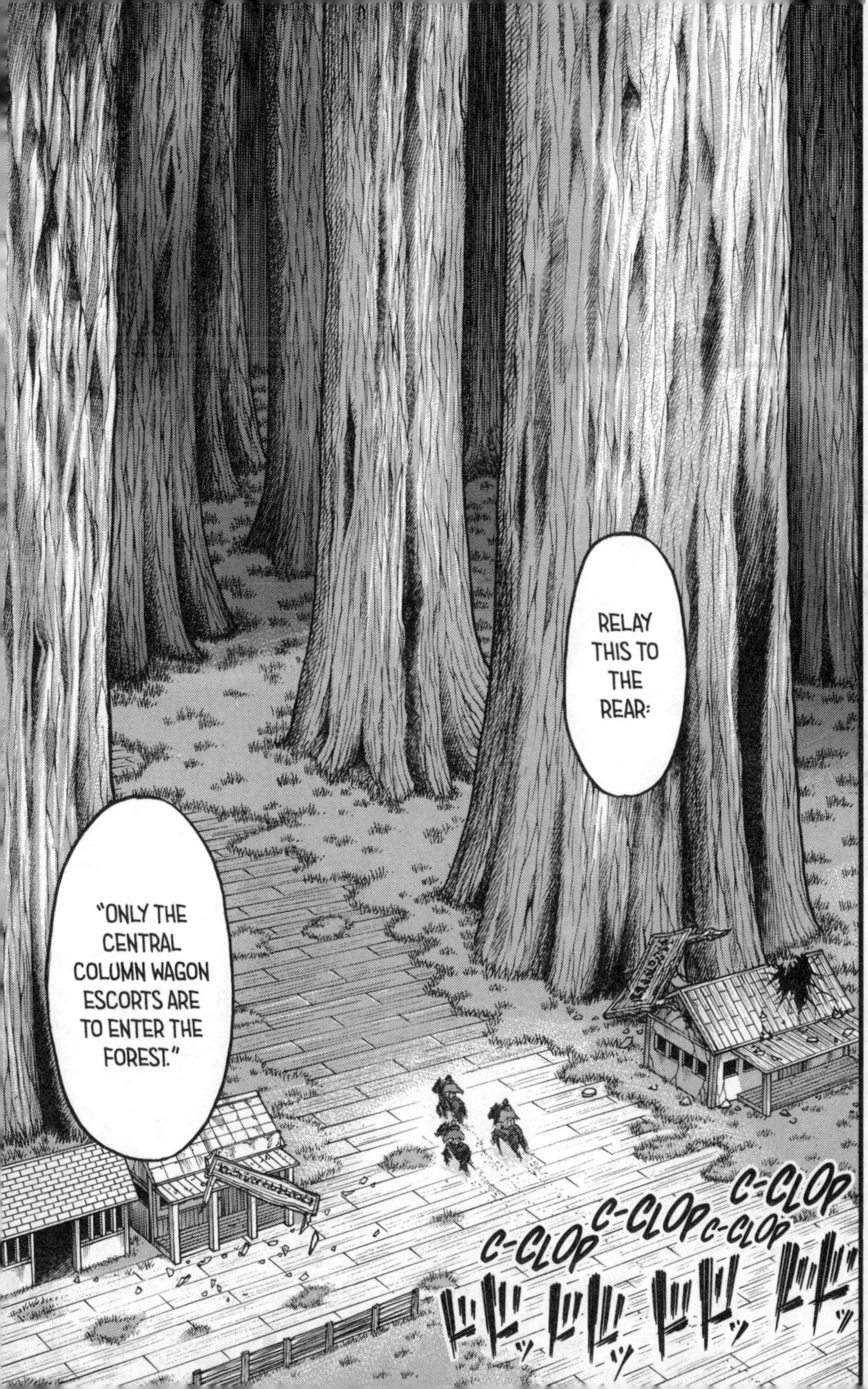
RELAY THIS TO THE REAR:
"ONLY THE CENTRAL COLUMN WAGON ESCORTS ARE TO ENTER THE FOREST."
C-CLOP C-CLOP C-CLOP C-CLOP

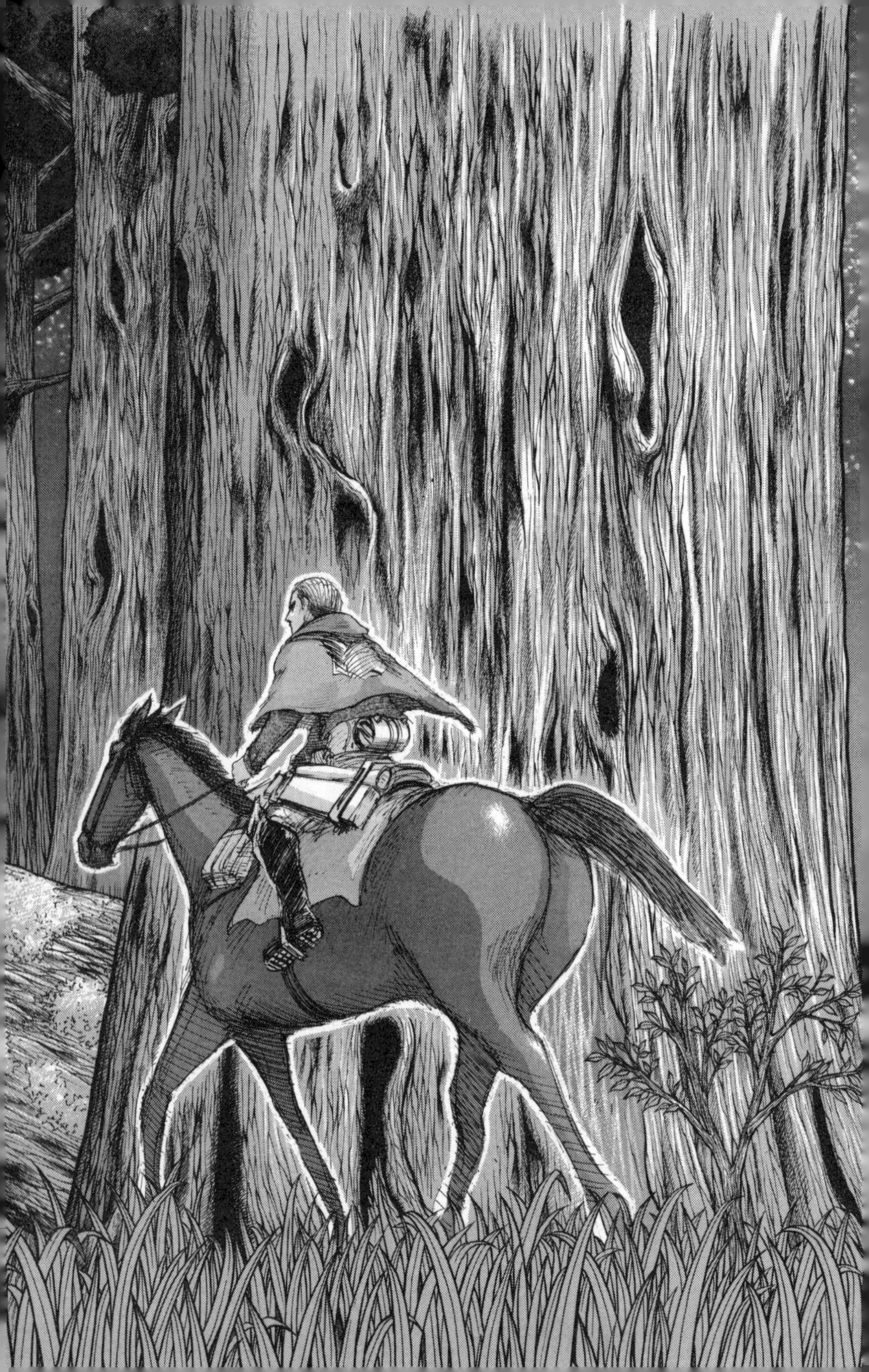

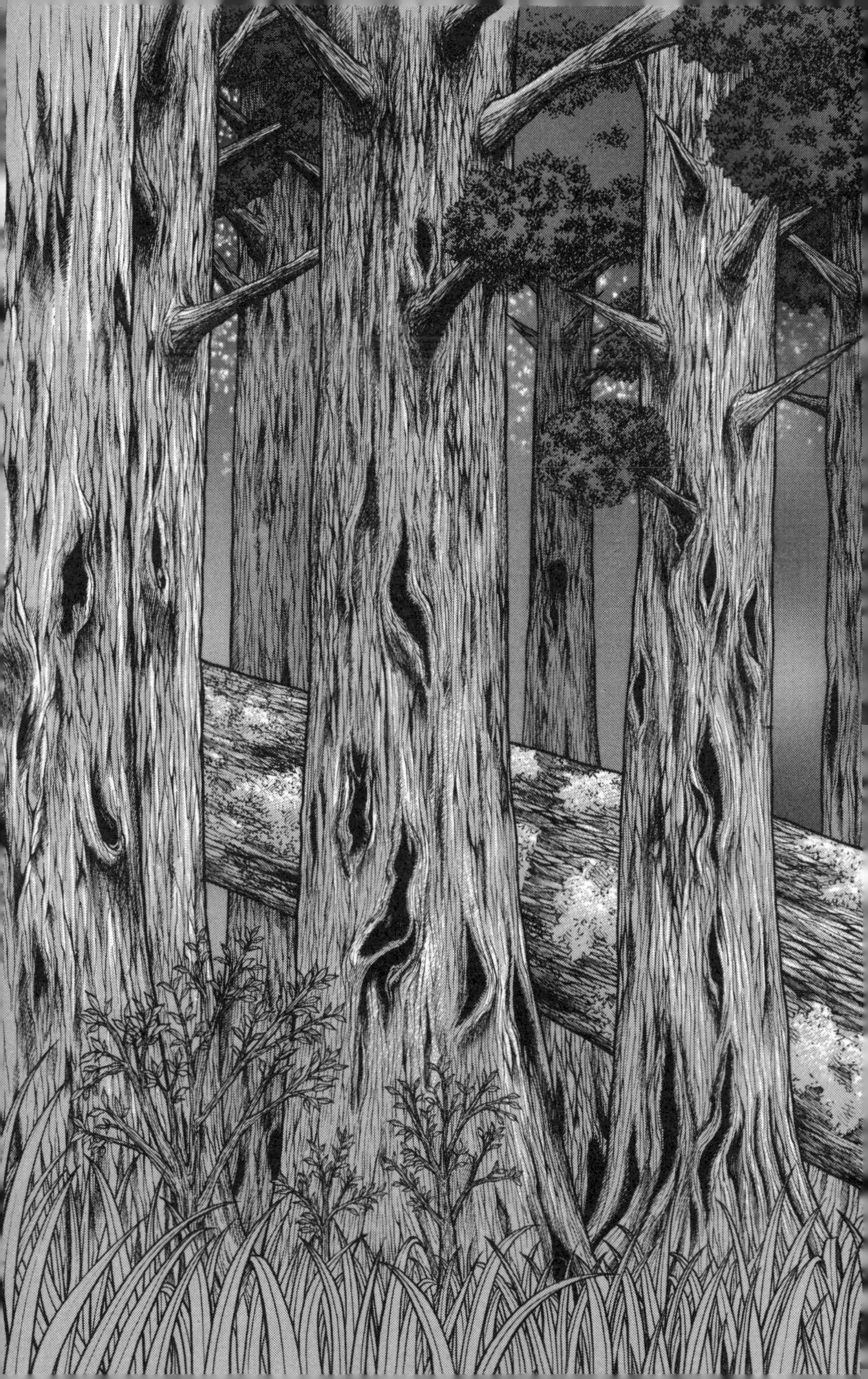

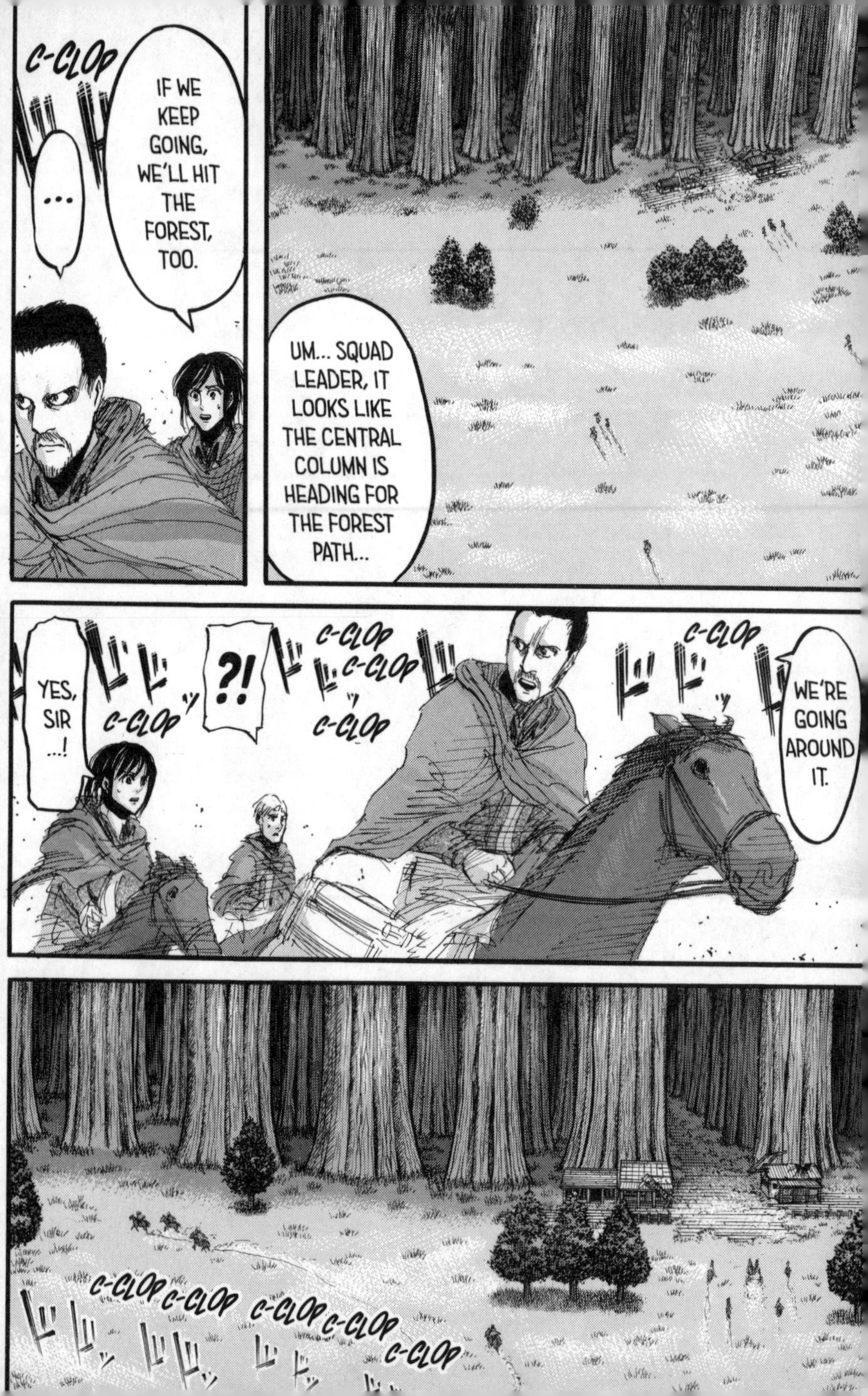
C-CLOP
IF WE KEEP GOING, WE'LL HIT THE FOREST, TOO.
...
UM... SQUAD LEADER, IT LOOKS LIKE THE CENTRAL COLUMN IS HEADING FOR THE FOREST PATH...
YES, SIR ...!
C-CLOP
?!
C-CLOP C-CLOP C-CLOP
C-CLOP
WE'RE GOING AROUND IT.
C-CLOP C-CLOP C-CLOP C-CLOP C-CLOP

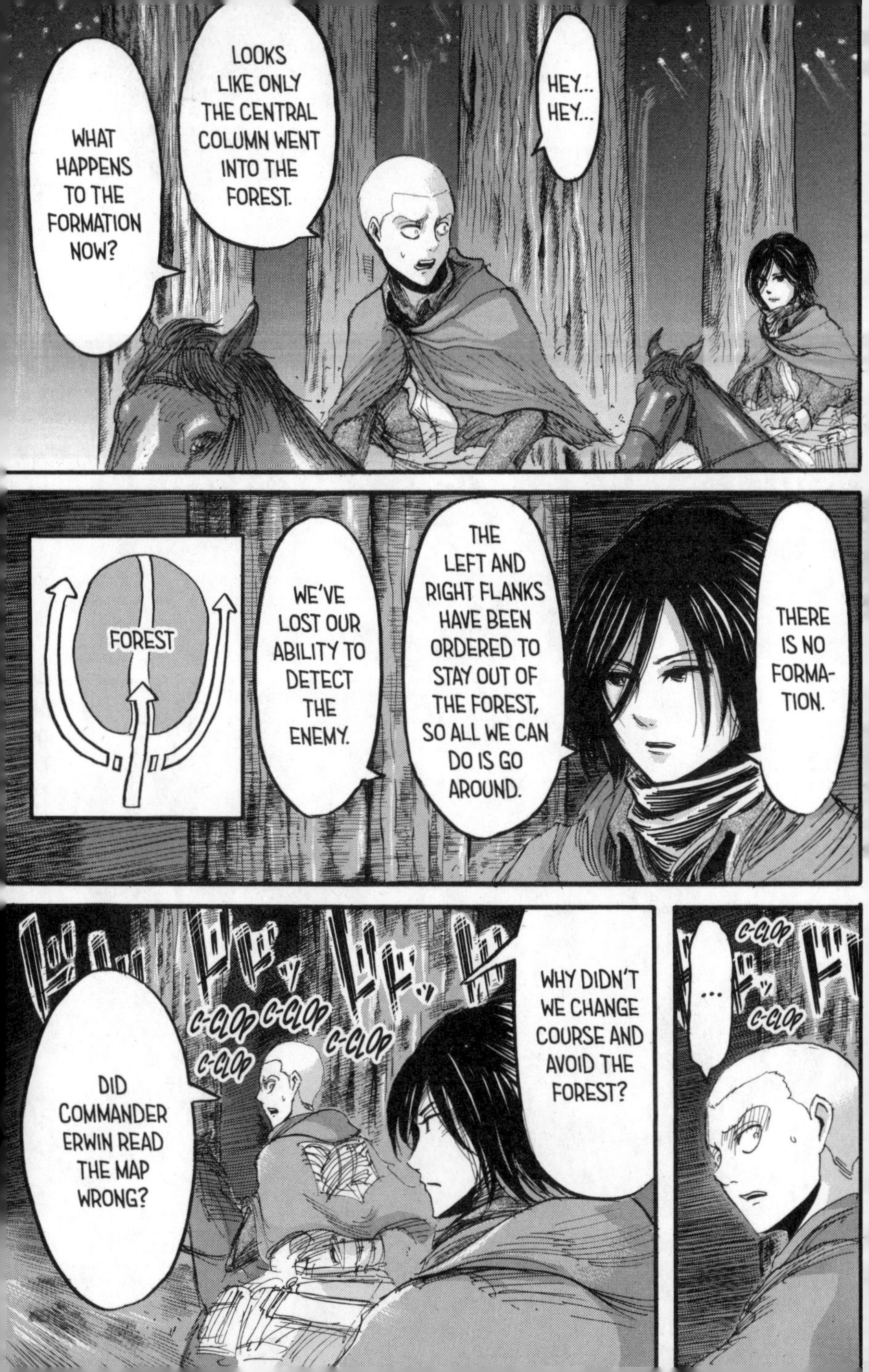
HEY... HEY...
LOOKS LIKE ONLY THE CENTRAL COLUMN WENT INTO THE FOREST.
WHAT HAPPENS TO THE FORMATION NOW?
THERE IS NO FORMATION.
THE LEFT AND RIGHT FLANKS HAVE BEEN ORDERED TO STAY OUT OF THE FOREST, SO ALL WE CAN DO IS GO AROUND.
WE'VE LOST OUR ABILITY TO DETECT THE ENEMY.
FOREST
C-CLOP
...
C-CLOP
WHY DIDN'T WE CHANGE COURSE AND AVOID THE FOREST?
C-CLOP C-CLOP C-CLOP C-CLOP
DID COMMANDER ERWIN READ THE MAP WRONG?

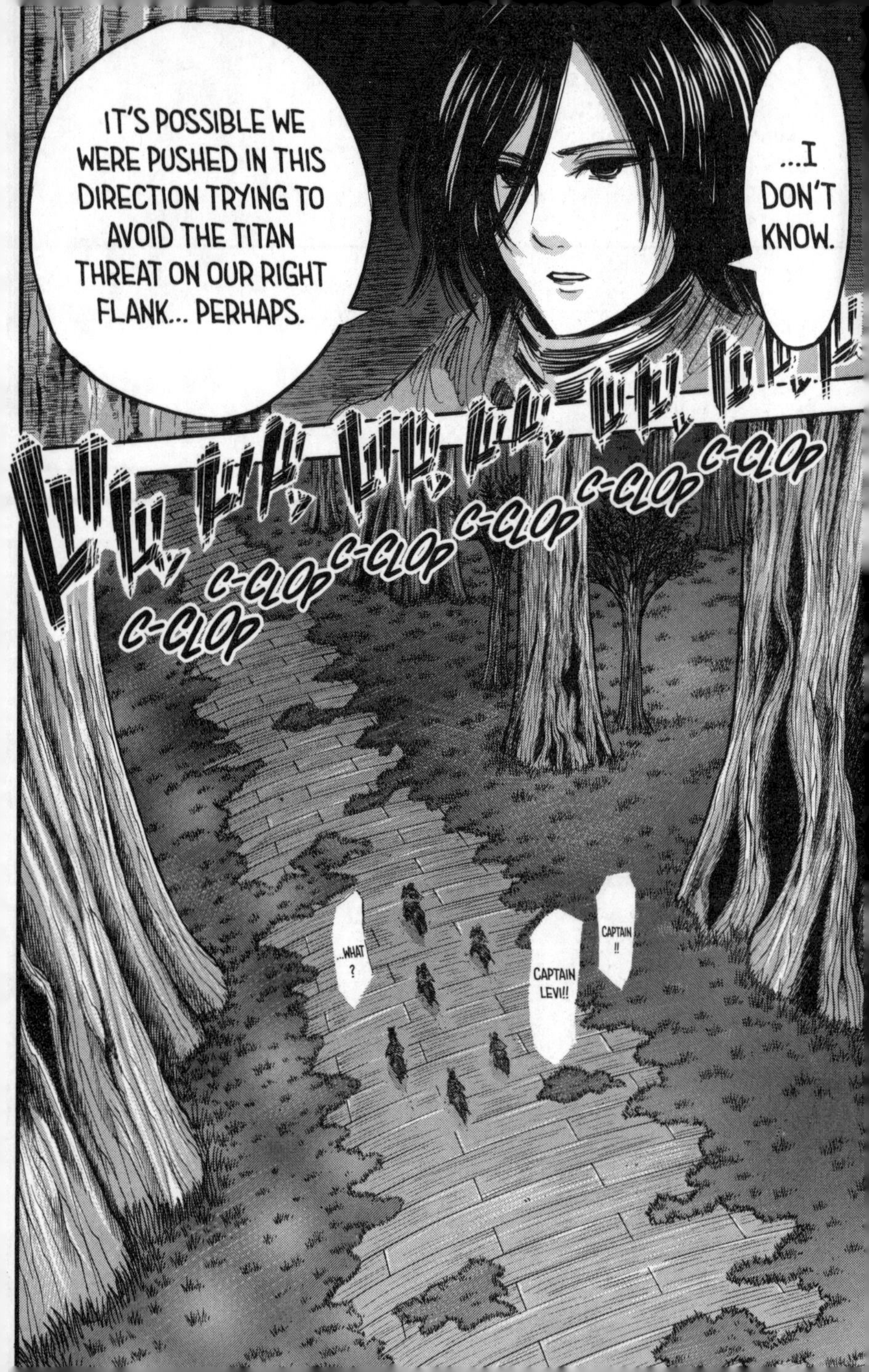
...I DON'T KNOW.
IT'S POSSIBLE WE WERE PUSHED IN THIS DIRECTION TRYING TO AVOID THE TITAN THREAT ON OUR RIGHT FLANK... PERHAPS.
C-CLOP
C-CLOP
C-CLOP
C-CLOP
C-CLOP
C-CLOP
CAPTAIN !!
CAPTAIN LEVI!!
...WHAT ?

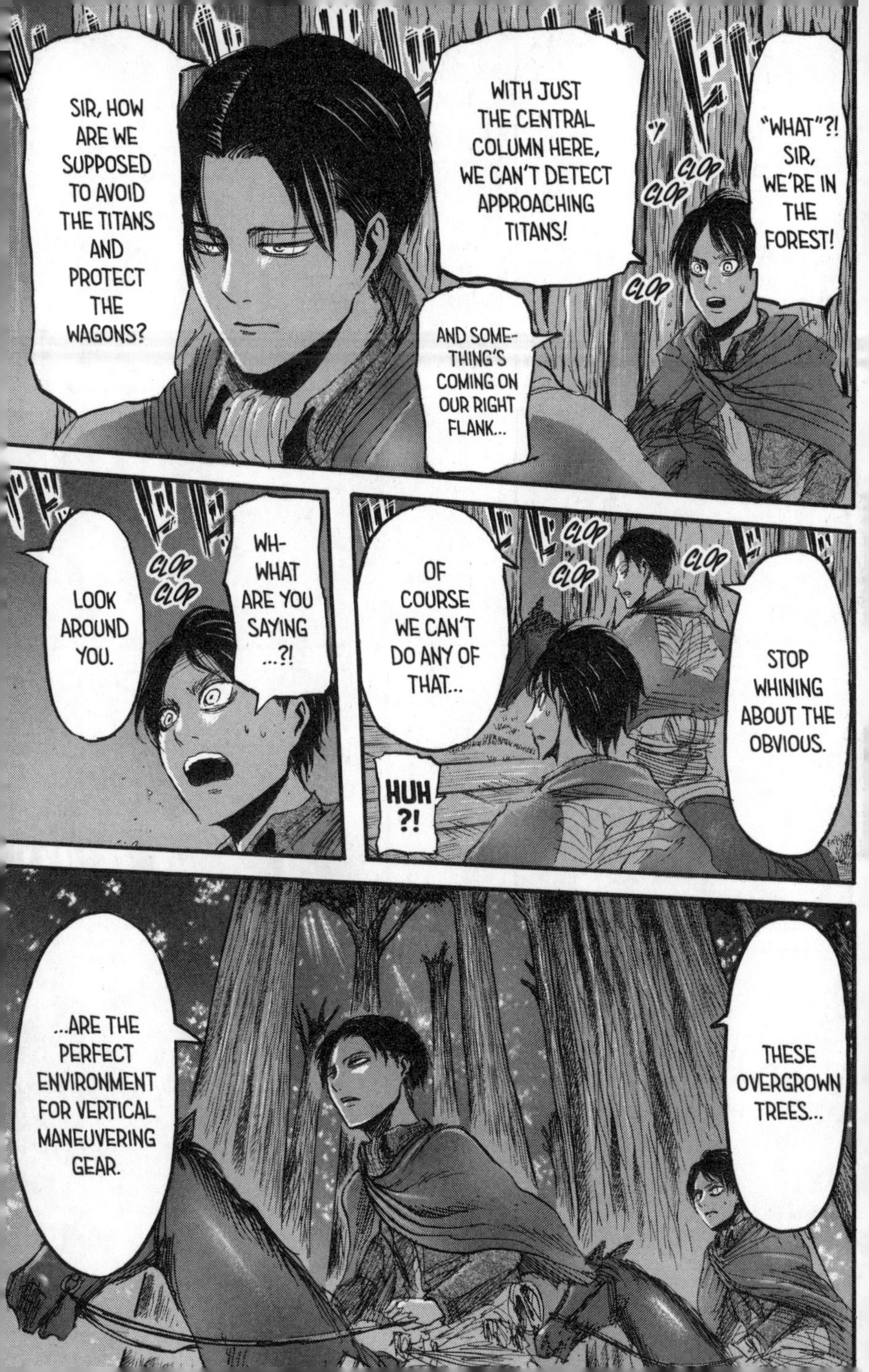
CLOP
CLOP
CLOP
"WHAT"?! SIR, WE'RE IN THE FOREST!
WITH JUST THE CENTRAL COLUMN HERE, WE CAN'T DETECT APPROACHING TITANS!
CLOP
AND SOME-THING'S COMING ON OUR RIGHT FLANK...
SIR, HOW ARE WE SUPPOSED TO AVOID THE TITANS AND PROTECT THE WAGONS?
CLOP
CLOP
CLOP
STOP WHINING ABOUT THE OBVIOUS.
OF COURSE WE CAN'T DO ANY OF THAT...
HUH ?!
CLOP
CLOP
WH-WHAT ARE YOU SAYING ...?!
LOOK AROUND YOU.
THESE OVERGROWN TREES...
...ARE THE PERFECT ENVIRONMENT FOR VERTICAL MANEUVERING GEAR.

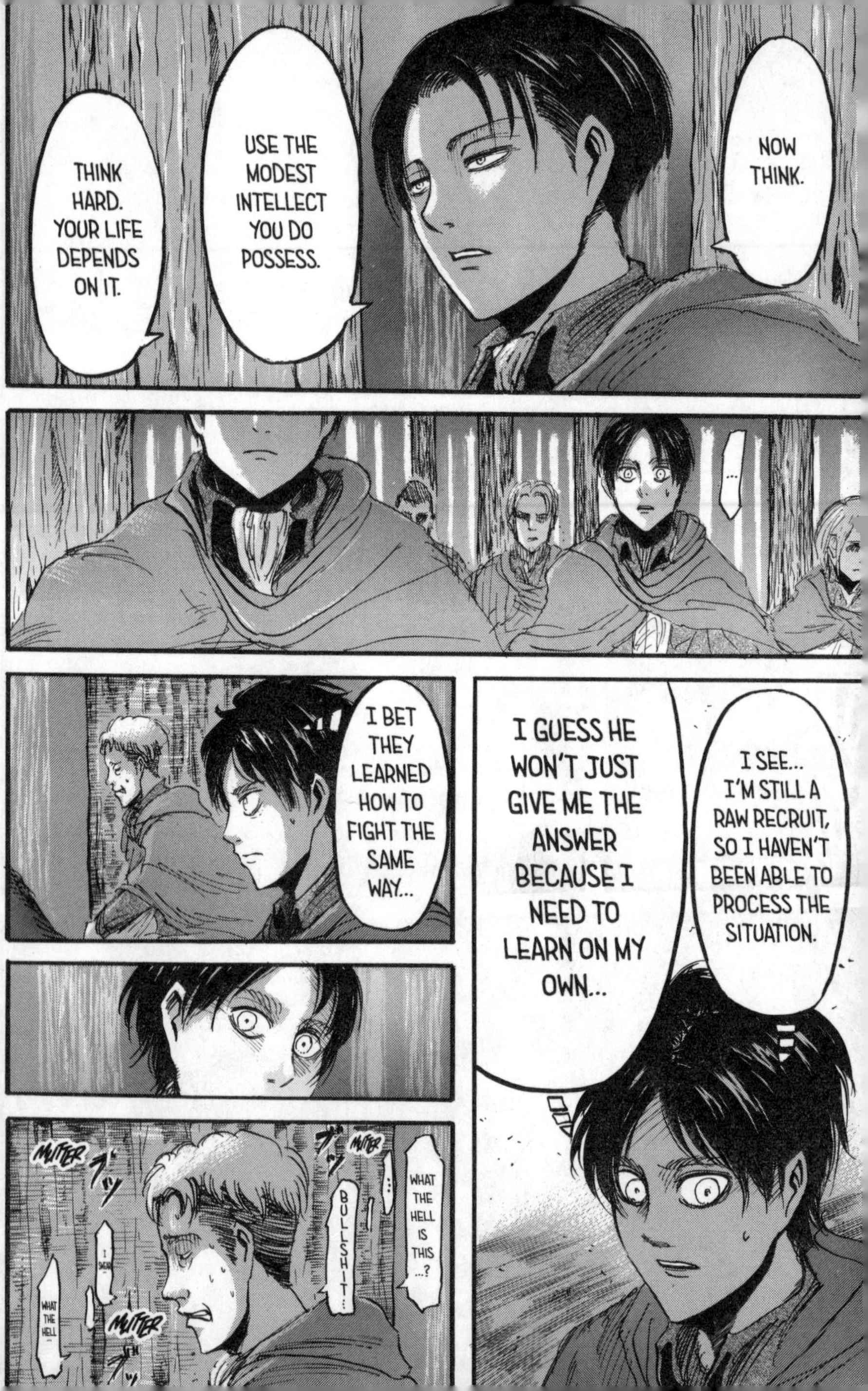
NOW THINK.
USE THE MODEST INTELLECT YOU DO POSSESS.
THINK HARD. YOUR LIFE DEPENDS ON IT.
...
I SEE... I'M STILL A RAW RECRUIT, SO I HAVEN'T BEEN ABLE TO PROCESS THE SITUATION.
I GUESS HE WON'T JUST GIVE ME THE ANSWER BECAUSE I NEED TO LEARN ON MY OWN...
I BET THEY LEARNED HOW TO FIGHT THE SAME WAY...
MUTTER
WHAT THE HELL IS THIS ...?
BULLSHIT...
...
MUTTER
WHAT THE HELL ...
MUTTER

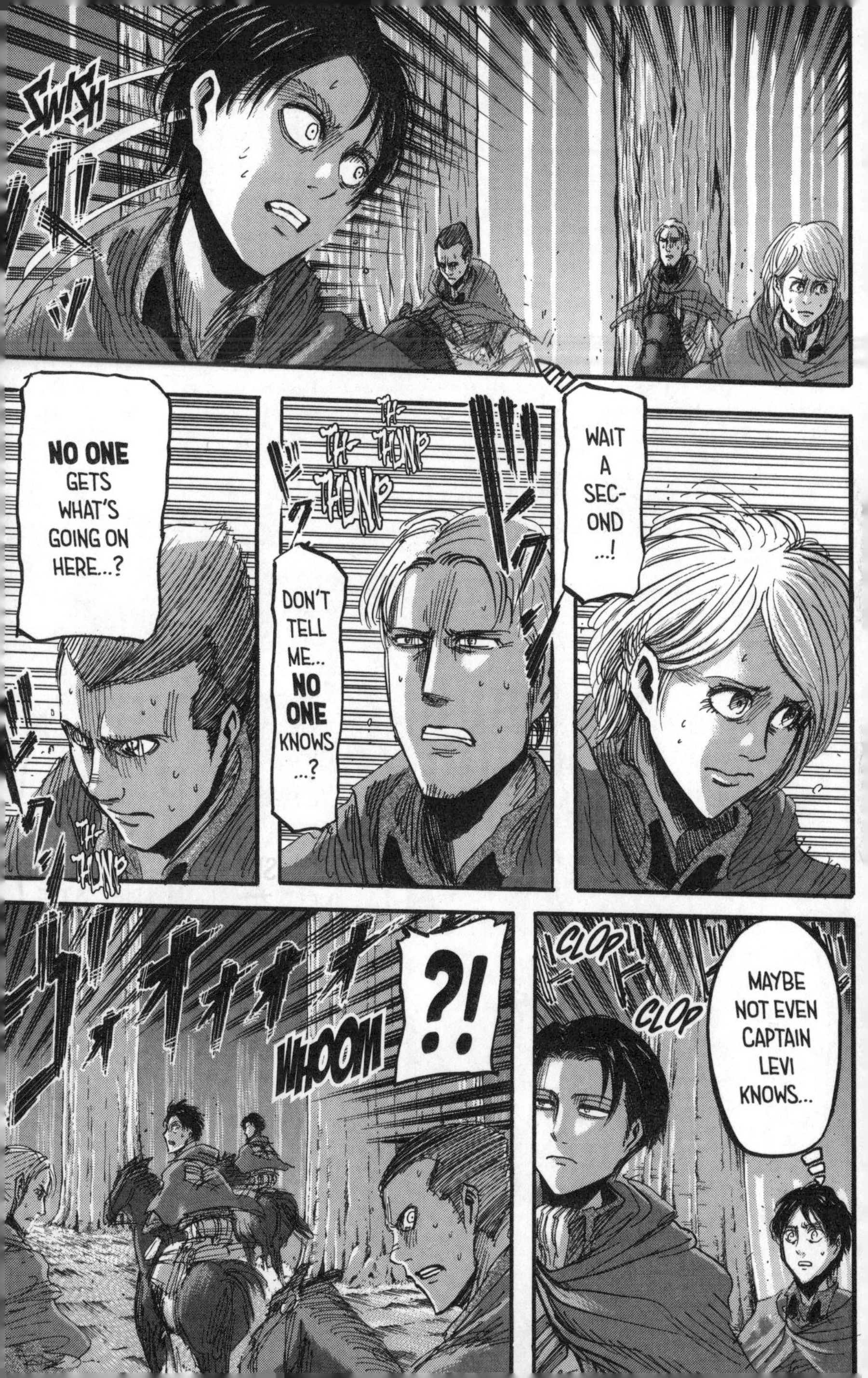
SWISH
WAIT A SEC-OND...!
TH-THUMP
TH-THUMP
DON'T TELL ME... **NO ONE** KNOWS...?
NO ONE GETS WHAT'S GOING ON HERE...?
TH-THUMP
CLOP
CLOP
MAYBE NOT EVEN CAPTAIN LEVI KNOWS...
?!
WHOOM

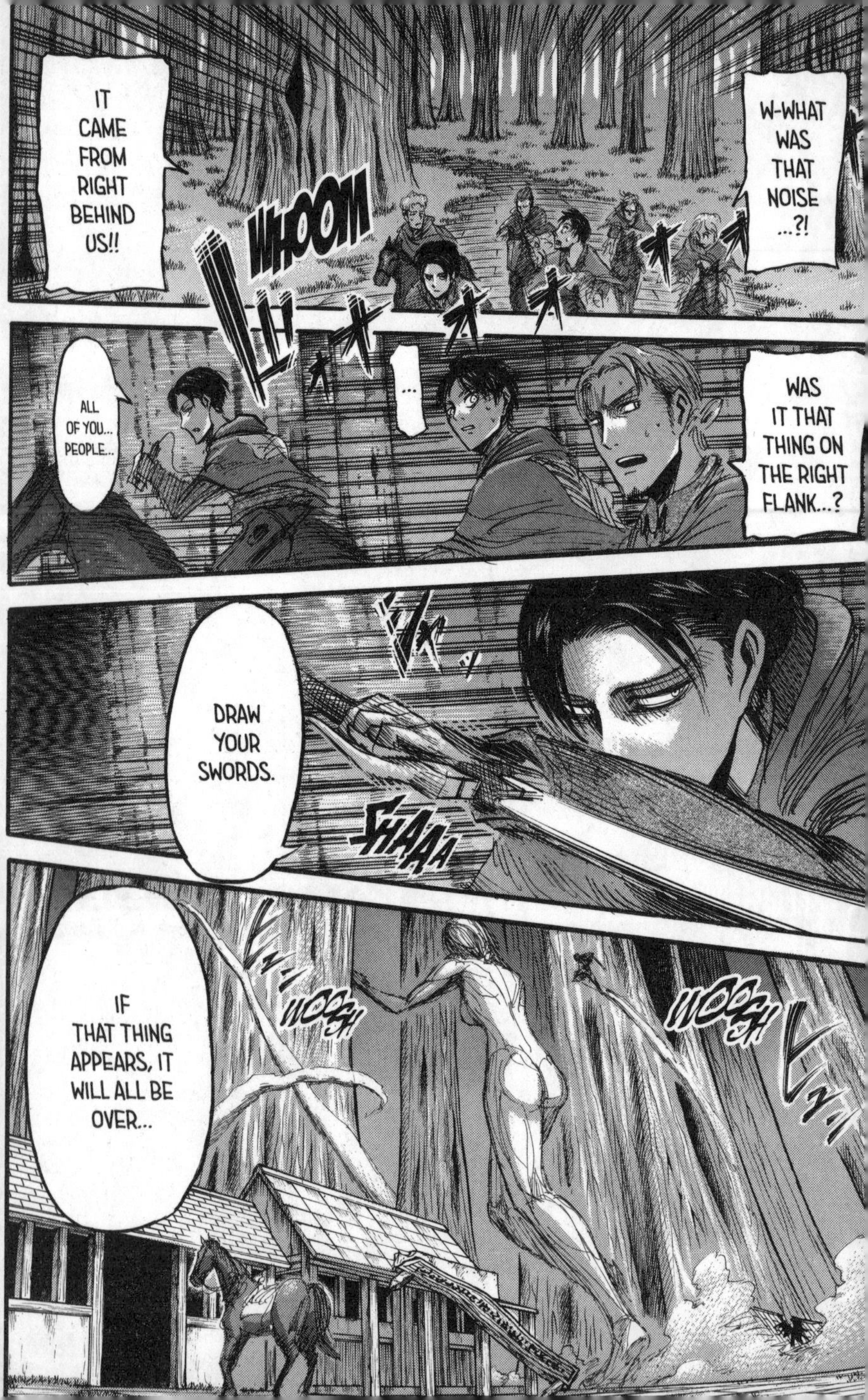
W-WHAT WAS THAT NOISE ...?!
IT CAME FROM RIGHT BEHIND US!!
WHOOM
WAS IT THAT THING ON THE RIGHT FLANK...?
...
ALL OF YOU... PEOPLE...
DRAW YOUR SWORDS.
SHAAA
WOOSH
WOOSH
IF THAT THING APPEARS, IT WILL ALL BE OVER...

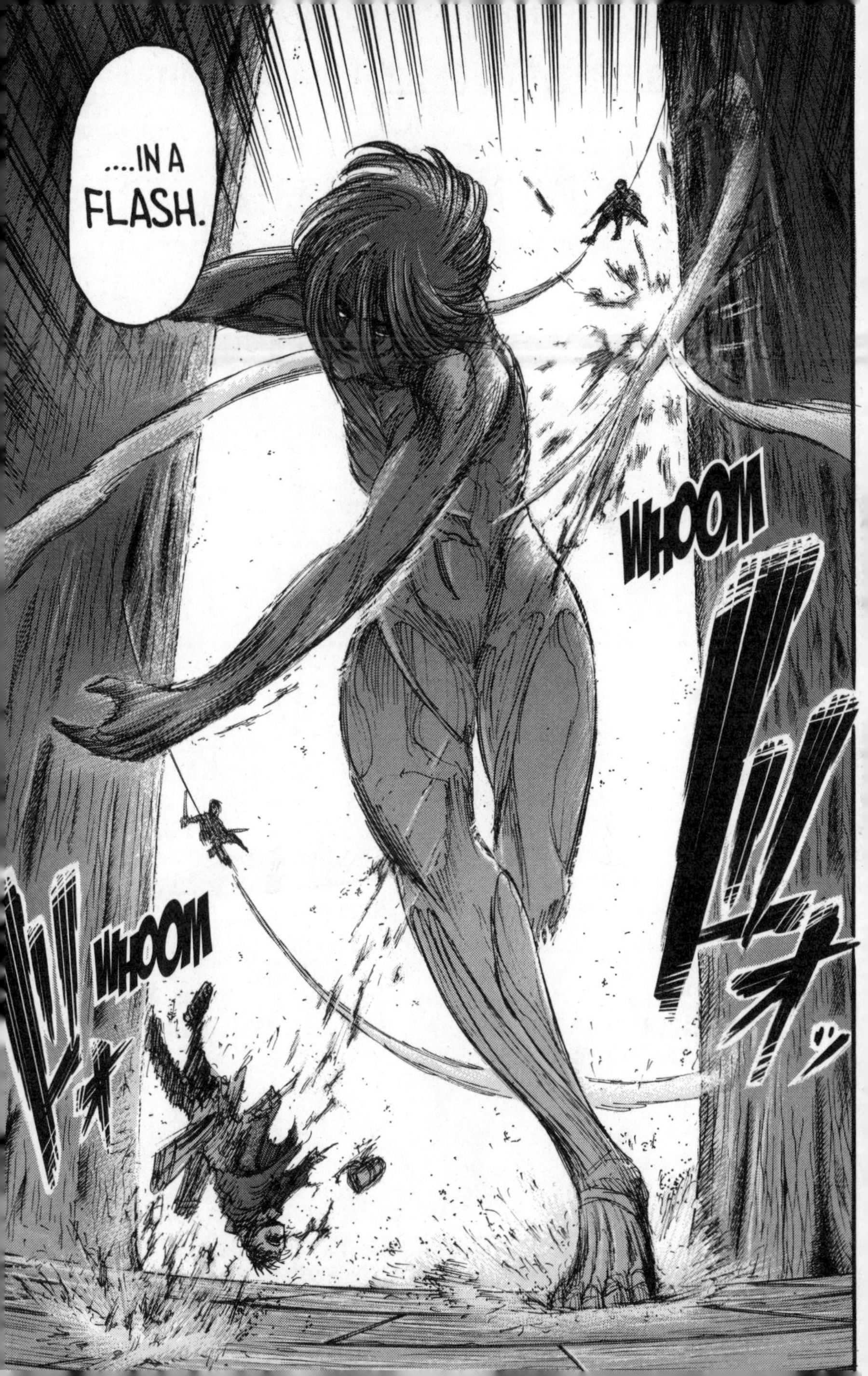
....IN A FLASH.
WHOOM
WHOOM

Current Publicly Available Information

12. The Titan Forest

THERE ARE FORESTS OF GIANT TREES BOTH INSIDE AND OUTSIDE THE WALL. THEY GROW WILD ALONG THE BORDER OF ONE DISTRICT, AVERAGING A HEIGHT OF OVER 80 METERS.* NO ONE KNOWS WHY TREES OF THIS SIZE EXIST, BUT SOME HAVE PROPOSED THE NATURE OF THE SOIL AS THE CAUSE. BEFORE THE FALL OF WALL MARIA, PEOPLE MAINTAINED THE FOREST AS A TOURIST ATTRACTION. WITHOUT HUMAN INTERCESSION IN THE LAST SEVERAL YEARS, THE AREA HAS FALLEN INTO RUIN, WITH THE FOREST PATH MOSTLY SWALLOWED UP BY WEEDS AND TREES, ALTHOUGH PARTS OF THE PATH REMAIN INTACT FROM THE COMINGS AND GOINGS OF THE TITANS THROUGH THE WOODS. THE FOREST HAS BECOME AN IMPORTANT BASE FOR THE SURVEY CORPS, USED TO PROTECT THEMSELVES FROM THE TITANS WHILE ON EXPEDITIONS OUTSIDE THE WALL. (WITH THANKS TO UKYŌ KODACHI AND KIYOMUNE MIWA.)

* ABOUT 260 FEET.

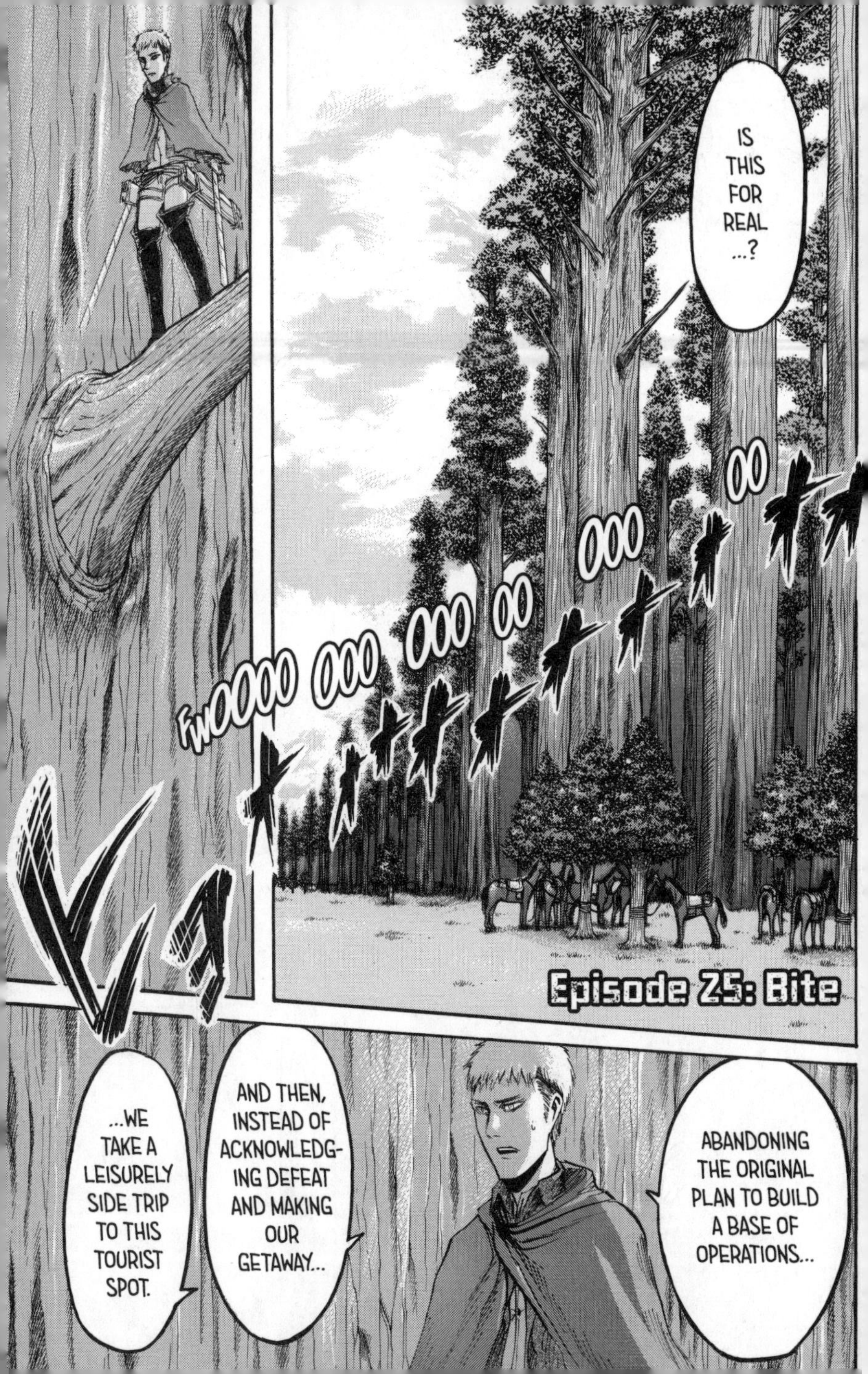
IS THIS FOR REAL ...?
FWOOOO OOO OOO OO OOO OO
Episode 25: Bite
ABANDONING THE ORIGINAL PLAN TO BUILD A BASE OF OPERATIONS...
AND THEN, INSTEAD OF ACKNOWLEDG-ING DEFEAT AND MAKING OUR GETAWAY...
...WE TAKE A LEISURELY SIDE TRIP TO THIS TOURIST SPOT.

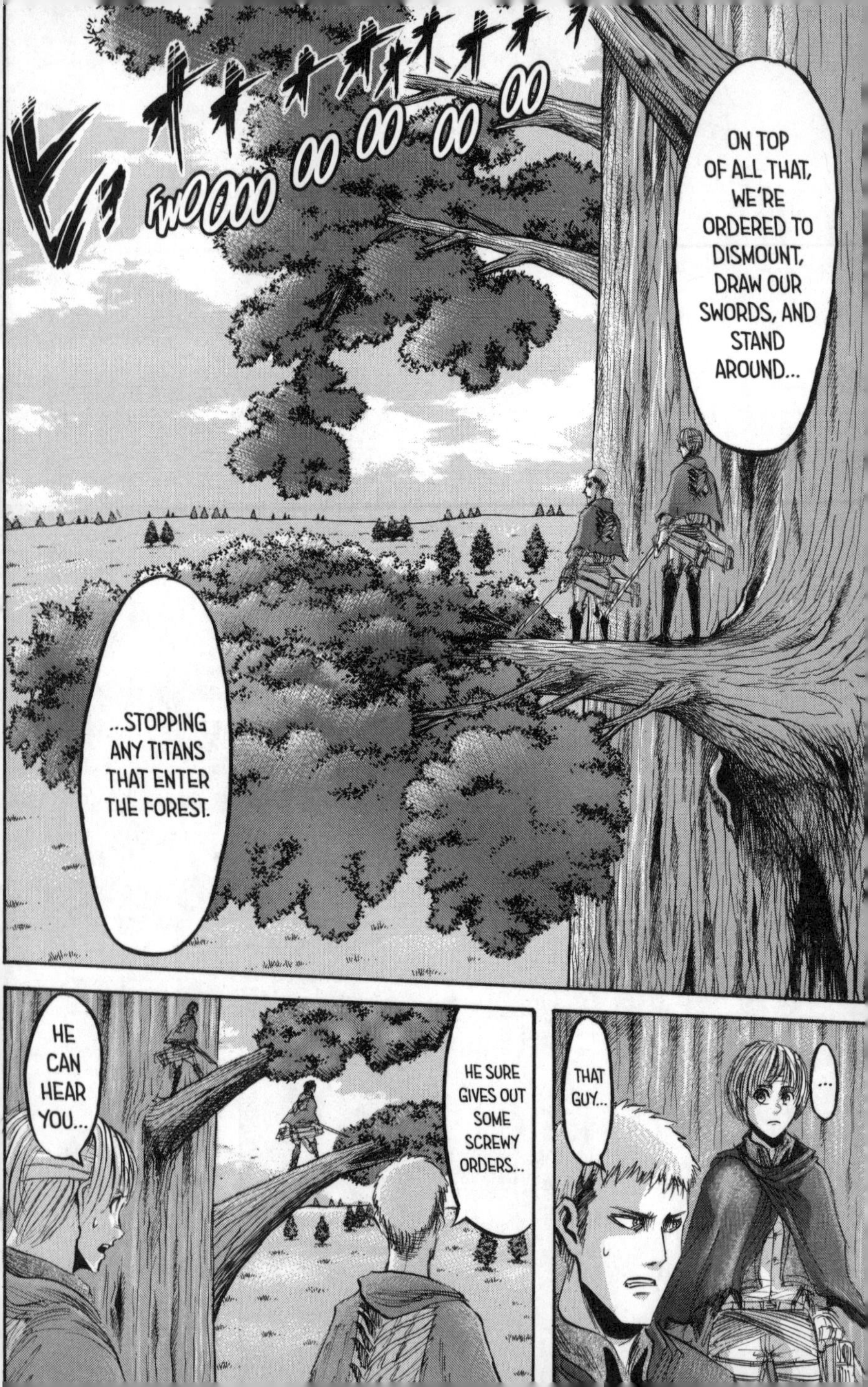
FWOOOO OO OO OO OO
ON TOP OF ALL THAT, WE'RE ORDERED TO DISMOUNT, DRAW OUR SWORDS, AND STAND AROUND...
...STOPPING ANY TITANS THAT ENTER THE FOREST.
...
THAT GUY...
HE SURE GIVES OUT SOME SCREWY ORDERS...
HE CAN HEAR YOU...

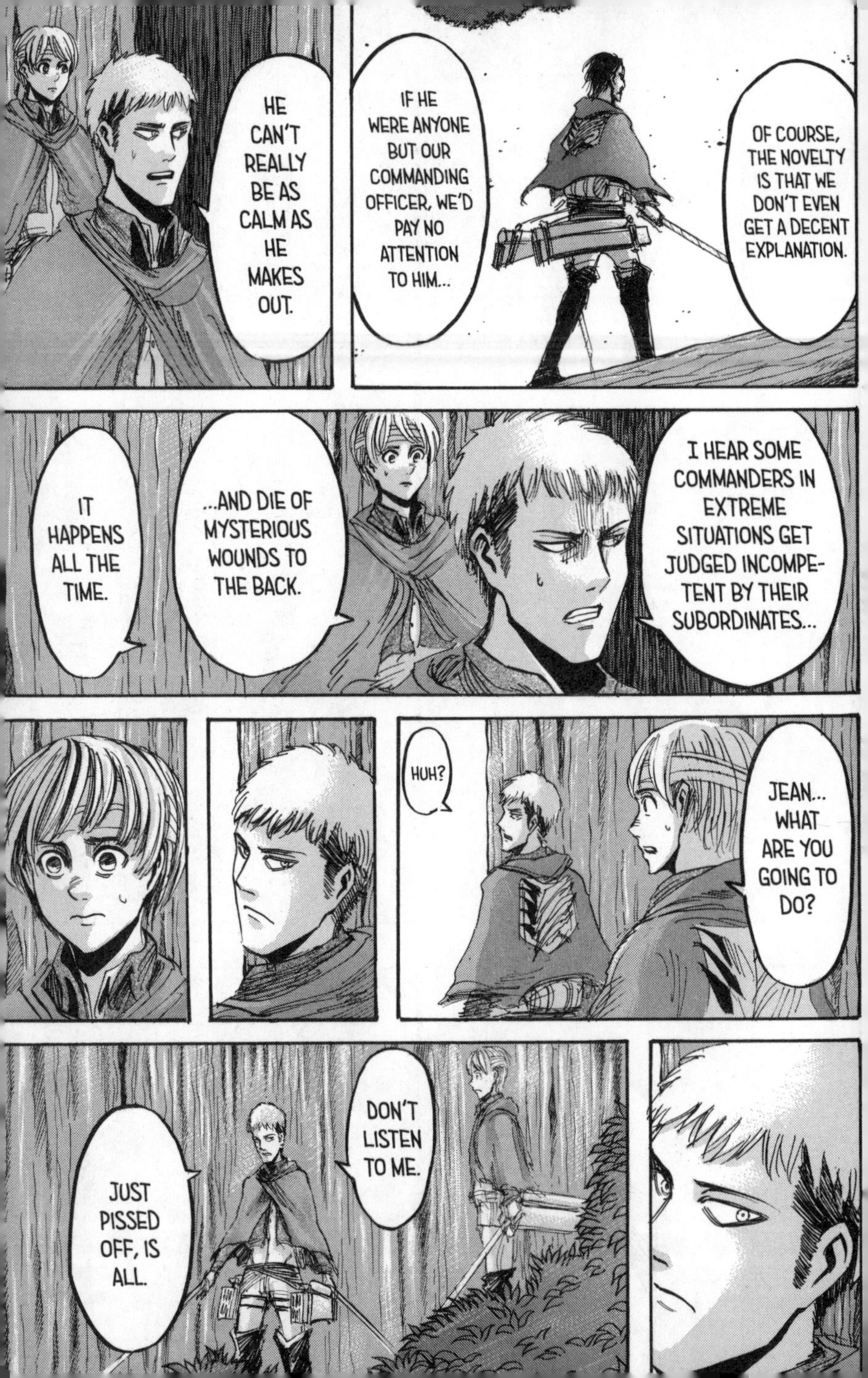
OF COURSE, THE NOVELTY IS THAT WE DON'T EVEN GET A DECENT EXPLANATION.
IF HE WERE ANYONE BUT OUR COMMANDING OFFICER, WE'D PAY NO ATTENTION TO HIM...
HE CAN'T REALLY BE AS CALM AS HE MAKES OUT.
I HEAR SOME COMMANDERS IN EXTREME SITUATIONS GET JUDGED INCOMPE-TENT BY THEIR SUBORDINATES...
...AND DIE OF MYSTERIOUS WOUNDS TO THE BACK.
IT HAPPENS ALL THE TIME.
JEAN... WHAT ARE YOU GOING TO DO?
HUH?
DON'T LISTEN TO ME.
JUST PISSED OFF, IS ALL.

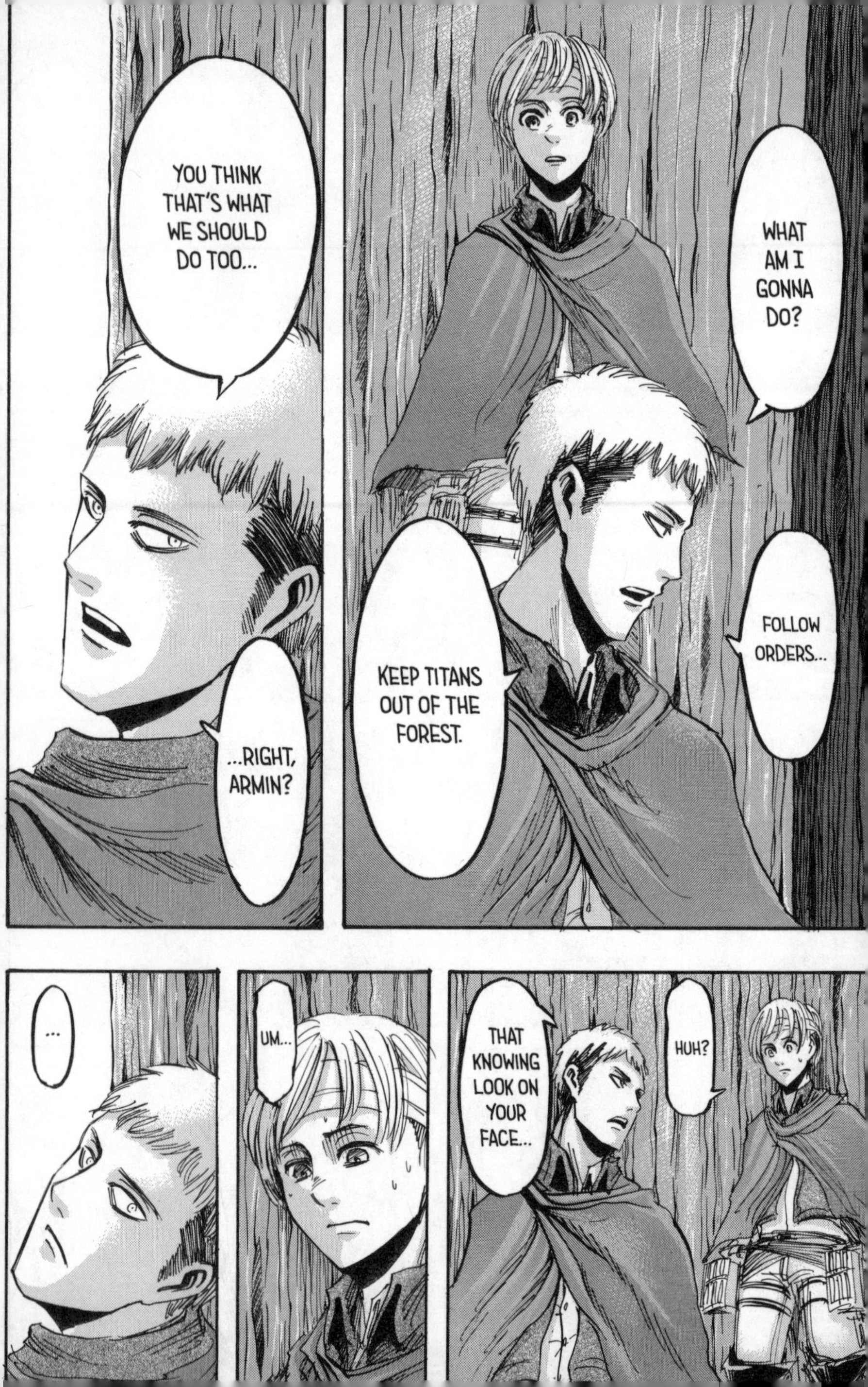
WHAT AM I GONNA DO?
FOLLOW ORDERS...
KEEP TITANS OUT OF THE FOREST.
YOU THINK THAT'S WHAT WE SHOULD DO TOO...
...RIGHT, ARMIN?
HUH?
THAT KNOWING LOOK ON YOUR FACE...
UM...
...

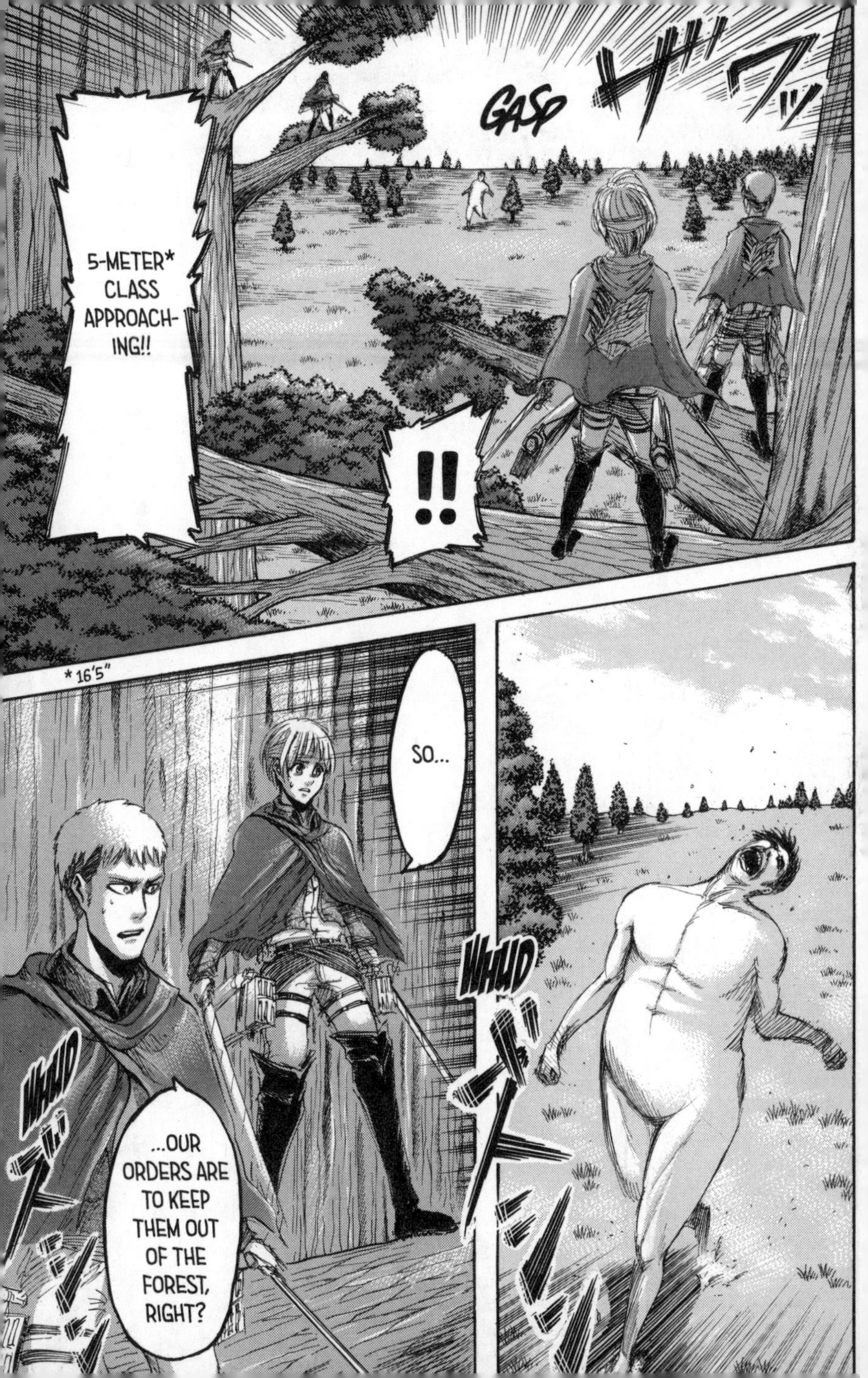
GASP
ザワッ
!!
5-METER* CLASS APPROACHING!!
*16'5"
WHUD
SO...
...OUR ORDERS ARE TO KEEP THEM OUT OF THE FOREST, RIGHT?
WHUD

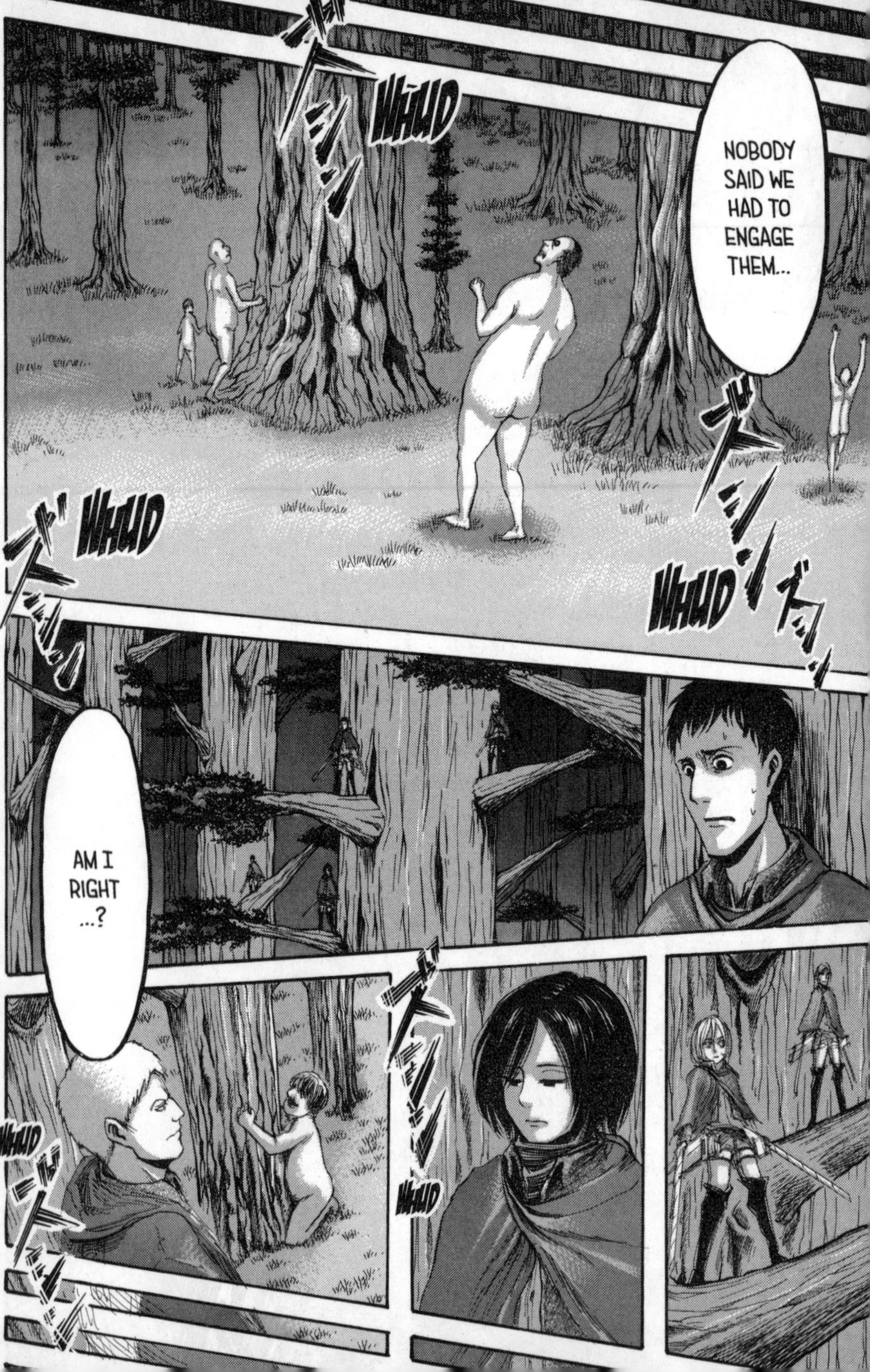
NOBODY SAID WE HAD TO ENGAGE THEM...
WHUD
WHUD
WHUD
AM I RIGHT ...?
WHUD
WHUD

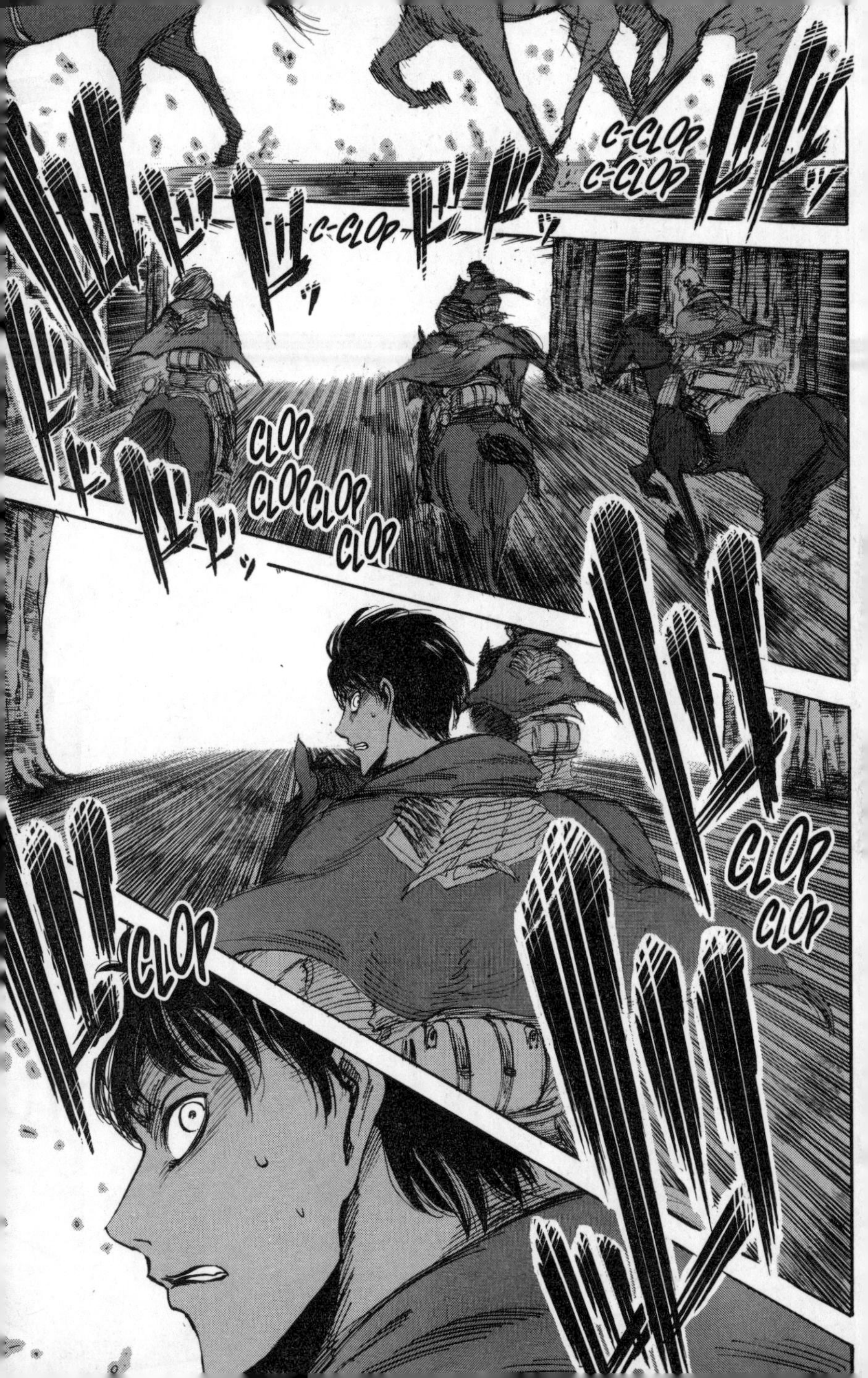
C-CLOP
C-CLOP
C-CLOP
CLOP
CLOPCLOP
CLOP
CLOP
CLOP
CLOP

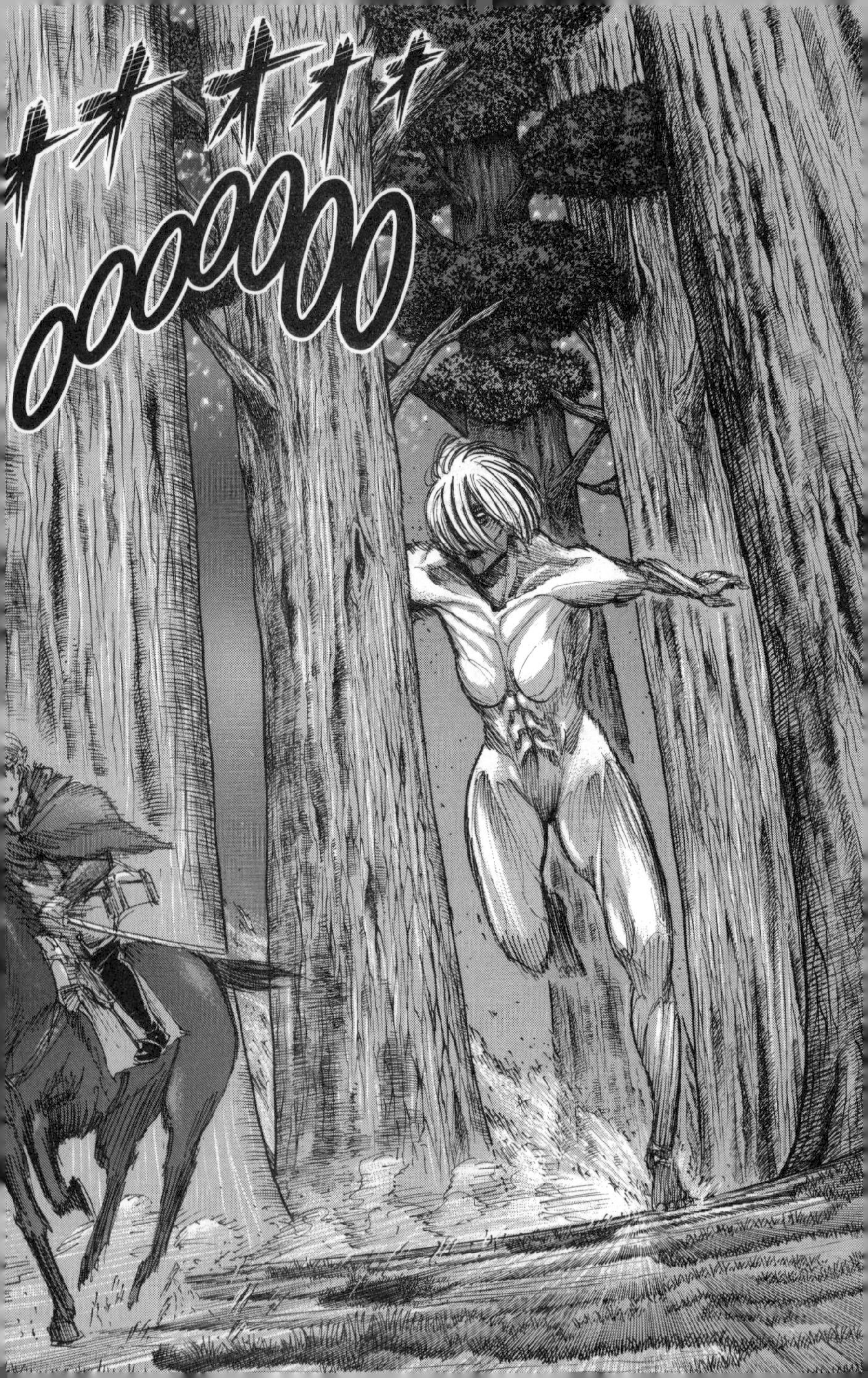
オオオオオ
OOOOOOO

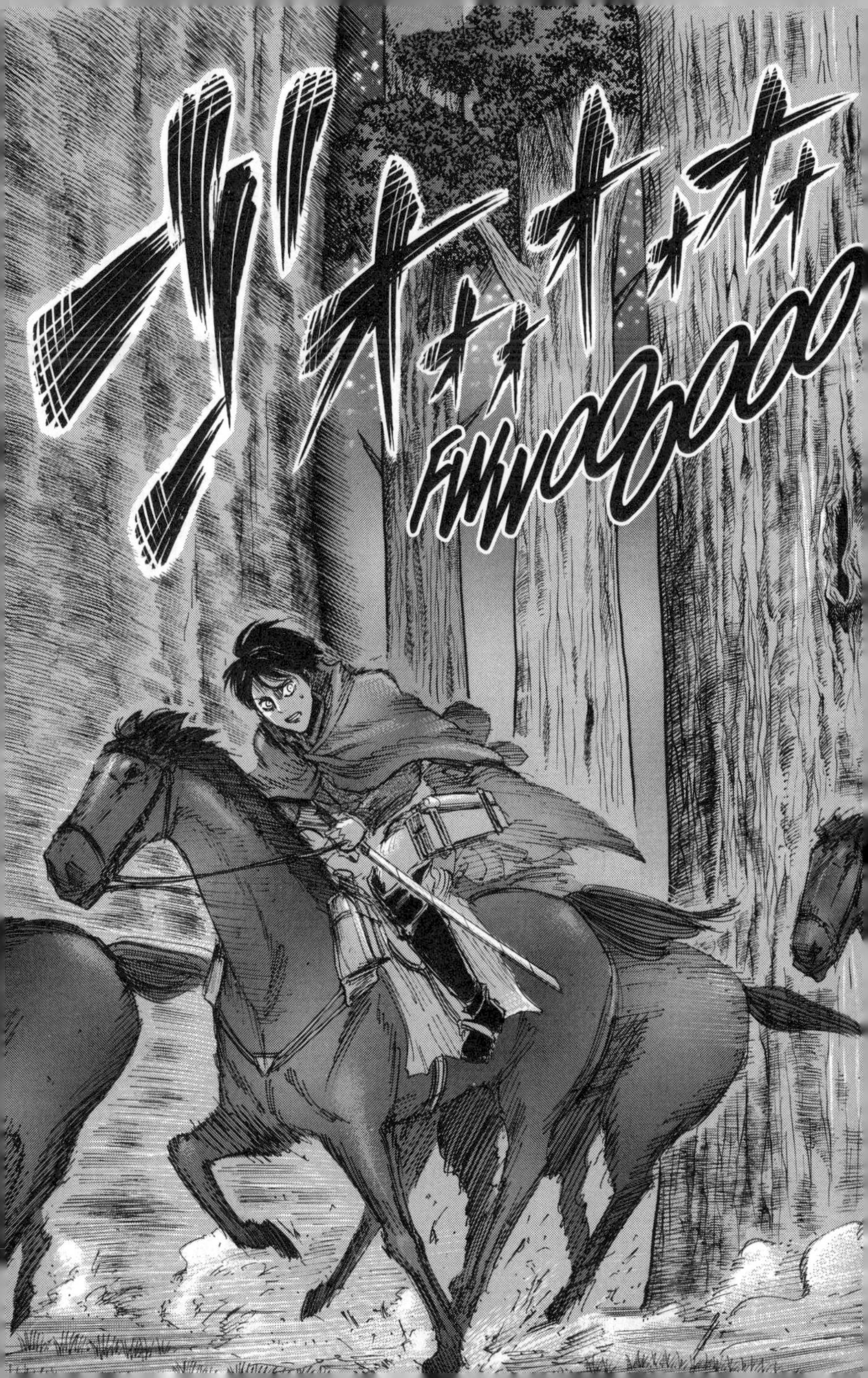
ブオォォオォオ
FWWOAAAA

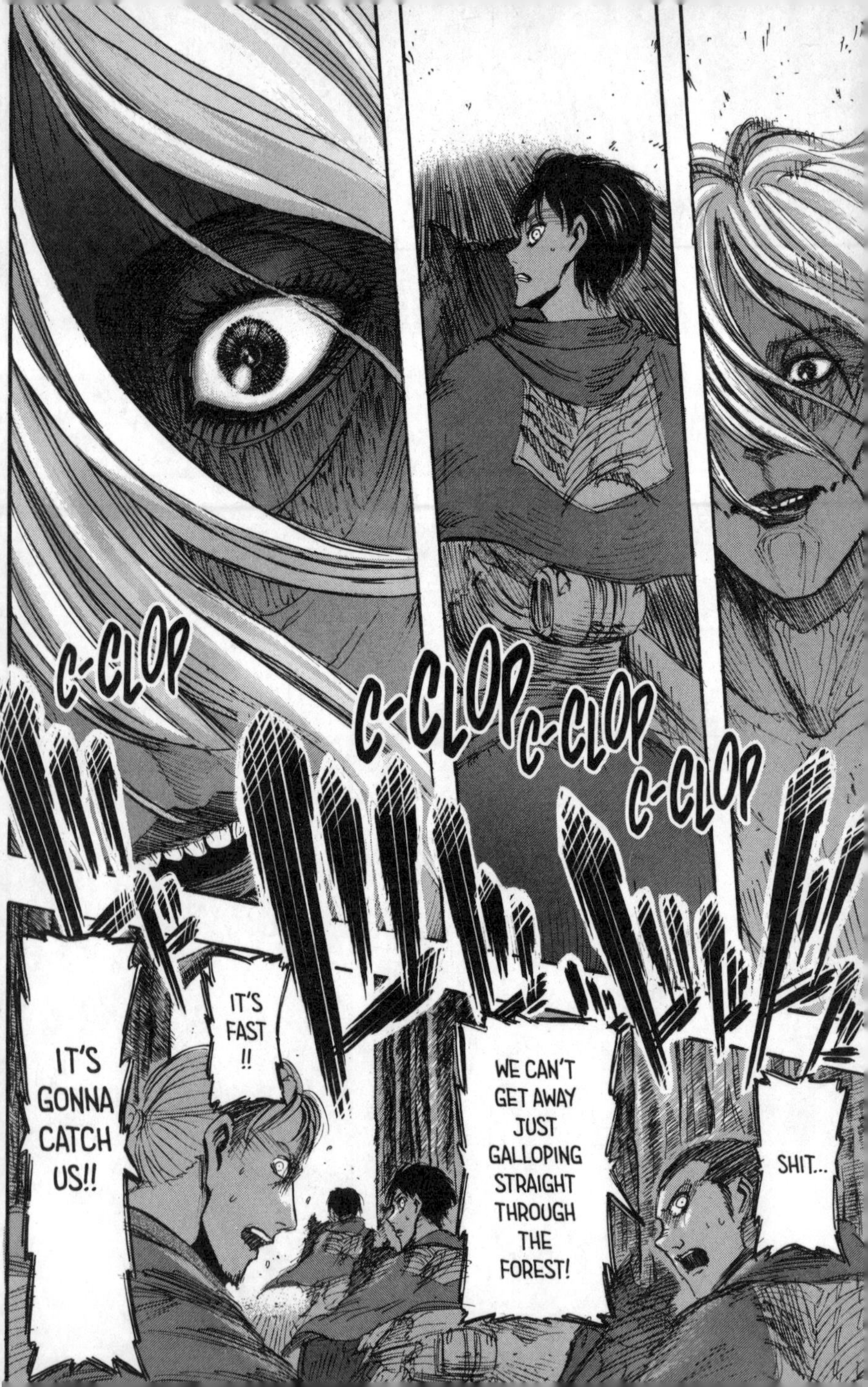
C-CLOP
C-CLOP
C-CLOP
C-CLOP
SHIT...
WE CAN'T GET AWAY JUST GALLOPING STRAIGHT THROUGH THE FOREST!
IT'S FAST!!
IT'S GONNA CATCH US!!

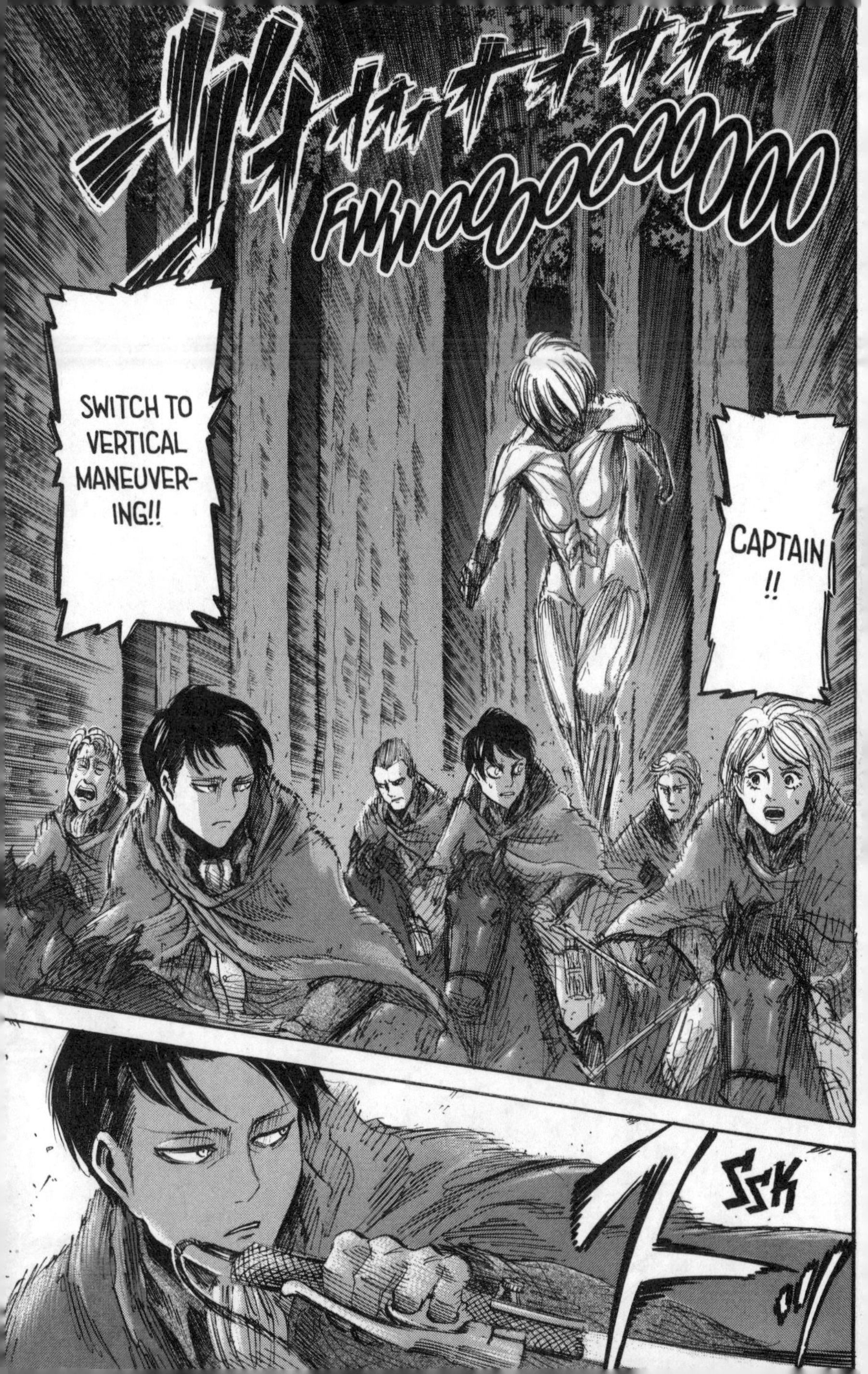
FWWOOOOOOOOO
CAPTAIN !!
SWITCH TO VERTICAL MANEUVER-ING!!
SSK

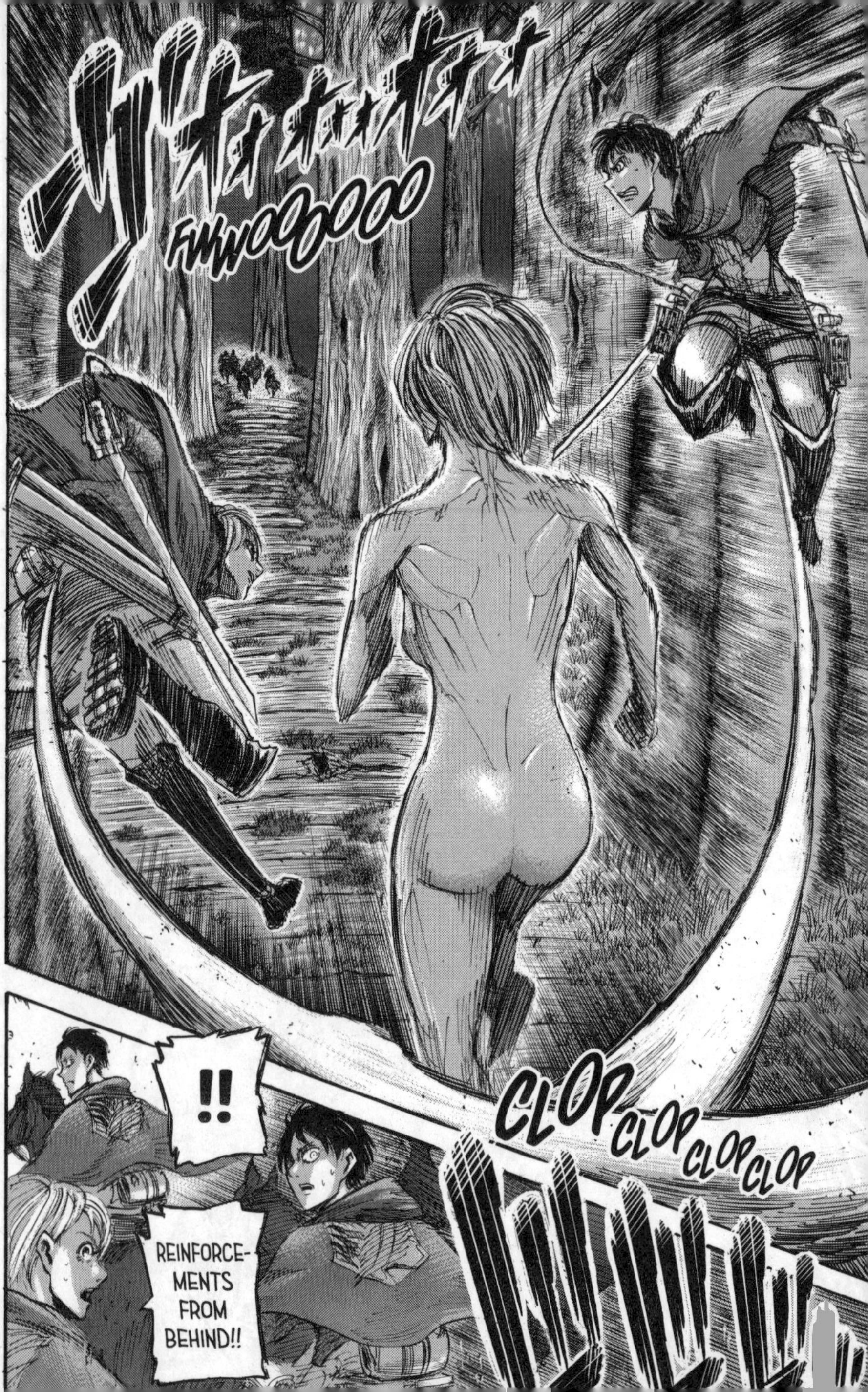
FWWOOOOOOO
CLOP CLOP CLOP CLOP
!!
REINFORCE-MENTS FROM BEHIND!!

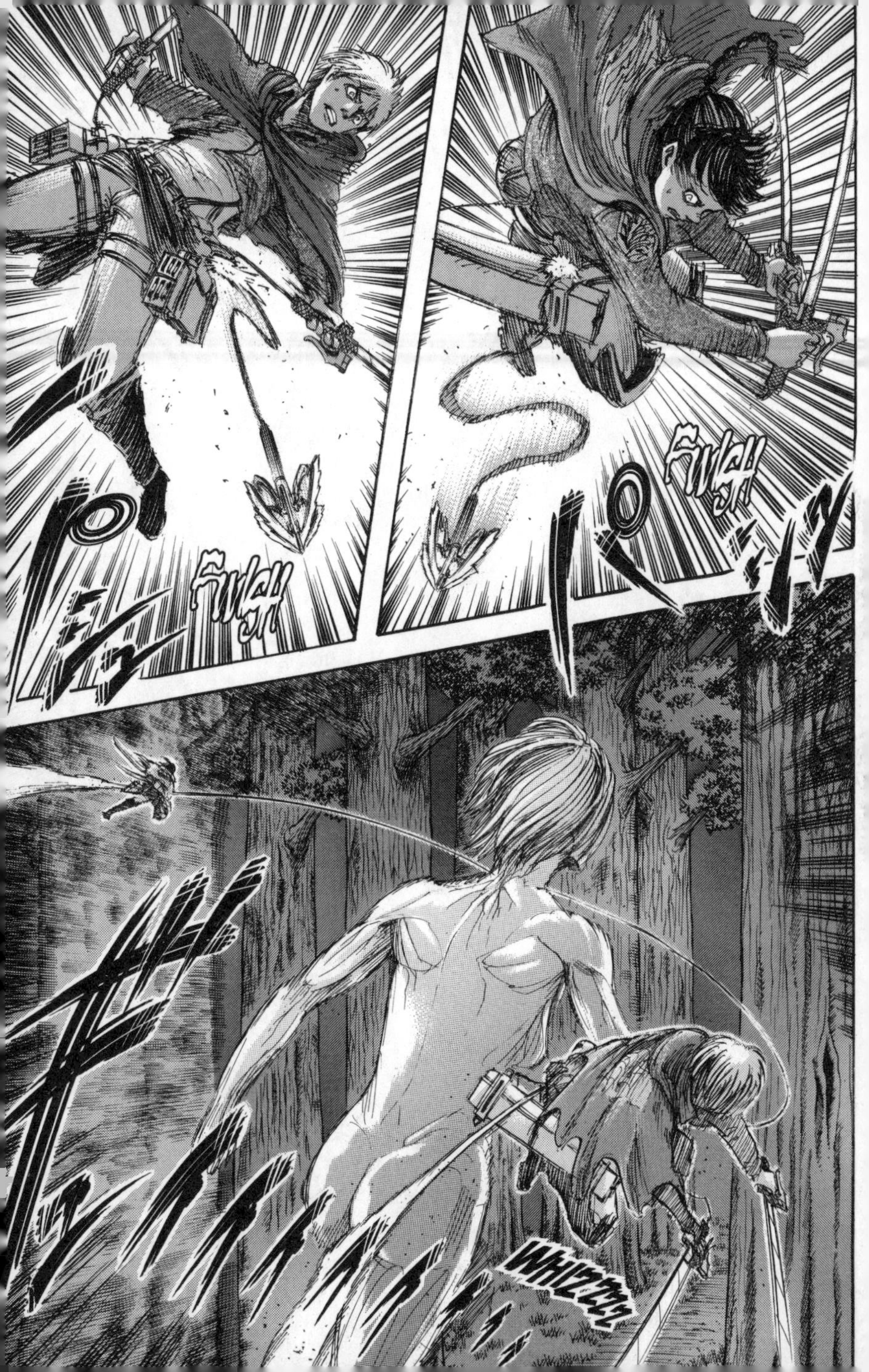
FWISH
FWISH
WHIZZZZ

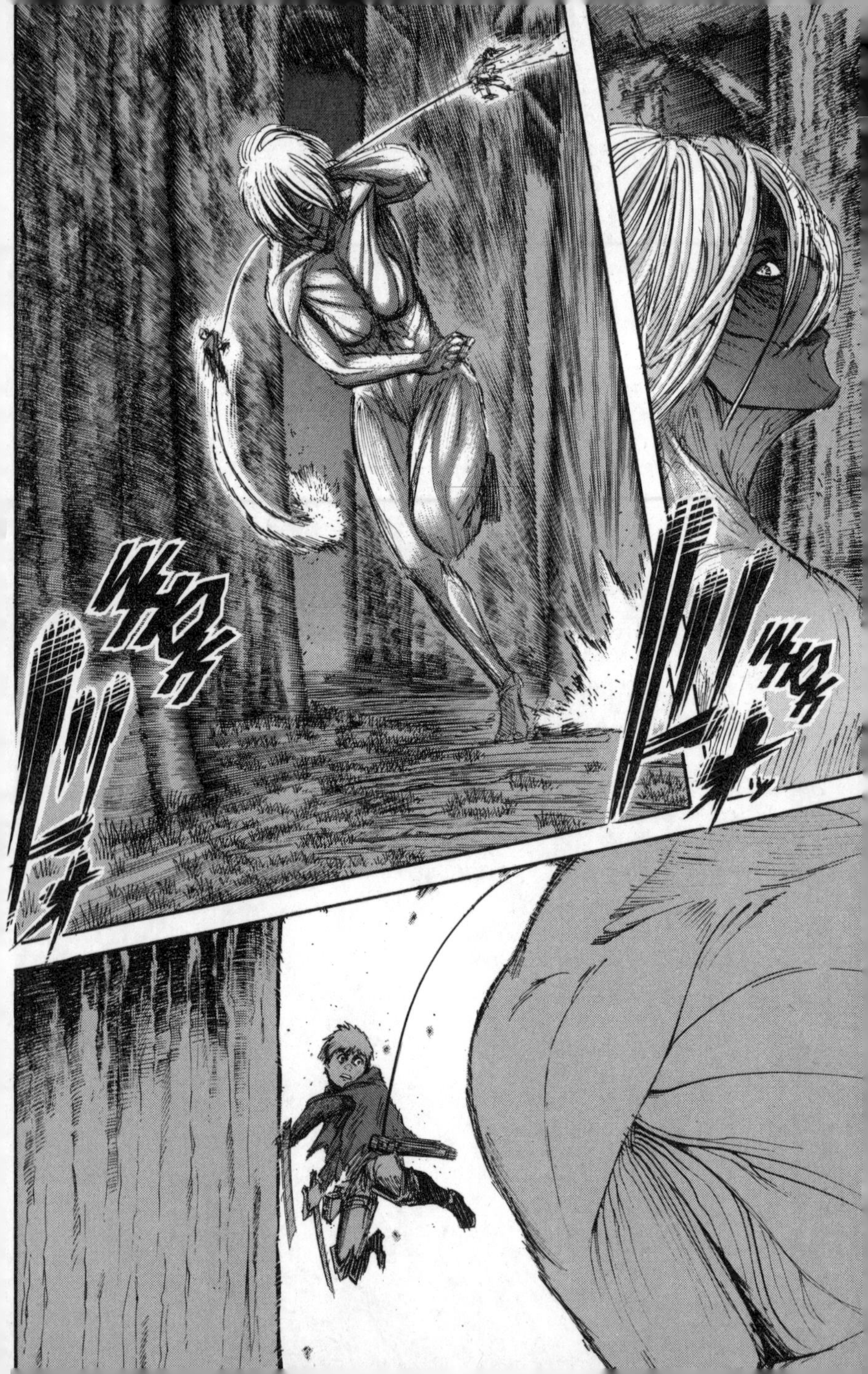

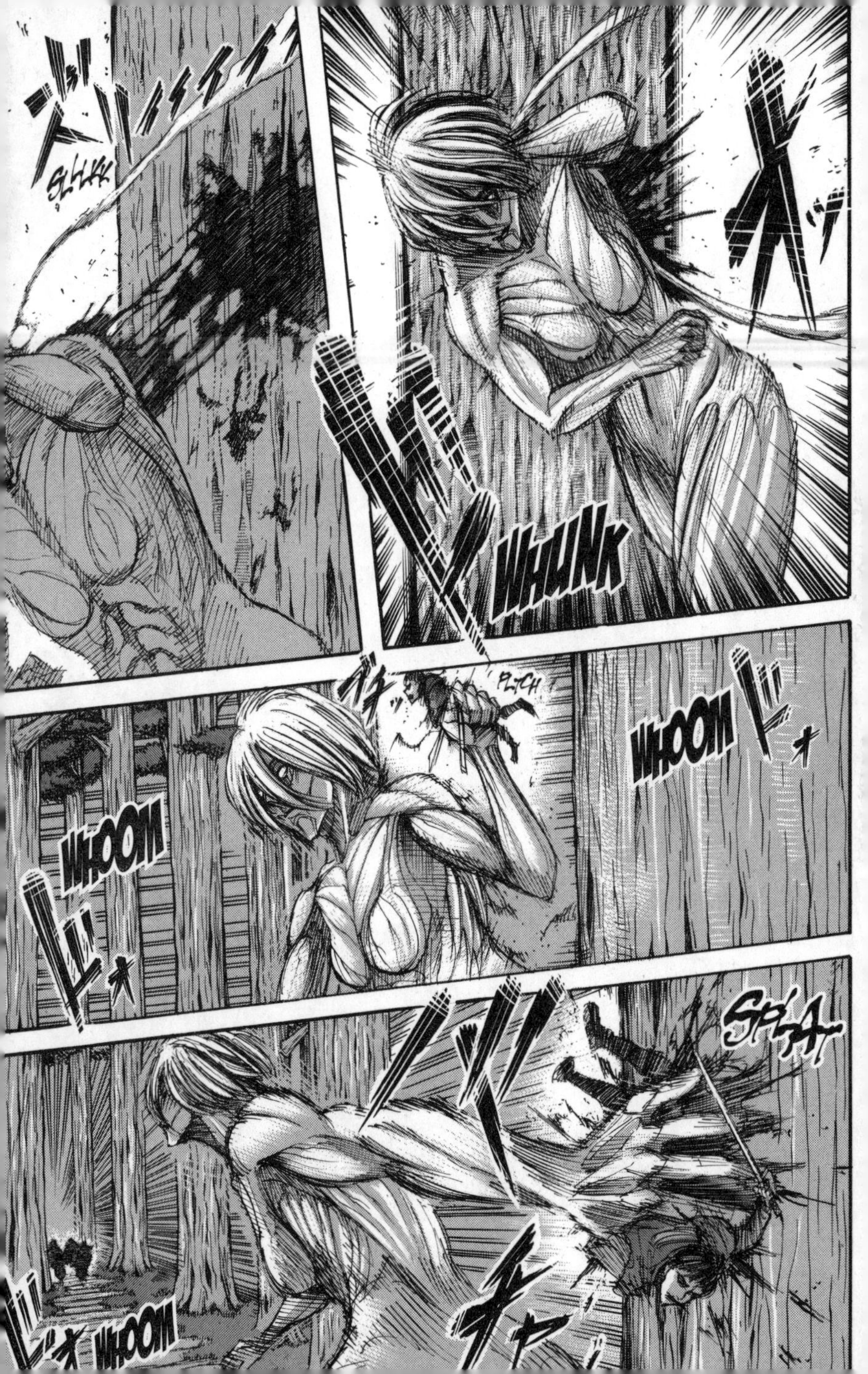
WHUNK
SLLLK
PLTCH
WHOOM
WHOOM
WHOOM

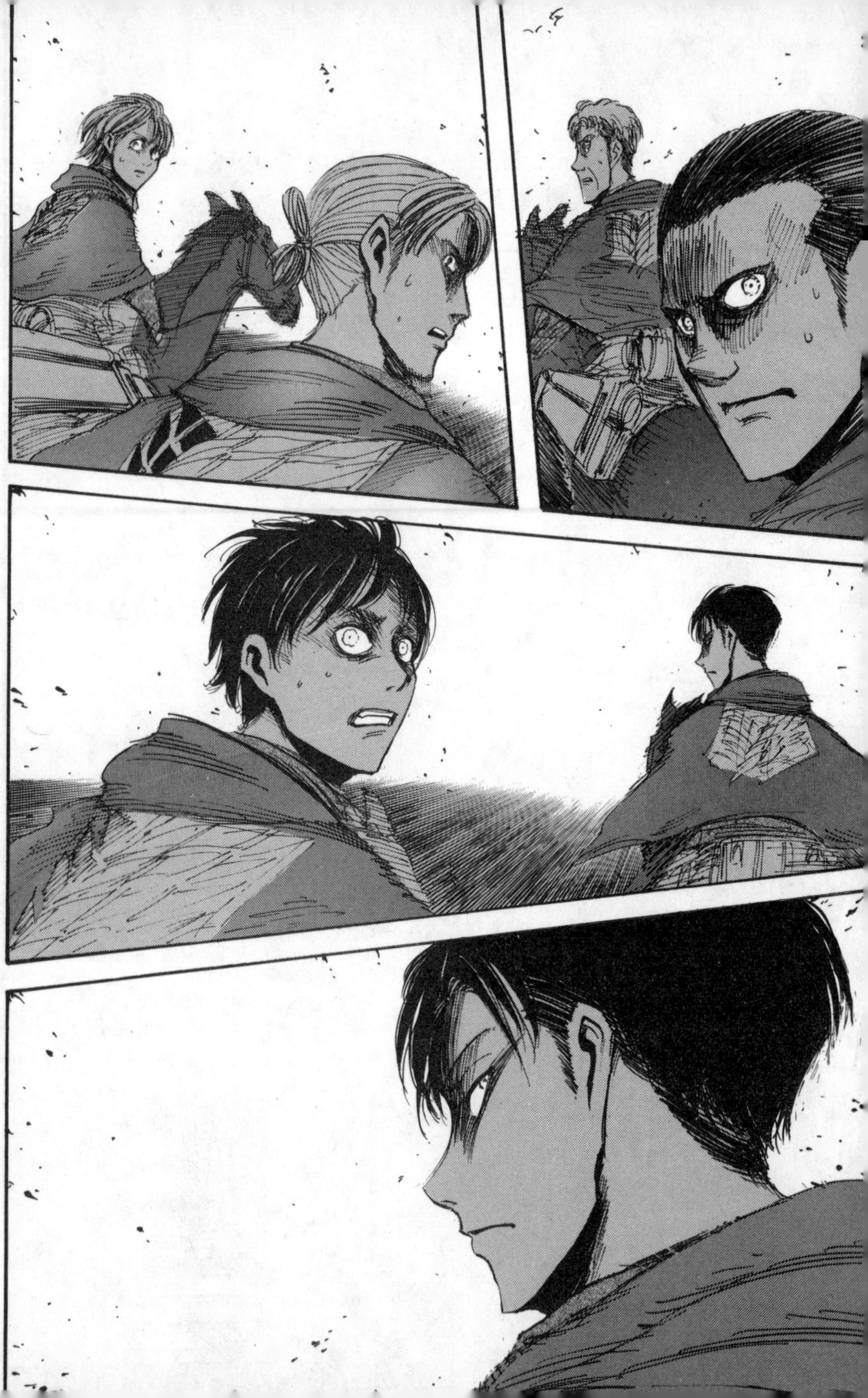

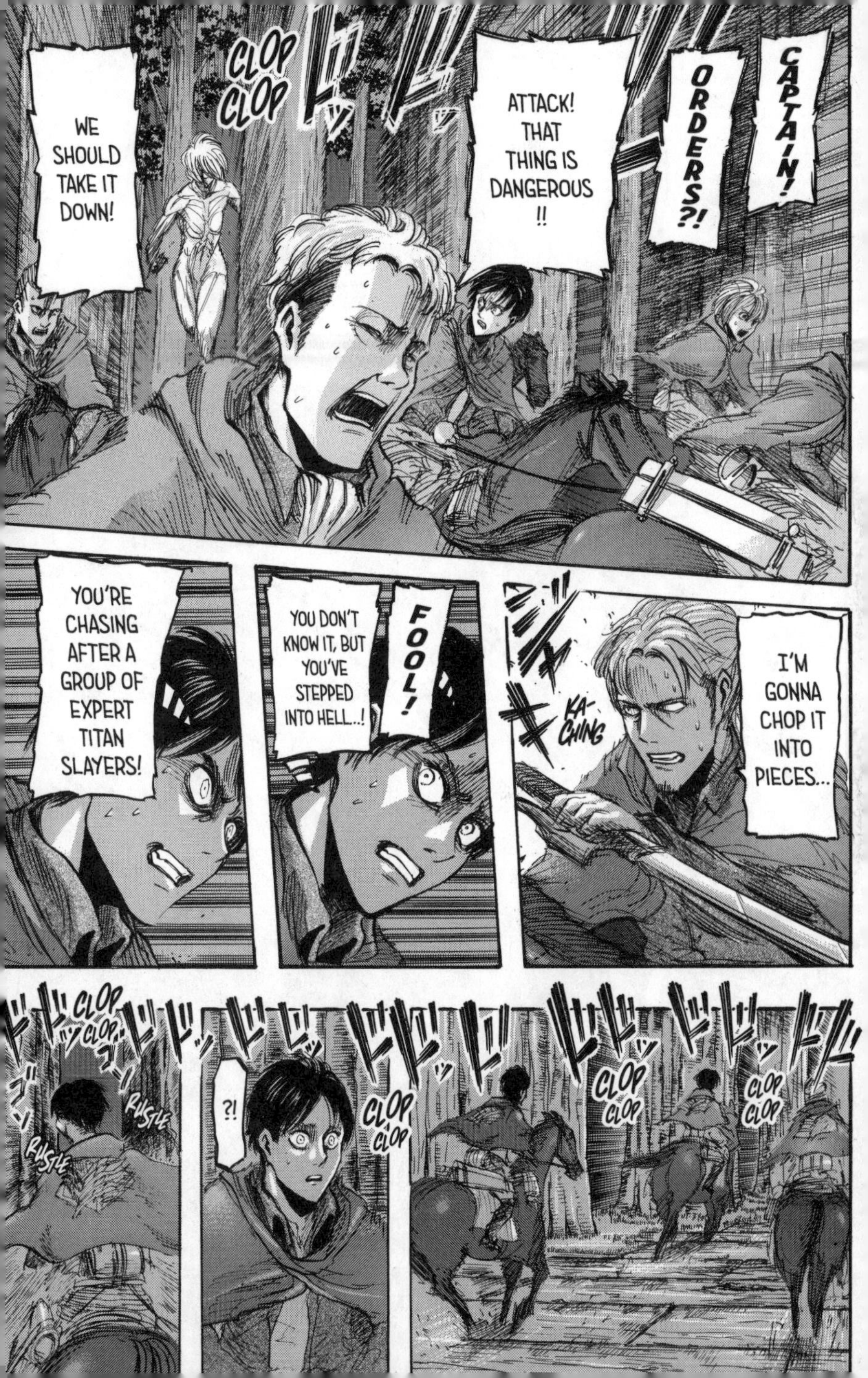
CAPTAIN!
ORDERS?!
ATTACK! THAT THING IS DANGEROUS!!
CLOP CLOP
WE SHOULD TAKE IT DOWN!
I'M GONNA CHOP IT INTO PIECES...
KA-CHING
FOOL!
YOU DON'T KNOW IT, BUT YOU'VE STEPPED INTO HELL..!
YOU'RE CHASING AFTER A GROUP OF EXPERT TITAN SLAYERS!
CLOP CLOP
CLOP CLOP
CLOP CLOP
?!
CLOP CLOP
RUSTLE
RUSTLE

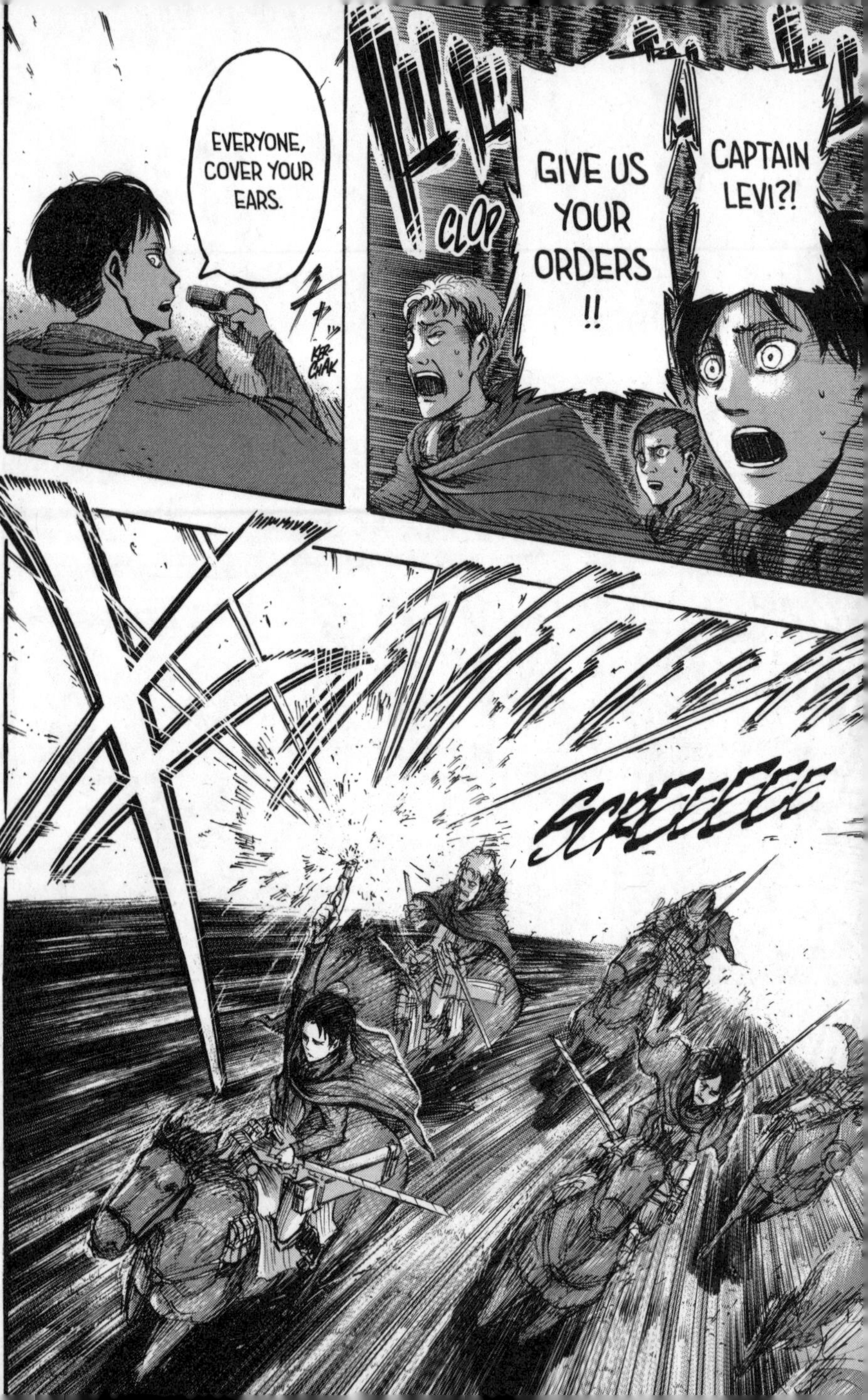
CAPTAIN LEVI?!
GIVE US YOUR ORDERS!!
CLOP
EVERYONE, COVER YOUR EARS.
KER-CHAK
SCREEEEEE

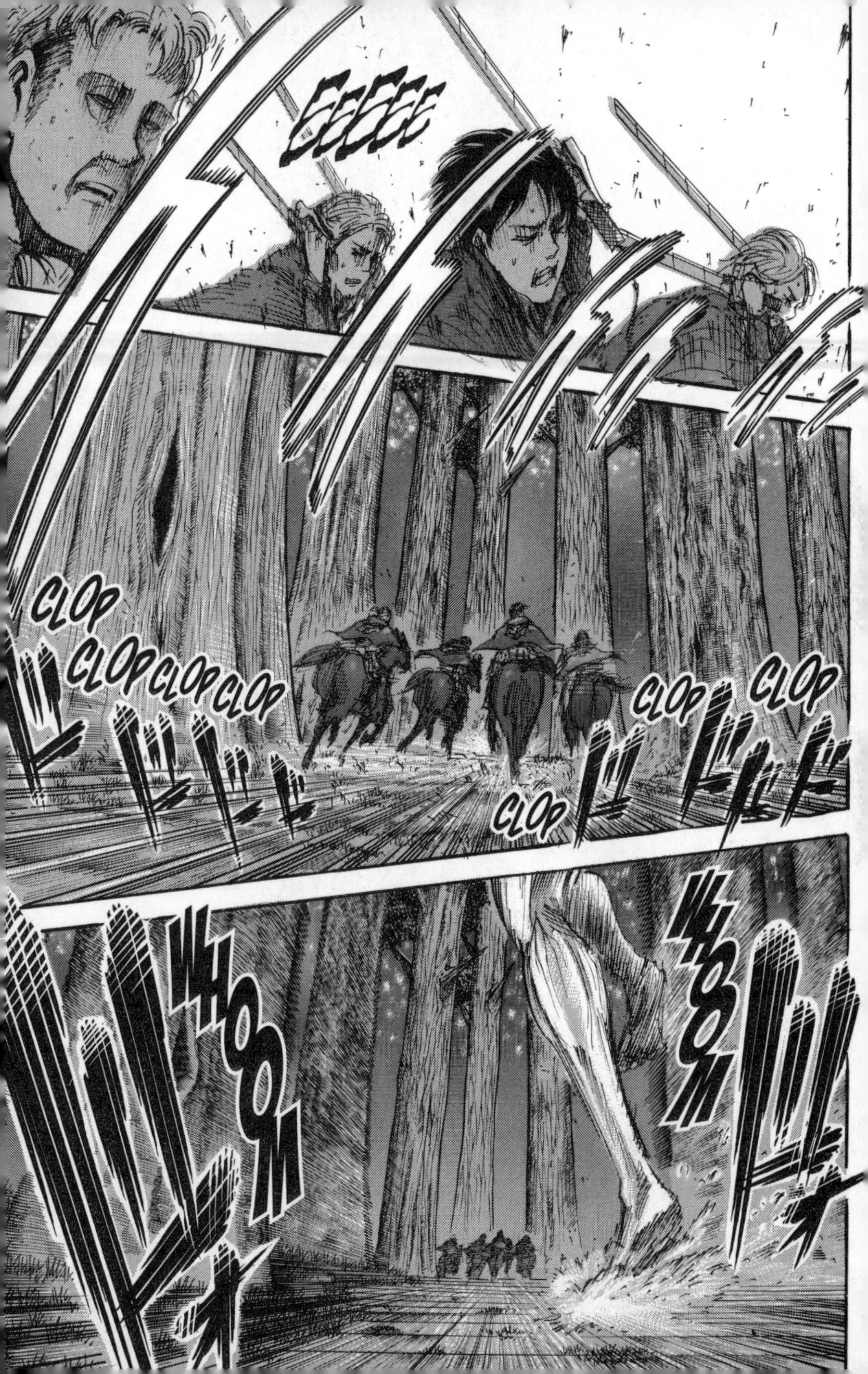
EEEEE
CLOP
CLOP
CLOP
CLOP
CLOP
CLOP
CLOP
CLOP
WHOOM
WHOOM

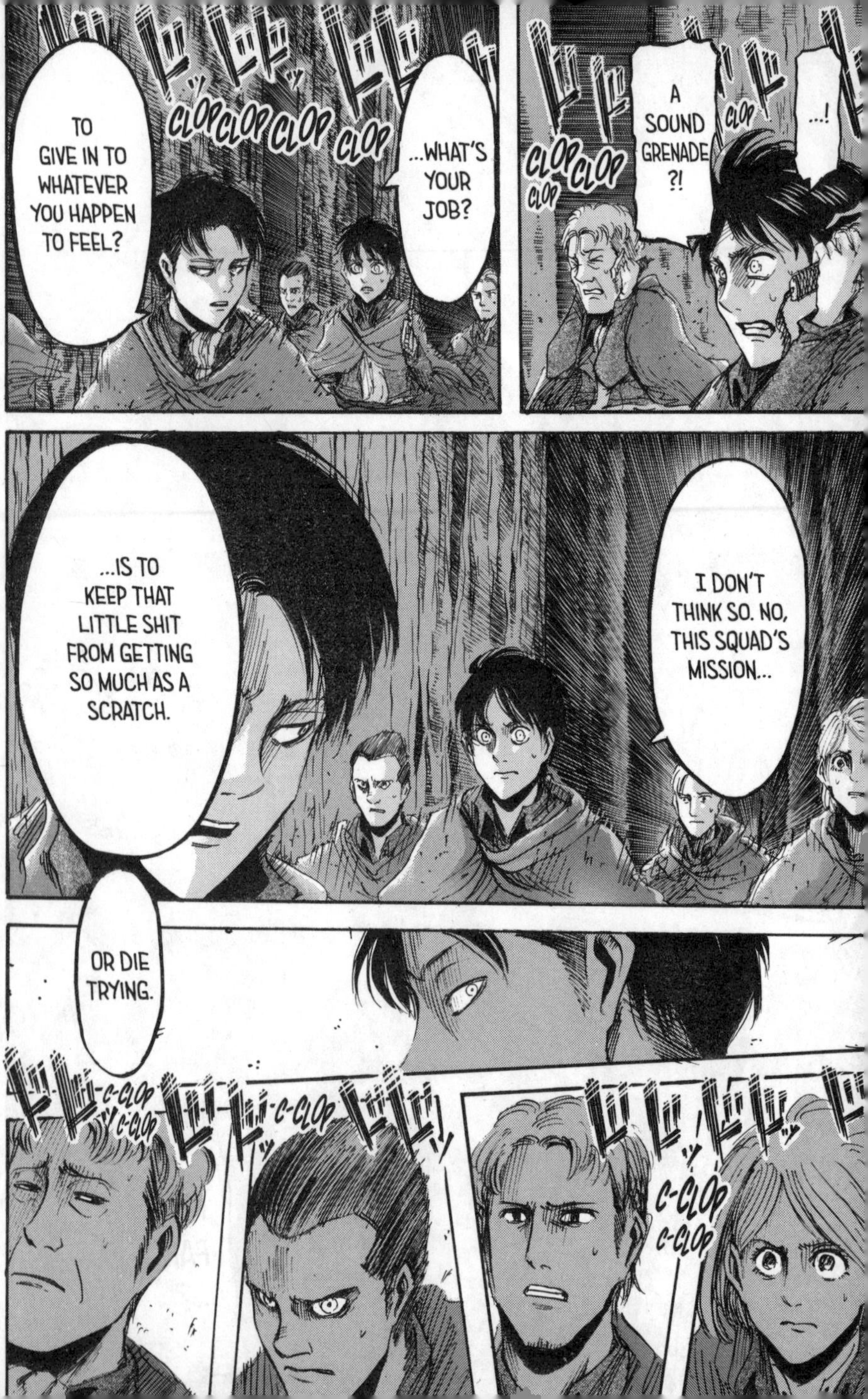
...!
CLOP
A SOUND GRENADE ?!
CLOP CLOP CLOP
...WHAT'S YOUR JOB?
TO GIVE IN TO WHATEVER YOU HAPPEN TO FEEL?
CLOP CLOP CLOP CLOP
I DON'T THINK SO. NO, THIS SQUAD'S MISSION...
...IS TO KEEP THAT LITTLE SHIT FROM GETTING SO MUCH AS A SCRATCH.
OR DIE TRYING.
C-CLOP C-CLOP
C-CLOP
C-CLOP C-CLOP

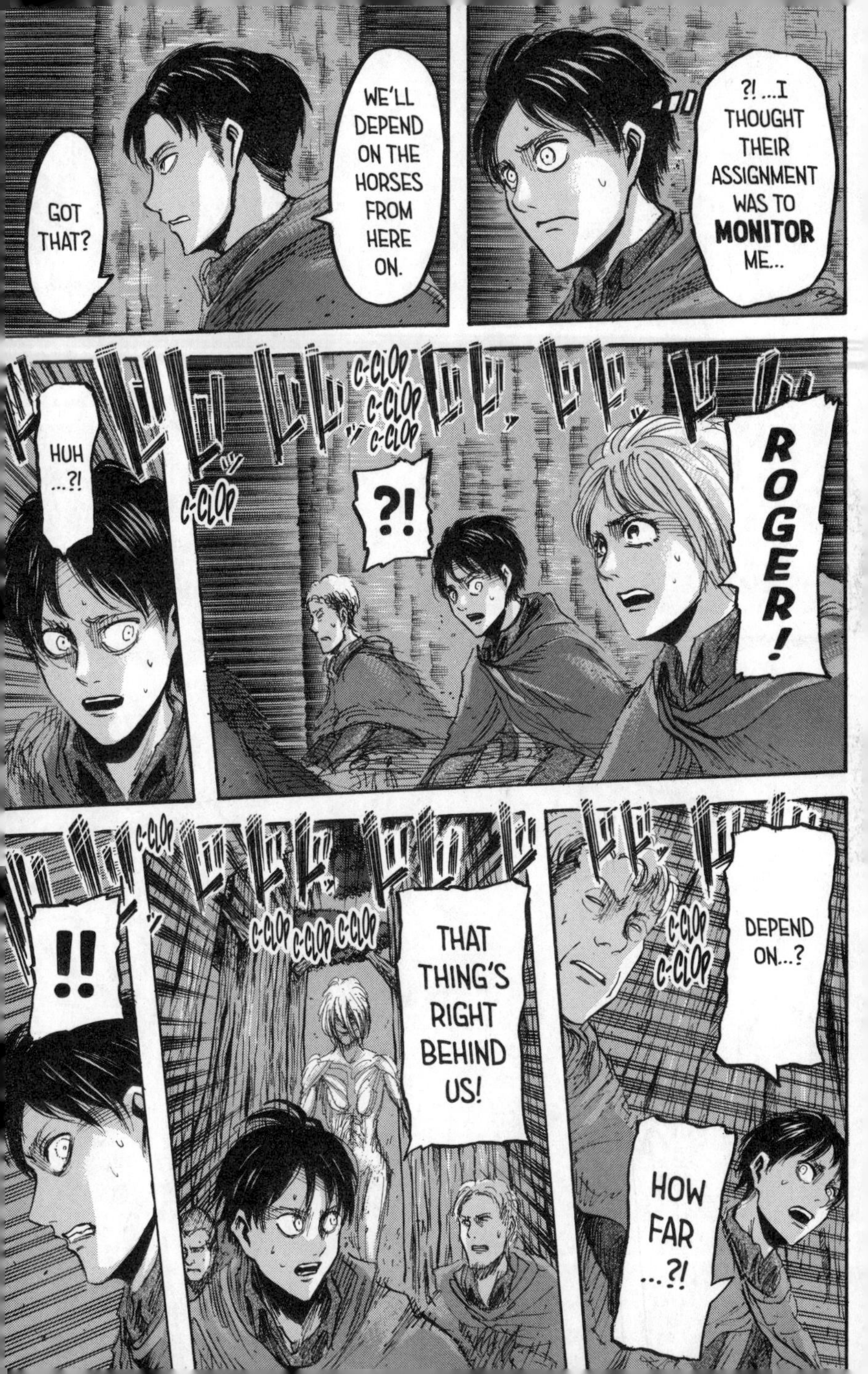
?! ...I THOUGHT THEIR ASSIGNMENT WAS TO **MONITOR** ME...
WE'LL DEPEND ON THE HORSES FROM HERE ON.
GOT THAT?
ROGER!
C-CLOP C-CLOP C-CLOP
?!
C-CLOP
HUH ...?!
C-CLOP C-CLOP
DEPEND ON...?
HOW FAR ...?!
THAT THING'S RIGHT BEHIND US!
C-CLOP C-CLOP C-CLOP
C-CLOP
!!

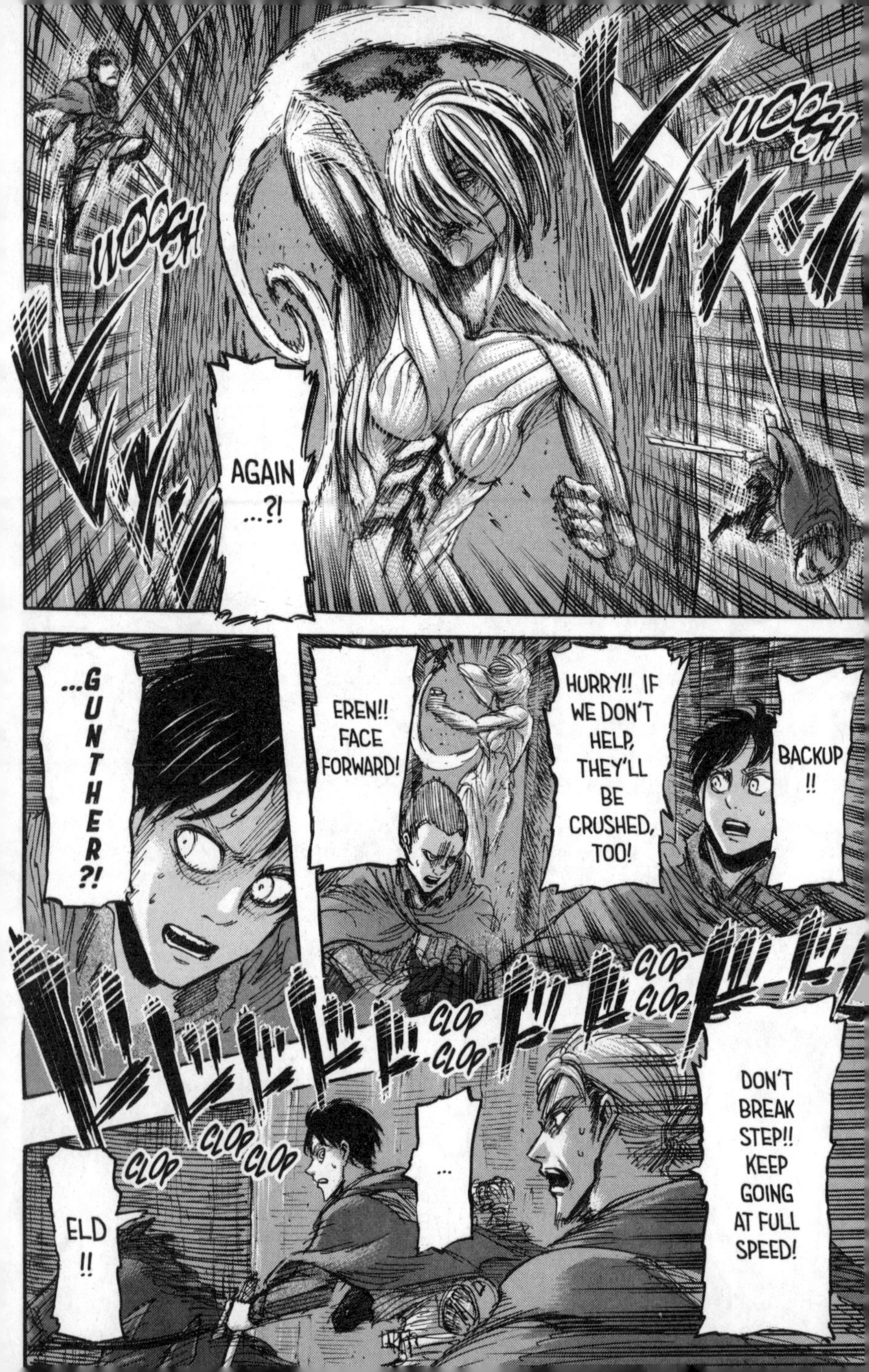

WOOSH
WOOSH
AGAIN ...?!
BACKUP !!
HURRY!! IF WE DON'T HELP, THEY'LL BE CRUSHED, TOO!
EREN!! FACE FORWARD!
...GUNTHER?!
CLOP CLOP
CLOP CLOP
CLOP CLOP
CLOP
DON'T BREAK STEP!! KEEP GOING AT FULL SPEED!
...
ELD !!

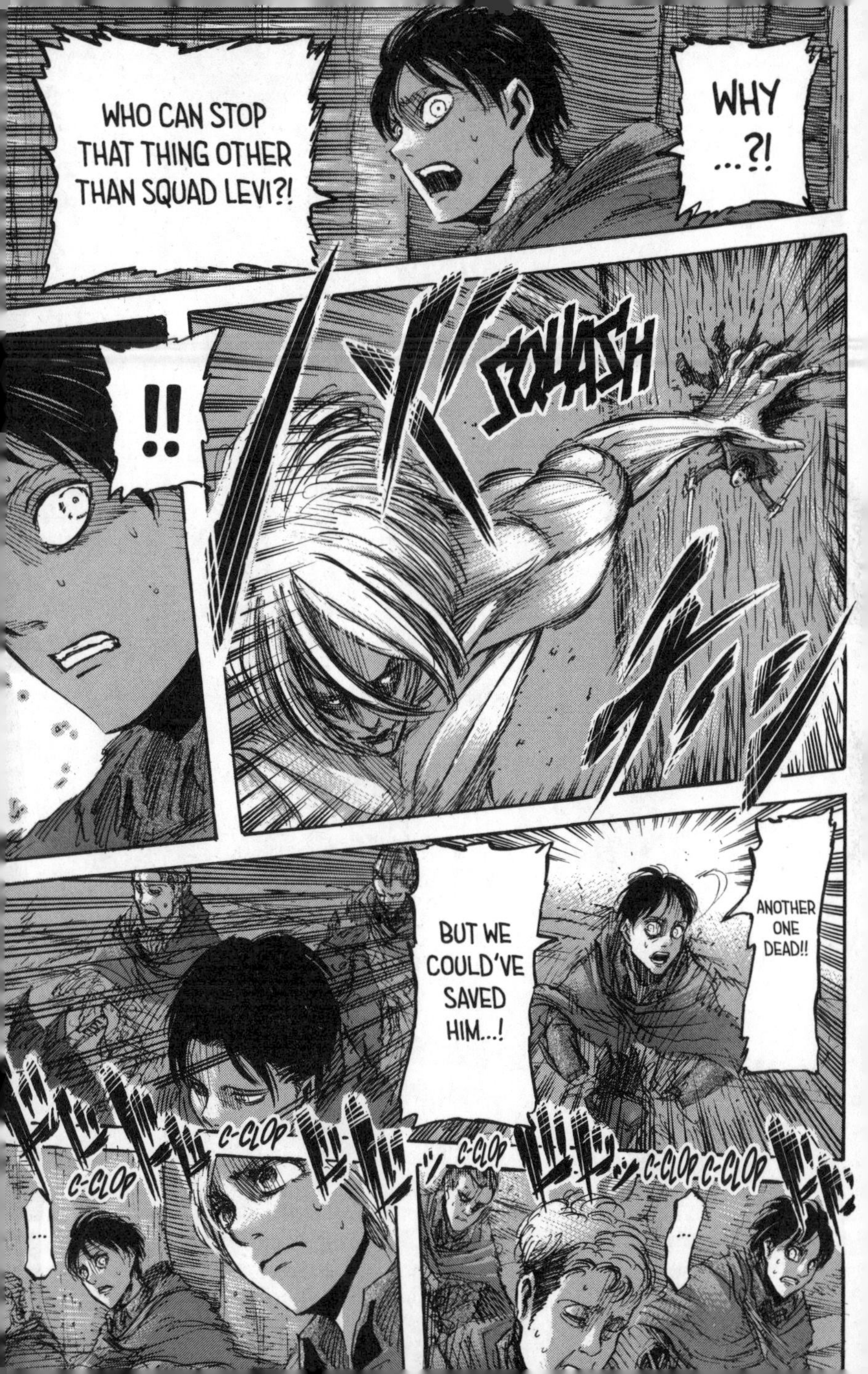
WHY ...?!
WHO CAN STOP THAT THING OTHER THAN SQUAD LEVI?!
SQUASH
!!
ANOTHER ONE DEAD!!
BUT WE COULD'VE SAVED HIM...!
C-CLOP C-CLOP
C-CLOP
...
C-CLOP
C-CLOP
...

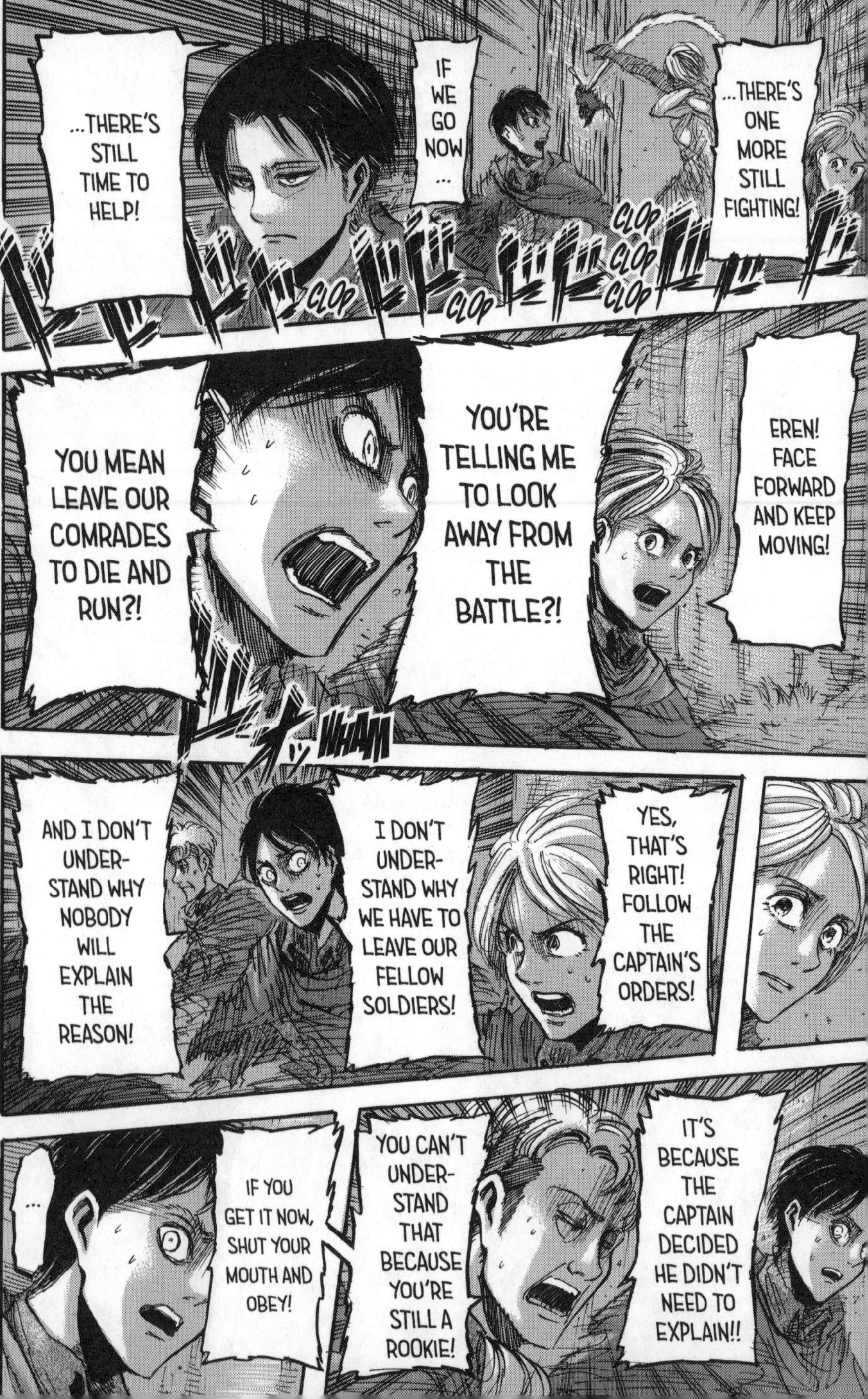
...THERE'S ONE MORE STILL FIGHTING!
IF WE GO NOW ...
...THERE'S STILL TIME TO HELP!
CLOP CLOP CLOP
CLOP
CLOP
CLOP
EREN! FACE FORWARD AND KEEP MOVING!
YOU'RE TELLING ME TO LOOK AWAY FROM THE BATTLE?!
YOU MEAN LEAVE OUR COMRADES TO DIE AND RUN?!
WHAM
YES, THAT'S RIGHT! FOLLOW THE CAPTAIN'S ORDERS!
I DON'T UNDER-STAND WHY WE HAVE TO LEAVE OUR FELLOW SOLDIERS!
AND I DON'T UNDER-STAND WHY NOBODY WILL EXPLAIN THE REASON!
IT'S BECAUSE THE CAPTAIN DECIDED HE DIDN'T NEED TO EXPLAIN!!
YOU CAN'T UNDER-STAND THAT BECAUSE YOU'RE STILL A ROOKIE!
IF YOU GET IT NOW, SHUT YOUR MOUTH AND OBEY!
...

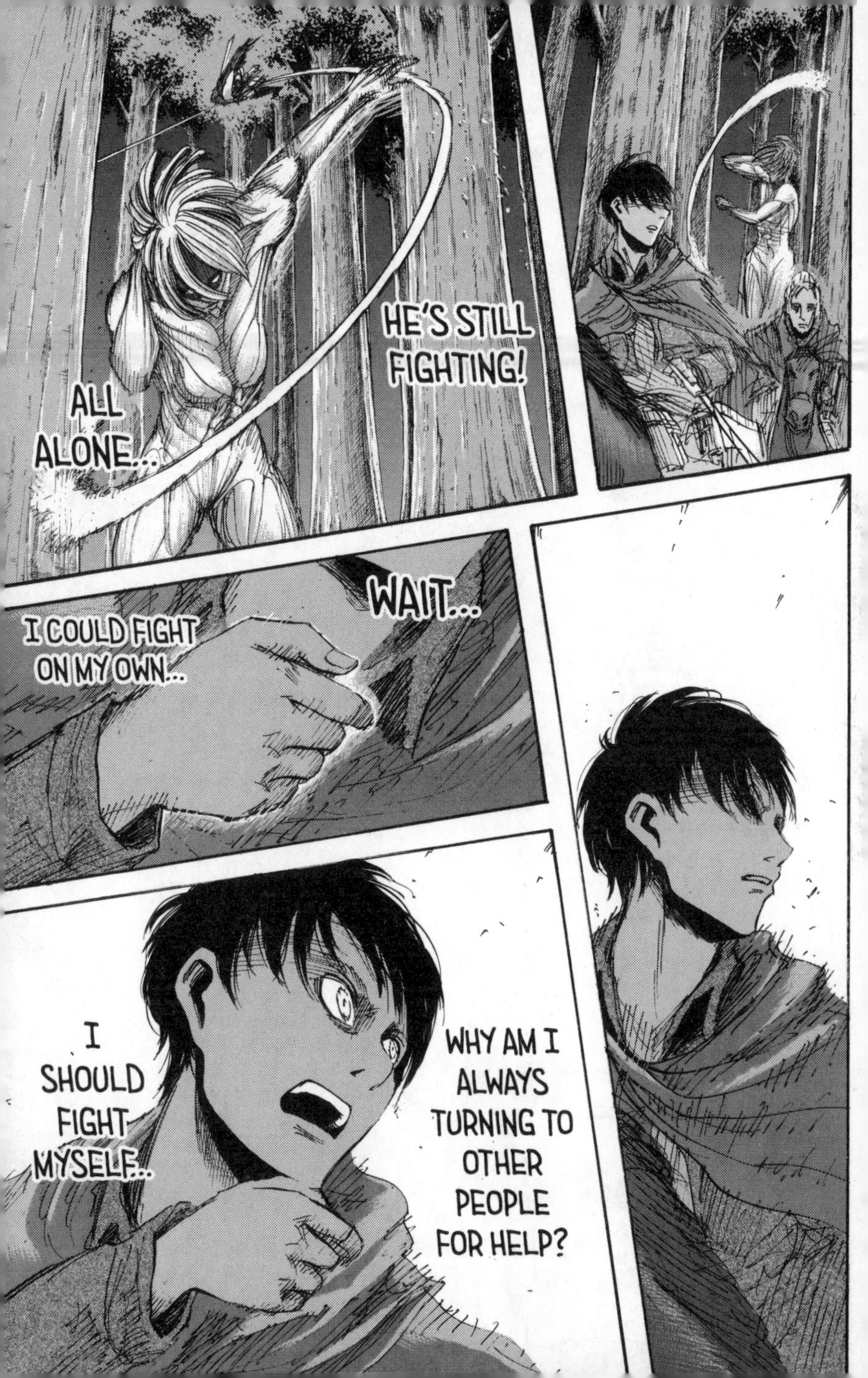
HE'S STILL FIGHTING!
ALL ALONE...
WAIT...
I COULD FIGHT ON MY OWN...
WHY AM I ALWAYS TURNING TO OTHER PEOPLE FOR HELP?
I SHOULD FIGHT MYSELF...

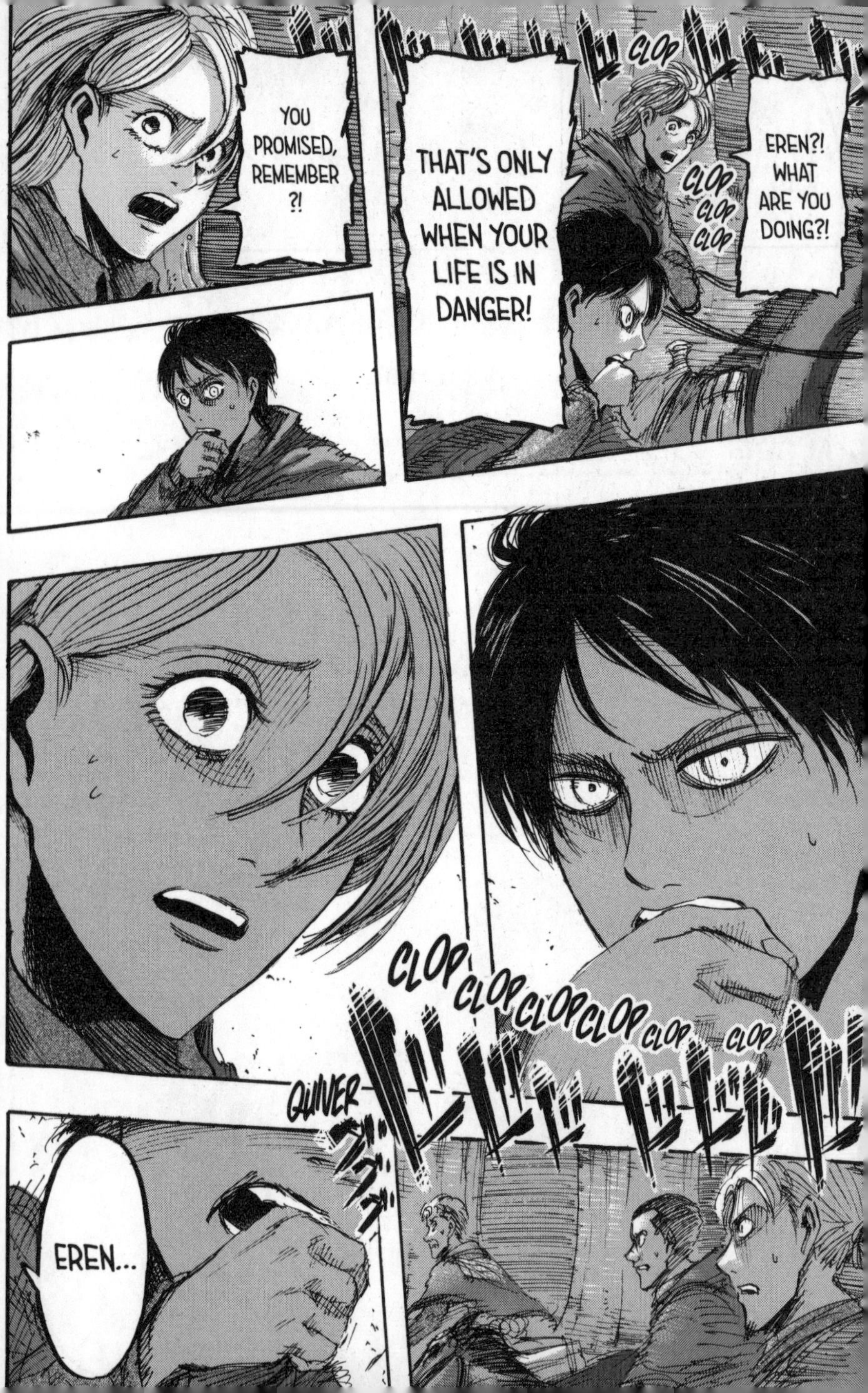
CLOP
EREN?! WHAT ARE YOU DOING?!
CLOP CLOP CLOP
THAT'S ONLY ALLOWED WHEN YOUR LIFE IS IN DANGER!
YOU PROMISED, REMEMBER ?!
CLOP CLOP CLOP CLOP CLOP CLOP
QUIVER
EREN...

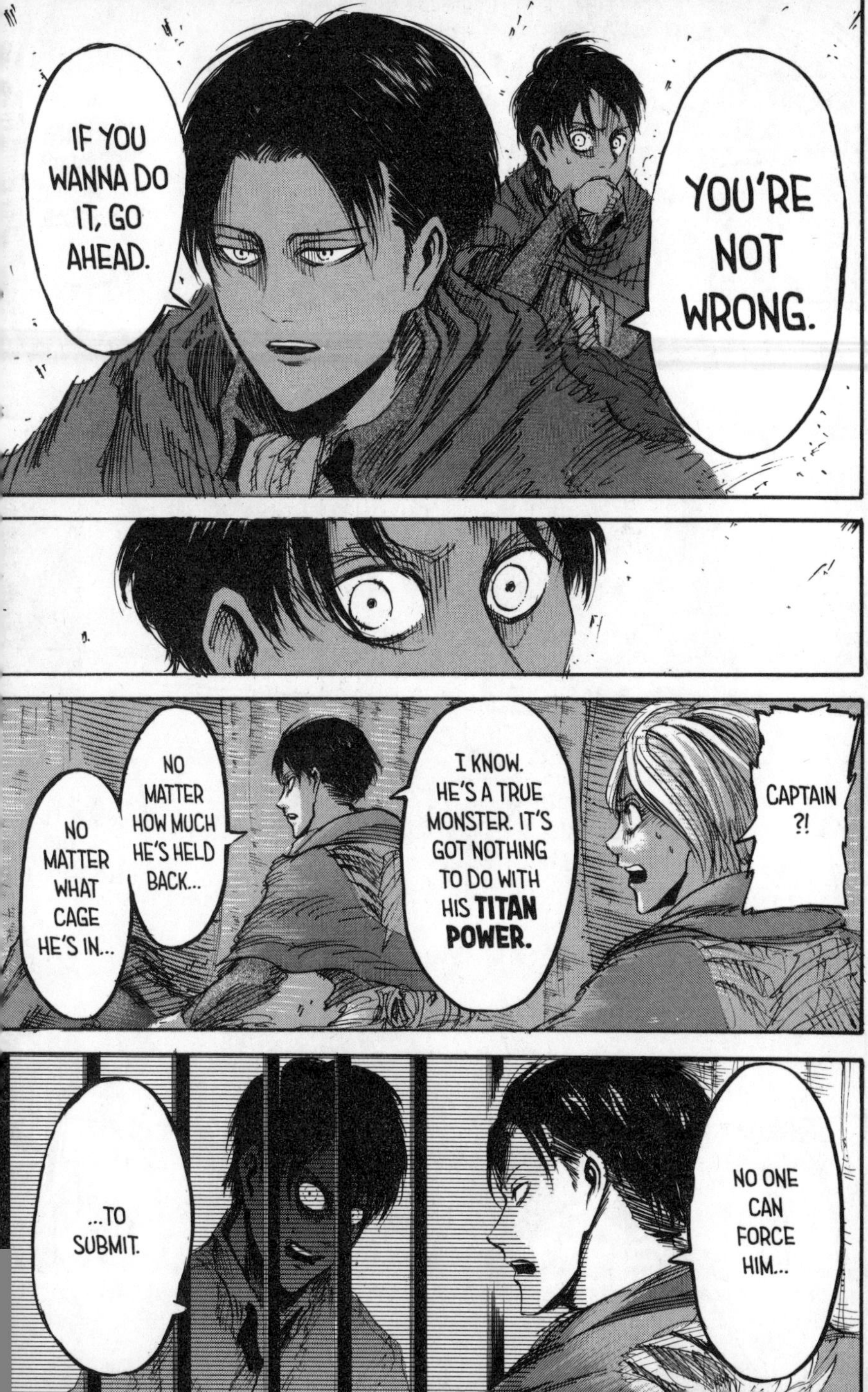
YOU'RE NOT WRONG.
IF YOU WANNA DO IT, GO AHEAD.
CAPTAIN?!
I KNOW. HE'S A TRUE MONSTER. IT'S GOT NOTHING TO DO WITH HIS **TITAN POWER.**
NO MATTER HOW MUCH HE'S HELD BACK...
NO MATTER WHAT CAGE HE'S IN...
NO ONE CAN FORCE HIM...
...TO SUBMIT.

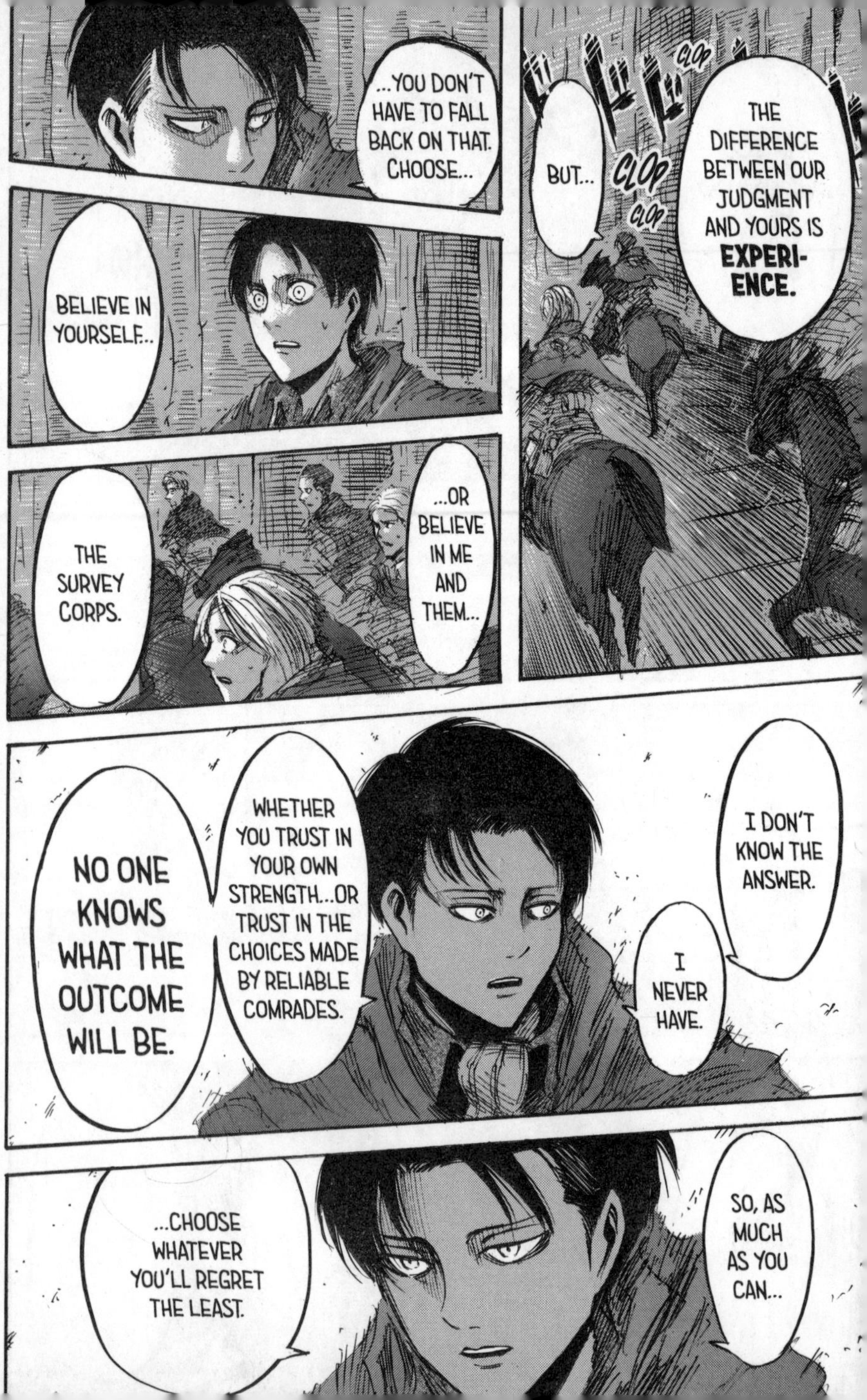
THE DIFFERENCE BETWEEN OUR JUDGMENT AND YOURS IS **EXPERIENCE.**
CLOP
CLOP
CLOP
BUT...
...YOU DON'T HAVE TO FALL BACK ON THAT. CHOOSE...
BELIEVE IN YOURSELF...
...OR BELIEVE IN ME AND THEM...
THE SURVEY CORPS.
I DON'T KNOW THE ANSWER.
I NEVER HAVE.
WHETHER YOU TRUST IN YOUR OWN STRENGTH...OR TRUST IN THE CHOICES MADE BY RELIABLE COMRADES.
NO ONE KNOWS WHAT THE OUTCOME WILL BE.
SO, AS MUCH AS YOU CAN...
...CHOOSE WHATEVER YOU'LL REGRET THE LEAST.

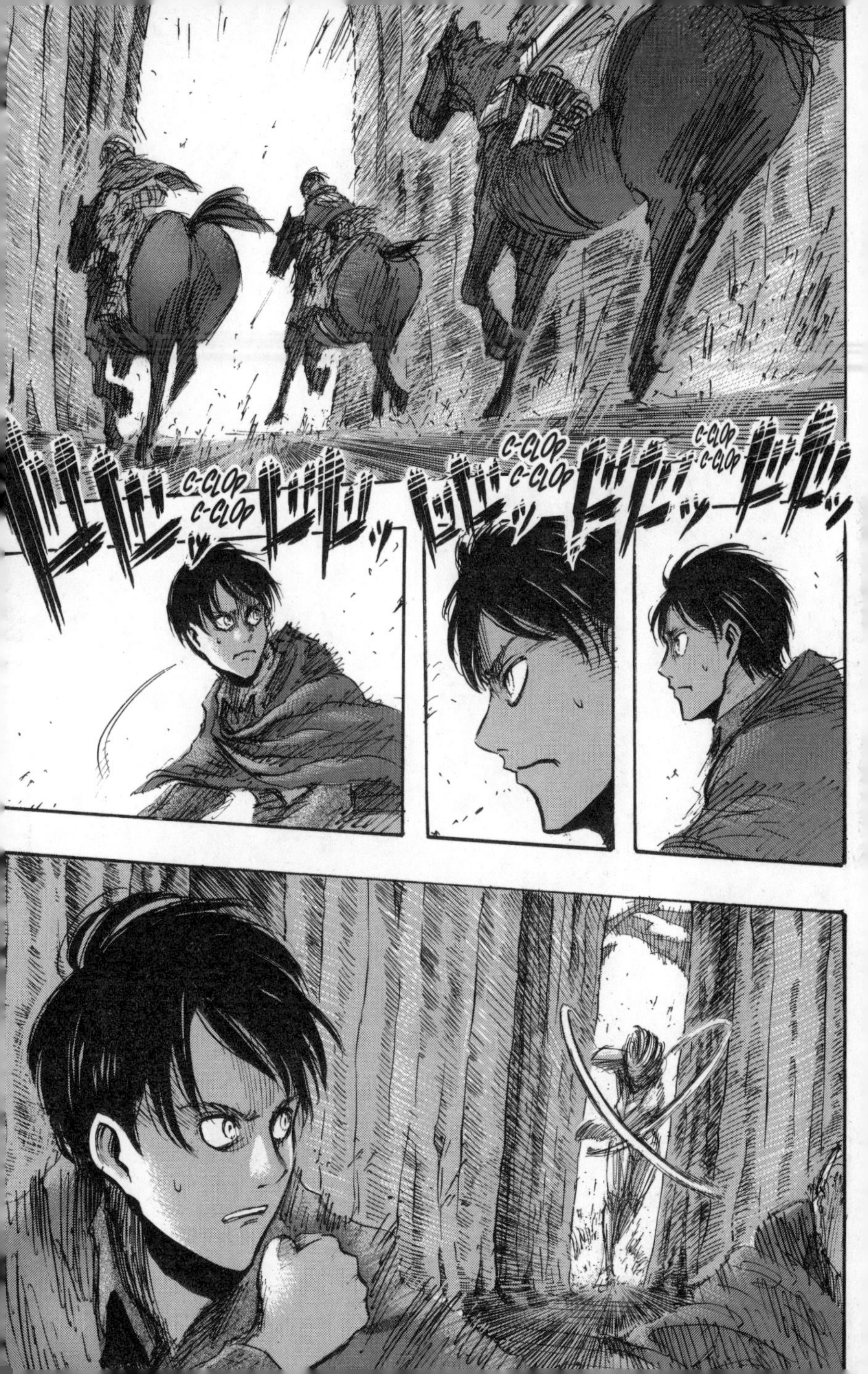
C-CLOP C-CLOP
C-CLOP C-CLOP
C-CLOP C-CLOP

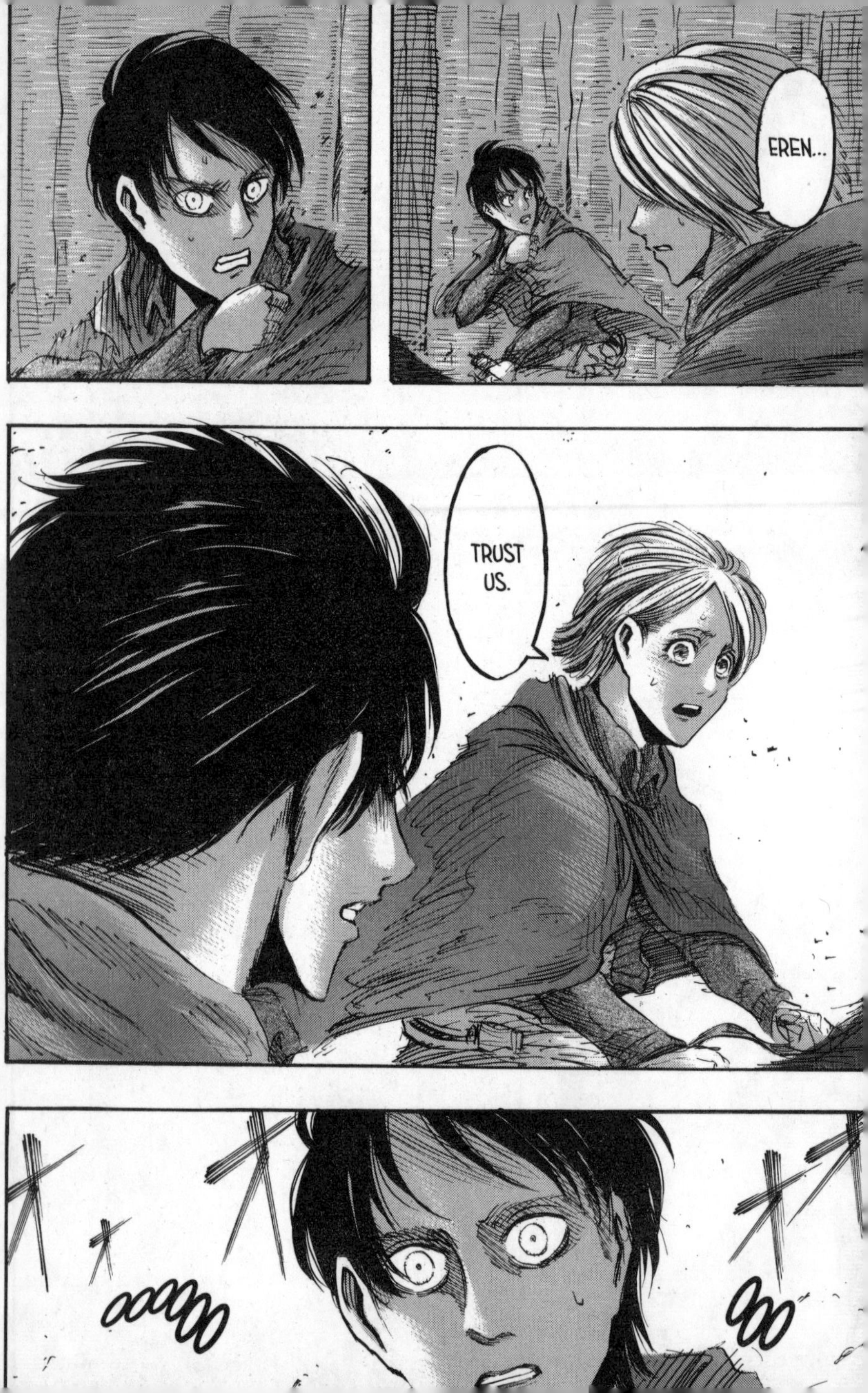
EREN...
TRUST US.
OO
OOOOOO

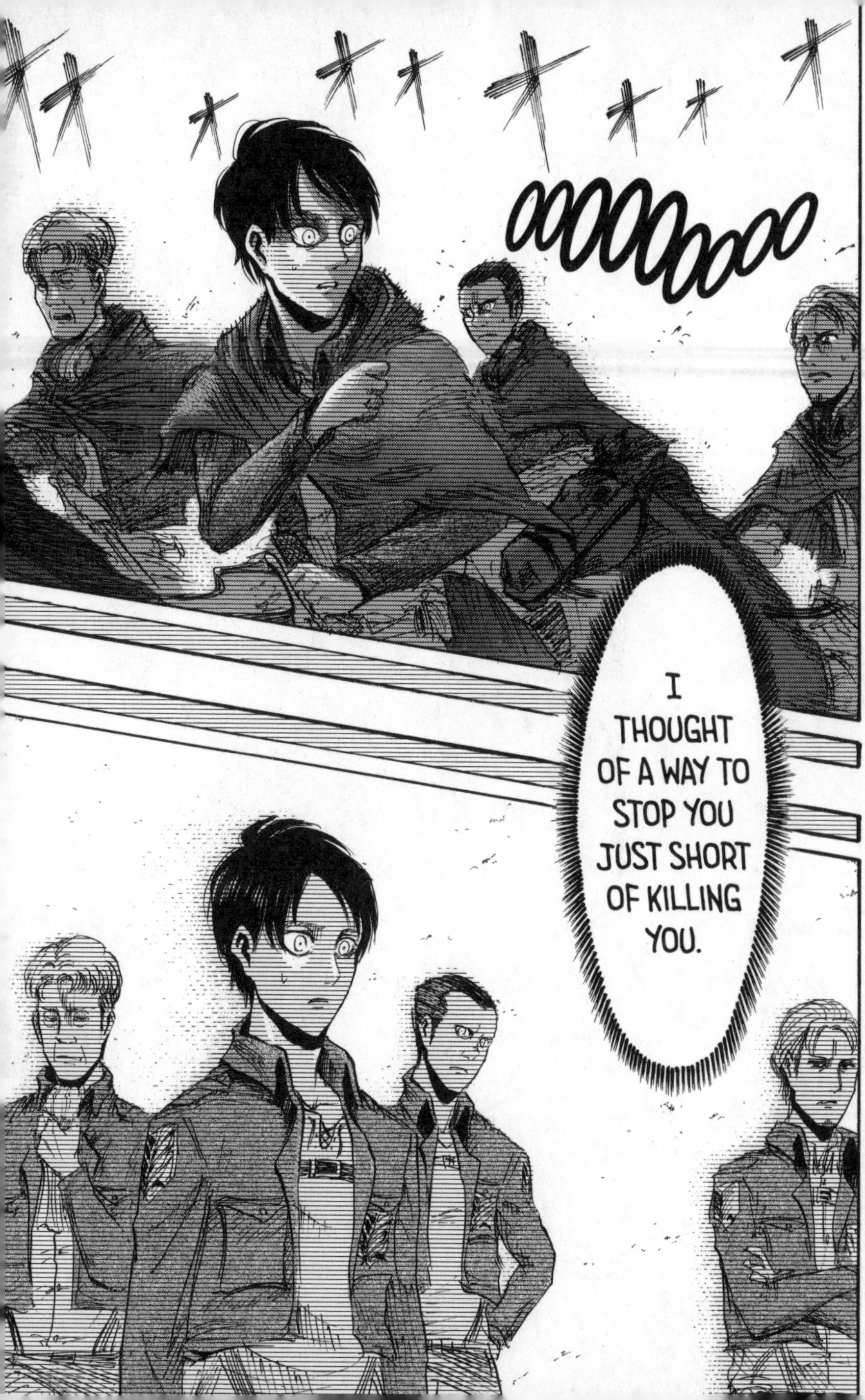
オオオオオオオオオ
OOOOOOOOOO
I THOUGHT OF A WAY TO STOP YOU JUST SHORT OF KILLING YOU.

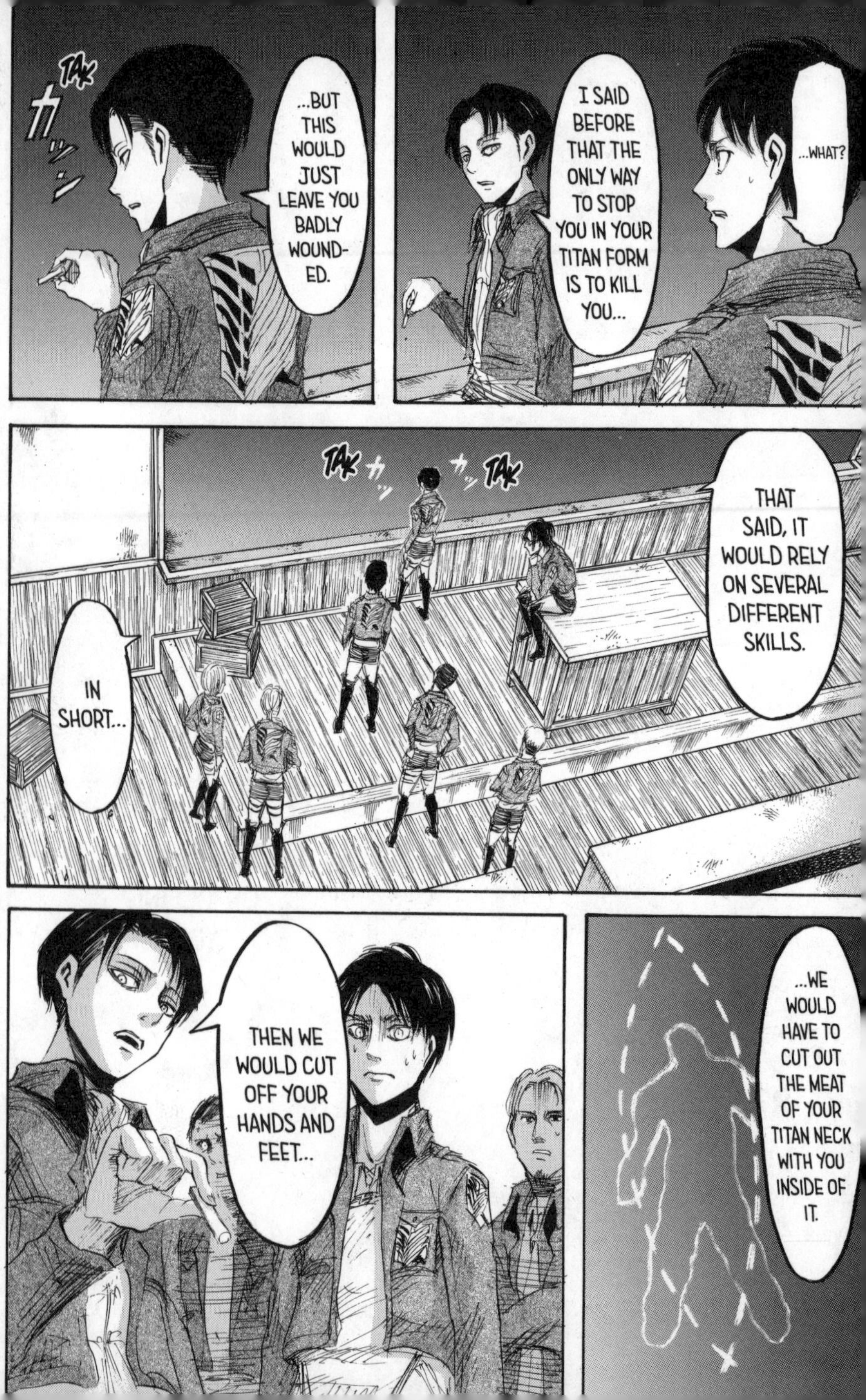
...WHAT?
I SAID BEFORE THAT THE ONLY WAY TO STOP YOU IN YOUR TITAN FORM IS TO KILL YOU...
TAK
...BUT THIS WOULD JUST LEAVE YOU BADLY WOUND-ED.
THAT SAID, IT WOULD RELY ON SEVERAL DIFFERENT SKILLS.
TAK
TAK
IN SHORT...
...WE WOULD HAVE TO CUT OUT THE MEAT OF YOUR TITAN NECK WITH YOU INSIDE OF IT.
THEN WE WOULD CUT OFF YOUR HANDS AND FEET...

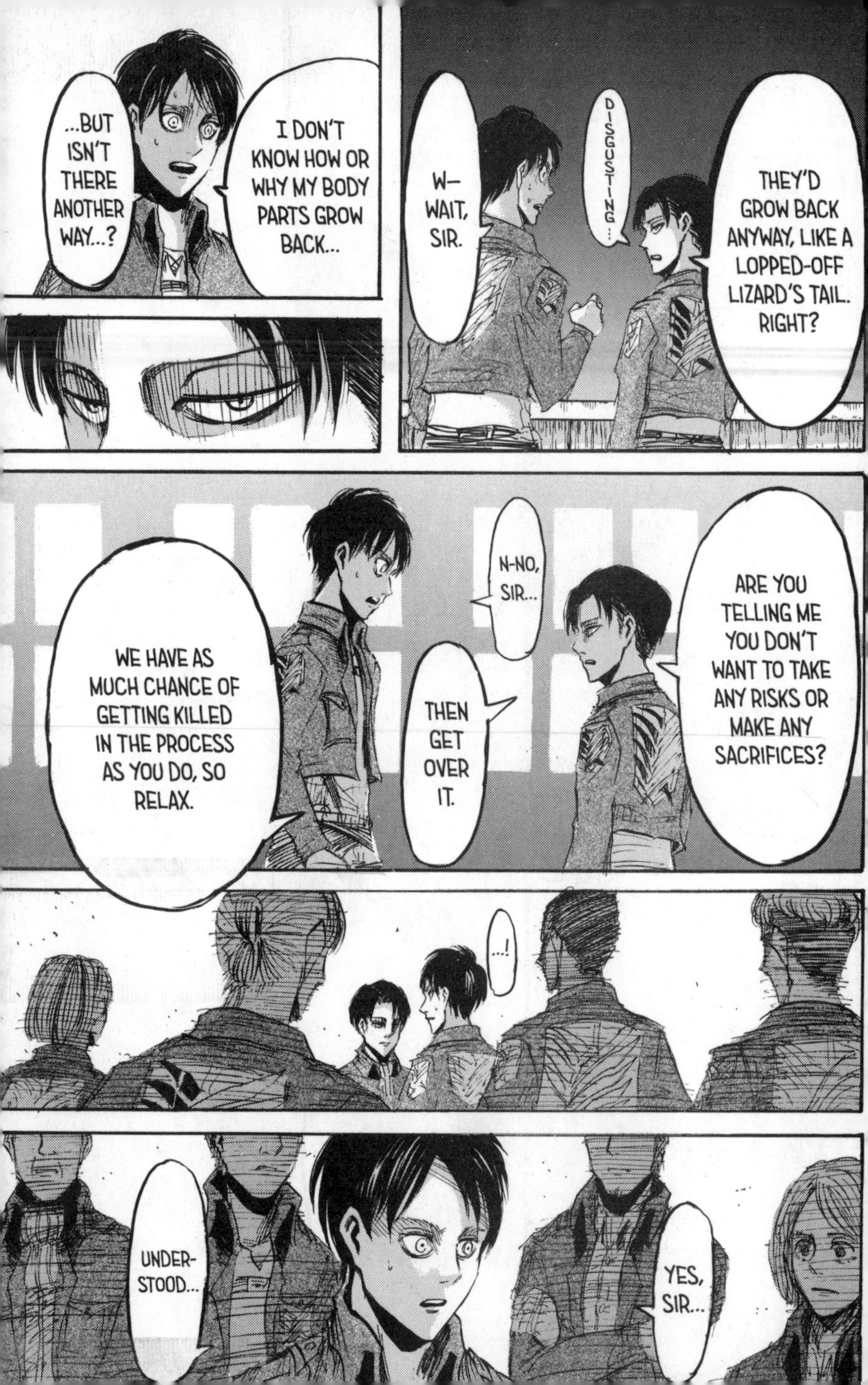
THEY'D GROW BACK ANYWAY, LIKE A LOPPED-OFF LIZARD'S TAIL. RIGHT?
DISGUSTING...
W— WAIT, SIR.
I DON'T KNOW HOW OR WHY MY BODY PARTS GROW BACK...
...BUT ISN'T THERE ANOTHER WAY...?
ARE YOU TELLING ME YOU DON'T WANT TO TAKE ANY RISKS OR MAKE ANY SACRIFICES?
N-NO, SIR...
THEN GET OVER IT.
WE HAVE AS MUCH CHANCE OF GETTING KILLED IN THE PROCESS AS YOU DO, SO RELAX.
...!
YES, SIR...
UNDER-STOOD...

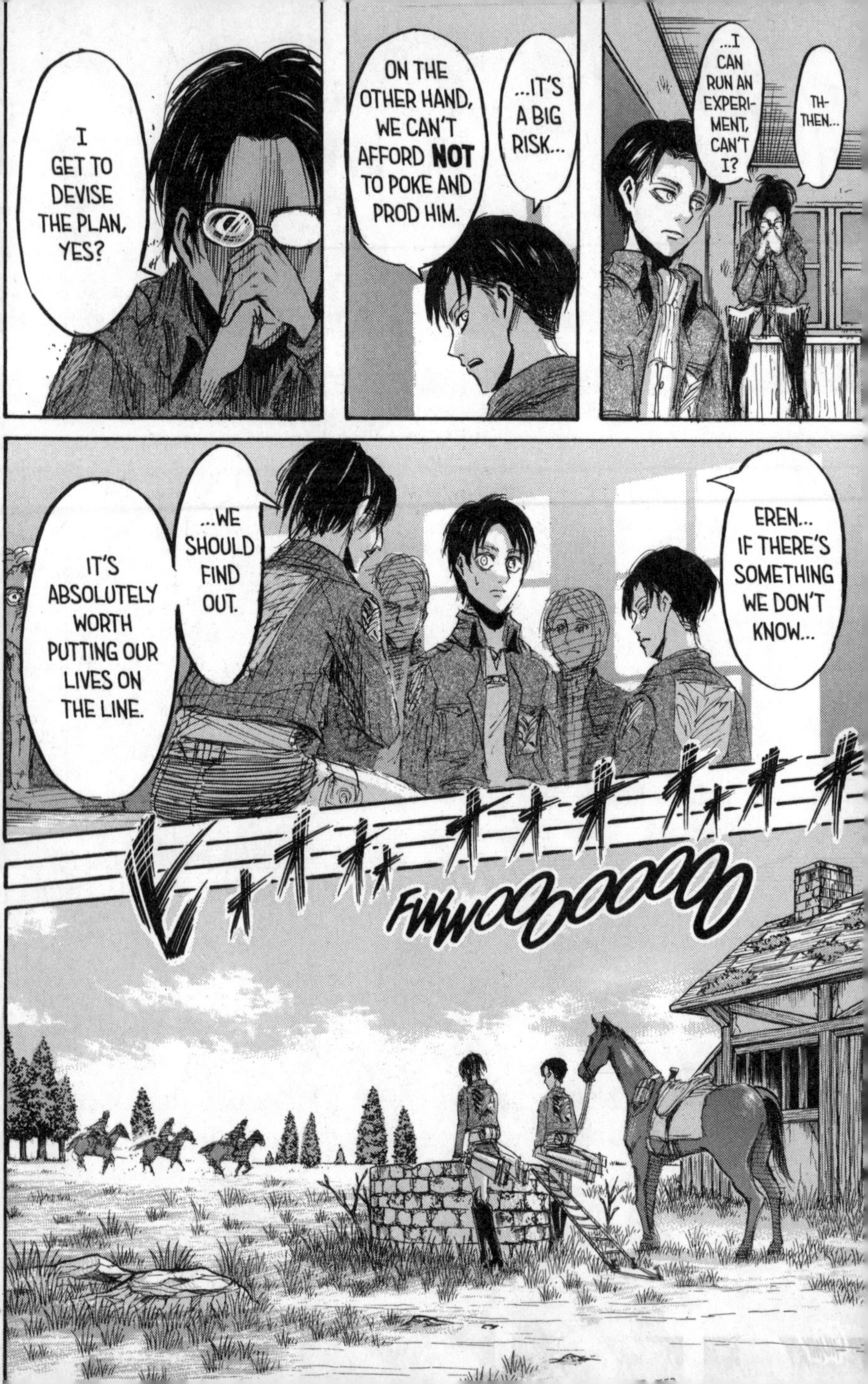
TH-THEN...
...I CAN RUN AN EXPERIMENT, CAN'T I?
...IT'S A BIG RISK...
ON THE OTHER HAND, WE CAN'T AFFORD **NOT** TO POKE AND PROD HIM.
I GET TO DEVISE THE PLAN, YES?
EREN... IF THERE'S SOMETHING WE DON'T KNOW...
...WE SHOULD FIND OUT.
IT'S ABSOLUTELY WORTH PUTTING OUR LIVES ON THE LINE.

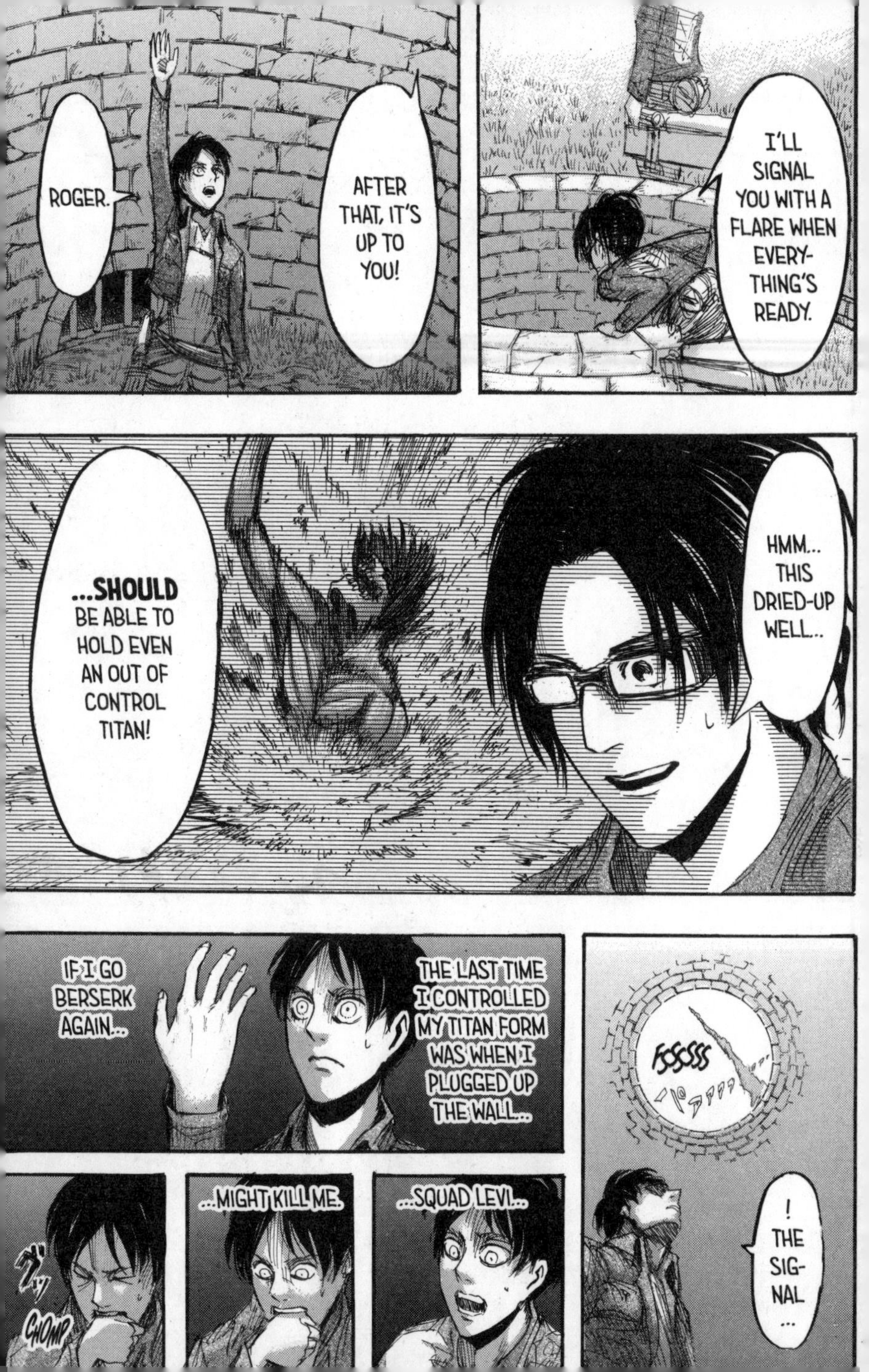
I'LL SIGNAL YOU WITH A FLARE WHEN EVERY-THING'S READY.
AFTER THAT, IT'S UP TO YOU!
ROGER.
HMM... THIS DRIED-UP WELL...
...SHOULD BE ABLE TO HOLD EVEN AN OUT OF CONTROL TITAN!
FSSSSS
! THE SIG-NAL ...
THE LAST TIME I CONTROLLED MY TITAN FORM WAS WHEN I PLUGGED UP THE WALL...
IF I GO BERSERK AGAIN...
...SQUAD LEVI...
...MIGHT KILL ME.
CHOMP

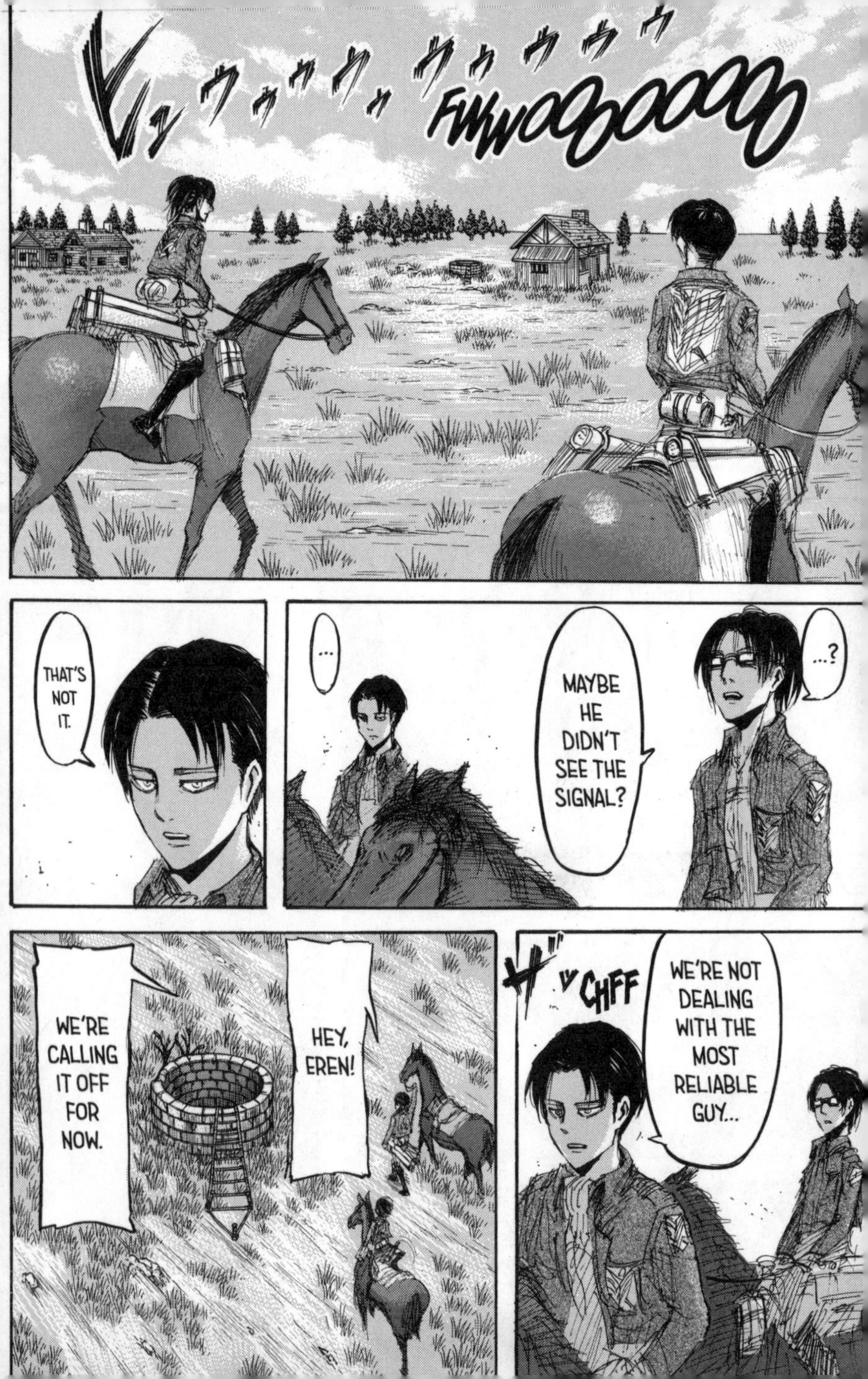
FWWOOOOOO
...?
MAYBE HE DIDN'T SEE THE SIGNAL?
...
THAT'S NOT IT.
CHFF
WE'RE NOT DEALING WITH THE MOST RELIABLE GUY...
HEY, EREN!
WE'RE CALLING IT OFF FOR NOW.

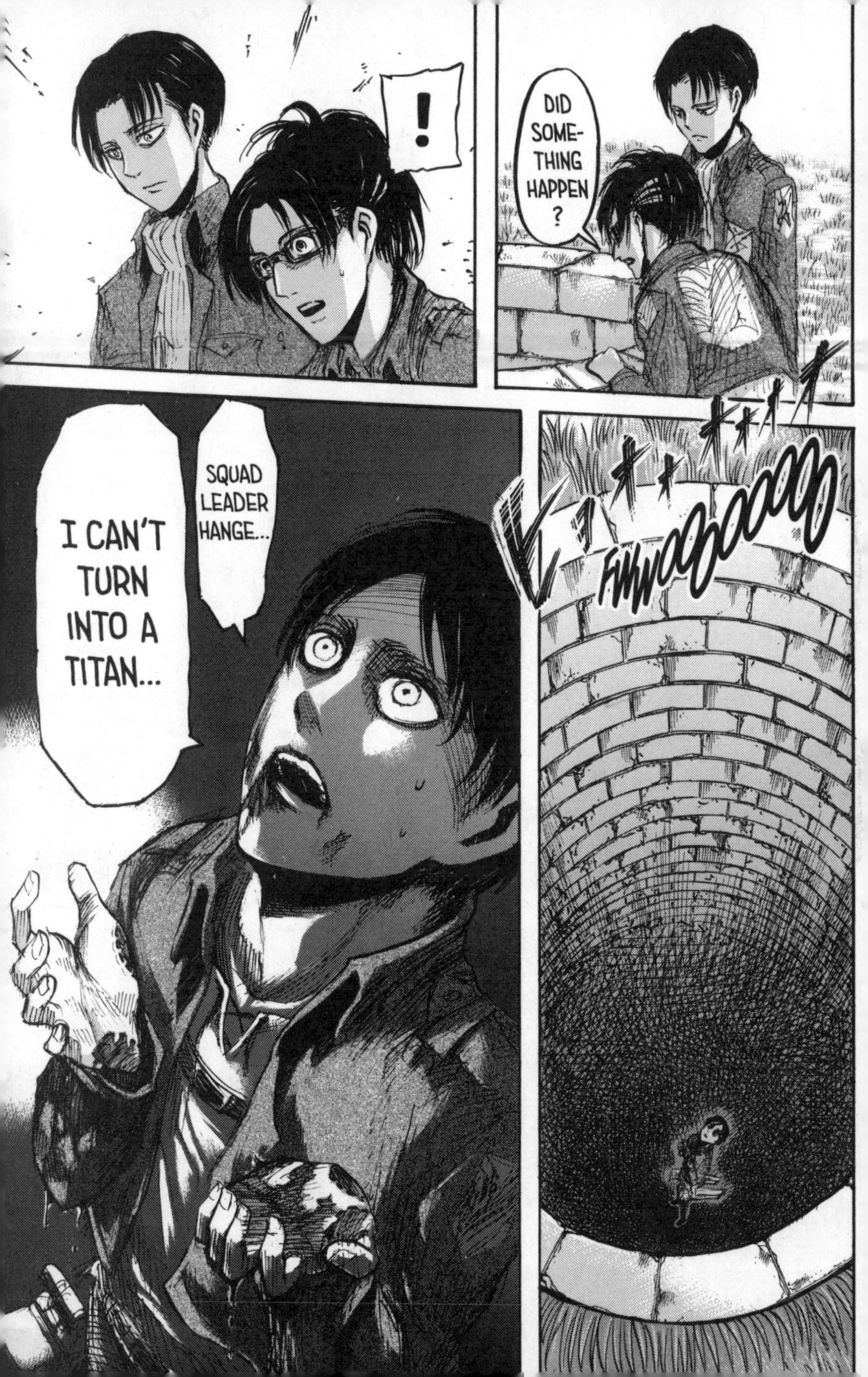
DID SOME-THING HAPPEN?
!
SQUAD LEADER HANGE...
I CAN'T TURN INTO A TITAN...

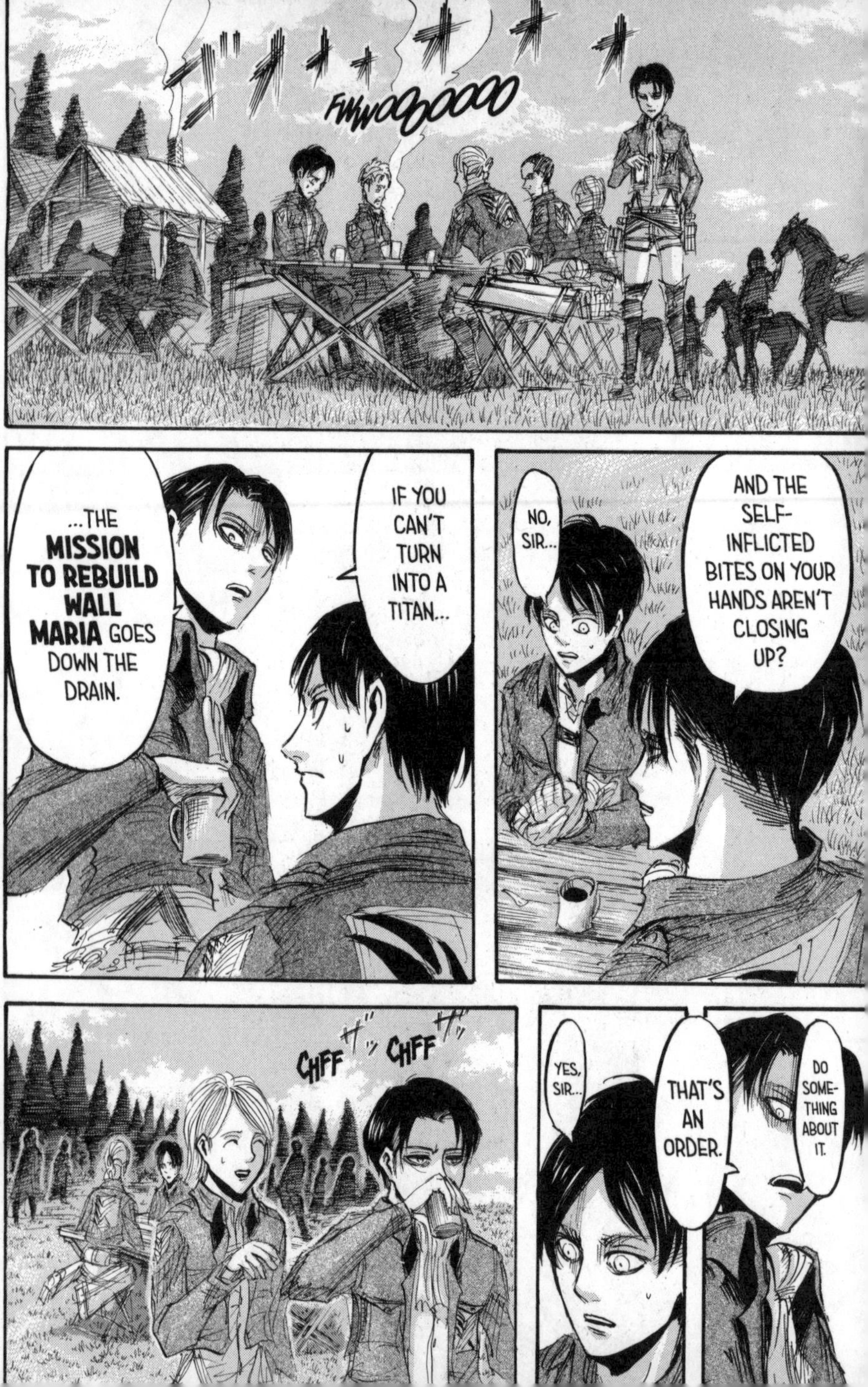
FWWOOOOOO
AND THE SELF-INFLICTED BITES ON YOUR HANDS AREN'T CLOSING UP?
NO, SIR...
IF YOU CAN'T TURN INTO A TITAN...
...THE **MISSION TO REBUILD WALL MARIA** GOES DOWN THE DRAIN.
DO SOMETHING ABOUT IT.
THAT'S AN ORDER.
YES, SIR...
CHFF CHFF

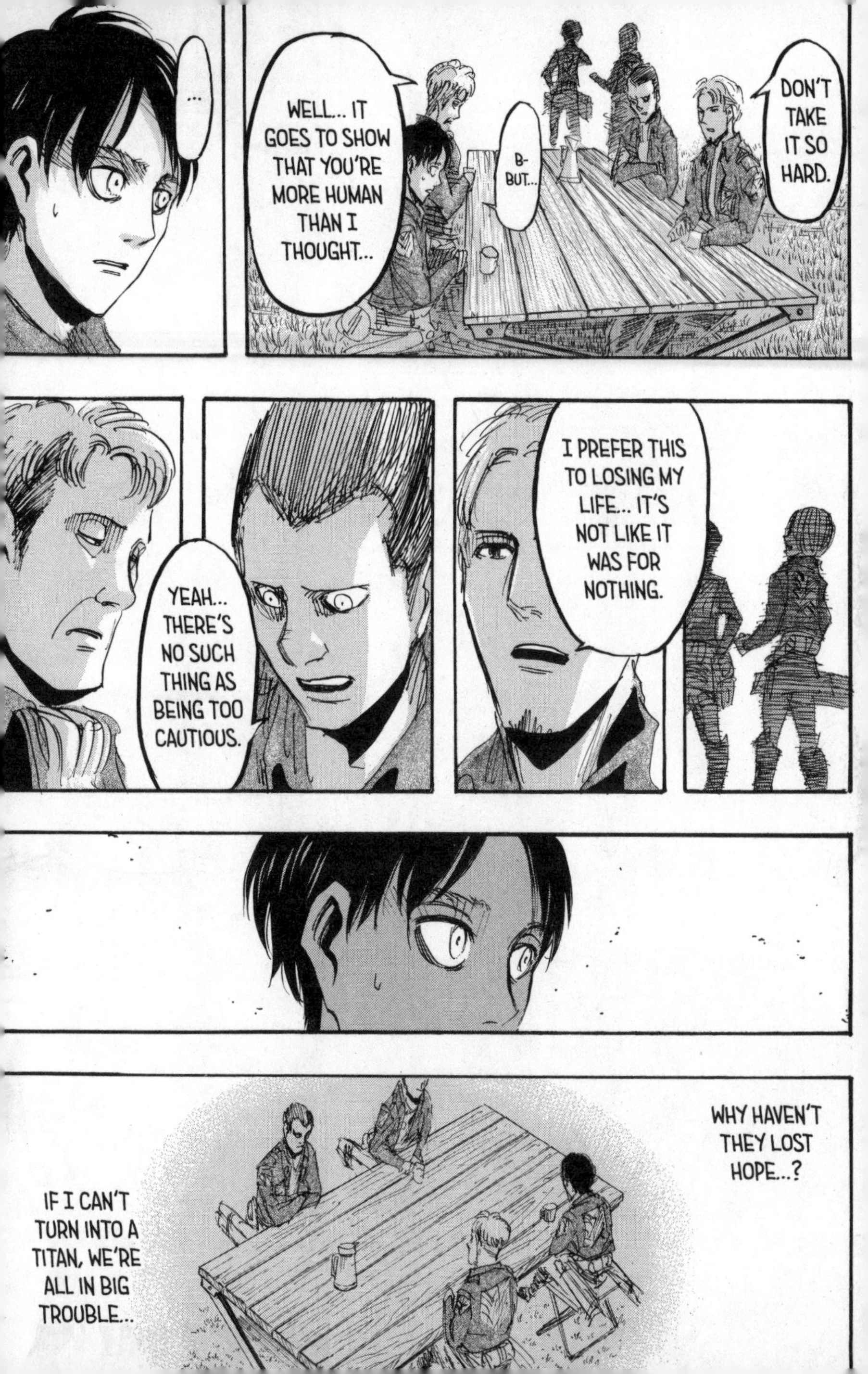
DON'T TAKE IT SO HARD.
B-BUT...
WELL... IT GOES TO SHOW THAT YOU'RE MORE HUMAN THAN I THOUGHT...
...
I PREFER THIS TO LOSING MY LIFE... IT'S NOT LIKE IT WAS FOR NOTHING.
YEAH... THERE'S NO SUCH THING AS BEING TOO CAUTIOUS.
WHY HAVEN'T THEY LOST HOPE...?
IF I CAN'T TURN INTO A TITAN, WE'RE ALL IN BIG TROUBLE...

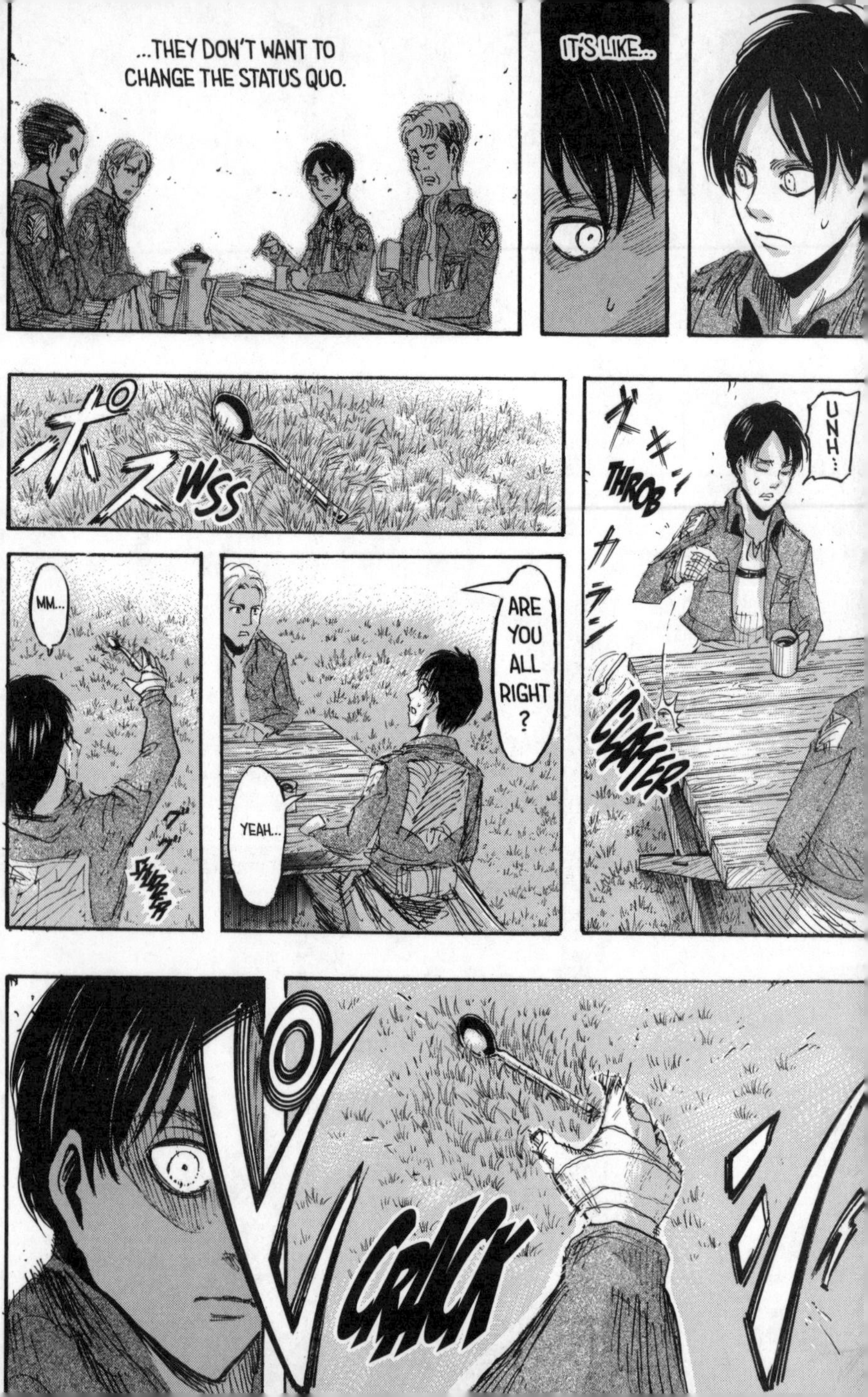
IT'S LIKE...
...THEY DON'T WANT TO CHANGE THE STATUS QUO.
UNH...
THROB
CLATTER
WSS
ARE YOU ALL RIGHT?
YEAH...
MM...
CRACK

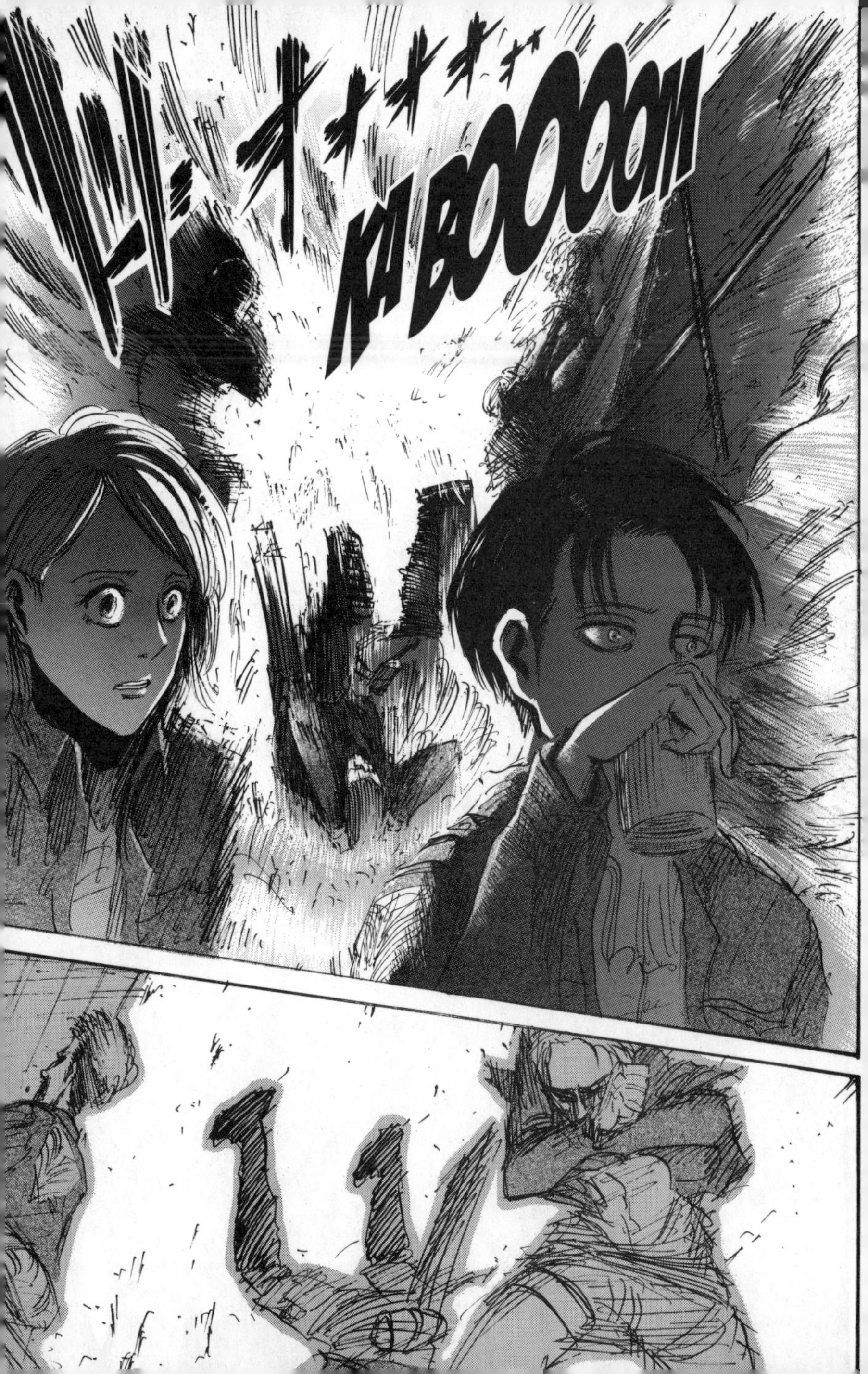
KABOOOM

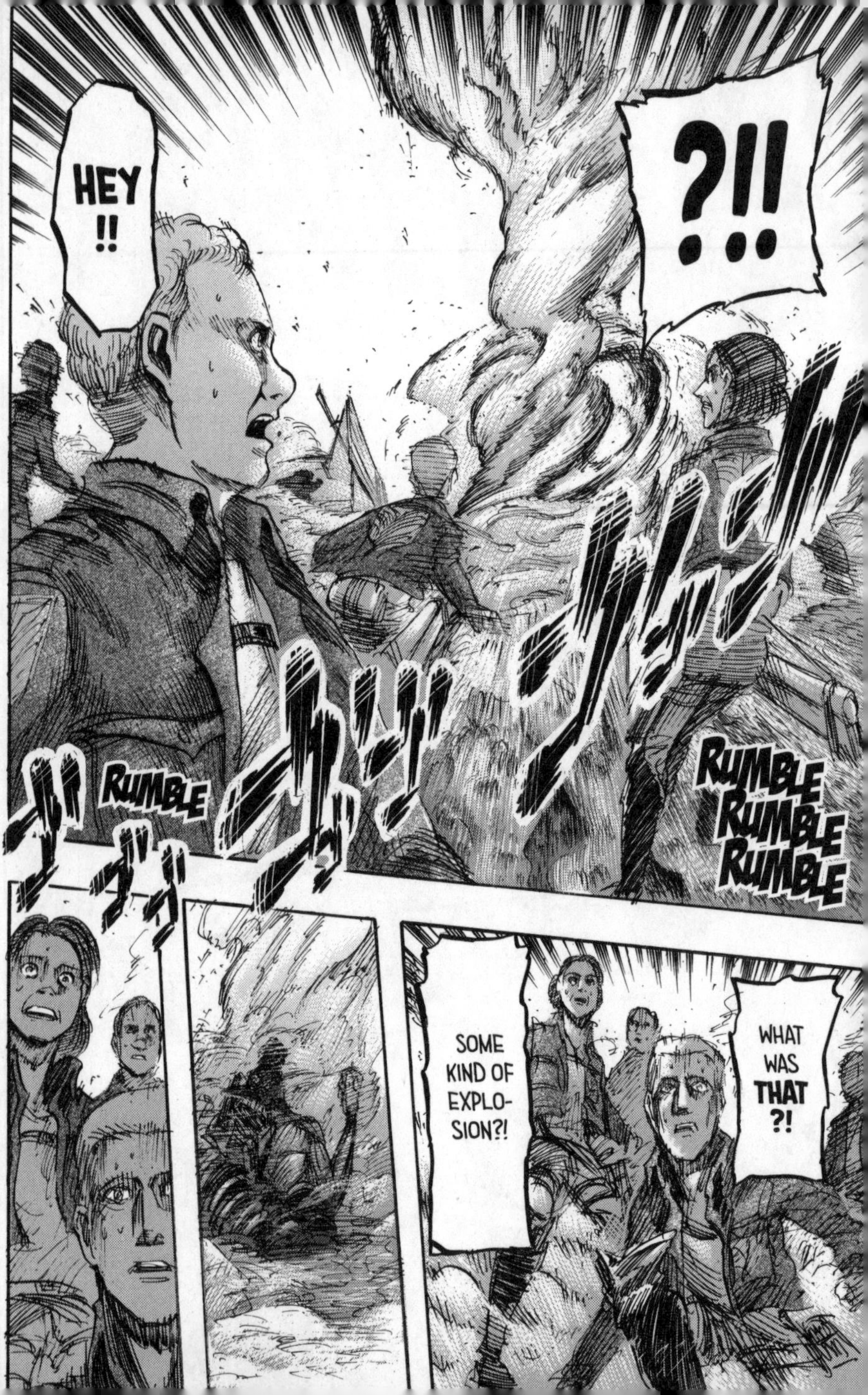
?!!
HEY !!
RUMBLE RUMBLE RUMBLE
RUMBLE
WHAT WAS THAT ?!
SOME KIND OF EXPLO-SION?!

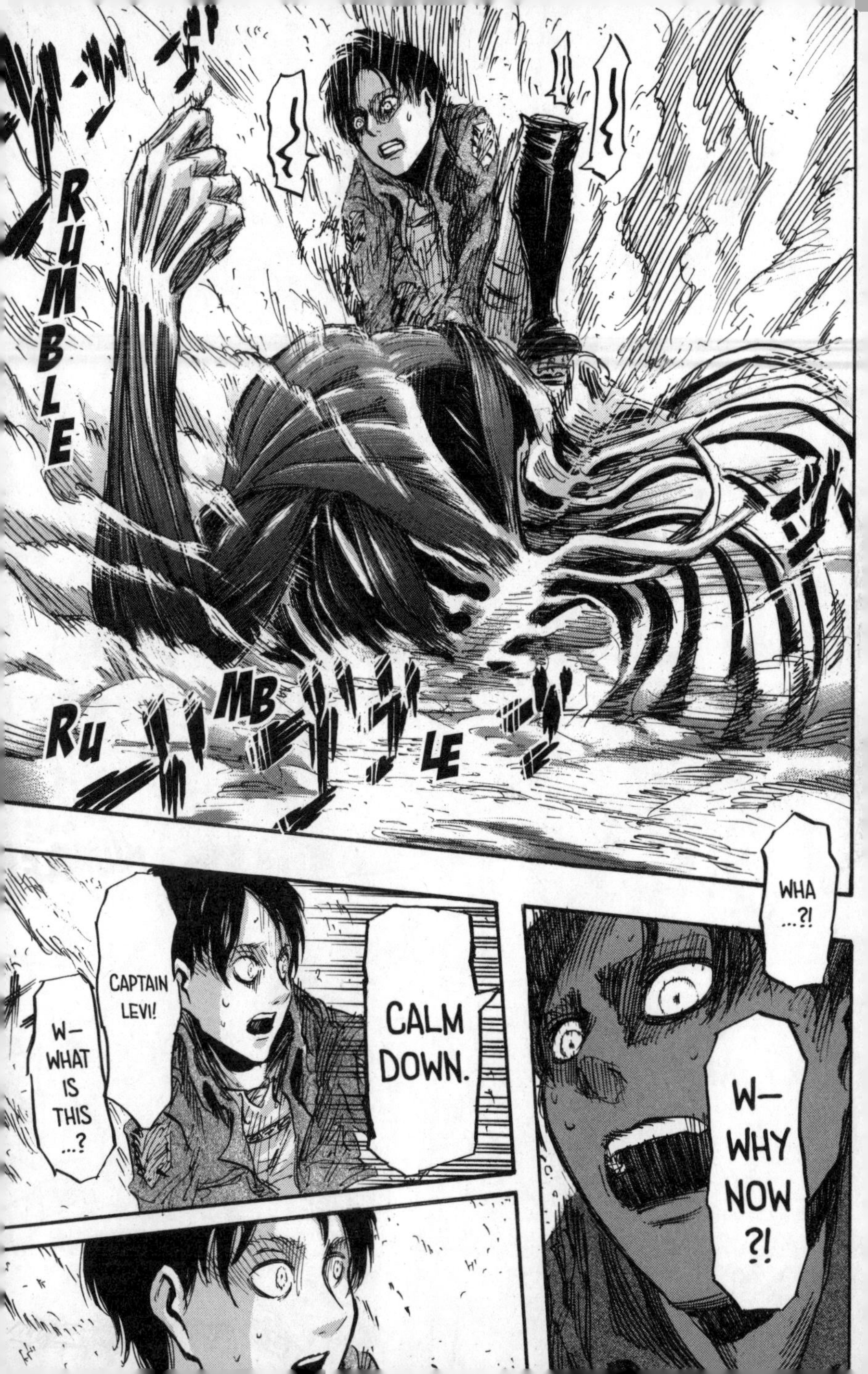
RUMBLE
Ru MB LE
WHA ...?!
W— WHY NOW ?!
CALM DOWN.
CAPTAIN LEVI!
W— WHAT IS THIS ...?

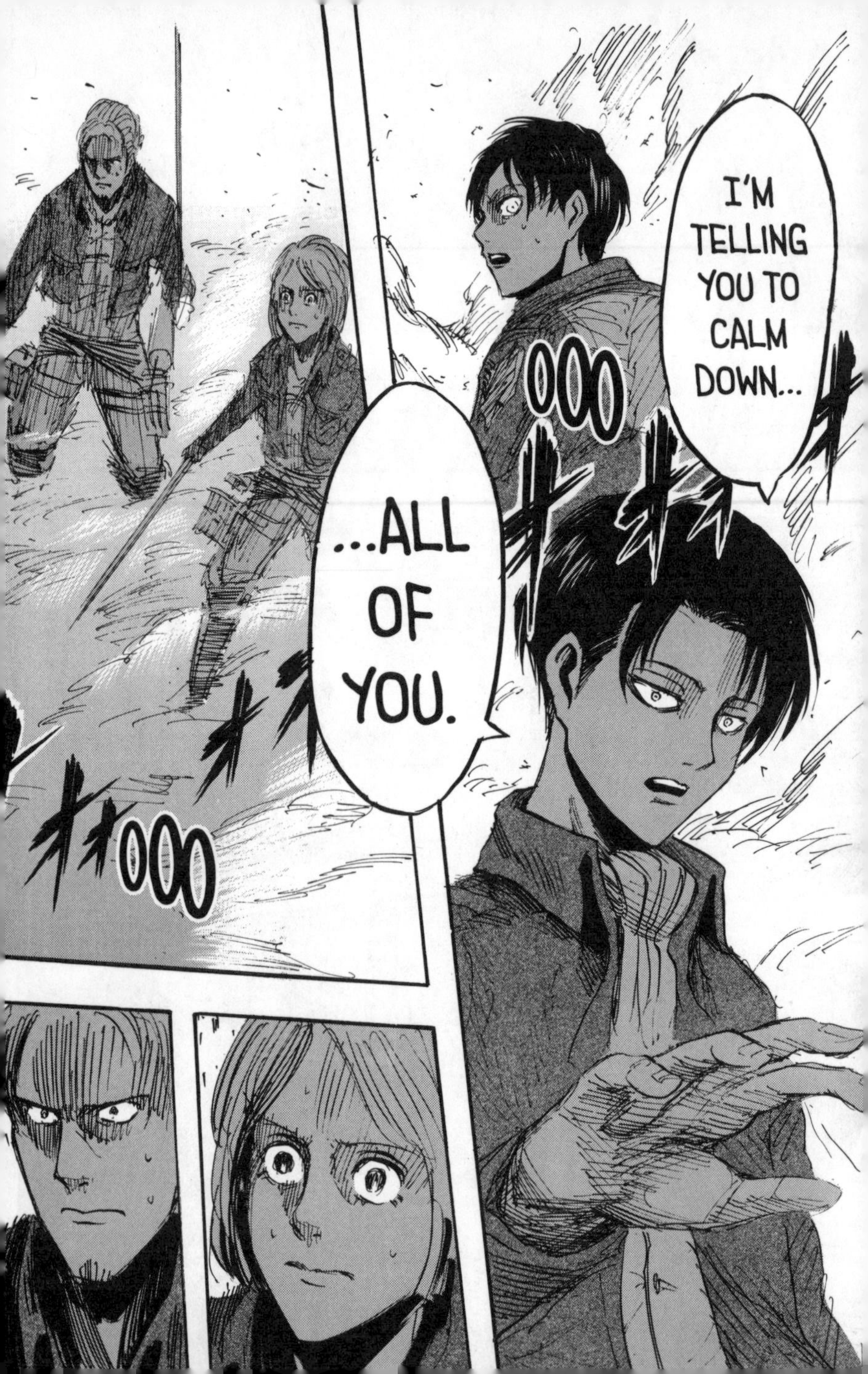
I'M TELLING YOU TO CALM DOWN...
...ALL OF YOU.
OOO
OOO

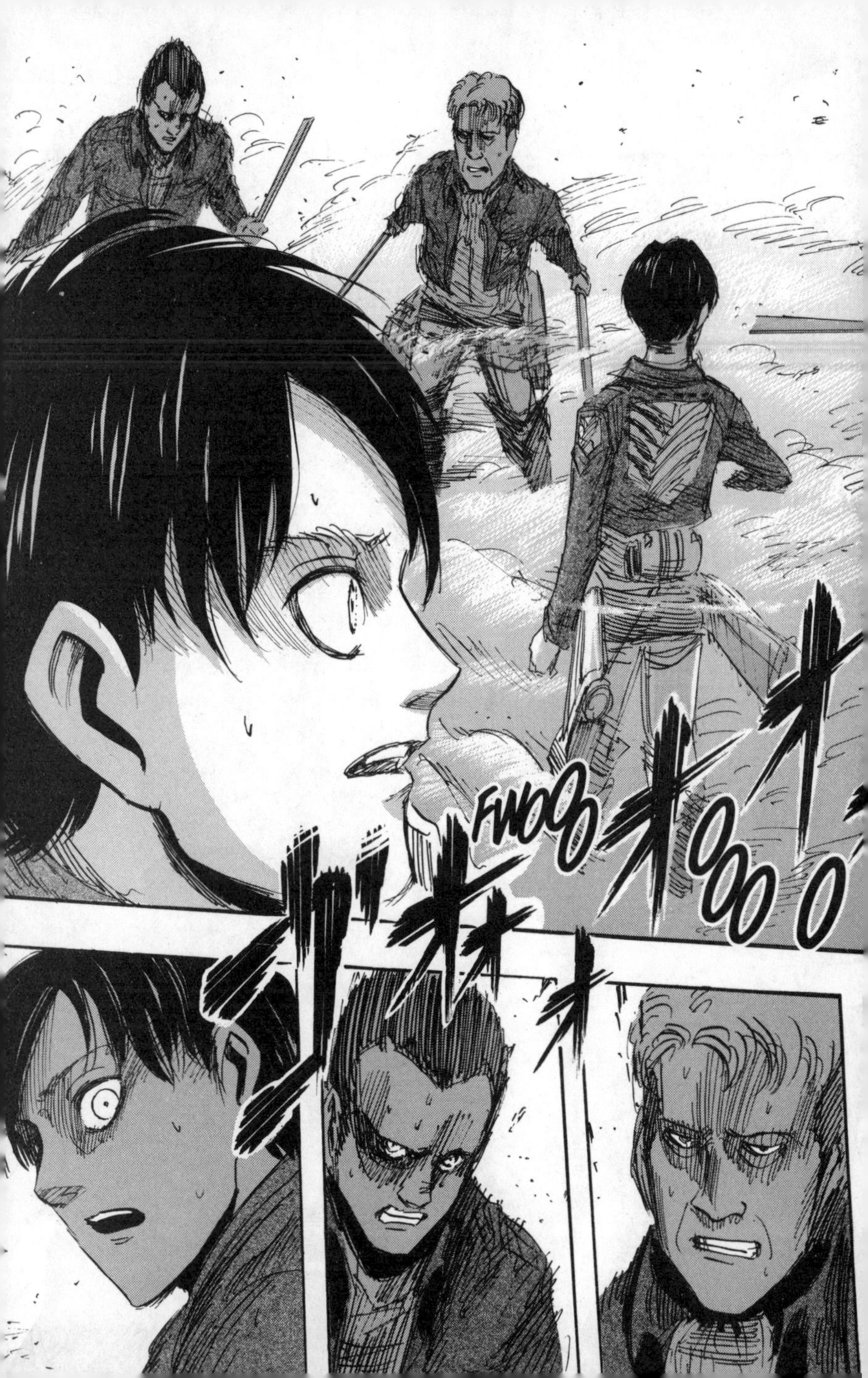
ゴオオオオ
FWOOOOOOO

ATTACK on TITAN

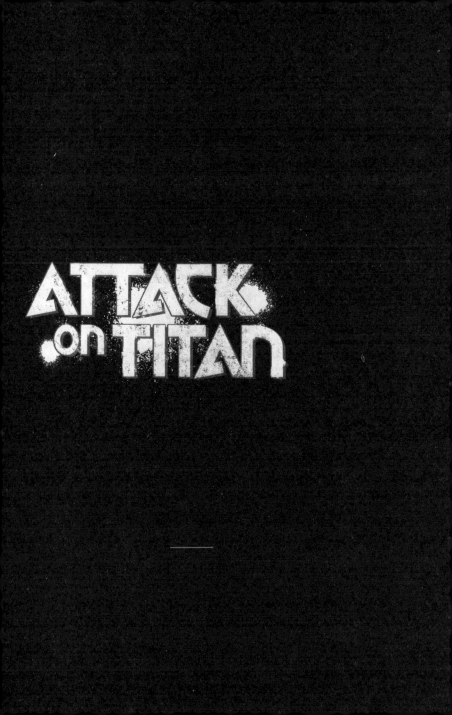

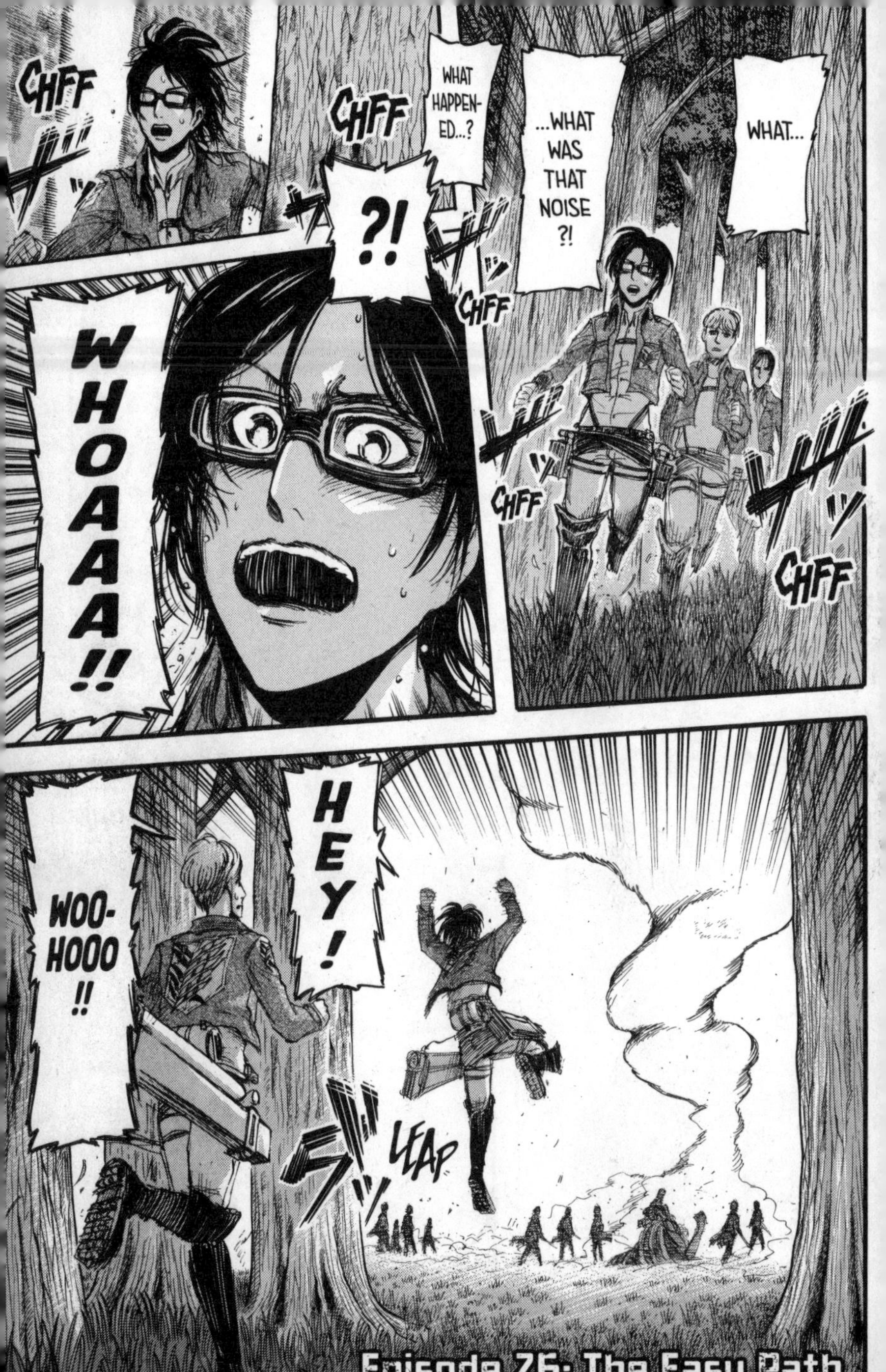
WHAT...
...WHAT WAS THAT NOISE ?!
CHFF
CHFF
WHAT HAPPEN-ED...?
CHFF
CHFF
CHFF
?!
WHOAAA!!
HEY!
WOO-HOOO!!
LEAP

Episode 26: The Easy Path

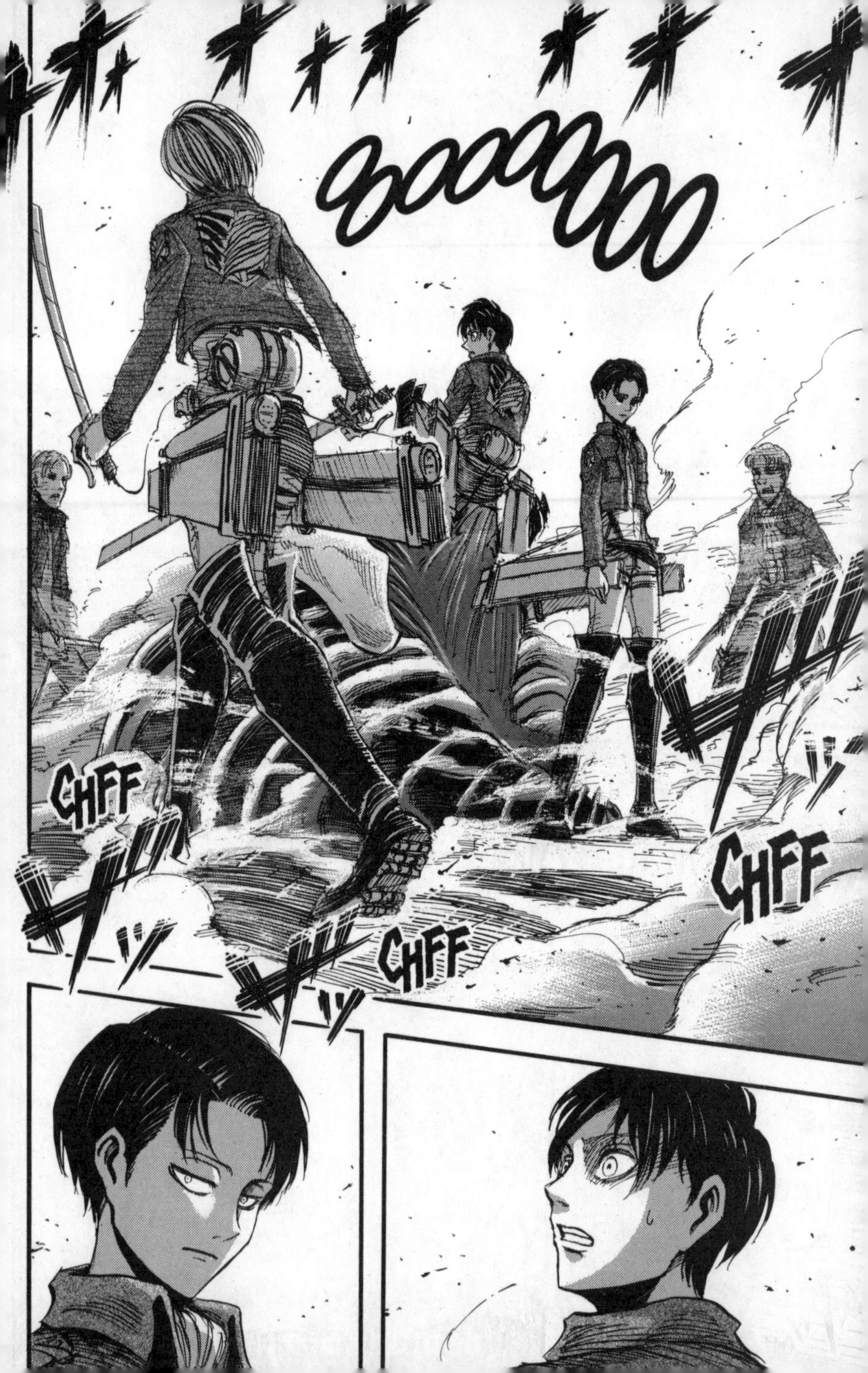
goooooo
CHFF
CHFF
CHFF

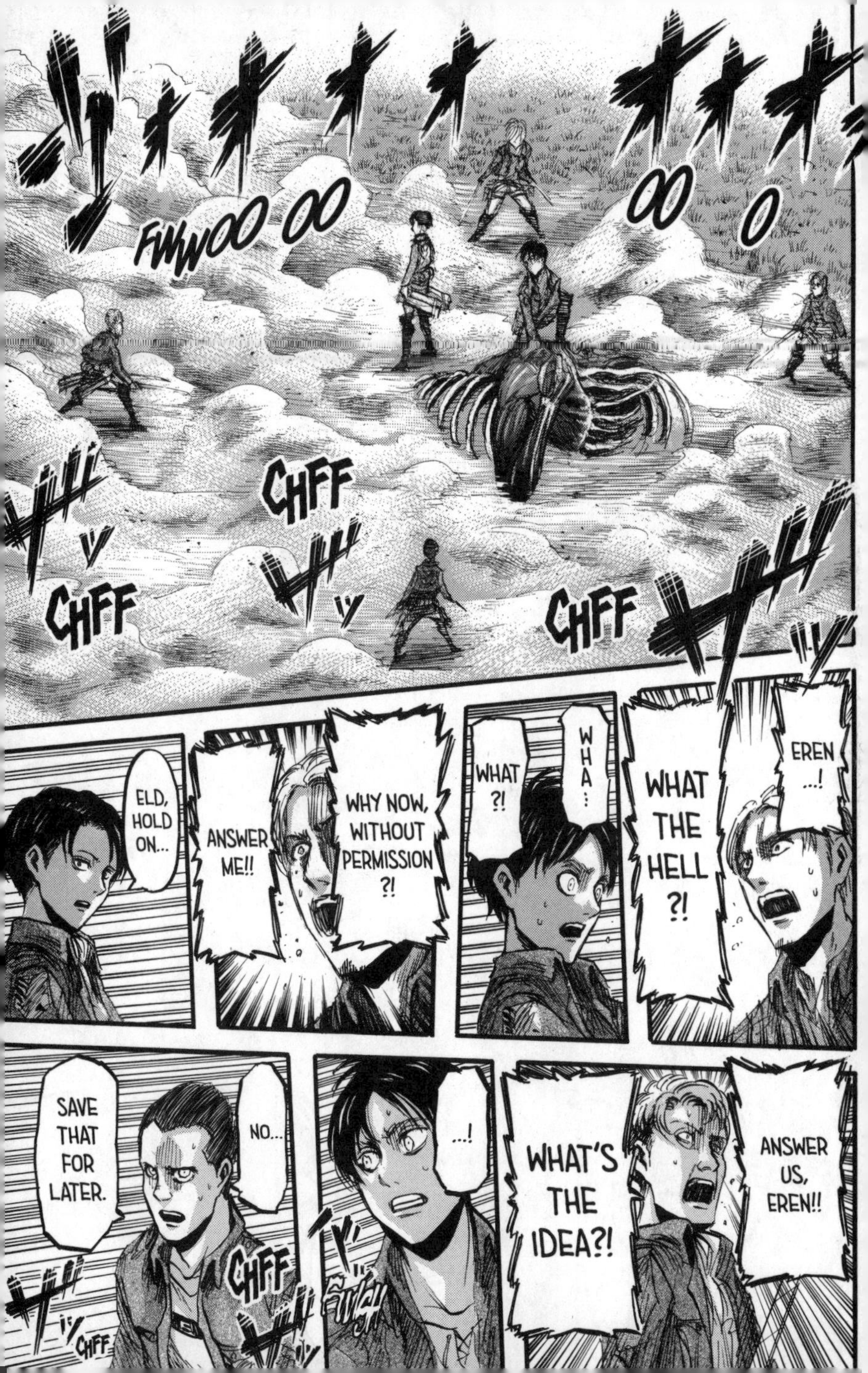
FWWOO OO
OO O
CHFF
CHFF
CHFF
EREN ...!
WHAT THE HELL ?!
WHA...
WHAT ?!
WHY NOW, WITHOUT PERMISSION ?!
ANSWER ME!!
ELD, HOLD ON...
ANSWER US, EREN!!
WHAT'S THE IDEA?!
...!
CHFF
NO...
SAVE THAT FOR LATER.
CHFF

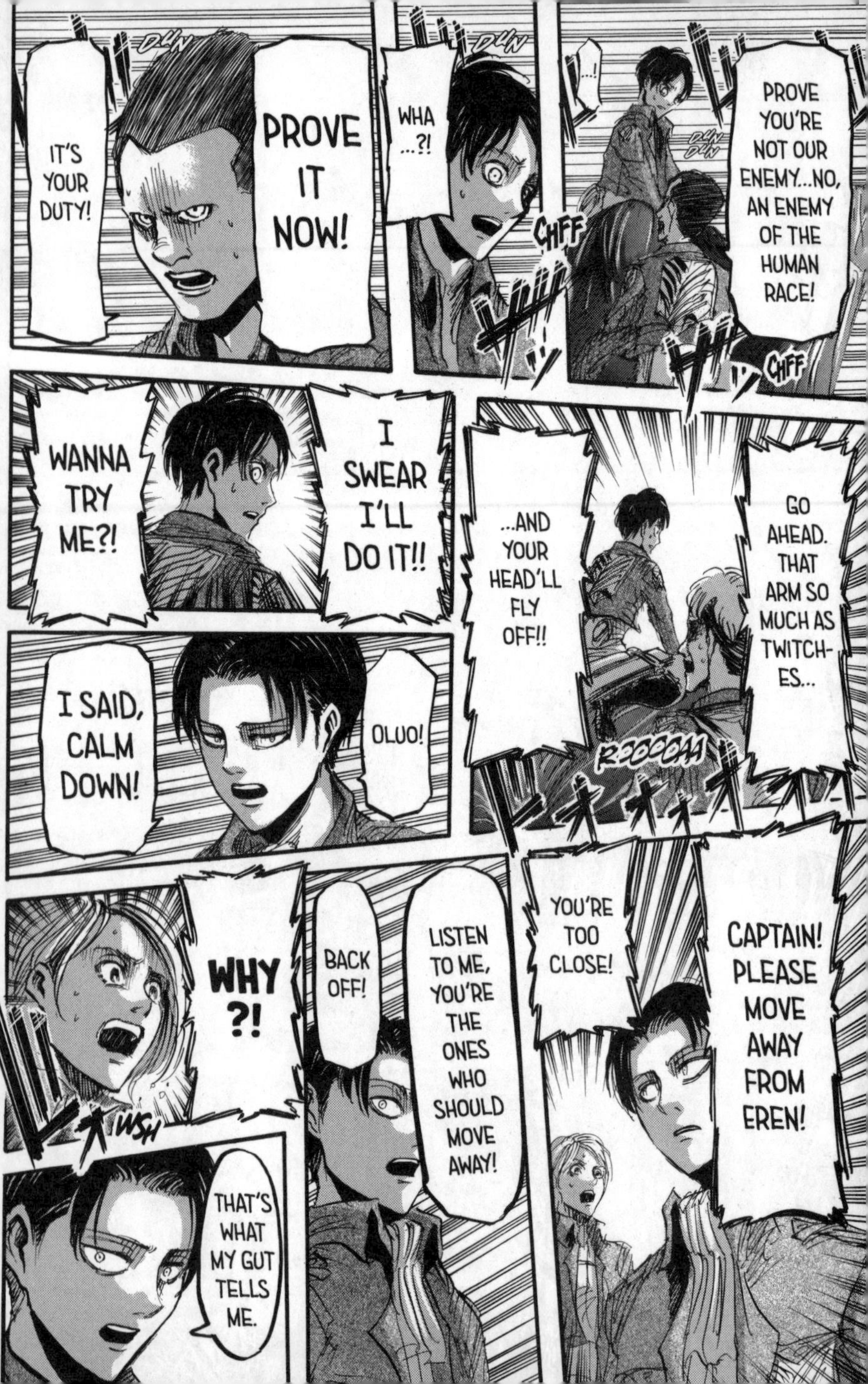
...!
PROVE YOU'RE NOT OUR ENEMY...NO, AN ENEMY OF THE HUMAN RACE!
DUN DUN
CHFF
CHFF
DUN
WHA ...?!
DUN
PROVE IT NOW!
IT'S YOUR DUTY!
GO AHEAD. THAT ARM SO MUCH AS TWITCH-ES...
...AND YOUR HEAD'LL FLY OFF!!
I SWEAR I'LL DO IT!!
WANNA TRY ME?!
OLUO!
I SAID, CALM DOWN!
CAPTAIN! PLEASE MOVE AWAY FROM EREN!
YOU'RE TOO CLOSE!
LISTEN TO ME, YOU'RE THE ONES WHO SHOULD MOVE AWAY!
BACK OFF!
WHY ?!
WSH
THAT'S WHAT MY GUT TELLS ME.

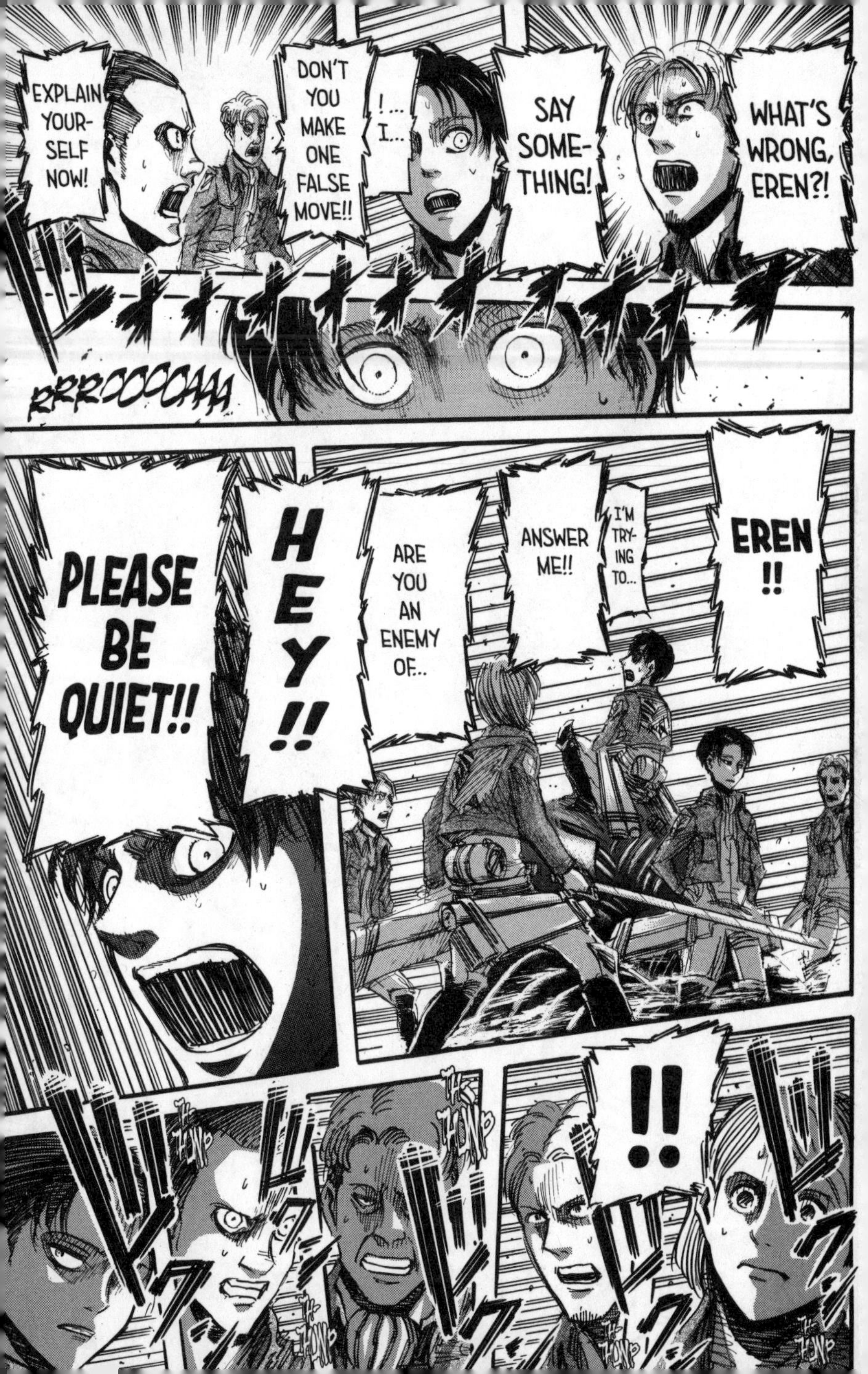
WHAT'S WRONG, EREN?!
SAY SOME-THING!
!... I...
DON'T YOU MAKE ONE FALSE MOVE!!
EXPLAIN YOUR-SELF NOW!
RRROOOOAAA
EREN!!
I'M TRY-ING TO...
ANSWER ME!!
ARE YOU AN ENEMY OF...
HEY!!
PLEASE BE QUIET!!
!!

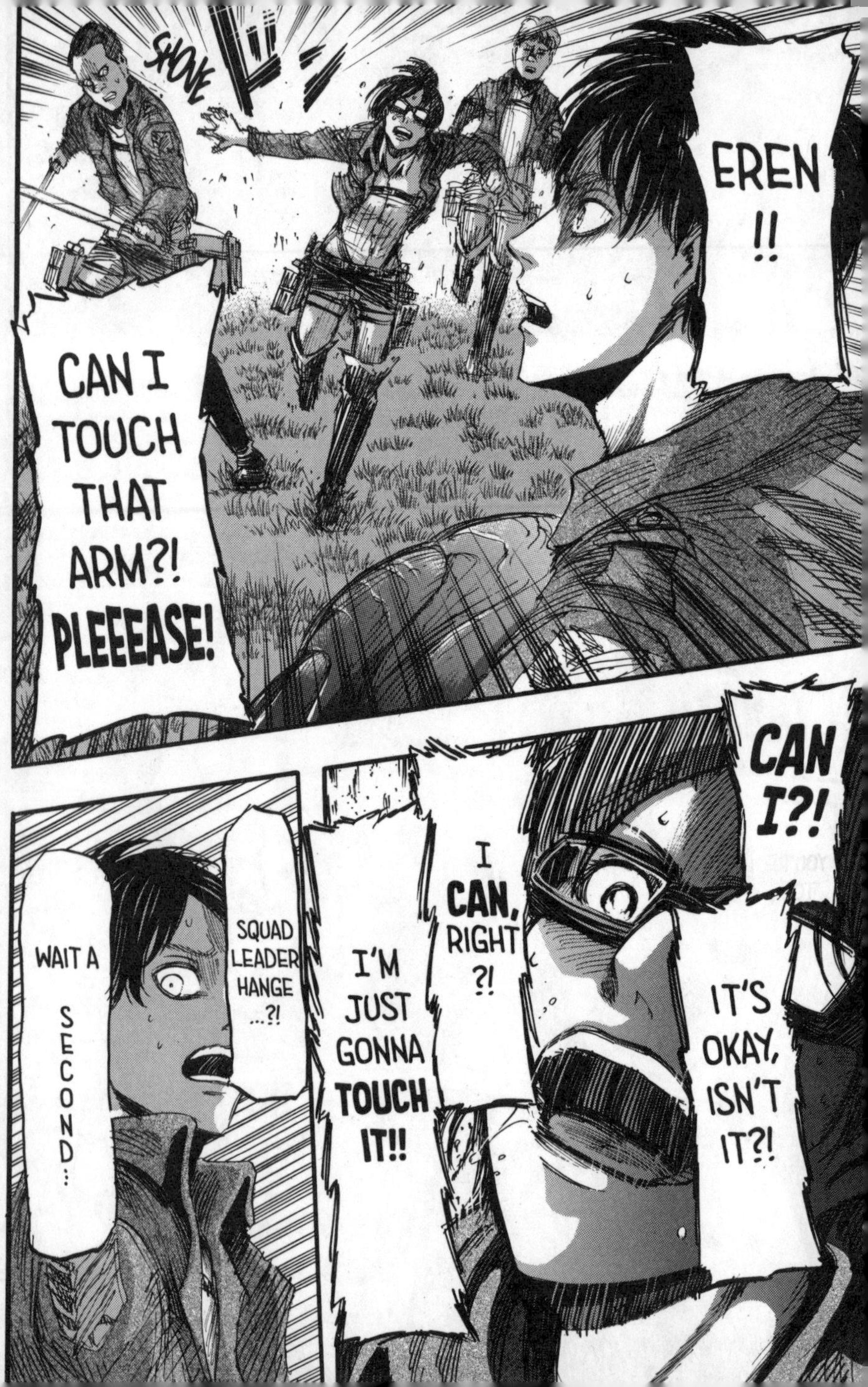
EREN!!
SHOVE
CAN I TOUCH THAT ARM?! PLEEEASE!
CAN I?!
IT'S OKAY, ISN'T IT?!
I CAN, RIGHT?!
I'M JUST GONNA TOUCH IT!!
SQUAD LEADER HANGE ...?!
WAIT A SECOND...

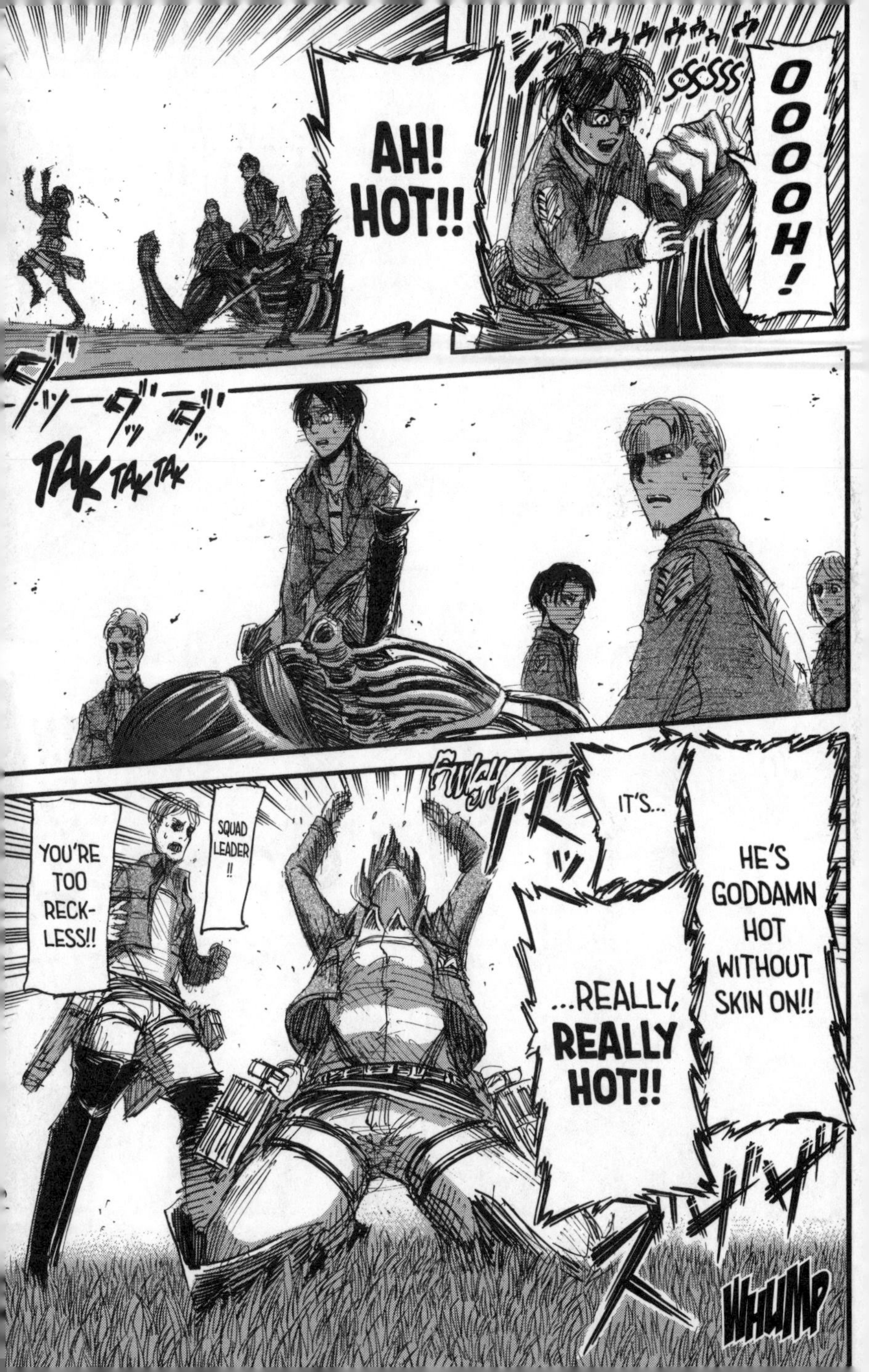

OOOOOH!
SSSSS
AH! HOT!!
TAK TAK TAK
HE'S GODDAMN HOT WITHOUT SKIN ON!!
IT'S...
...REALLY, REALLY HOT!!
FWUSH
SQUAD LEADER!!
YOU'RE TOO RECK-LESS!!
WHUMP

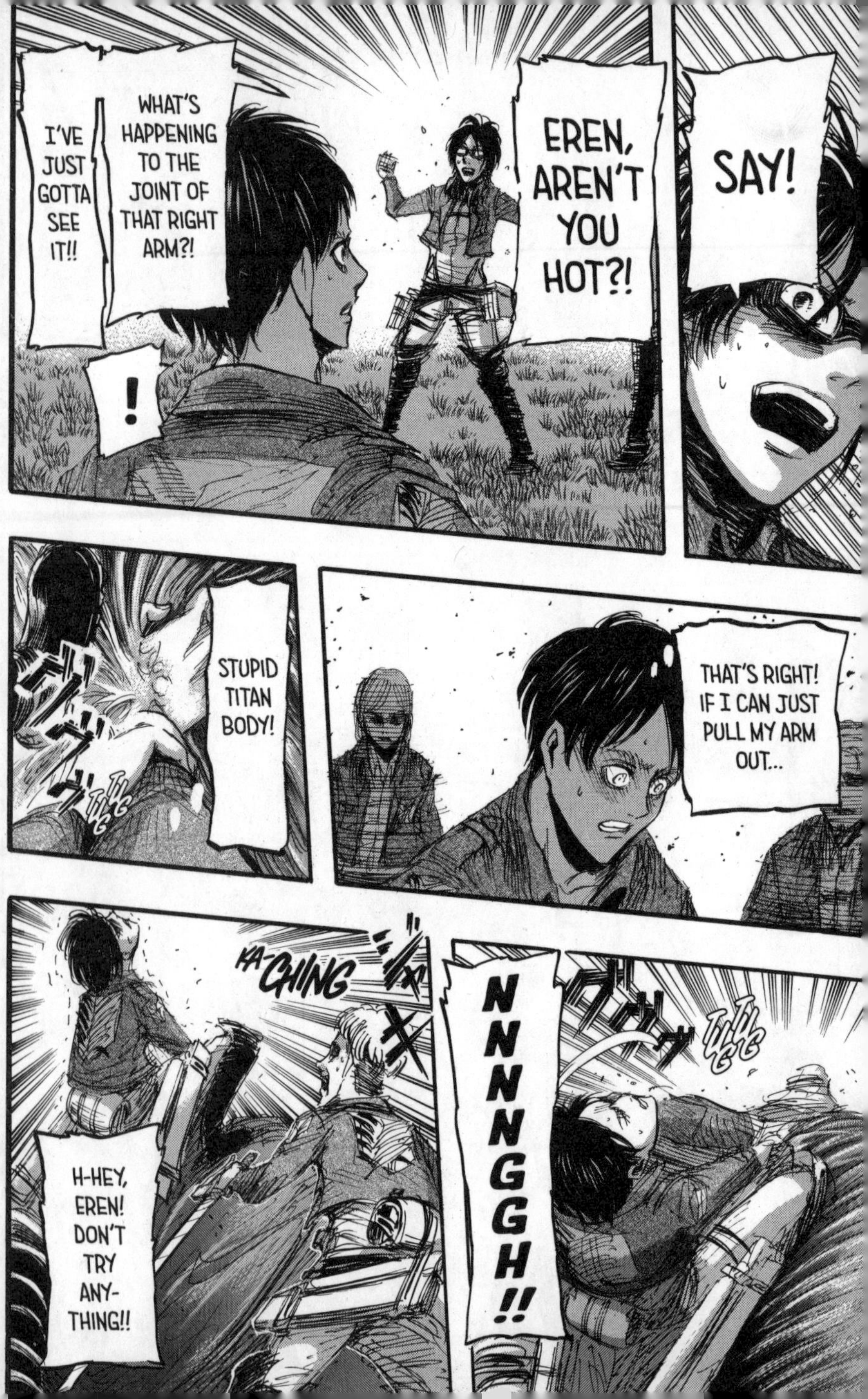
SAY!
EREN, AREN'T YOU HOT?!
WHAT'S HAPPENING TO THE JOINT OF THAT RIGHT ARM?!
I'VE JUST GOTTA SEE IT!!
!
THAT'S RIGHT! IF I CAN JUST PULL MY ARM OUT...
STUPID TITAN BODY!
TUG TUG
NNNNGGH!!
TUG TUG
KA-CHING
H-HEY, EREN! DON'T TRY ANY-THING!!

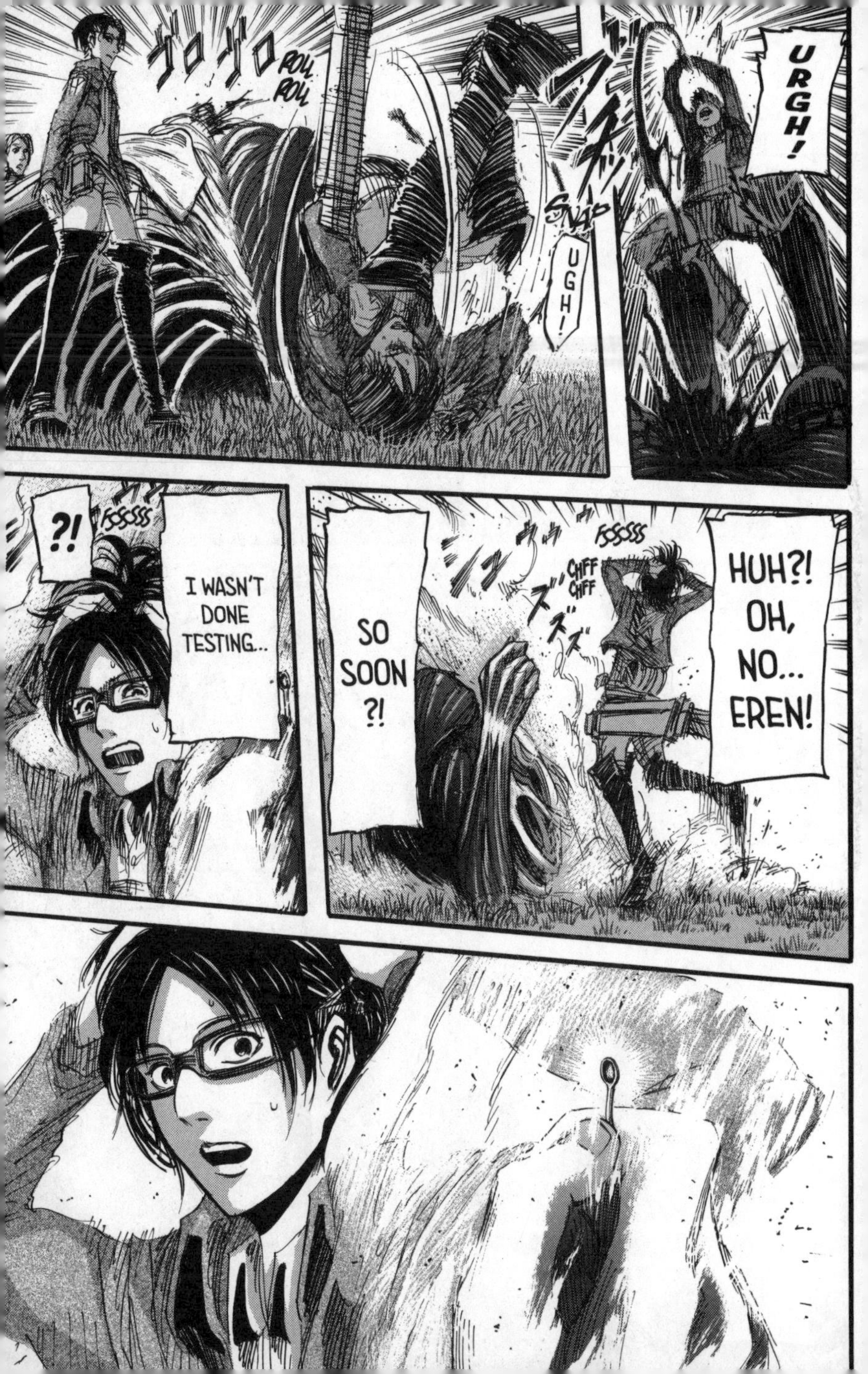
URGH!
SNAP
UGH!
ROLL ROLL
HUH?! OH, NO... EREN!
FSSSSS
CHFF CHFF
SO SOON?!
I WASN'T DONE TESTING...
FSSSSS
?!

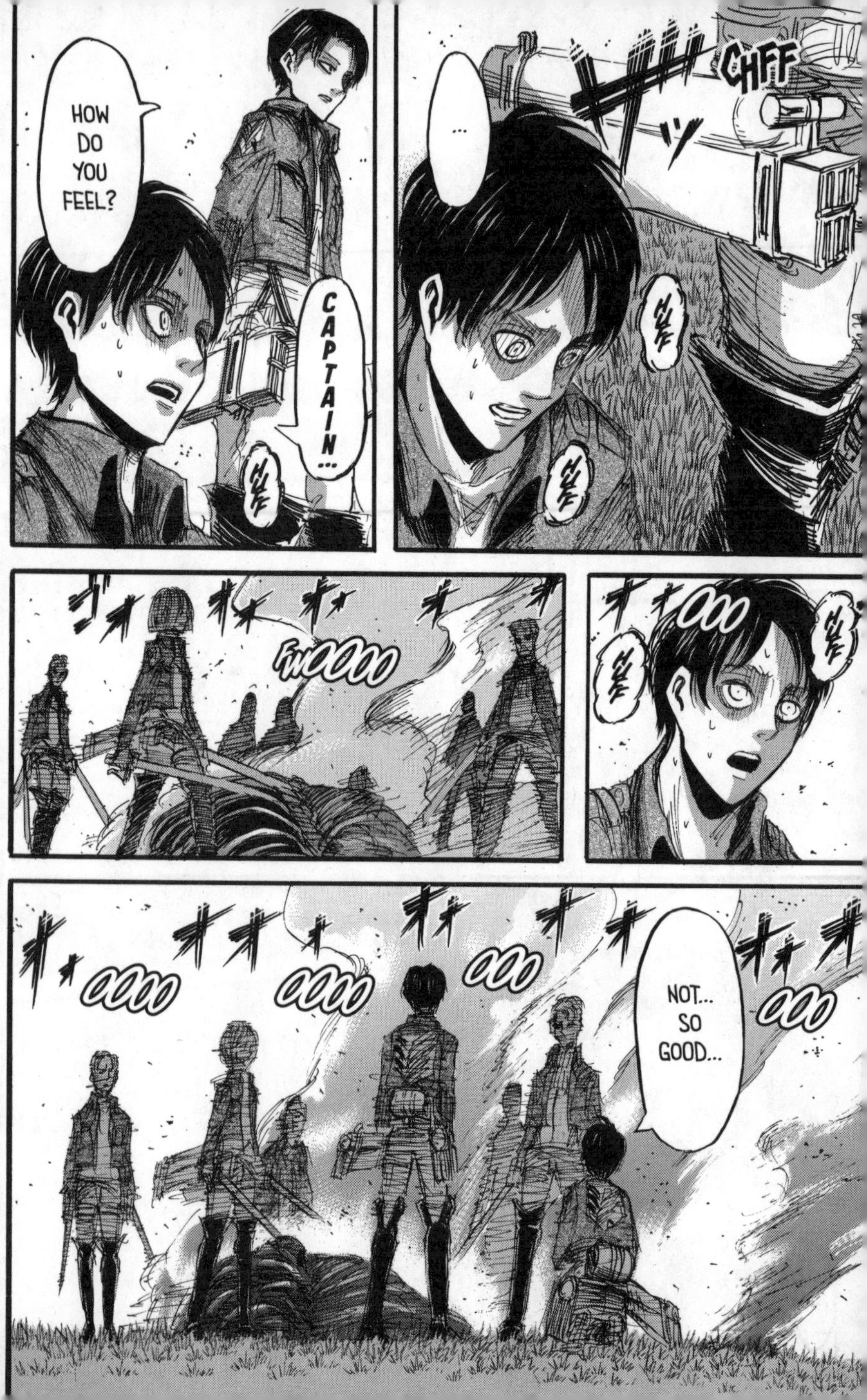

...
CHFF
HUFF
HUFF
HOW DO YOU FEEL?
CAPTAIN...
HUFF
HUFF
HUFF
OOO
FWOOOO
OOO
NOT... SO GOOD...
OOO
OOOO
OOOO

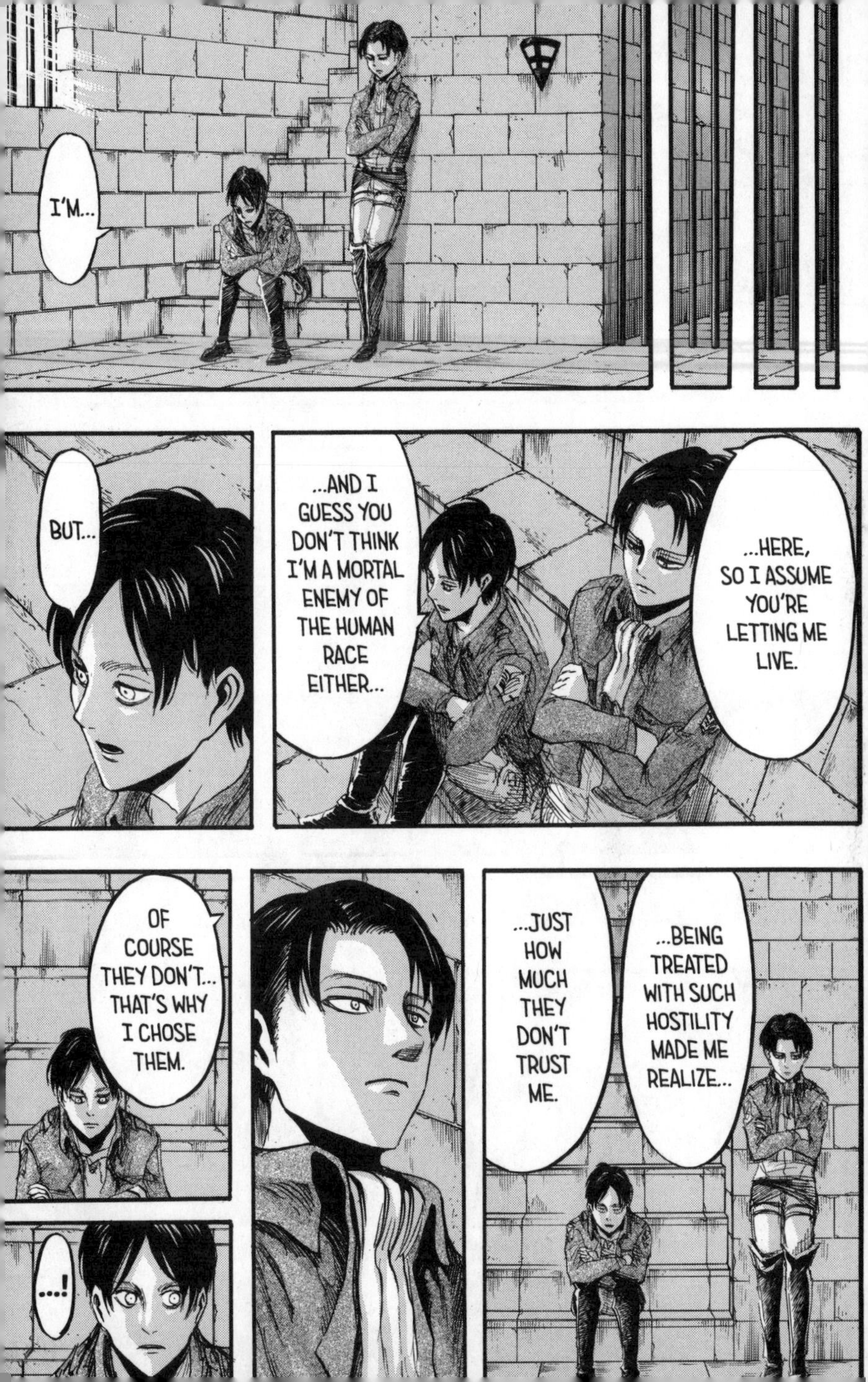
I'M...
...HERE, SO I ASSUME YOU'RE LETTING ME LIVE.
...AND I GUESS YOU DON'T THINK I'M A MORTAL ENEMY OF THE HUMAN RACE EITHER...
BUT...
...BEING TREATED WITH SUCH HOSTILITY MADE ME REALIZE...
...JUST HOW MUCH THEY DON'T TRUST ME.
OF COURSE THEY DON'T... THAT'S WHY I CHOSE THEM.
...!

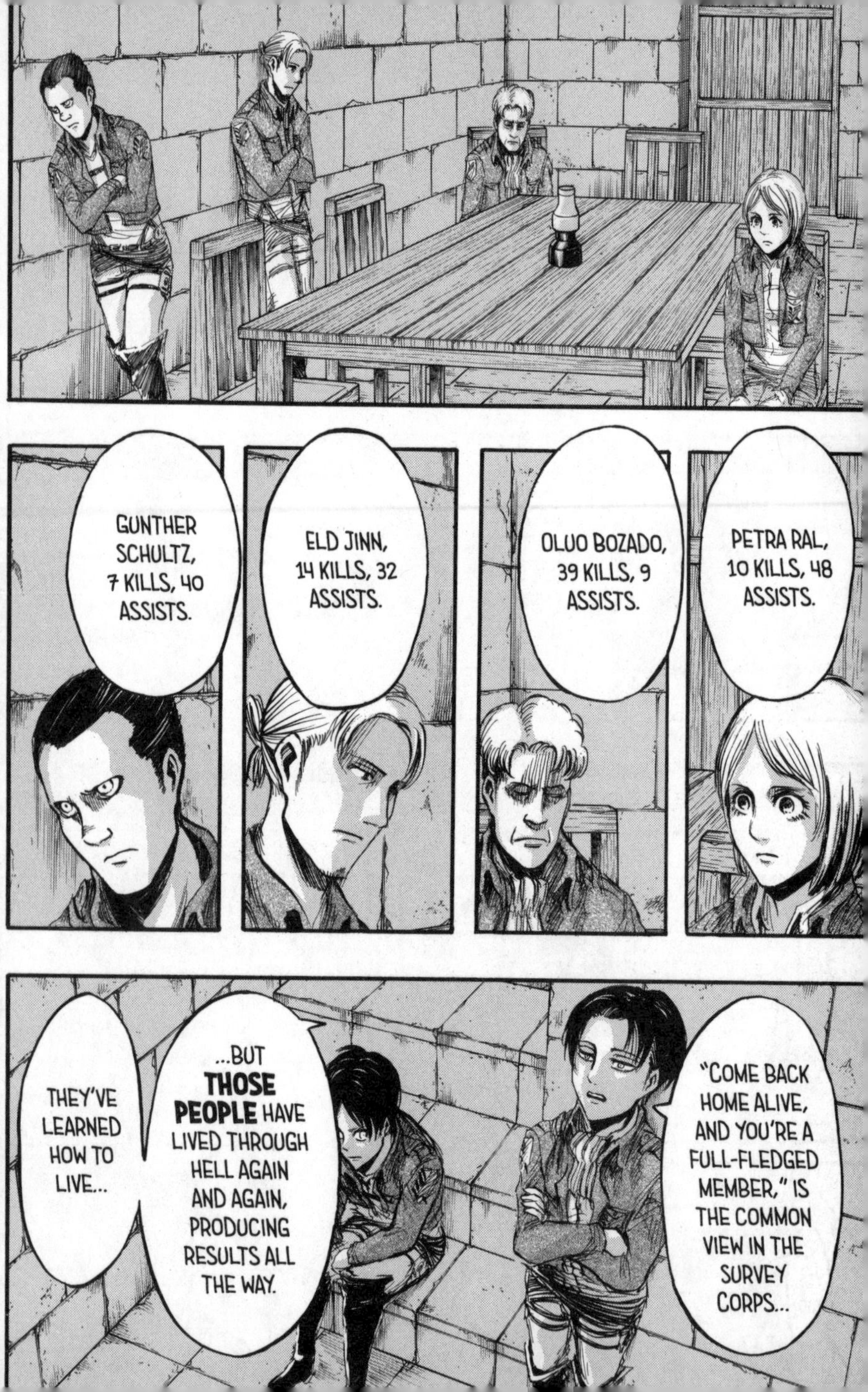
PETRA RAL, 10 KILLS, 48 ASSISTS.
OLUO BOZADO, 39 KILLS, 9 ASSISTS.
ELD JINN, 14 KILLS, 32 ASSISTS.
GUNTHER SCHULTZ, 7 KILLS, 40 ASSISTS.
"COME BACK HOME ALIVE, AND YOU'RE A FULL-FLEDGED MEMBER," IS THE COMMON VIEW IN THE SURVEY CORPS...
...BUT **THOSE PEOPLE** HAVE LIVED THROUGH HELL AGAIN AND AGAIN, PRODUCING RESULTS ALL THE WAY.
THEY'VE LEARNED HOW TO LIVE...

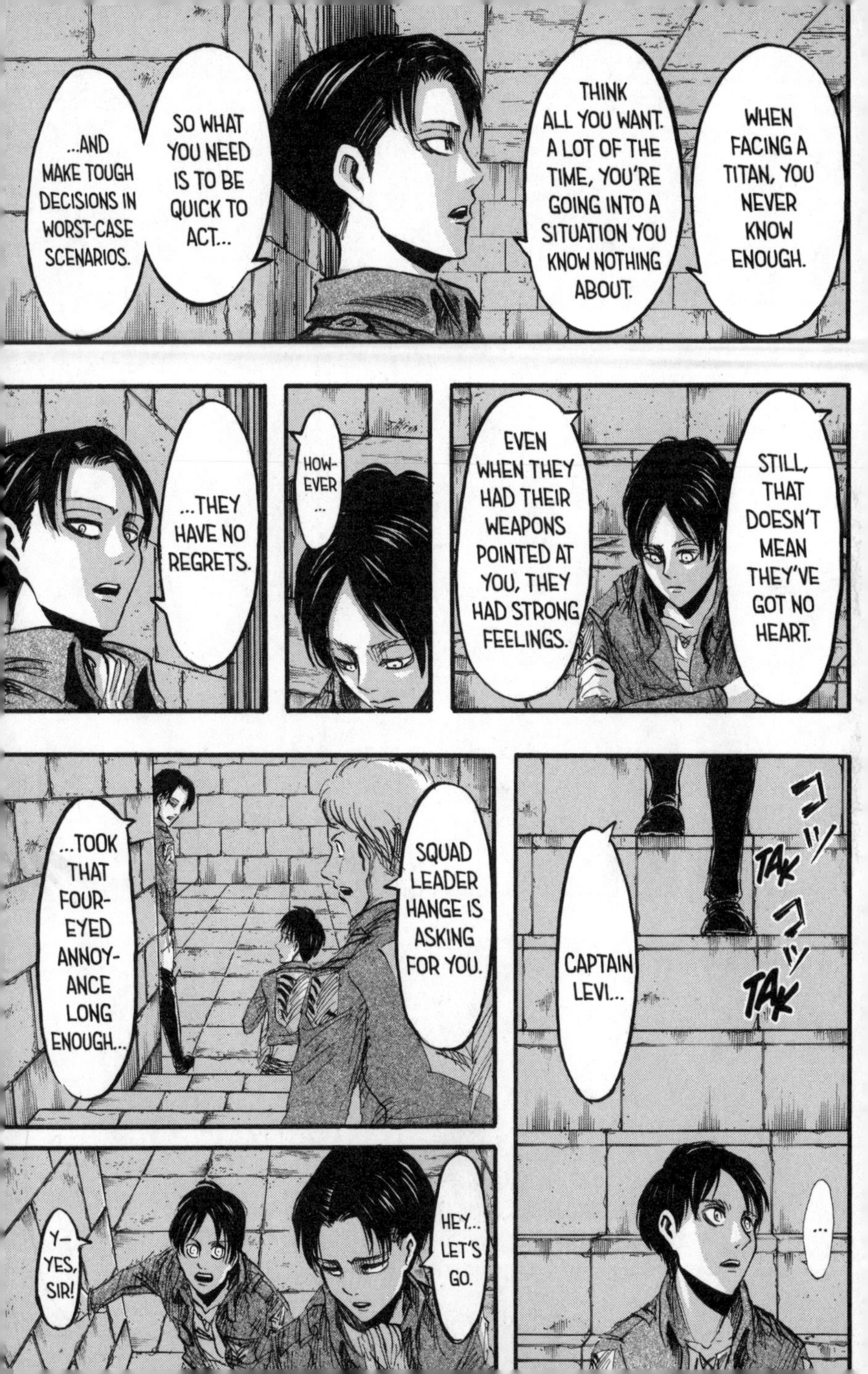
WHEN FACING A TITAN, YOU NEVER KNOW ENOUGH.
THINK ALL YOU WANT. A LOT OF THE TIME, YOU'RE GOING INTO A SITUATION YOU KNOW NOTHING ABOUT.
SO WHAT YOU NEED IS TO BE QUICK TO ACT...
...AND MAKE TOUGH DECISIONS IN WORST-CASE SCENARIOS.
STILL, THAT DOESN'T MEAN THEY'VE GOT NO HEART.
EVEN WHEN THEY HAD THEIR WEAPONS POINTED AT YOU, THEY HAD STRONG FEELINGS.
HOW-EVER ...
...THEY HAVE NO REGRETS.
コッ TAK
コッ TAK
CAPTAIN LEVI...
SQUAD LEADER HANGE IS ASKING FOR YOU.
...TOOK THAT FOUR-EYED ANNOY-ANCE LONG ENOUGH...
...
HEY... LET'S GO.
Y-YES, SIR!

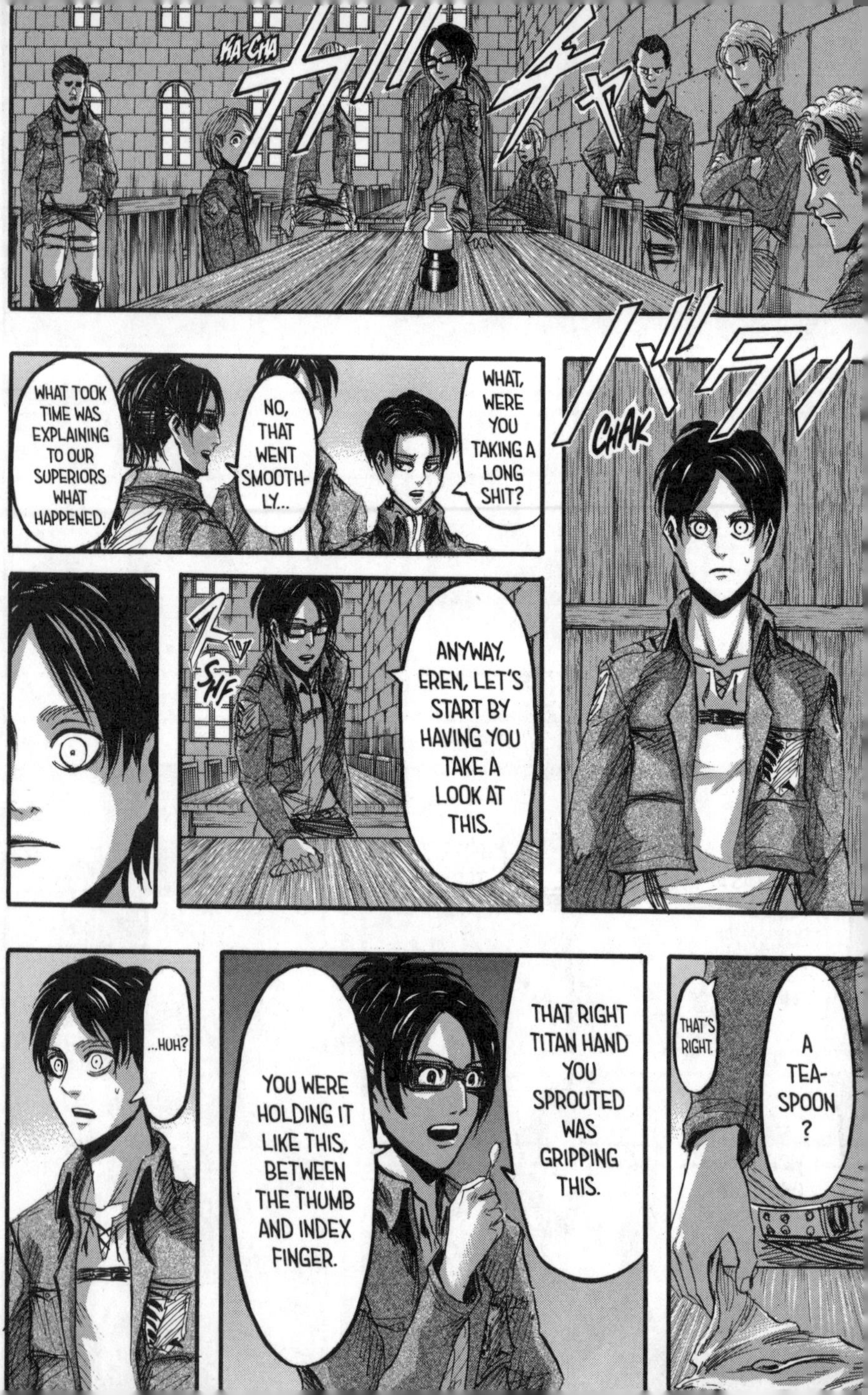
KA-CHA
CHAK
WHAT, WERE YOU TAKING A LONG SHIT?
NO, THAT WENT SMOOTH-LY...
WHAT TOOK TIME WAS EXPLAINING TO OUR SUPERIORS WHAT HAPPENED.
SHF
ANYWAY, EREN, LET'S START BY HAVING YOU TAKE A LOOK AT THIS.
A TEA-SPOON?
THAT'S RIGHT.
THAT RIGHT TITAN HAND YOU SPROUTED WAS GRIPPING THIS.
YOU WERE HOLDING IT LIKE THIS, BETWEEN THE THUMB AND INDEX FINGER.
...HUH?

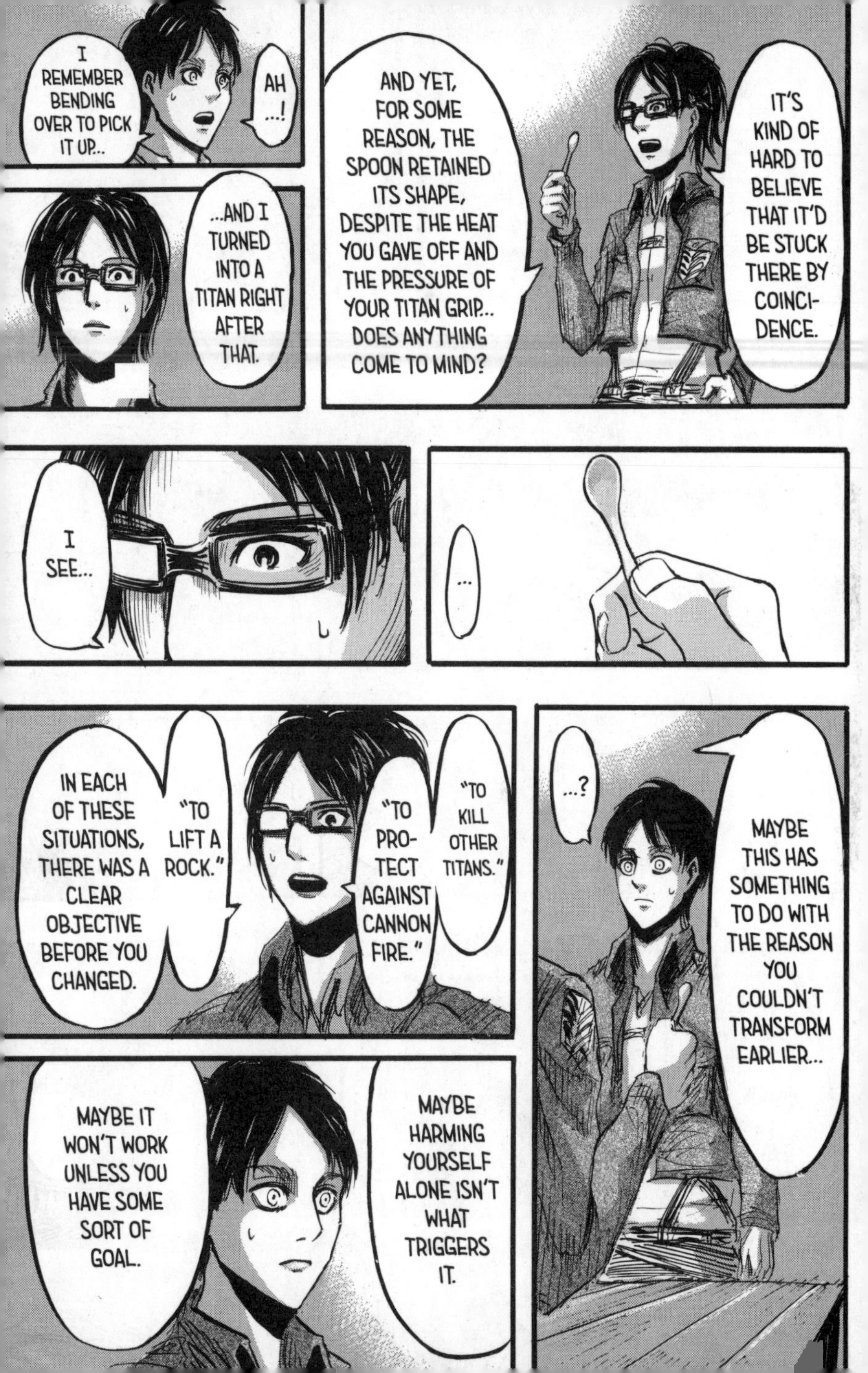
IT'S KIND OF HARD TO BELIEVE THAT IT'D BE STUCK THERE BY COINCIDENCE.
AND YET, FOR SOME REASON, THE SPOON RETAINED ITS SHAPE, DESPITE THE HEAT YOU GAVE OFF AND THE PRESSURE OF YOUR TITAN GRIP... DOES ANYTHING COME TO MIND?
AH ...!
I REMEMBER BENDING OVER TO PICK IT UP...
...AND I TURNED INTO A TITAN RIGHT AFTER THAT.
...
I SEE...
...?
MAYBE THIS HAS SOMETHING TO DO WITH THE REASON YOU COULDN'T TRANSFORM EARLIER...
"TO KILL OTHER TITANS."
"TO PROTECT AGAINST CANNON FIRE."
"TO LIFT A ROCK."
IN EACH OF THESE SITUATIONS, THERE WAS A CLEAR OBJECTIVE BEFORE YOU CHANGED.
MAYBE HARMING YOURSELF ALONE ISN'T WHAT TRIGGERS IT.
MAYBE IT WON'T WORK UNLESS YOU HAVE SOME SORT OF GOAL.

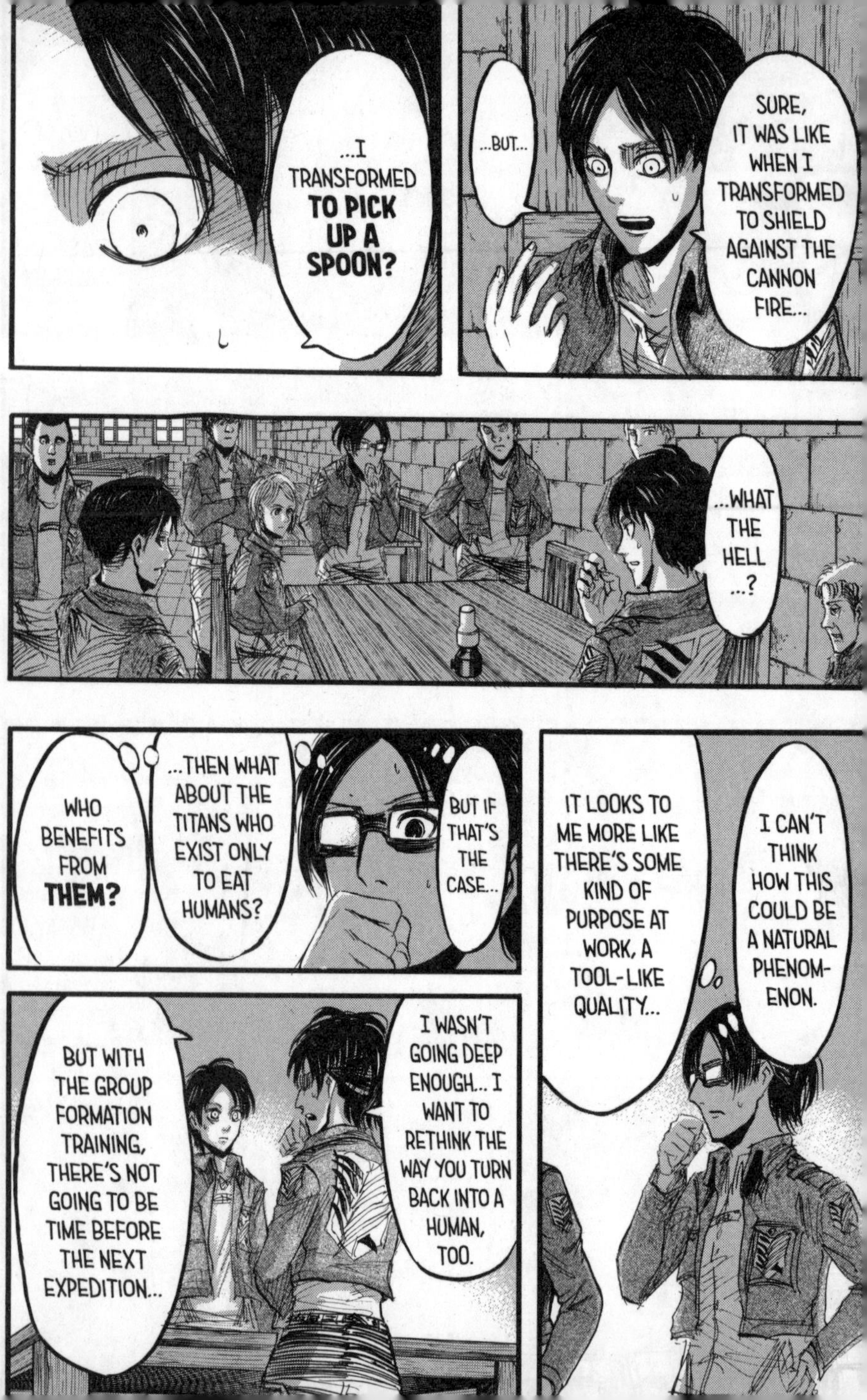
SURE, IT WAS LIKE WHEN I TRANSFORMED TO SHIELD AGAINST THE CANNON FIRE...
...BUT...
...I TRANSFORMED **TO PICK UP A SPOON?**
...WHAT THE HELL ...?
I CAN'T THINK HOW THIS COULD BE A NATURAL PHENOM-ENON.
IT LOOKS TO ME MORE LIKE THERE'S SOME KIND OF PURPOSE AT WORK, A TOOL-LIKE QUALITY...
BUT IF THAT'S THE CASE...
...THEN WHAT ABOUT THE TITANS WHO EXIST ONLY TO EAT HUMANS?
WHO BENEFITS FROM **THEM?**
I WASN'T GOING DEEP ENOUGH... I WANT TO RETHINK THE WAY YOU TURN BACK INTO A HUMAN, TOO.
BUT WITH THE GROUP FORMATION TRAINING, THERE'S NOT GOING TO BE TIME BEFORE THE NEXT EXPEDITION...

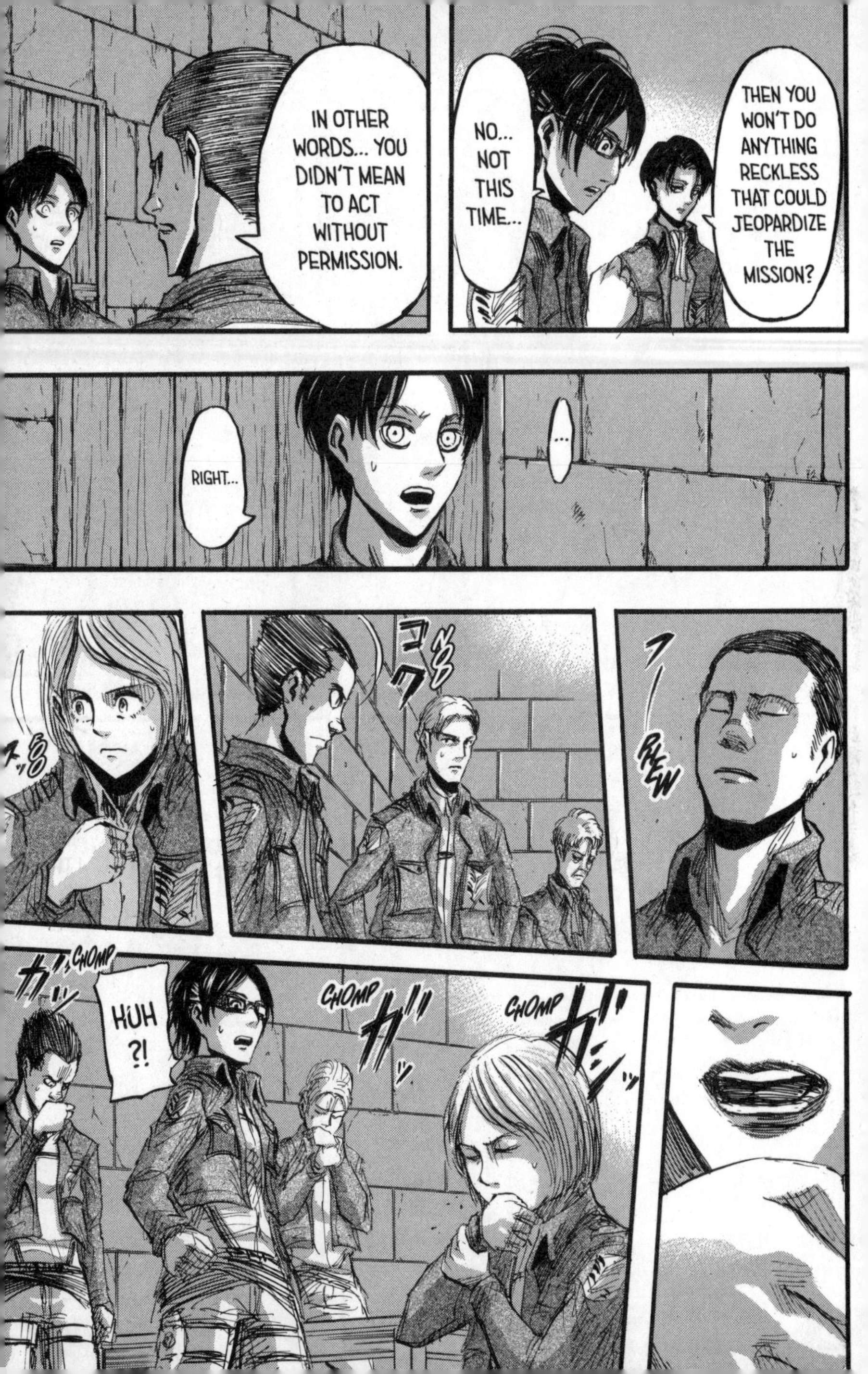
THEN YOU WON'T DO ANYTHING RECKLESS THAT COULD JEOPARDIZE THE MISSION?
NO... NOT THIS TIME...
IN OTHER WORDS... YOU DIDN'T MEAN TO ACT WITHOUT PERMISSION.
...
RIGHT...
PHEW
CHOMP
CHOMP
CHOMP
HUH ?!

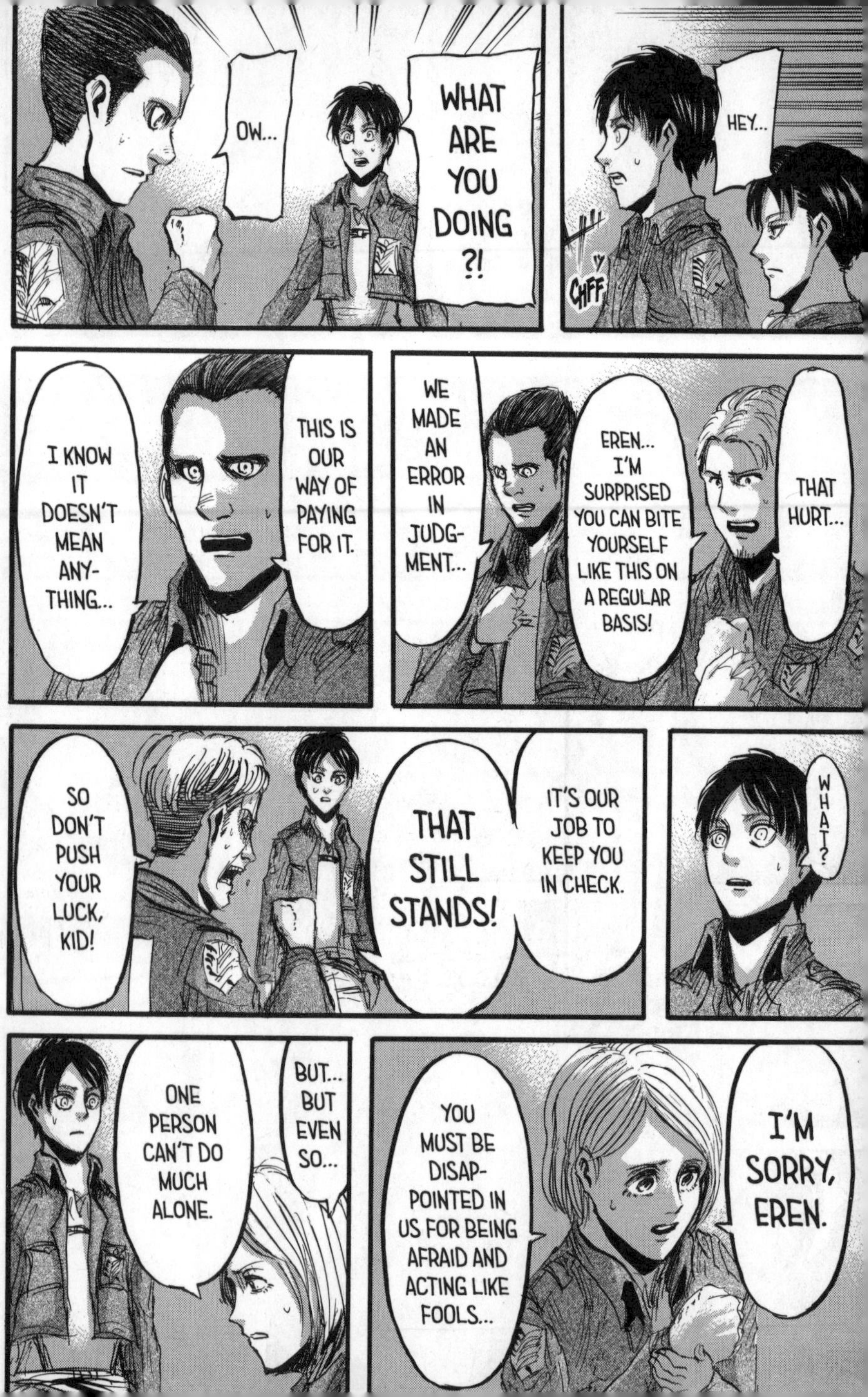
HEY...
CHFF
WHAT ARE YOU DOING ?!
OW...
THAT HURT...
EREN... I'M SURPRISED YOU CAN BITE YOURSELF LIKE THIS ON A REGULAR BASIS!
WE MADE AN ERROR IN JUDG-MENT...
THIS IS OUR WAY OF PAYING FOR IT.
I KNOW IT DOESN'T MEAN ANY-THING...
WHAT?
IT'S OUR JOB TO KEEP YOU IN CHECK.
THAT STILL STANDS!
SO DON'T PUSH YOUR LUCK, KID!
I'M SORRY, EREN.
YOU MUST BE DISAP-POINTED IN US FOR BEING AFRAID AND ACTING LIKE FOOLS...
BUT... BUT EVEN SO...
ONE PERSON CAN'T DO MUCH ALONE.

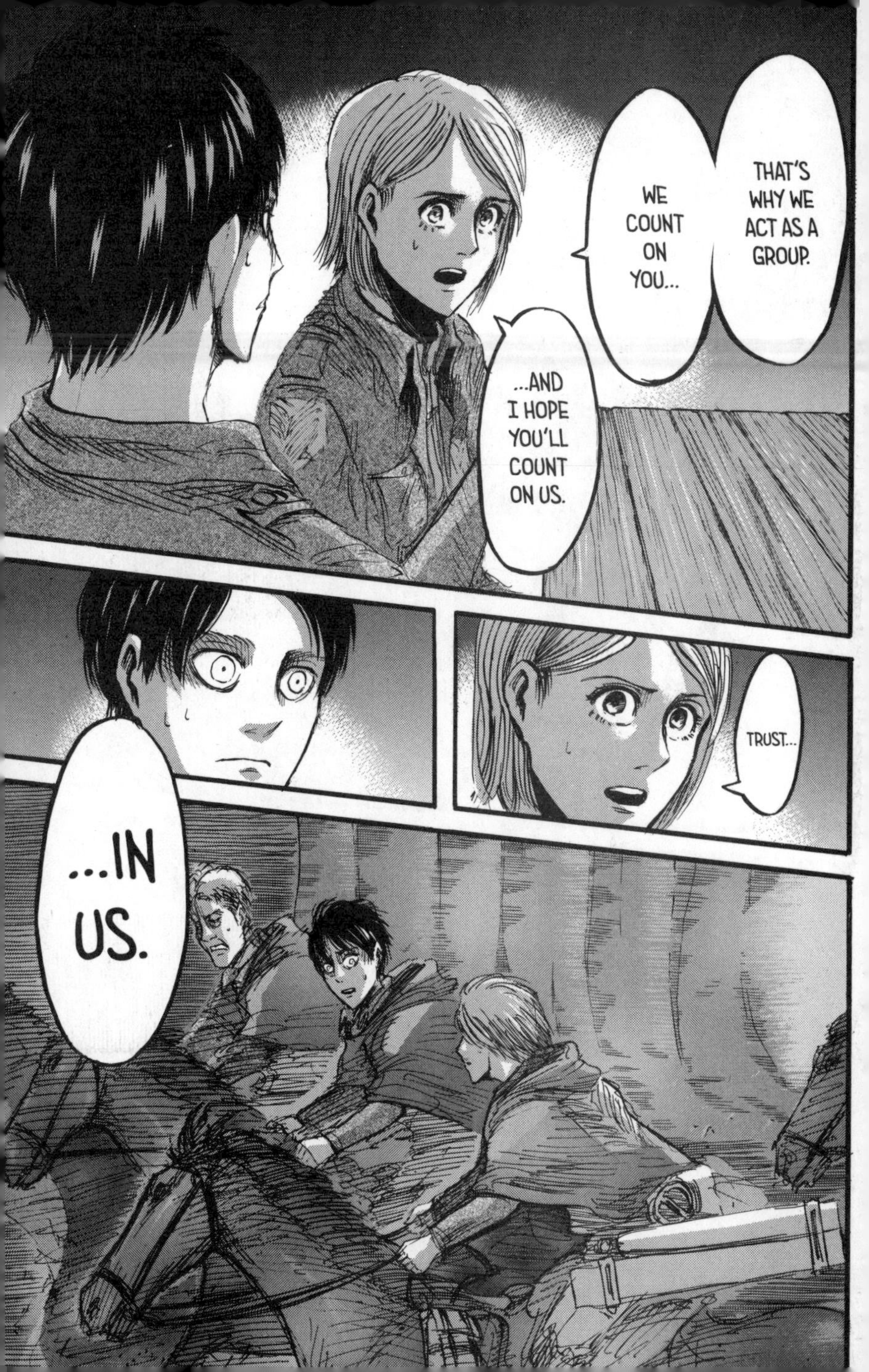
THAT'S WHY WE ACT AS A GROUP.
WE COUNT ON YOU...
...AND I HOPE YOU'LL COUNT ON US.
TRUST...
...IN US.

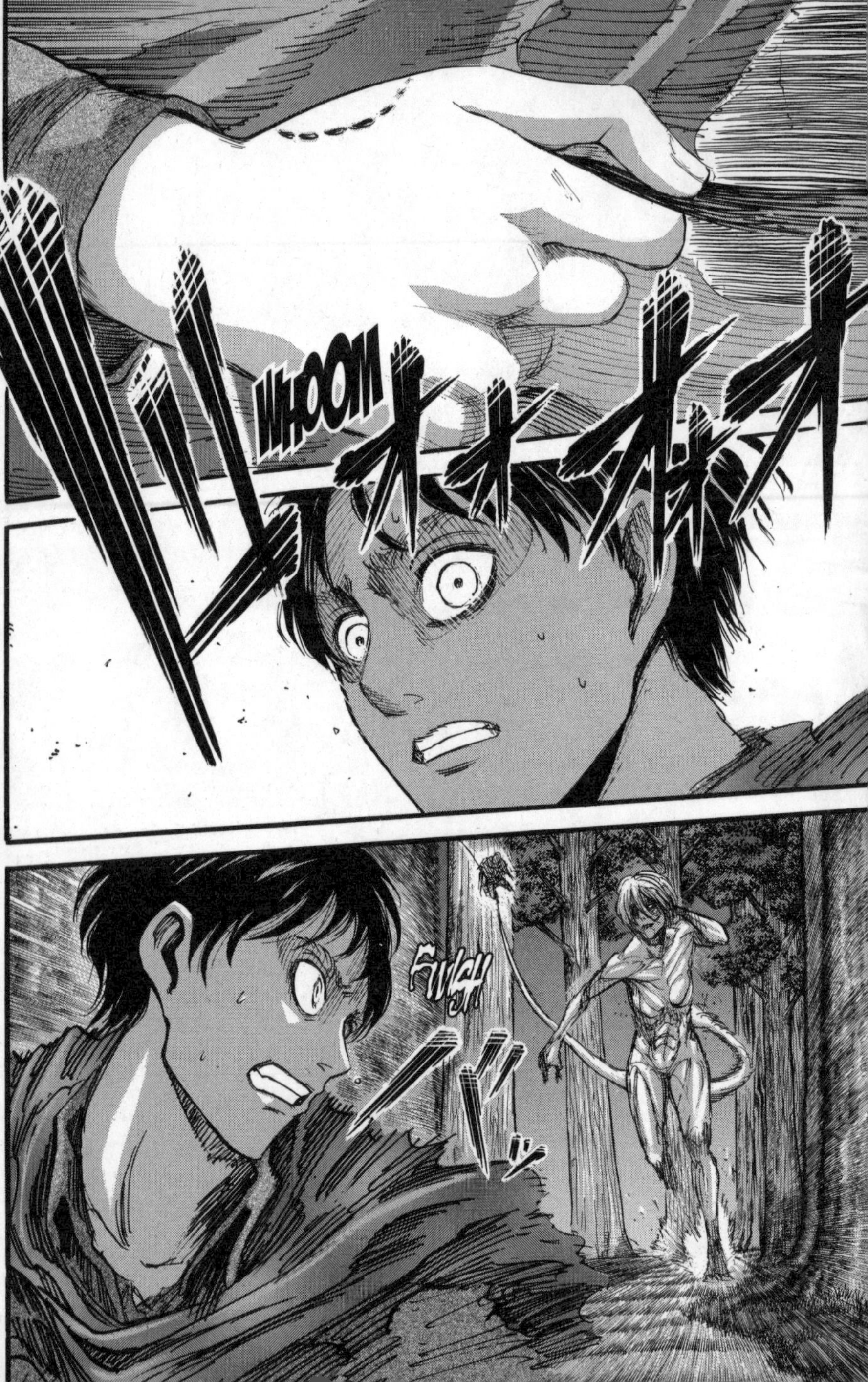
WHOOM
FWISH

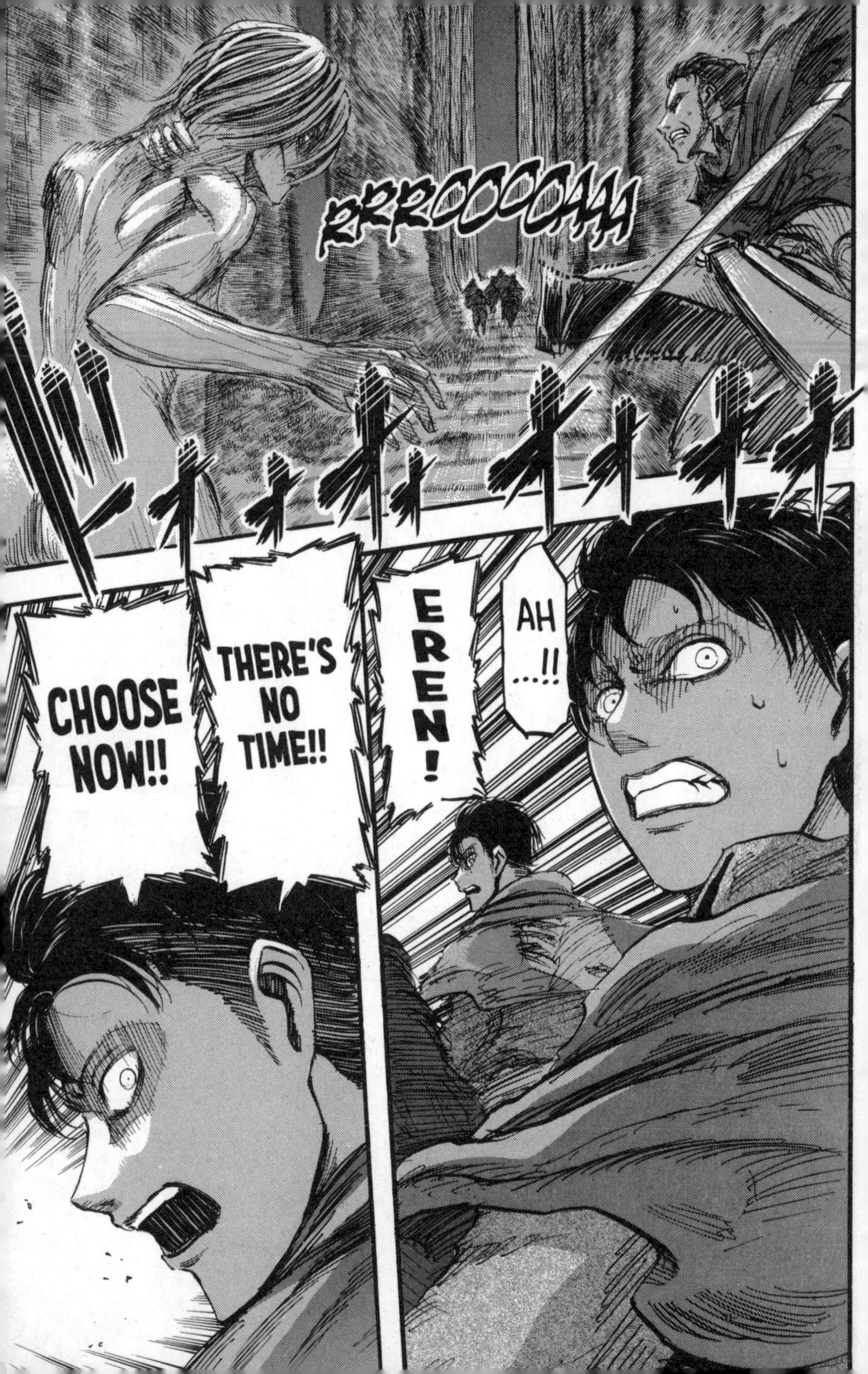
KRRROOOOAAA
AH
...!!
EREN!
THERE'S NO TIME!!
CHOOSE NOW!!

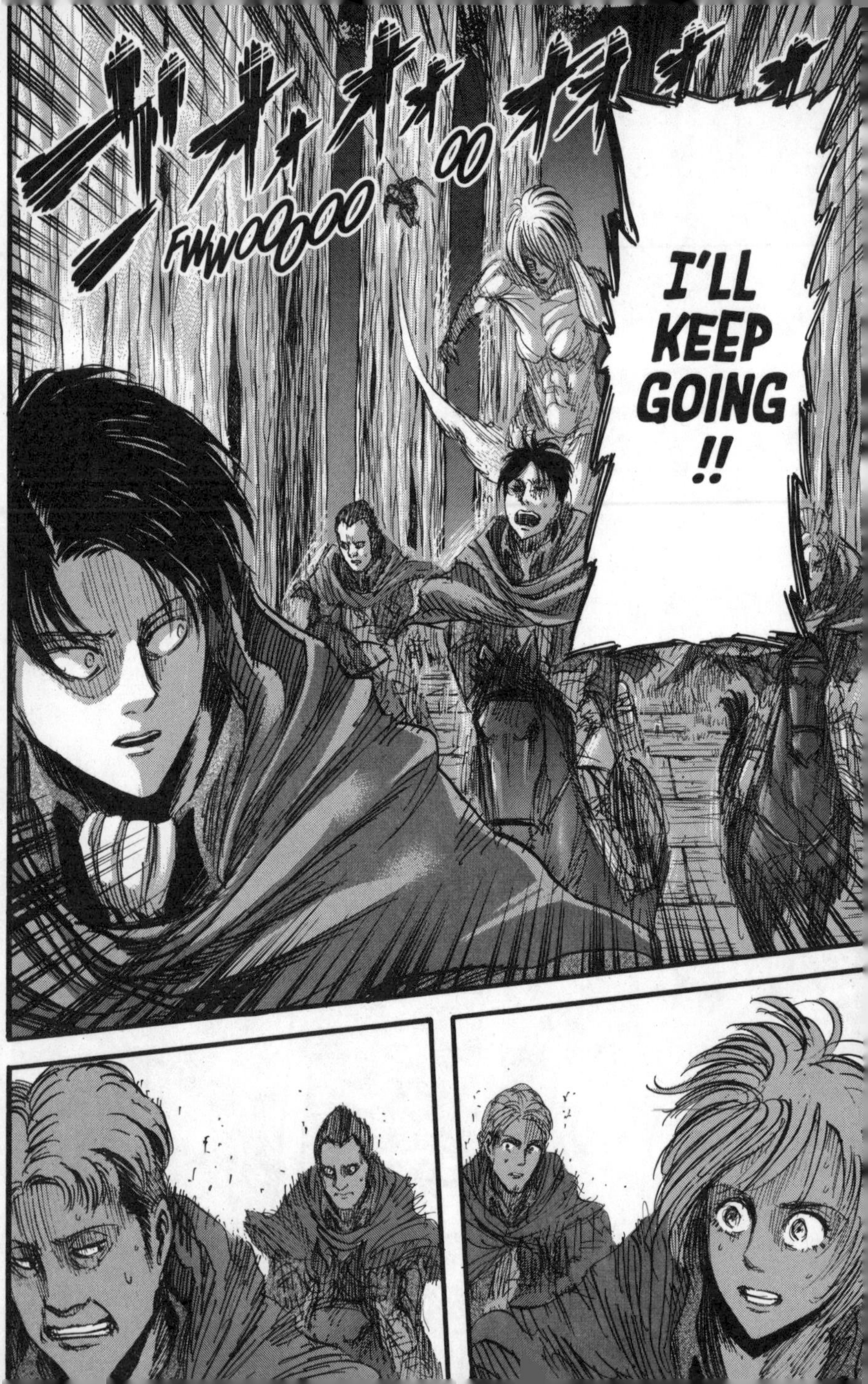
FWWOOOOOOO
I'LL KEEP GOING !!

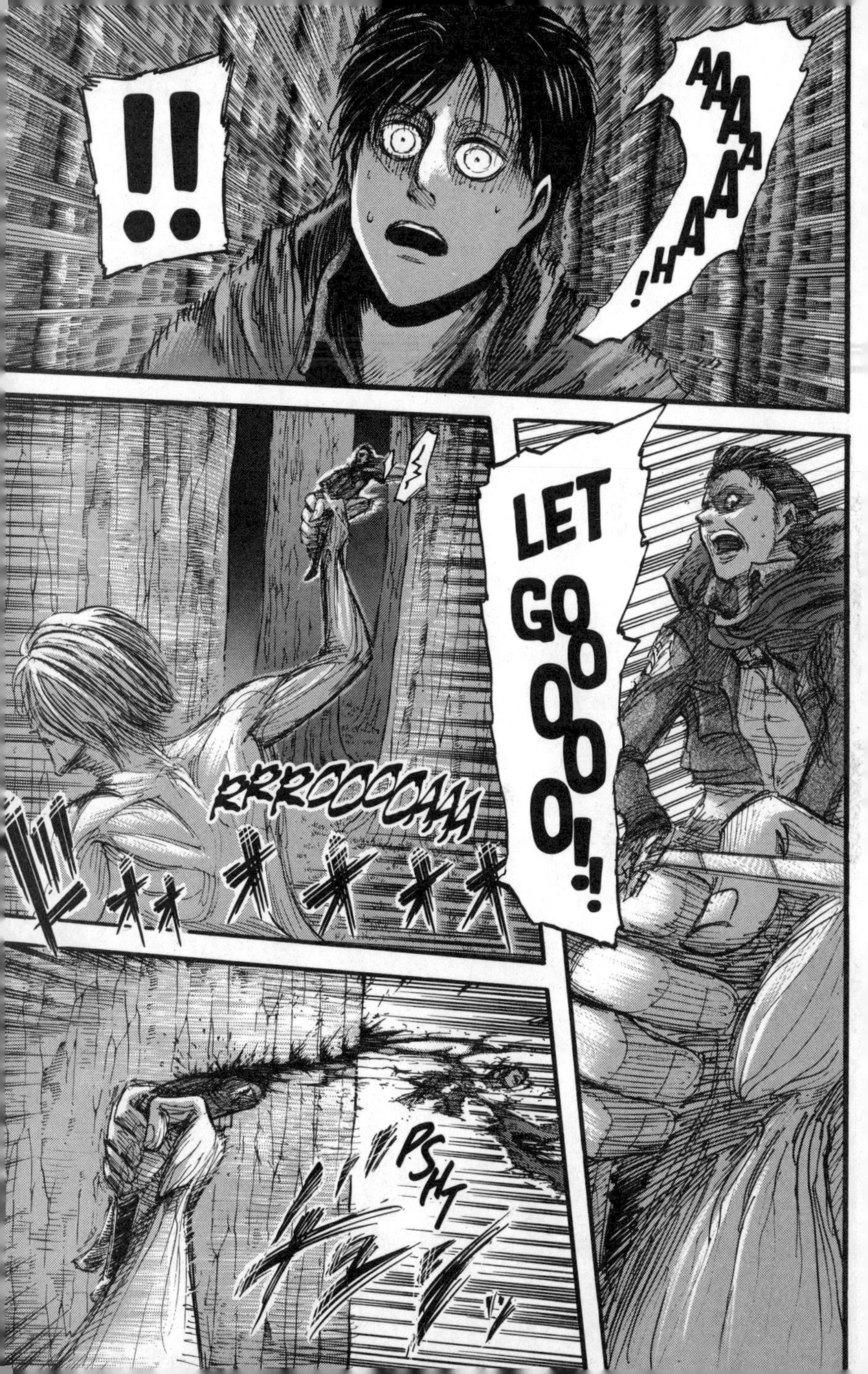
AAAAAAAH!
!!
LET GOOOOOOO!!
RRRROOOOAAA
PSHT

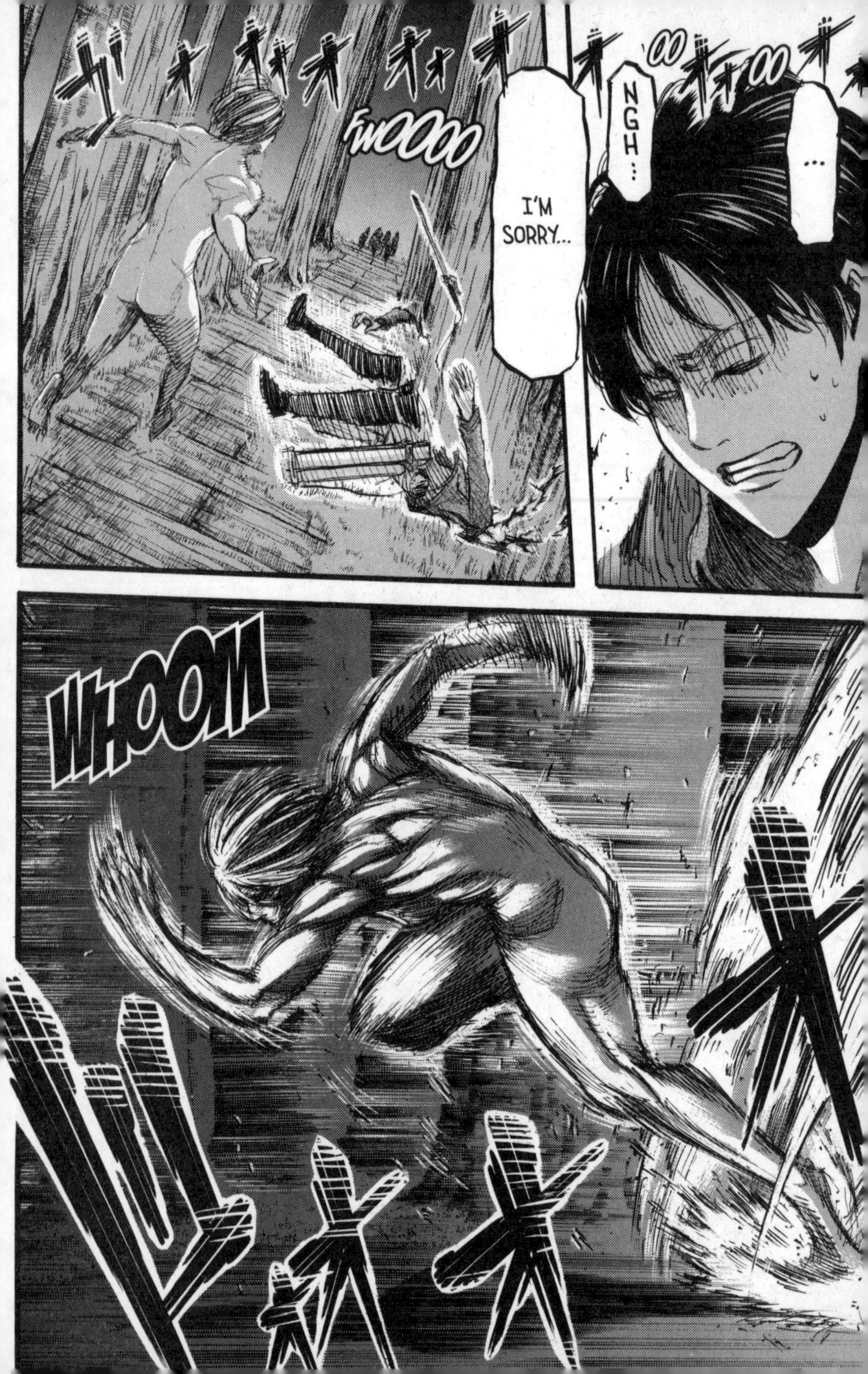
...
OO
OO
NGH...
I'M SORRY...
FWOOOO
WHOOM

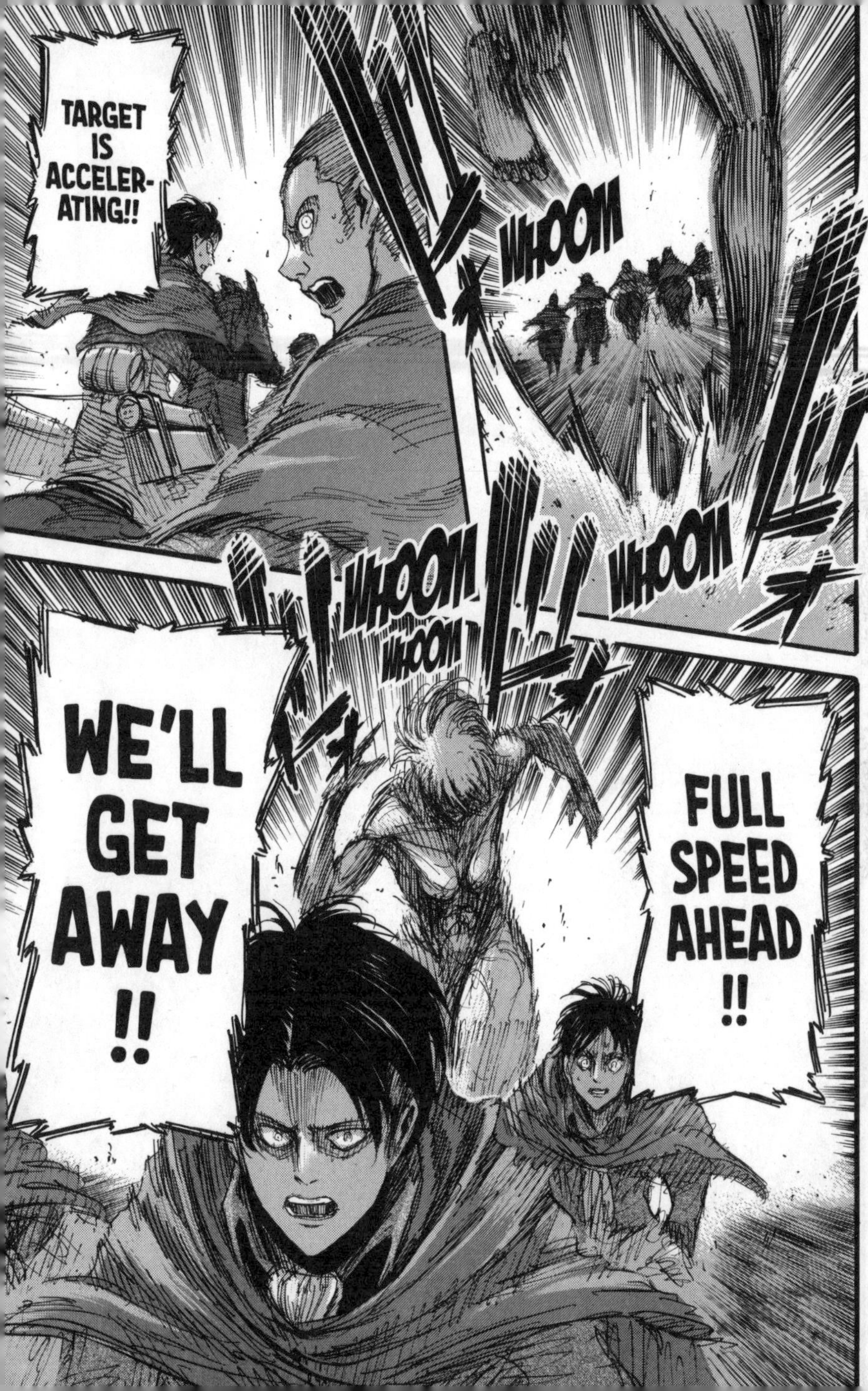
WHOOM
WHOOM
WHOOM
WHOOM
TARGET IS ACCELERATING!!
FULL SPEED AHEAD!!
WE'LL GET AWAY!!

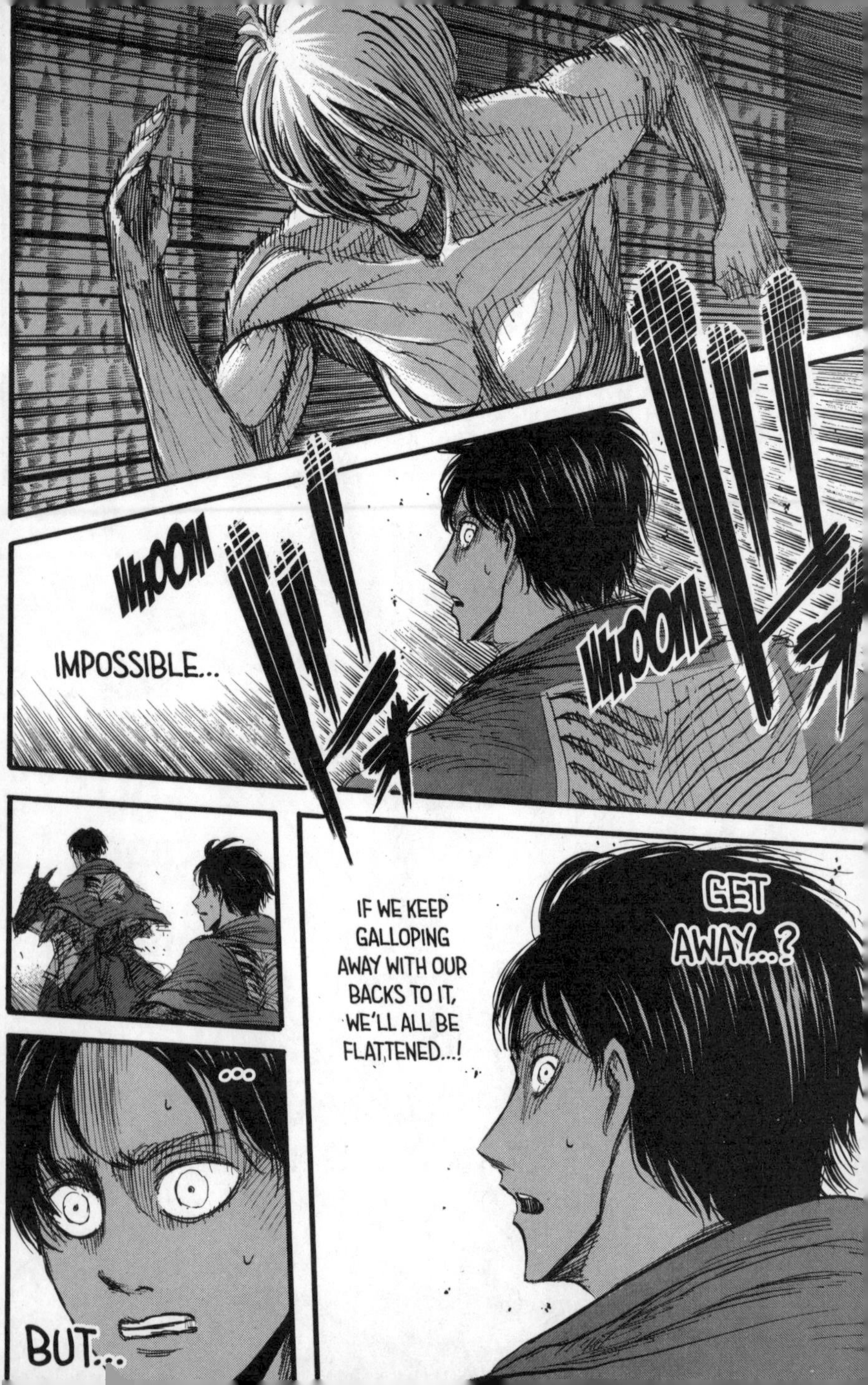
WHOOM
WHOOM
IMPOSSIBLE...
GET AWAY...?
IF WE KEEP GALLOPING AWAY WITH OUR BACKS TO IT, WE'LL ALL BE FLATTENED...!
BUT...

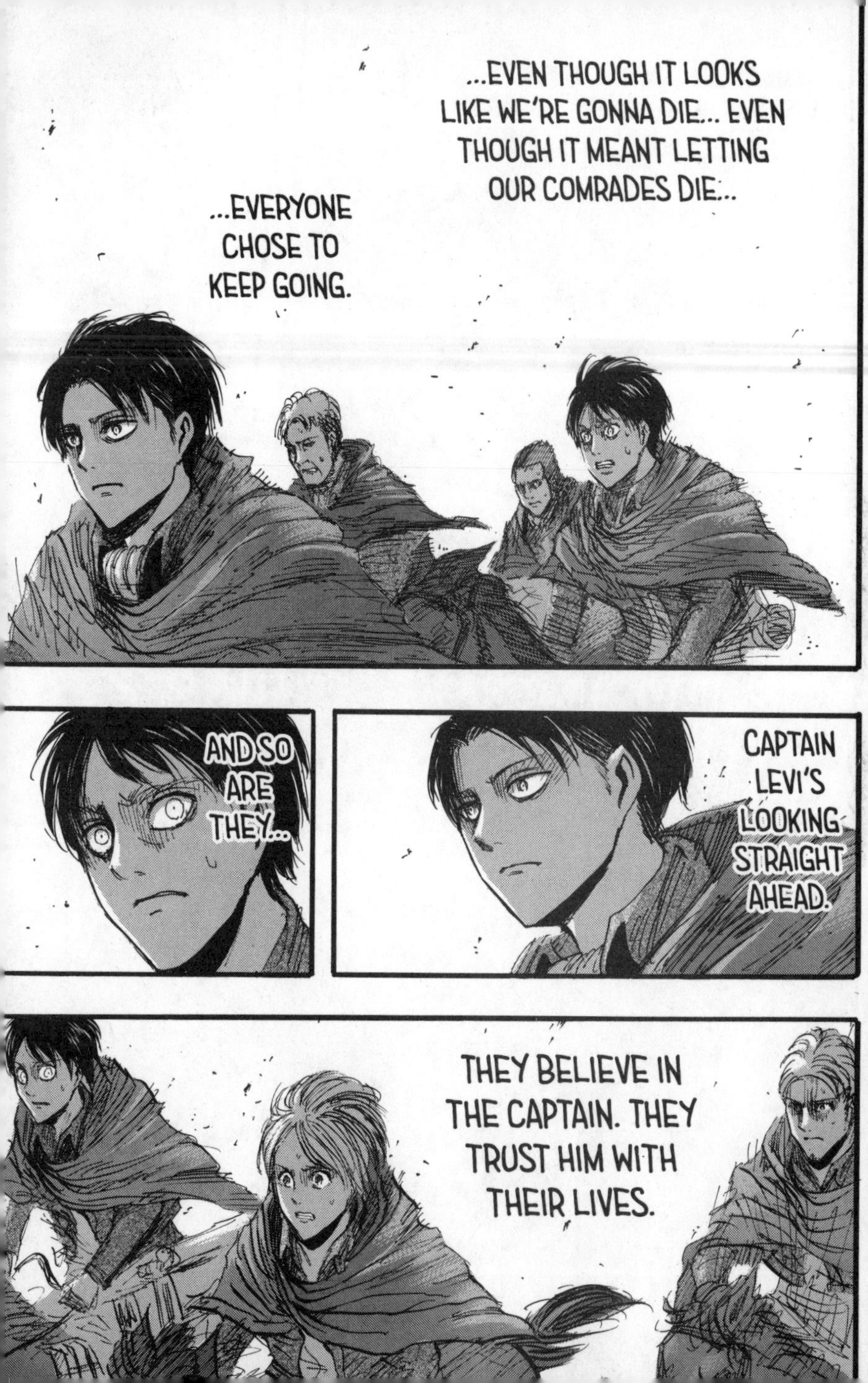
...EVEN THOUGH IT LOOKS LIKE WE'RE GONNA DIE... EVEN THOUGH IT MEANT LETTING OUR COMRADES DIE...
...EVERYONE CHOSE TO KEEP GOING.
CAPTAIN LEVI'S LOOKING STRAIGHT AHEAD.
AND SO ARE THEY...
THEY BELIEVE IN THE CAPTAIN. THEY TRUST HIM WITH THEIR LIVES.

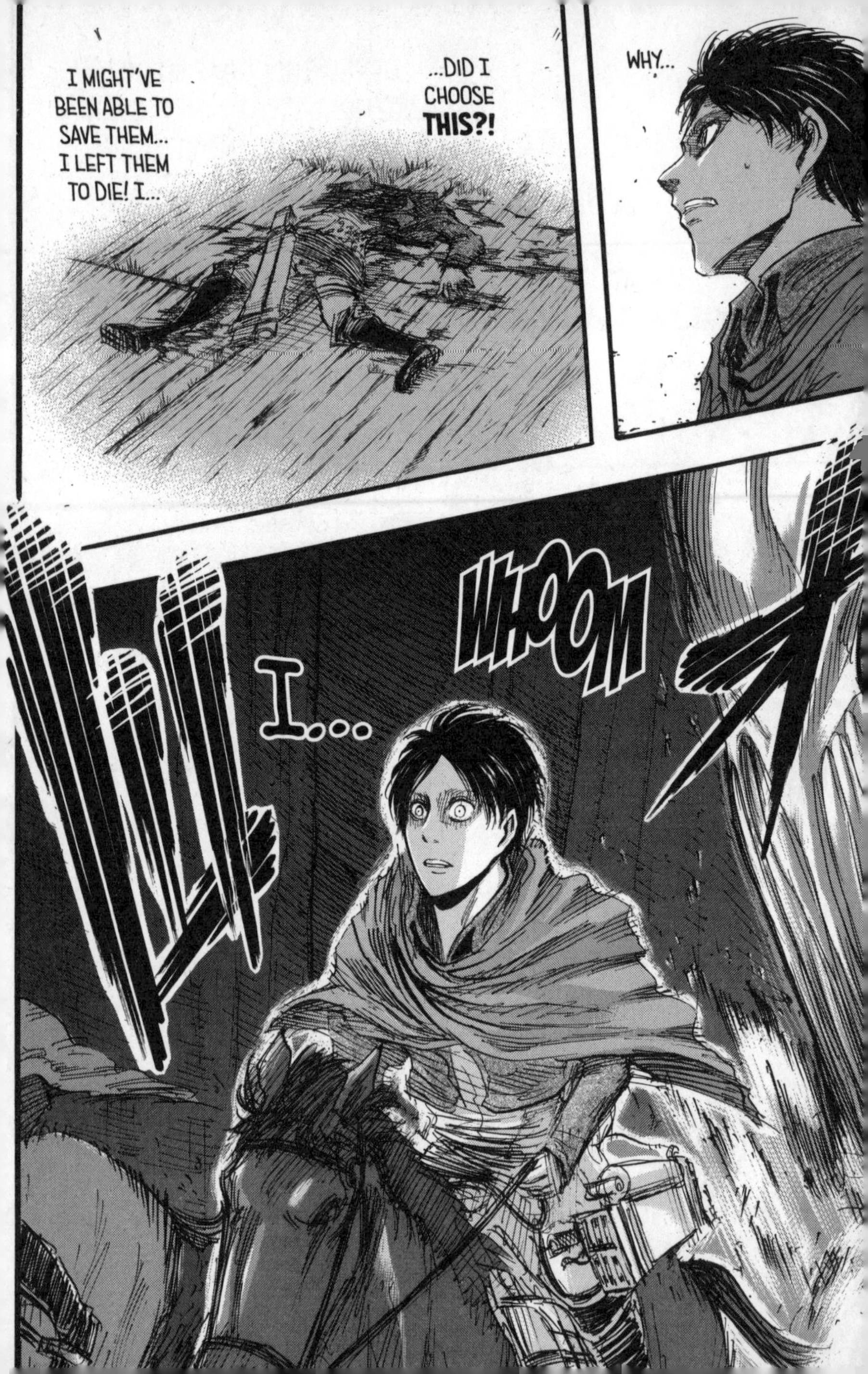

WHY...
...DID I CHOOSE THIS?!
I MIGHT'VE BEEN ABLE TO SAVE THEM... I LEFT THEM TO DIE! I...
WHOOM
I...

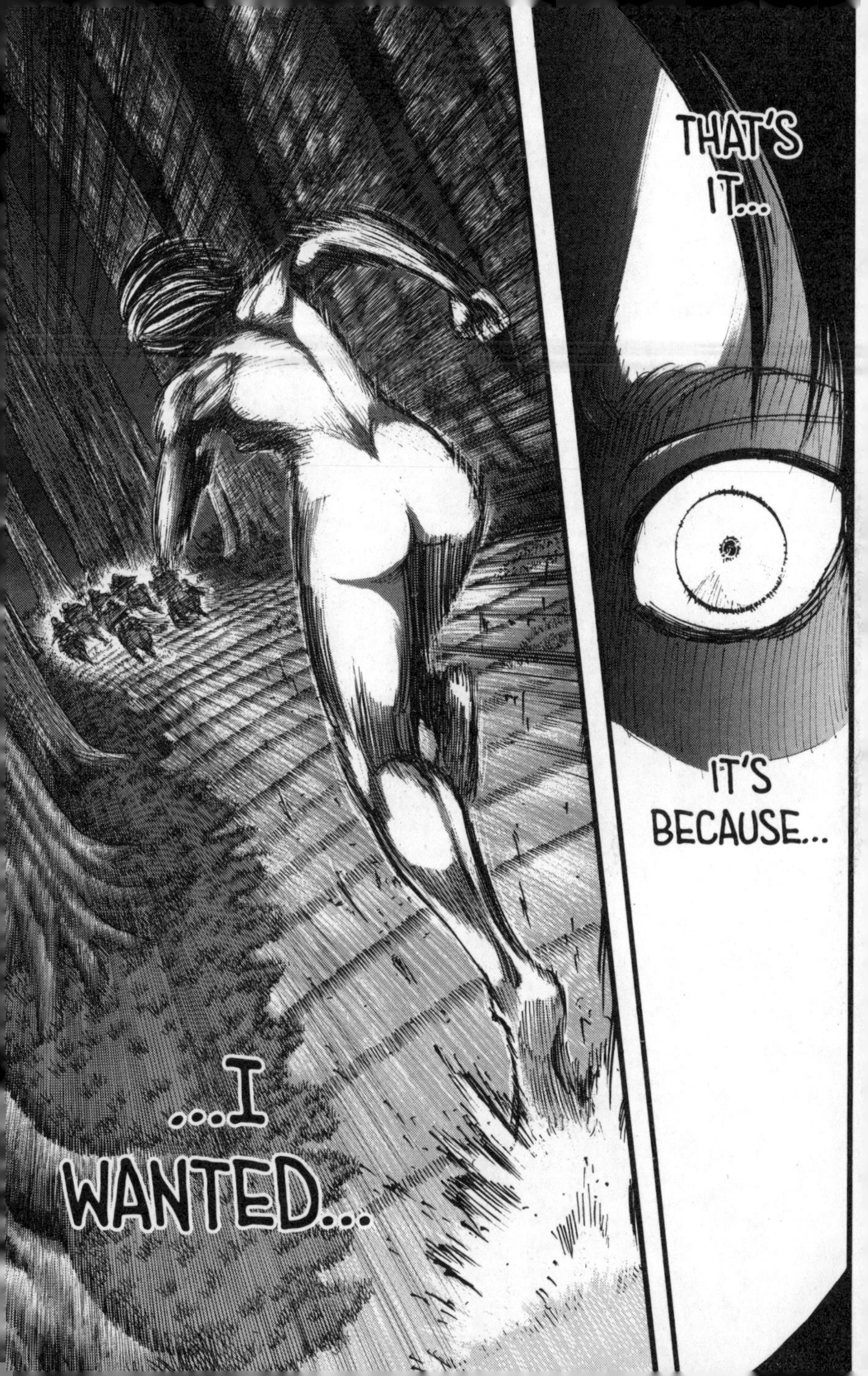
THAT'S IT...
IT'S BECAUSE...
...I WANTED...

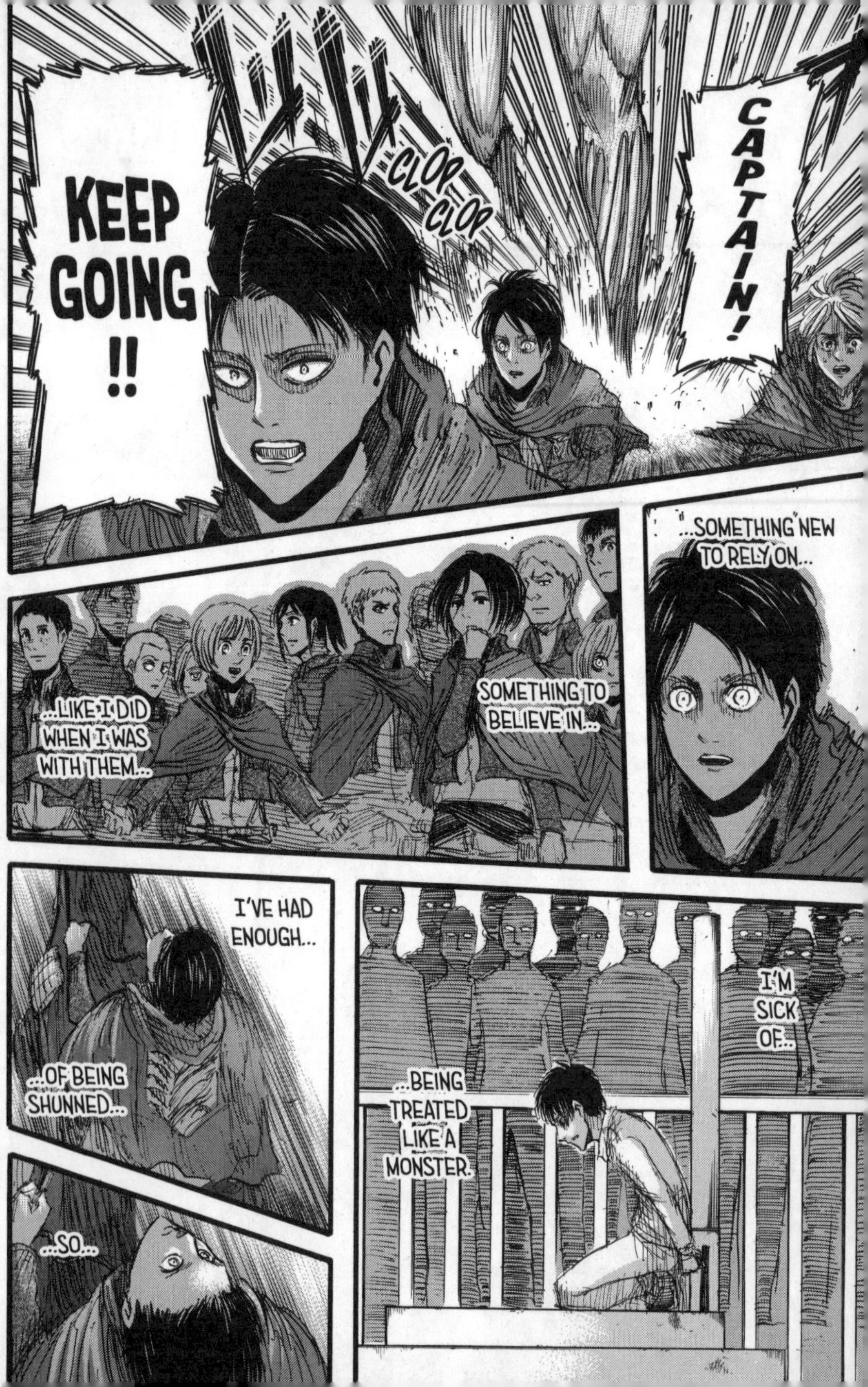
CAPTAIN!
CLOP CLOP
KEEP GOING!!
...SOMETHING NEW TO RELY ON...
SOMETHING TO BELIEVE IN...
...LIKE I DID WHEN I WAS WITH THEM...
I'M SICK OF...
...BEING TREATED LIKE A MONSTER.
I'VE HAD ENOUGH...
...OF BEING SHUNNED...
...SO...

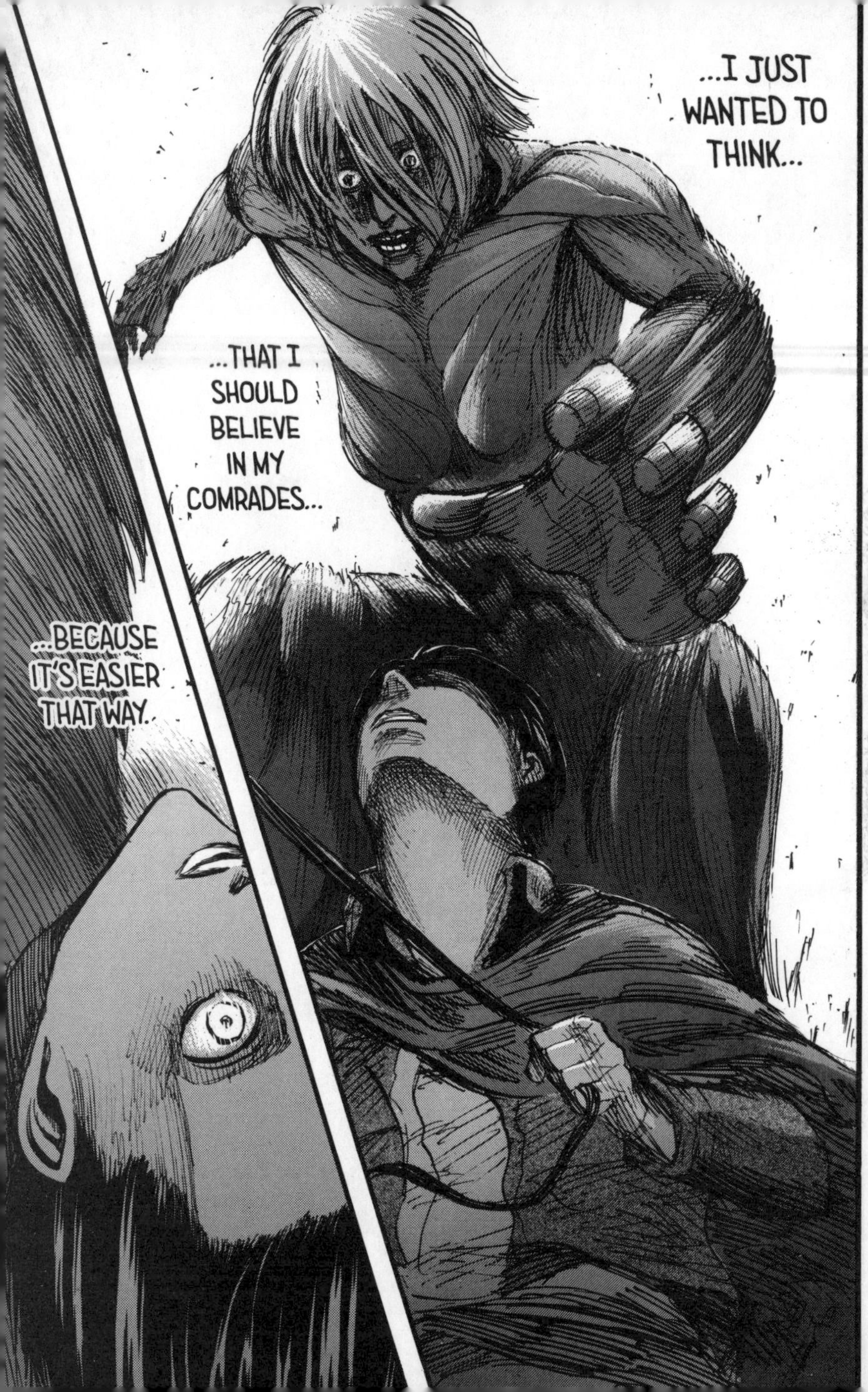
...I JUST WANTED TO THINK...
...THAT I SHOULD BELIEVE IN MY COMRADES...
...BECAUSE IT'S EASIER THAT WAY.

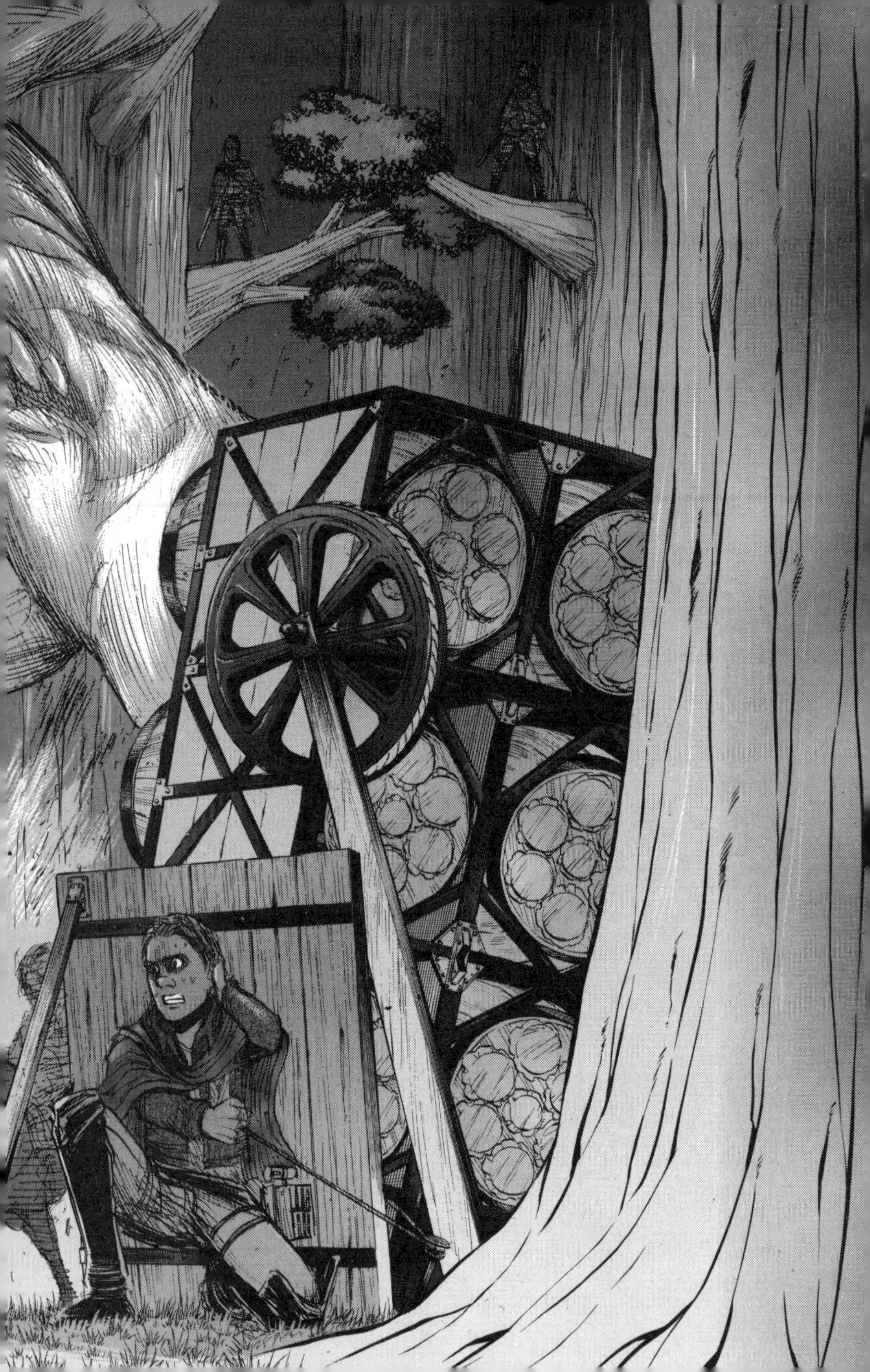

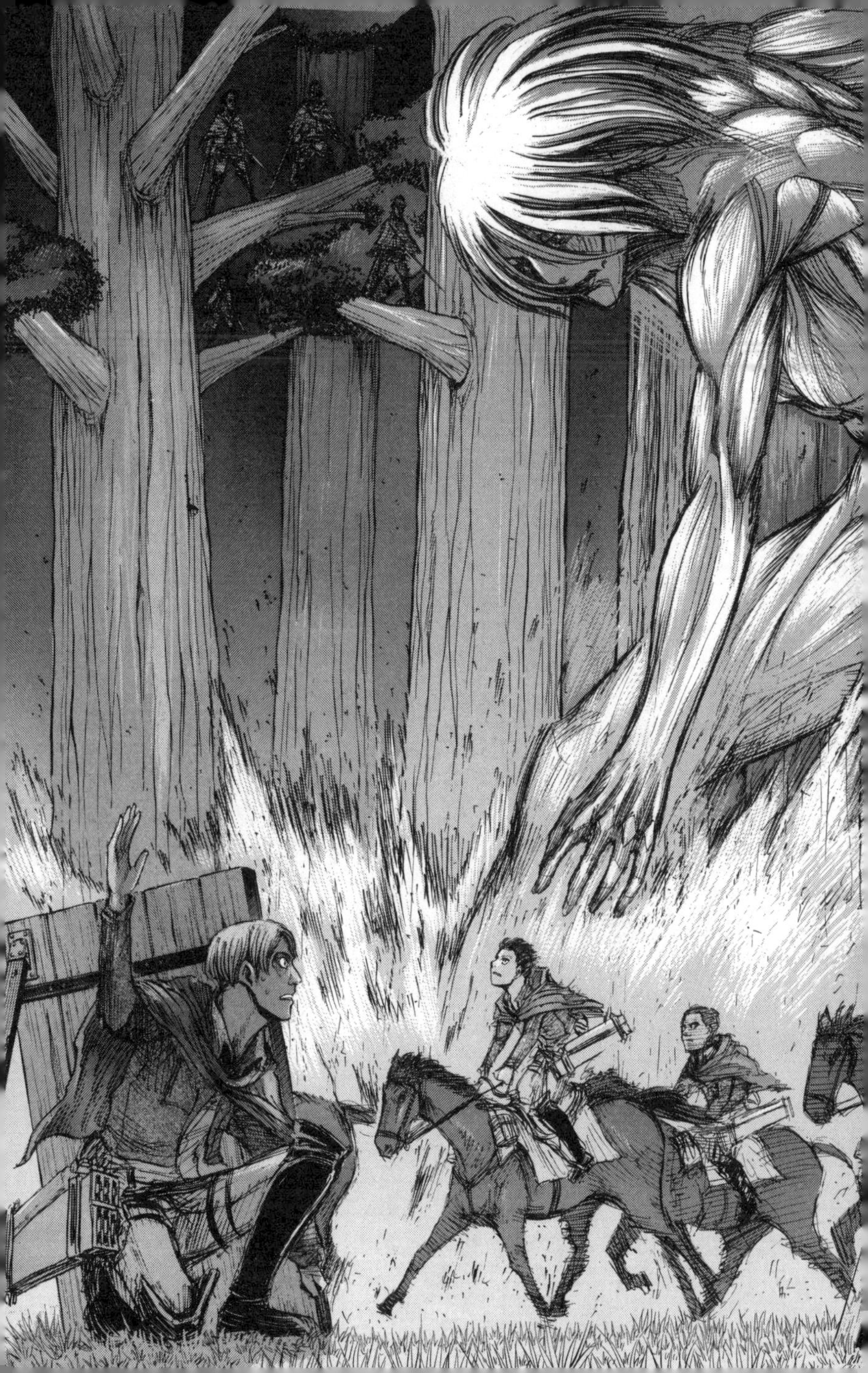

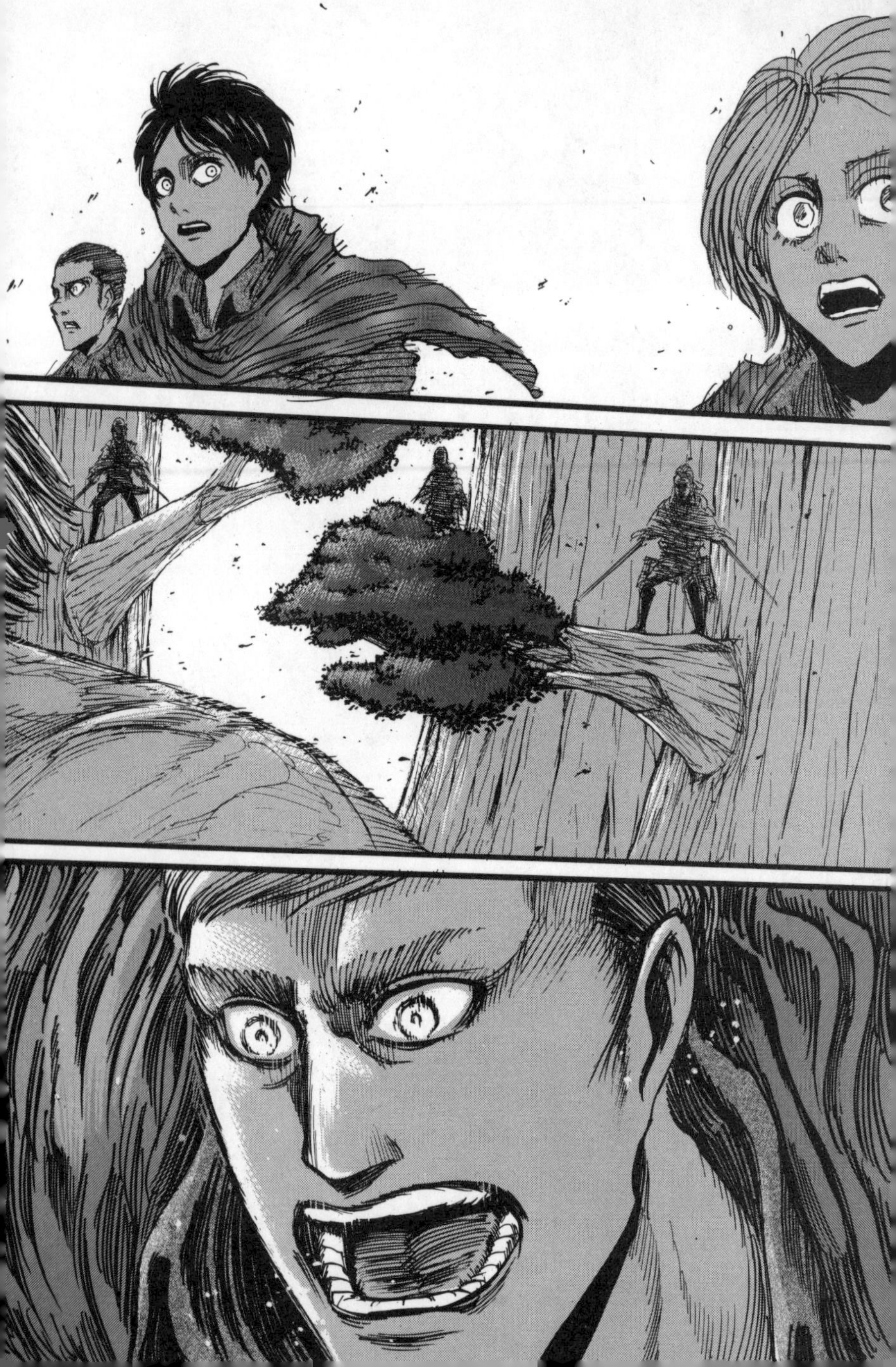

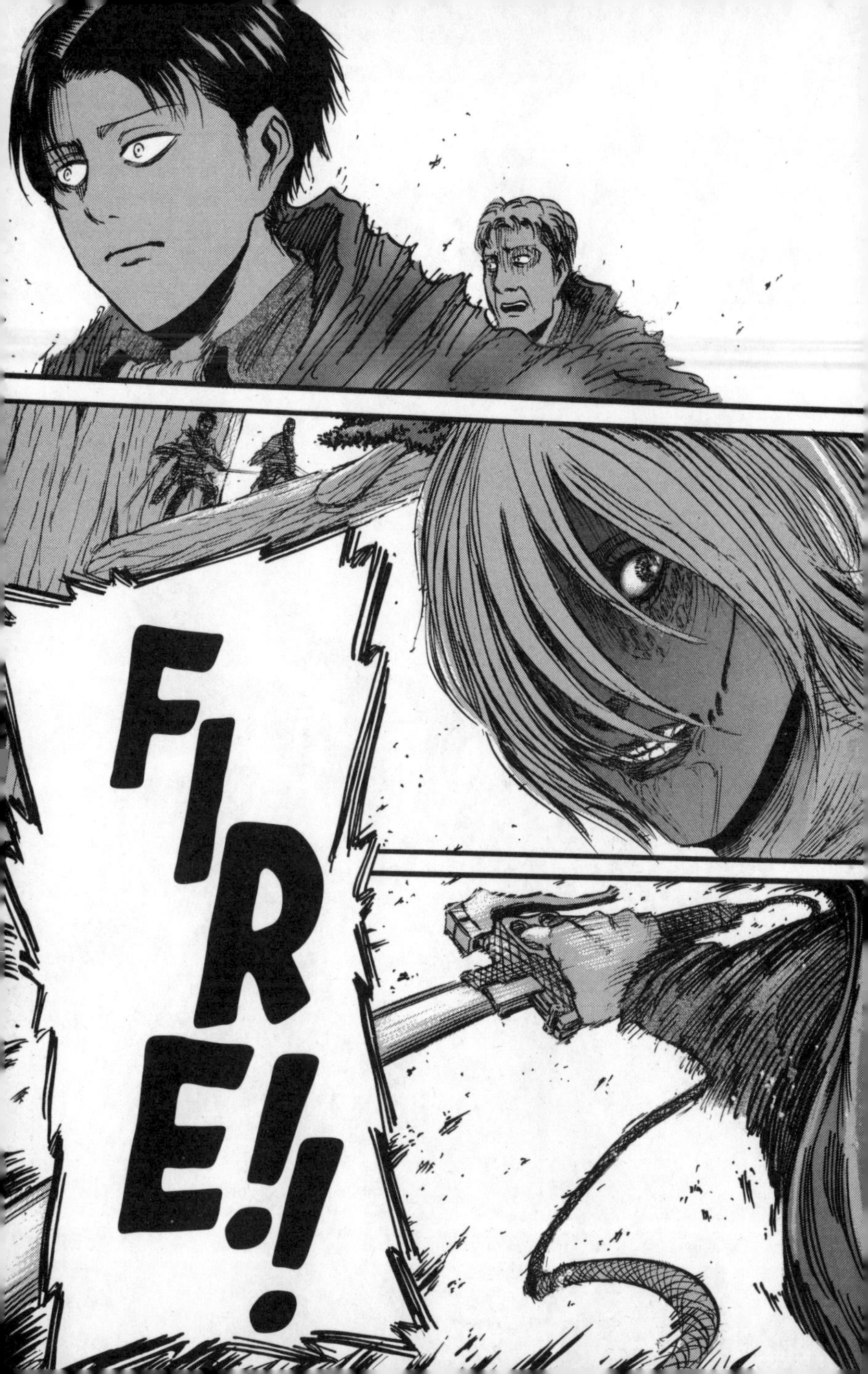
FIRE!!

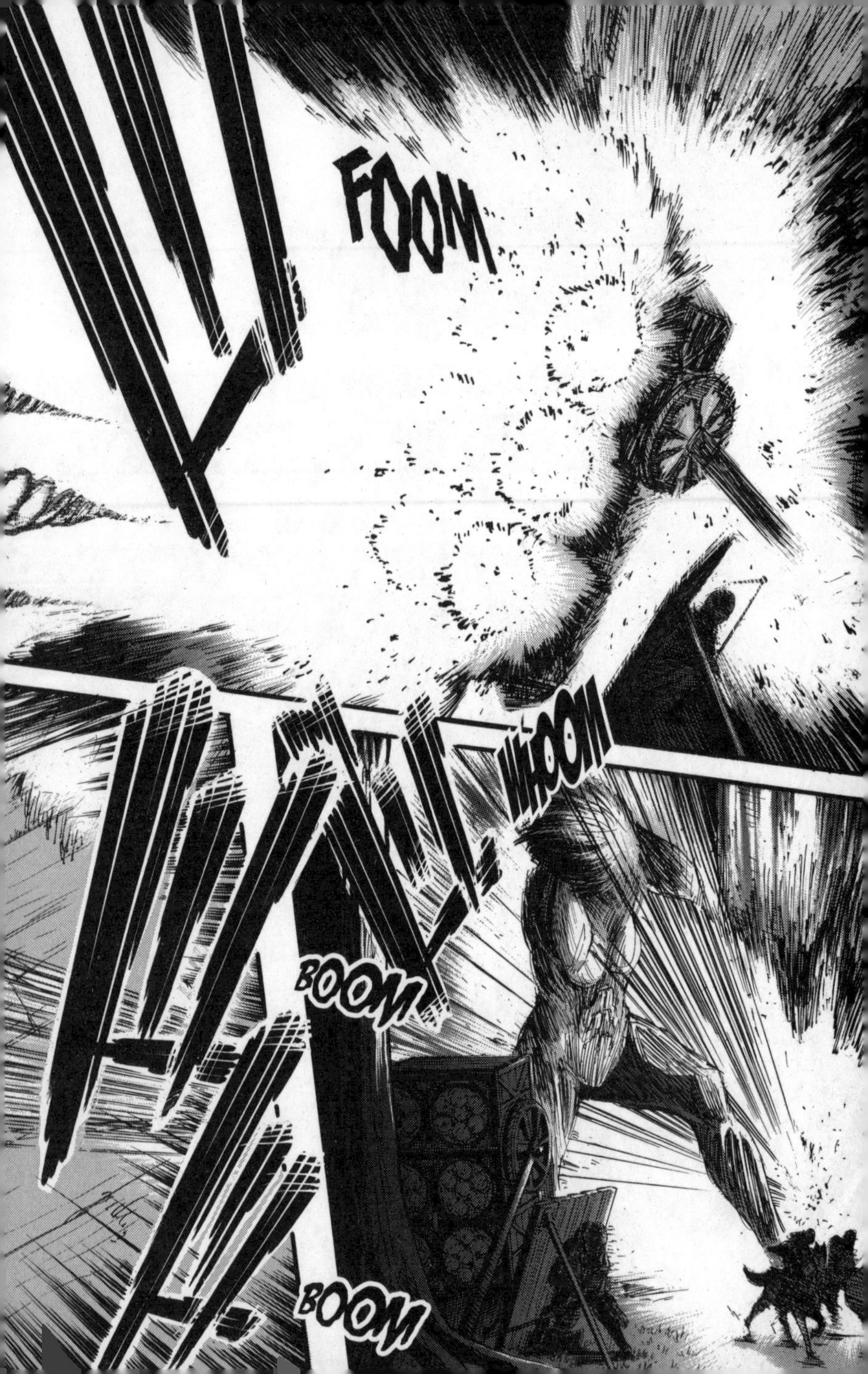
FOOM
WHOOM
BOOM
BOOM

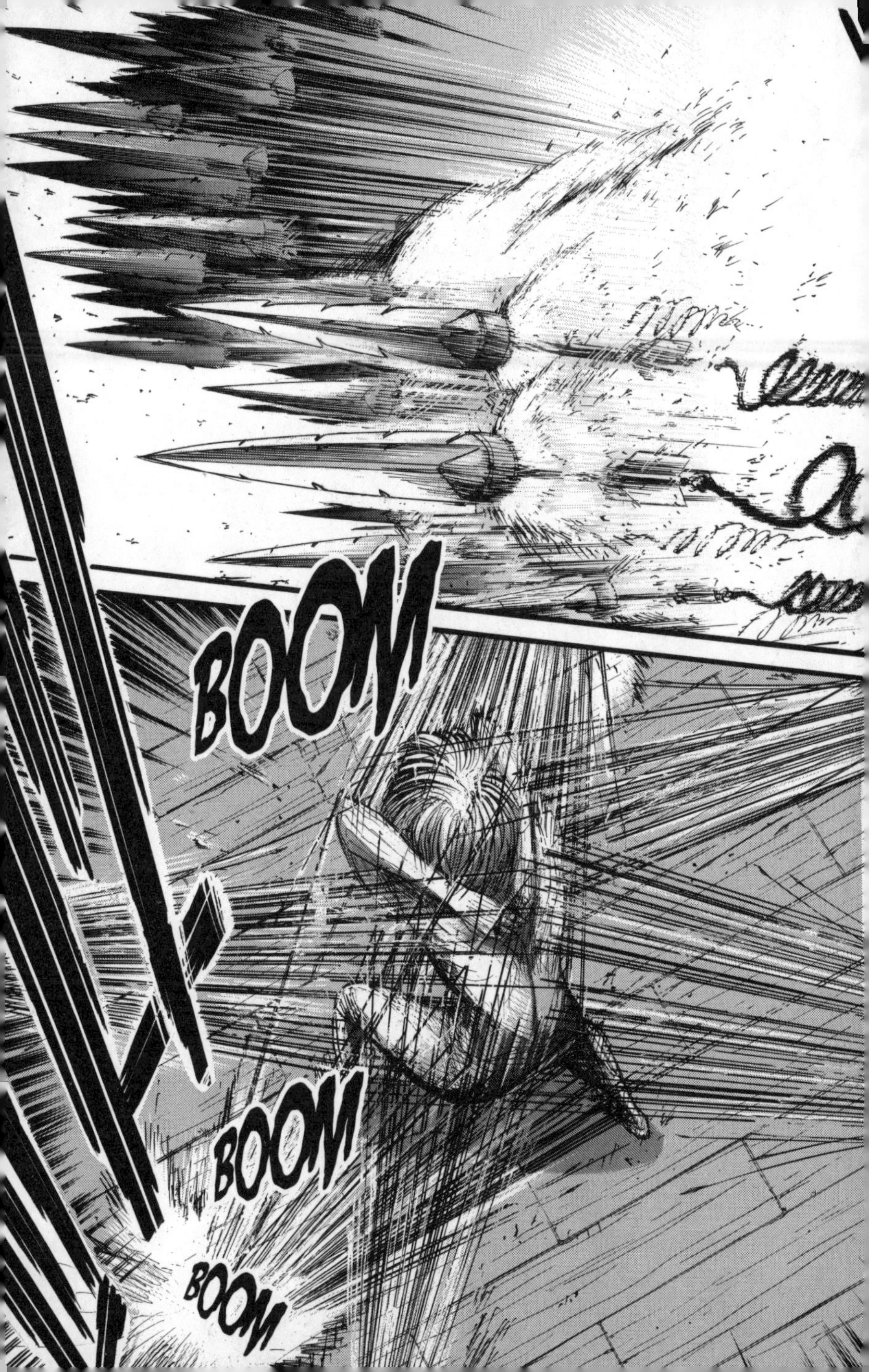
BOOM
BOOM
BOOM

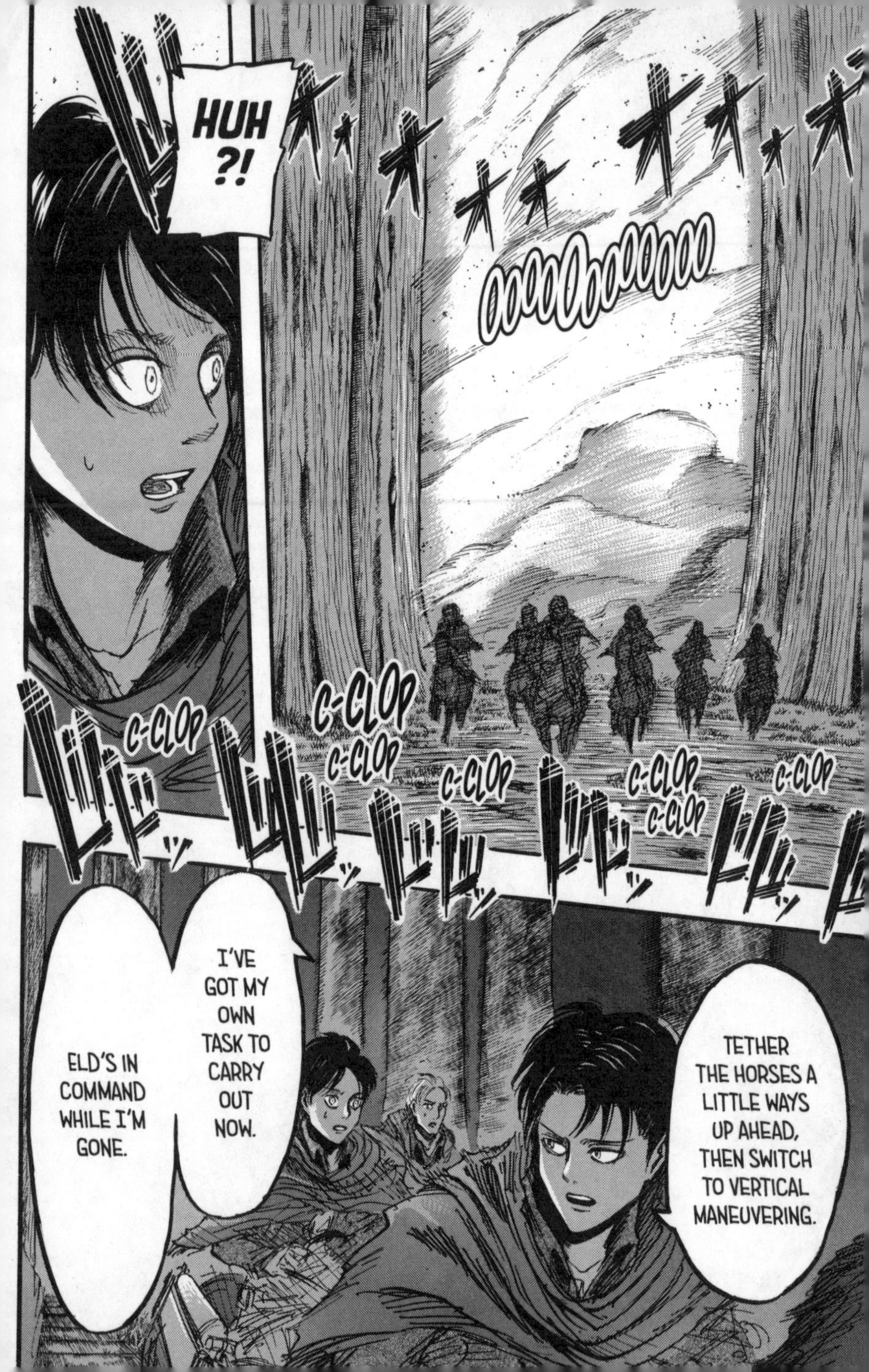
OOOOOOOOOOOO
C-CLOP C-CLOP
C-CLOP
C-CLOP C-CLOP
C-CLOP
C-CLOP
HUH ?!
TETHER THE HORSES A LITTLE WAYS UP AHEAD, THEN SWITCH TO VERTICAL MANEUVERING.
I'VE GOT MY OWN TASK TO CARRY OUT NOW.
ELD'S IN COMMAND WHILE I'M GONE.

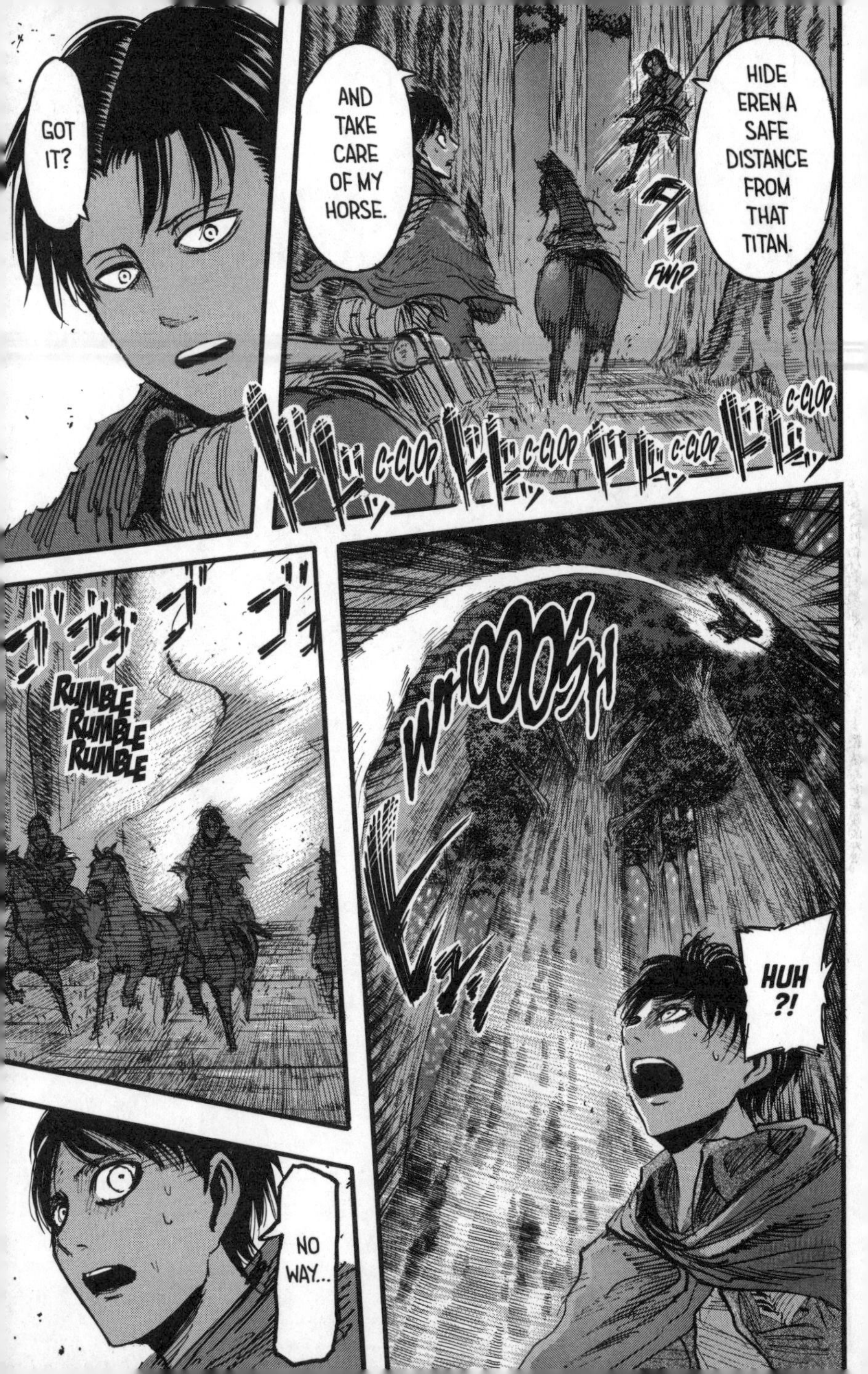
HIDE EREN A SAFE DISTANCE FROM THAT TITAN.
FWIP
AND TAKE CARE OF MY HORSE.
C-CLOP C-CLOP C-CLOP C-CLOP
GOT IT?
WHOOOOSH
HUH ?!
RUMBLE RUMBLE RUMBLE
NO WAY...

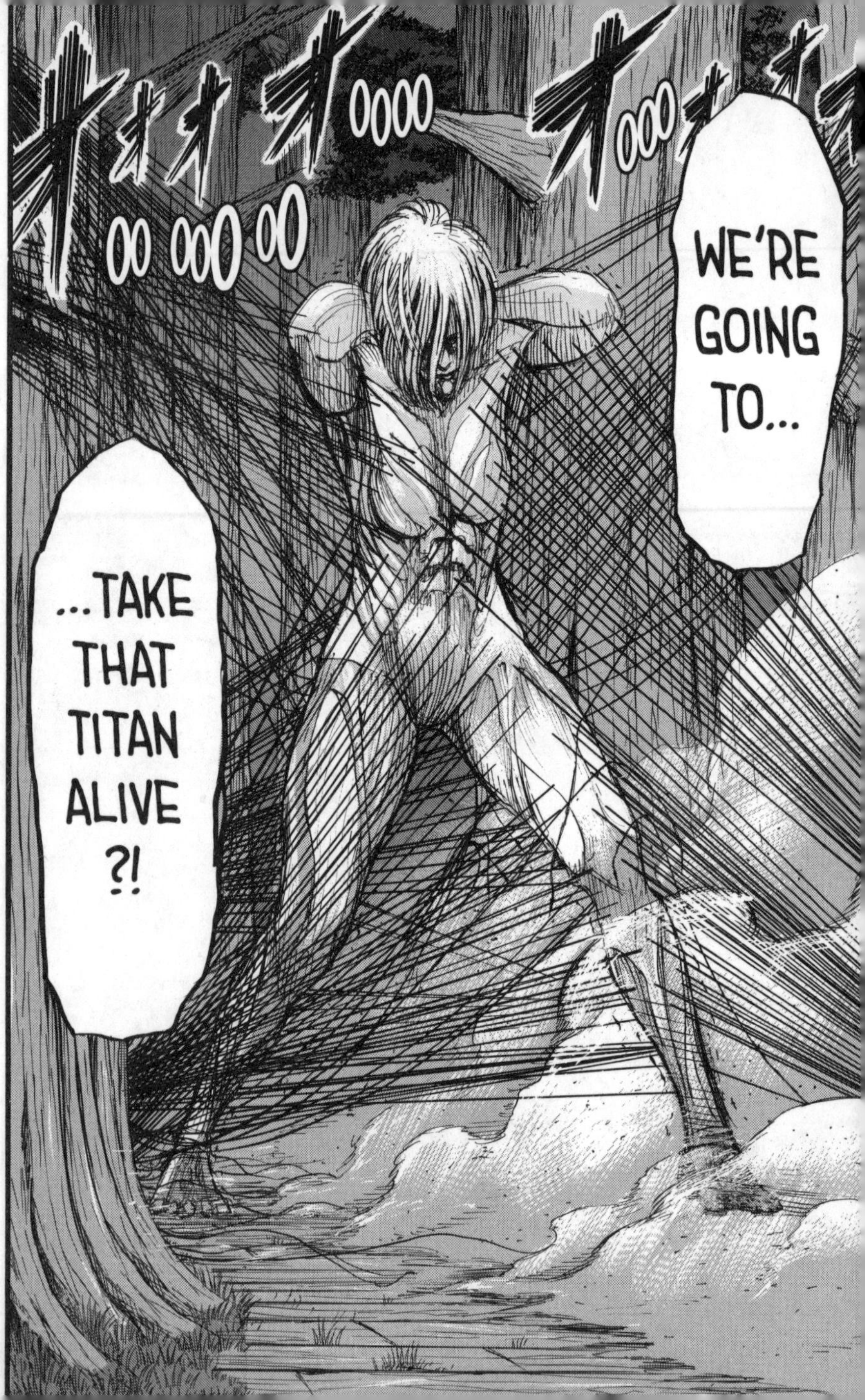
OOO
WE'RE GOING TO...
OOOO
OO OOO OO
...TAKE THAT TITAN ALIVE ?!

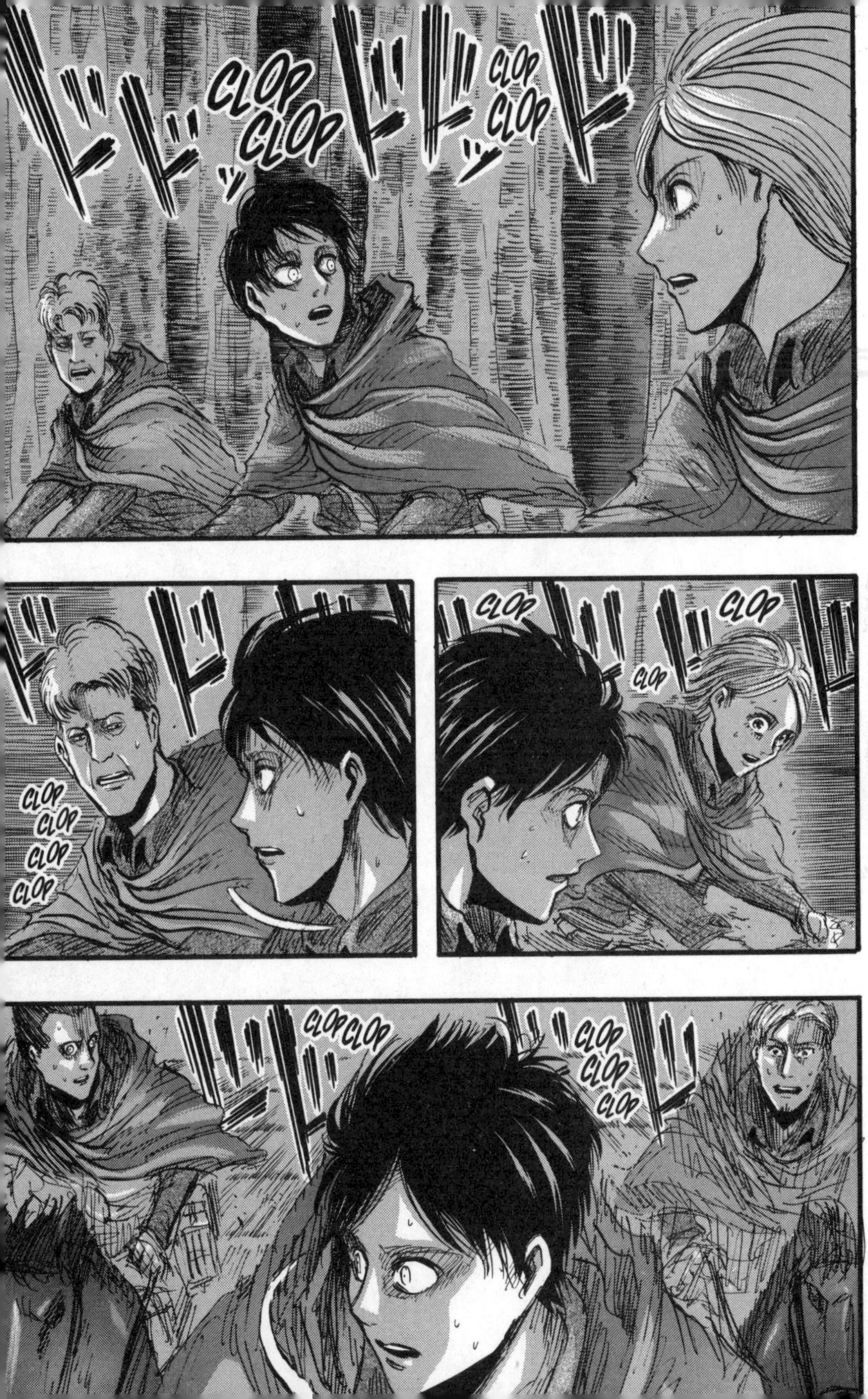
CLOP
CLOP
CLOP
CLOP
CLOP
CLOP
CLOP
CLOP
CLOP
CLOP
CLOP
CLOP
CLOP
CLOP
CLOP
CLOP

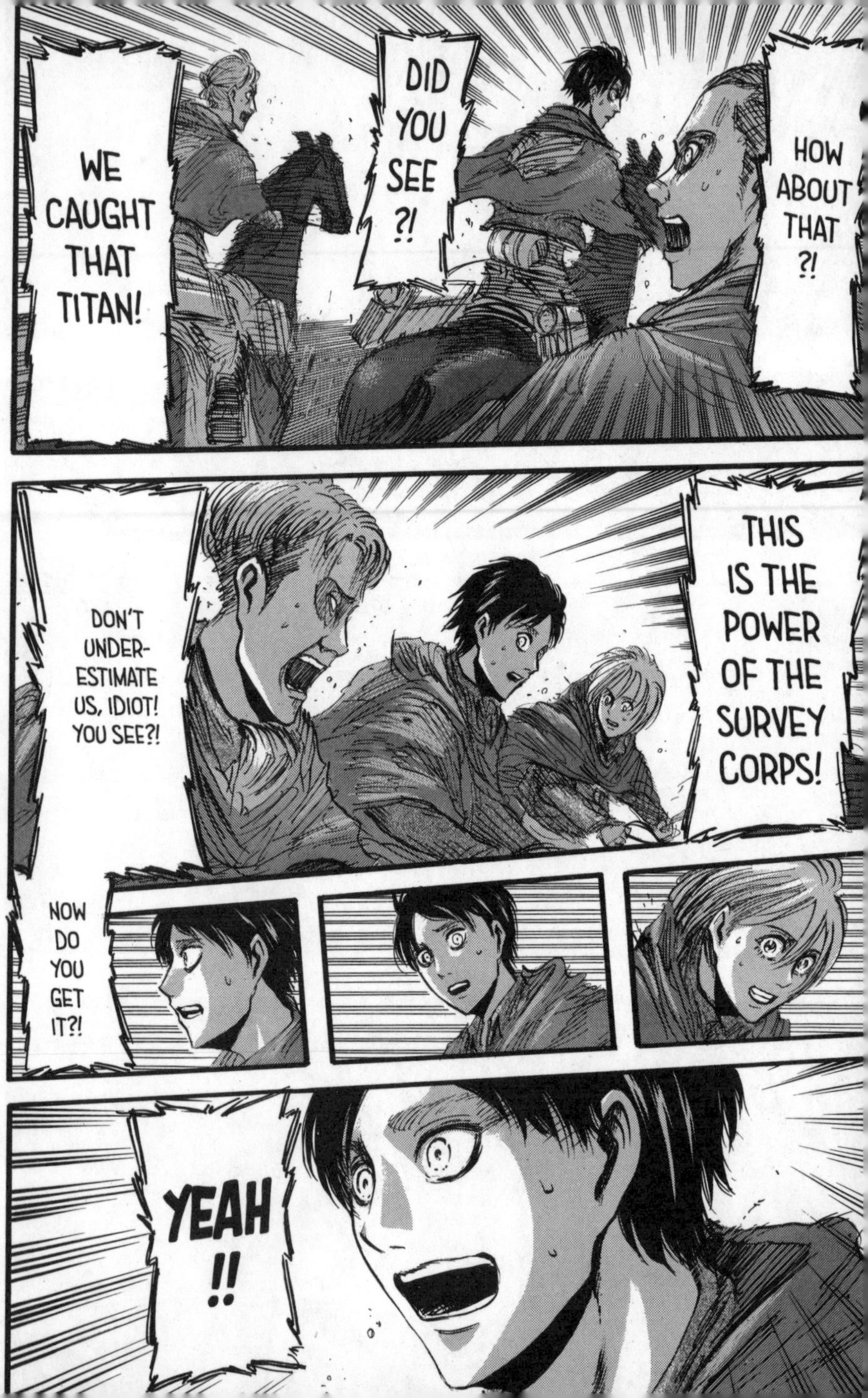
HOW ABOUT THAT ?!
DID YOU SEE ?!
WE CAUGHT THAT TITAN!
THIS IS THE POWER OF THE SURVEY CORPS!
DON'T UNDER-ESTIMATE US, IDIOT! YOU SEE?!
NOW DO YOU GET IT?!
YEAH !!

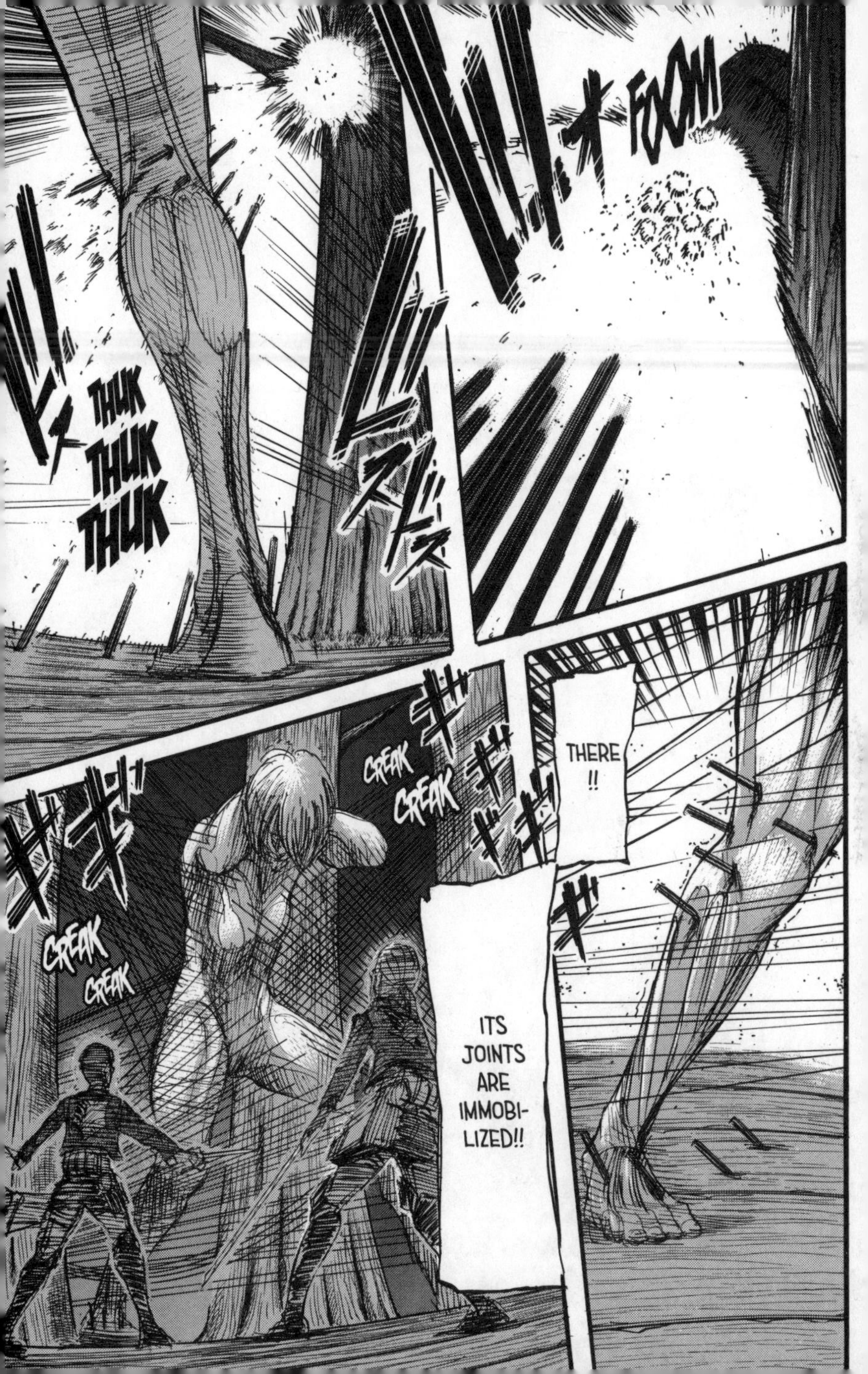
FOOM
THUK THUK THUK
THERE!!
ITS JOINTS ARE IMMOBI-LIZED!!
CREAK CREAK
CREAK CREAK

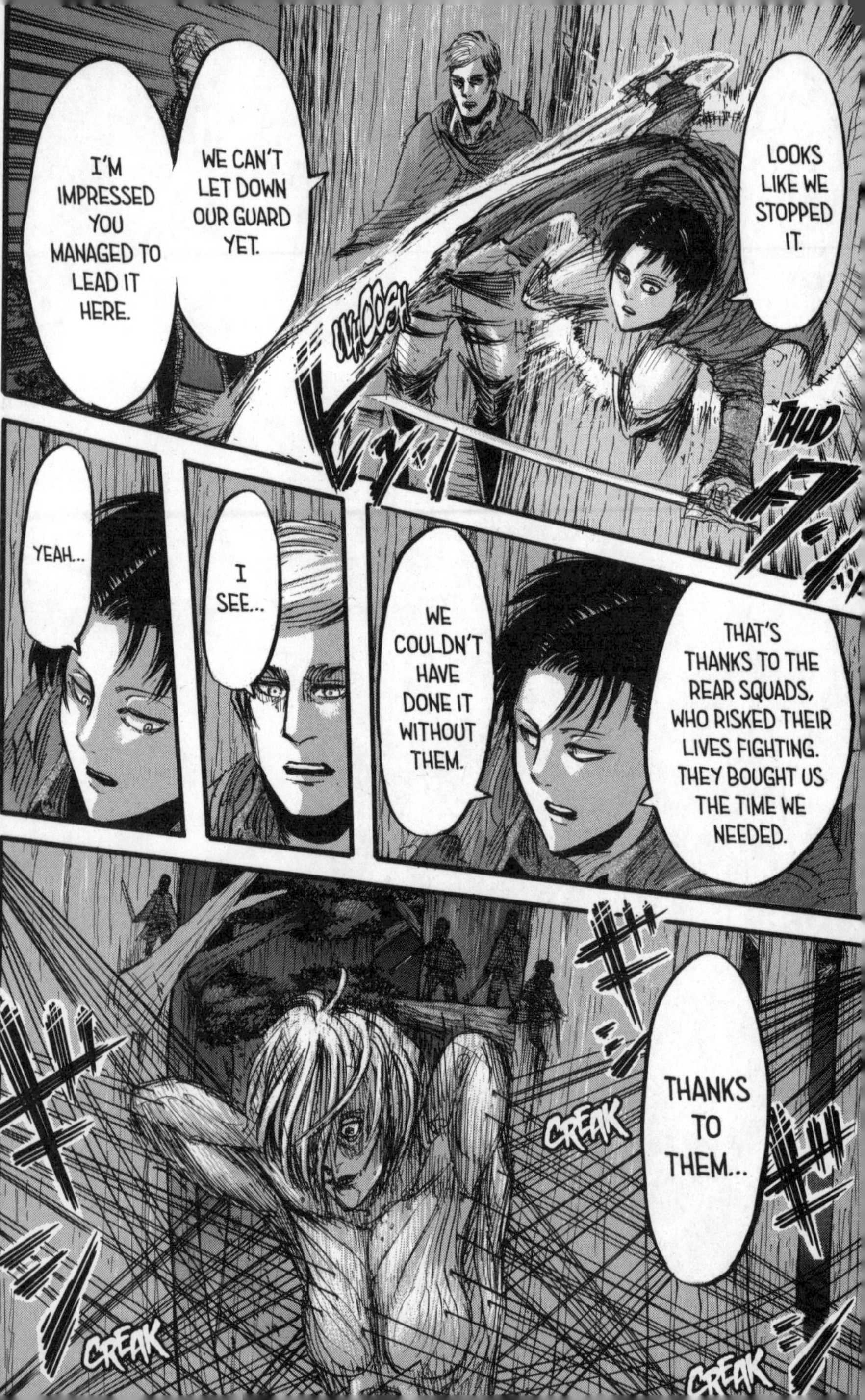
LOOKS LIKE WE STOPPED IT.
WHOOSH
THUD
WE CAN'T LET DOWN OUR GUARD YET.
I'M IMPRESSED YOU MANAGED TO LEAD IT HERE.
THAT'S THANKS TO THE REAR SQUADS, WHO RISKED THEIR LIVES FIGHTING. THEY BOUGHT US THE TIME WE NEEDED.
WE COULDN'T HAVE DONE IT WITHOUT THEM.
I SEE...
YEAH...
THANKS TO THEM...
CREAK
CREAK
CREAK

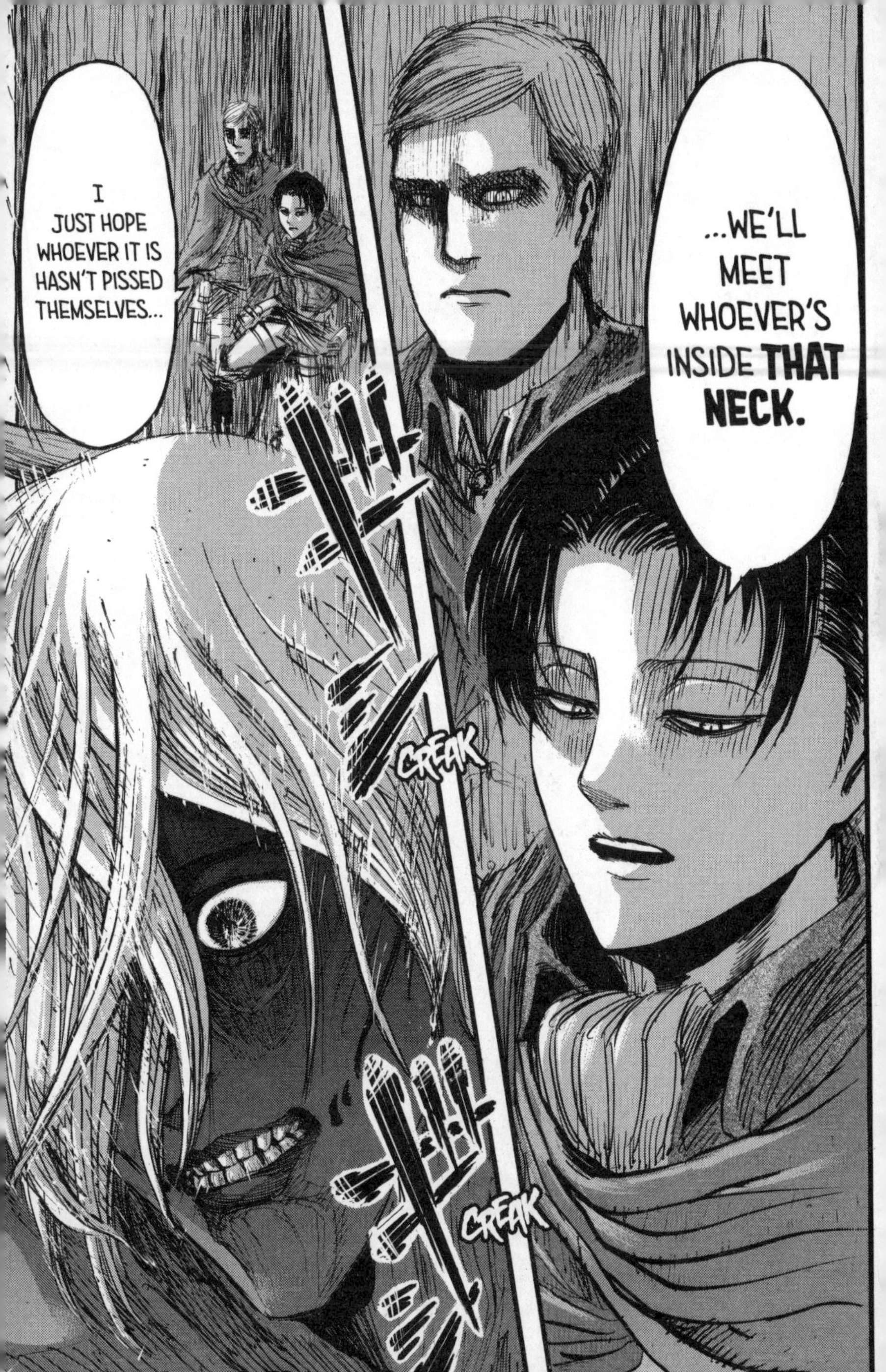
...WE'LL MEET WHOEVER'S INSIDE **THAT NECK.**
I JUST HOPE WHOEVER IT IS HASN'T PISSED THEMSELVES...
CREAK
CREAK
To Be Continued in Volume 7

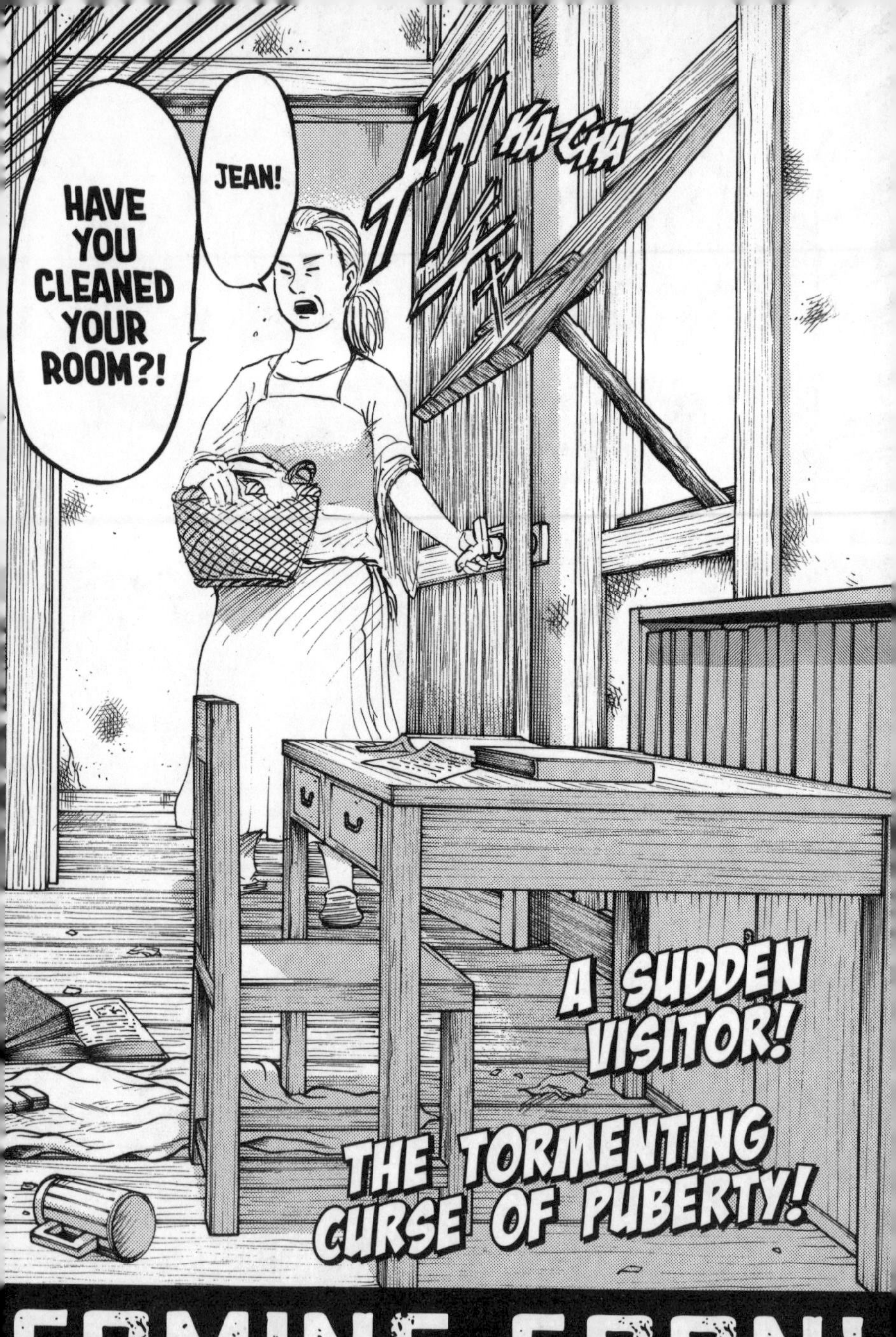
KA-CHA
JEAN!
HAVE YOU CLEANED YOUR ROOM?!
A SUDDEN VISITOR!
THE TORMENTING CURSE OF PUBERTY!

COMING SOON!

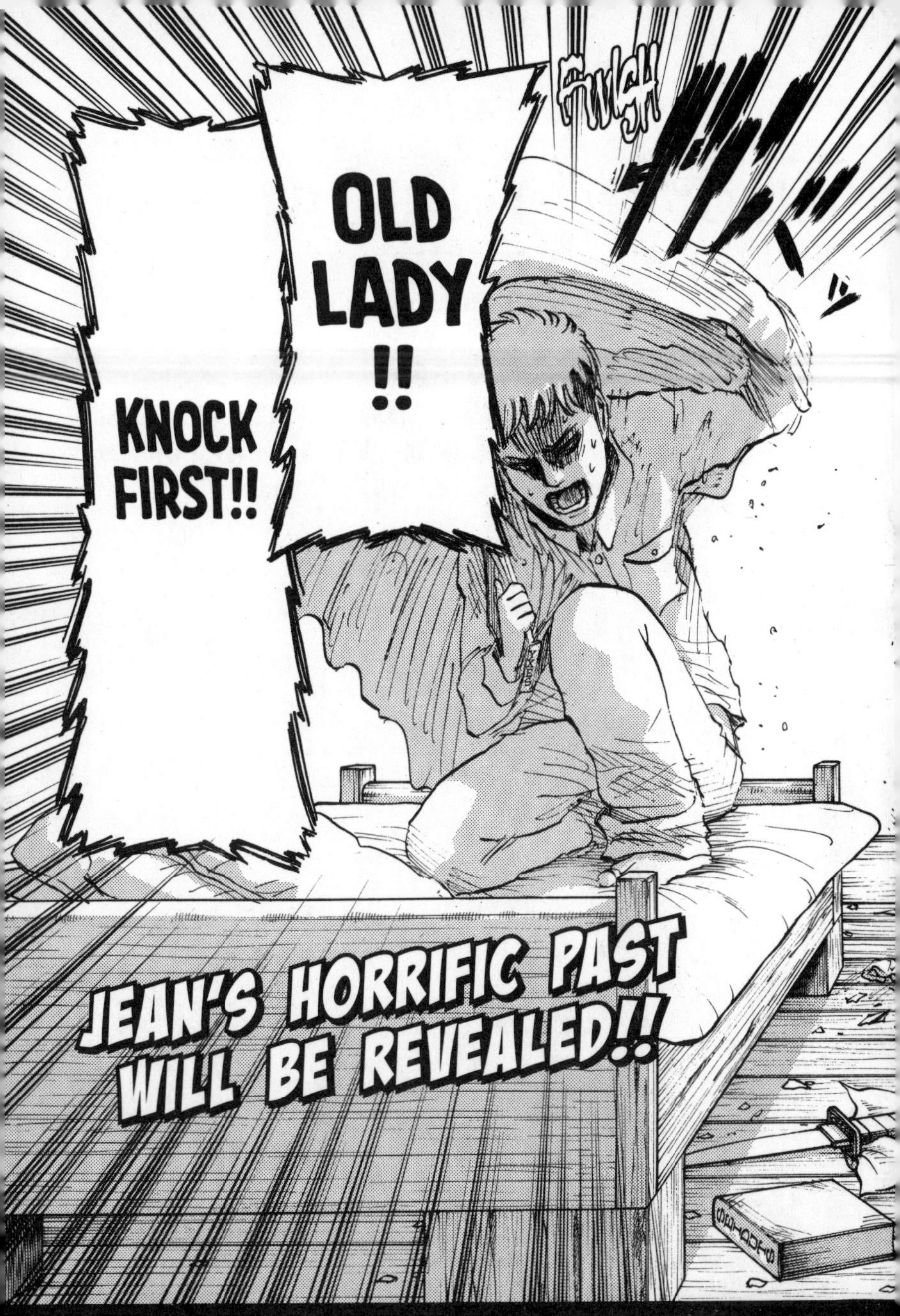
Fwish
OLD LADY!!
KNOCK FIRST!!
JEAN'S HORRIFIC PAST WILL BE REVEALED!!

* Not a real preview.

VOLUME 7

Translation Notes

SEIDUTS, PAGE 189 [189.1]

IN THE ORIGINAL, THIS BOOK WAS TITLED "OKYONBEO."
THE OTHER BOOK WAS "UNONKA." GO READ THE ENGLISH
TITLES AGAIN, THEN PLUG THE REAL TITLES INTO AN
ENGLISH-JAPANESE DICTIONARY. YOU DON'T GET ANY
MORE HELP!